Lowell Edmunds
Greek Myth

Trends in Classics – Key Perspectives on Classical Research

General Editors
Franco Montanari and Antonios Rengakos

Series Editors
P. J. Finglass, S. J. V. Malloch, Christos Tsagalis

Associate Editors
Anna Marmodoro and Elena Isayev

Volume 2

Lowell Edmunds

Greek Myth

—

DE GRUYTER

ISBN 978-3-11-068233-5
e-ISBN (PDF) 978-3-11-069620-2
e-ISBN (EPUB) 978-3-11-069624-0
ISSN 2626-1030

Library of Congress Control Number: 2021931471

Bibliographic information published by the Deutsche Nationalbibliothek
The Deutsche Nationalbibliothek lists this publication in the Deutsche Nationalbibliografie;
detailed bibliographic data are available on the Internet at http://dnb.dnb.de.

© 2021 Walter de Gruyter GmbH, Berlin/Boston
Cover image: Domenico Spinosa, Fondo Marino, courtesy of Nicola Spinosa
Printing and binding: CPI books GmbH, Leck

www.degruyter.com

Preface

In writing this book I have had the benefit of much excellent work on Greek myth, in particular the collections edited by Richard Buxton (1999), Roger Woodard (2007), and Ken Dowden and Niall Livingstone (2011). Most of the articles in these collections, like the five topical chapters in Delattre's manual (2005), use reliable formulas for the study of Greek myth. They are: myth in y, where y is Homer or another poet, tragedy, lyric, Alexandrian verse, visual media, or mythography; x in myth, where x is women, history, geography, or any number of smaller-sized subjects, such as dolphins; myth and z, where z is religion, politics, or some other, non-Greek body or bodies of myth, such as Biblical narratives, seen in a comparative perspective.

The author of such an article can rightly assume that everyone will agree that the myth under discussion is a myth. If, however, one asks what a Greek myth is, scholars disagree, as my survey of opinions in the Introduction shows. I argue that the answer to this question depends partly on the sources that one is using. The poets were once primary and perhaps still are. With the turn to mythography in the present generation, a new source claims attention. (I mean the early Greek mythographers and also a second phase, beginning in Alexandrian times and extending down to the early centuries C.E.). Myths in visual media have become sources in a new sense, as independent witnesses to myths, not the reflexes of poetry. My first chapter discusses Theseus in visual media (thus an instance of the myth in y formula) as a large counter-example to the art historians' old truism that poetry "tends to inspire artistic representation."

As for the question of what a myth is, if it is identified with a poem or a passage in a poem, then the myth is a text to be interpreted like any other text. But a myth and a poem are not the same thing (Introduction, p. XXI n. 24). If, as is often the case, a myth is a common story-pattern drawn from a set of "mythemes" ch. 7.3) or some construal of a myth's basic units, then the further question of interpretation arises. The scholar may look, in one direction, for an explanation in society. Another scholar may look in another direction, into the human mind. These diverging approaches have their long histories in the three great theories discussed in chapter 7: the myth-ritual, the psychoanalytic (principally in the work of Freud and Jung), and the structuralist. In addition, there are the three main fields of comparison, Indo-European myth, ancient Near Eastern myth, and folklore, discussed in chapter 8. As I point out in chapter 9, classicists have no shared terminology for either story-patterns or basic constituent units nor do they have an agreed upon method for the segmentation that yields the patterns and the units.

Most of my chapters take a position on the topic I am discussing or make an argument. My intention is not to settle the matter, whatever it may be, for the foreseeable future but, in keeping with the goals of the series in which this book appears, to offer a *mise au point* from which others will continue. For once, an author welcomes a reader's or reviewer's "he was wrong about..." As for the citation of other scholars, omissions are inevitable. Having written most of this book after the university libraries near me closed in mid-March of 2020, I have a special excuse. (Not everything is available in electronic form.) I also have the usual excuse, especially good in the case of Greek myth, that one cannot cite everything.

I have usually cited translations of books in modern languages, if available, and have put the year of the first publication in brackets, e.g., Calame 2003 [1996]. I have also listed the first publication in Works Cited. My abbreviations of ancient titles and authors' names are as in *OCD*⁴. For the most part, I use Latin or Latinized transliterations of Greek words and proper names.

For help of various kinds I thank Ruth Barringer, Fiorenza Bevilacqua, William Hansen, Giorgio Ieranò, Jordi Pàmias, Maria Pretzler, Alan Shapiro, Nereida Villagra, Roger Woodard and, as always and especially, Susan Edmunds. At the end Patrick Finglass and Christos Tsagalis read the whole manuscript and to them I am especially indebted.

Lowell Edmunds
Highland Park, NJ
July 2020

Contents

Preface —— V
Abbreviations —— XI
Introduction —— XV

1	Myth in Visual Media: The Example of Theseus —— 1	
2	Greek Myth as Story-Telling and in Oratory —— 15	
2.1	Story-telling and variation —— 15	
2.2	Myths in daily life in the polis —— 17	
2.3	Myths and places —— 21	
2.4	Myth in oratory —— 23	
2.5	Longer and shorter myths —— 29	
2.6	Conclusion —— 31	
3	Characters and Names in Myth, Epic and Fiction —— 33	
3.1	Inconsistency of character in myth —— 33	
3.2	Character and action in tragedy —— 35	
3.3	Character and narrative in epic —— 37	
3.4	Character in the novel —— 38	
3.5	The inner as emotion —— 40	
3.6	Names —— 41	
3.7	Names in genealogies —— 44	
3.8	Conclusion —— 47	
4	Mythography —— 49	
4.1	The two periods —— 50	
4.2	Mythography outside mythographers —— 52	
4.3	Hecataeus, Acusilaus, and the goals of writing down the myths —— 54	
4.4	The taste for collections —— 55	
4.5	Hellenistic and Imperial mythography —— 56	
4.6	The example of Palaephatus —— 60	
4.7	Conclusion —— 62	
5	The Question of Belief in Myth —— 64	
5.1	Belief and the gods in Homer and Hesiod —— 65	
5.2	A word for belief-that: πείθεσθαι —— 68	

5.3	Belief and Cult —— 70
5.4	The scholarly debate on belief —— 72
5.5	The Erythraean Paean —— 75
5.6	Conclusion —— 79

6 Myth and Religion, Myth and Cult, Myth and Ritual —— 80
6.1	Double existence —— 81
6.2	Myths explain origin of cults —— 83
6.3	The myth of the sacrifice at Mecone —— 85
6.4	Myths of transportable cult images —— 90
6.5	Conclusion —— 93

7 Three Great Theories of Myth —— 94
7.1	The myth-ritual school —— 94
7.2	Psychoanalytic interpretation of myth —— 98
7.3	Structuralism —— 102
7.4	Conclusion —— 108

8 Three Comparative Approaches —— 110
8.1	Indo-European —— 111
8.2	Near East —— 116
8.3	Folklore —— 121
8.4	Conclusion —— 124

9 Typology, Morphology and Segmentation —— 125
9.1	Typology —— 126
9.2	Morphology —— 127
9.2.1	After Propp —— 128
9.3	Segmentation —— 131
9.4	Structural narratology —— 138
9.5	Conclusion —— 141

10 Conclusion —— 142

11 Appendix: *Muthos* and Myth. From Homer to Plato and Aristotle —— 156
11.1	*Muthos* and *logos* from Homer and Hesiod to Herodotus —— 157
11.1.1	*Historia* in Herodotus —— 162
11.2	Thucydides —— 164
11.3	Plato —— 168

11.4	Beast fable (αἶνος)	170
11.5	Aristotle	170
11.6	Conclusion	171

Works Cited —— 173
Index Nominum et Rerum —— 197
Index Locorum —— 205

Abbreviations

ABV	Beazley, J.D. 1956. *Attic Black-Figure Vase Painters*. Oxford.
ANET	Pritchard, James B. 1969. *Ancient Near Eastern Texts Relating to the Old Testament*. 3rd ed. Princeton, NJ.
AT	Aarne, Antti, and Stith Thompson. 1981. *The Types of the Folktale: A Classification and Bibliography*. 2nd ed. FF Communications 184. Helsinki.
ATU	Uther, Hans-Jörg. 2004. *The Types of International Folktales: A Classification and Bibliography*. 3 vols. FF Communications 284, 285, 286. Helsinki.
B	Bernabé, Albertus, ed. 1987. *Poetarum epicorum Graecorum: testimonia et fragmenta*. Leipzig.
CGRN	Jan-Mathieu Carbon, Saskia Peels and Vinciane Pirenne-Delforge. 2016- . *A Collection of Greek Ritual Norms*. Liège. http://cgrn.ulg.ac.be.
D	Davies, Malcolm, ed. 1988. *Epicorum Graecorum fragmenta*. Göttingen.
DELG	Chantraine, Pierre. 1968. *Dictionaire étymologique de la langue grecque: histoire des mots*. 2 vols. Paris.
D-F	Davies, Malcolm/P.J. Finglass. 2014. *Stesichorus: The Poems*. Cambridge. [See also F]
D-K	Diels, Hermann/Walther Kranz. 1952[1903]. 6th ed., rev. Kranz. *Die Fragmente der Vorsokratiker*. Berlin.
EGM	Fowler, Robert L. 2000–2013. *Early Greek Mythography*. 2 vols. Oxford.
EM	Ranke, Kurt, ed. 1977– . *Enzyklopädie des Märchens: Handwörterbuch zur historischen und vergleichenden Erzählforschung*. 14 vols. Berlin.
F	Text and critical apparatus in Davies, Malcolm/P.J. Finglass. 2014. *Stesichorus: The Poems*. Cambridge.
Festa	Festa, Nicolaus. 1902. *Palaephati Peri apiston*. Teubner.
FGrH	Jacoby, Felix. 1923–59. *Die Fragmente der griechischen Historiker*. 15 vols. Leiden.
Gow-Page	Gow, A.S.F./D.L. Page. 1965. *Hellenistic Epigrams: The Greek Anthology*. 2 vols. Cambridge.
H	Hirschberger, Martina. 2004. *Gynaikon Katalogos und Megalai Ehoiai: Ein Kommentar zu den Fragmenten zweier hesiodeischer Epen*. Beiträge zur Altertumskunde 198. Munich.
HE	*Homer Encyclopedia* = Finkelberg, Margalit, ed. 2011. *The Homer Encyclopedia*. 3 vols. Chichester.
IG I^3	Lewis, D. Malcolm. 1981. *Inscriptiones Atticae Euclidis anno anteriores*. 3rd ed. Berlin.
K-A	Kassel, Rudolf/Colin Austin. 1983–. *Poetae Comici Graeci*. 8 vols. Berlin.
Kannicht	Kannicht, Richard. 2004. *Tragicorum Graecorum Fragmenta*. Vol. 5.1 (Euripides). Göttingen.
K-G	Kühner, Raphael/Friedrich Blass/Bernhard Gerth. 1890–1904. *Ausführliche Grammatik der griechischen Sprache*. 3rd ed. 2 vols. in 4. 1. Elementar- und Formenlehre (2 vols.) by Kühner/Blass. 2. Satzlehre (2 vols.) by Kühner/Gerth. Repr. 1976–1978. Hannover.
L-M	Laks, André/Glenn W. Most, eds. 2016. *Early Greek Philosophy*. Trans. by eds. Cambridge MA.

	Latacz, Joachim/Anton Bierl, eds. 2000– . *Homers Ilias, Gesamtkommentar: Basler Kommentar (BK)*. Auf der Grundlage der Ausgabe von Ameis-Hentze-Cauer (1868–1913). Munich/Berlin.
LfgrE	Snell, Bruno et al. 1955–2010. *Lexikon des frühgriechischen Epos*. 4 vols. Göttingen.
LIMC "Ai."	"Aigeus" = Kron, Uta. 1981. In *LIMC* I.1, 359–67.
LIMC "Ak. and Dem."	"Akamas and Demophon" = Kron, Uta. 1981. In *LIMC* I.1, 435–46.
LIMC "Am."	"Amphitrite II" = Kaempe-Dimitriadou, Sophia. 1981. In *LIMC* I.1, 724–35.
LIMC "Ar."	"Ariadne" = Bernhard, Mary-Louise/Wiktor A. Daszewski. 1986. In *LIMC* III.1 (Addenda), 1050–70.
LIMC "Hel."	"Hélène" = Kahil, Lilly. 1988. In LIMC IV.1, 498– 563.
LIMC "Mi."	"Minotaurus" = Woodford, Susan. 1992. In *LIMC* VI.1, 574–81.
LIMC "Th."	"Theseus" = Neils, Jennifer. 1994. In *LIMC* VIII.1, 923–51.
LIMC	Boardman, John, et al. 1981– 99. *Lexicon Iconographicum Mythologiae Classicae*. 9 vols. Zurich.
L-N-S	Latacz, Joachim/René Nünlist/Magdalena Stoevesandt. 2000. In Bierl/Latacz, eds. 2000– . Vol. 1 (Book 1). Fasc. 2 (Commentary). Munich.
L-S-J	Liddell, Henry George/Robert Scott/Henry Stuart Jones/Roderick McKenzie. 1996. *A Greek-English Lexicon*. With rev. suppl. Oxford.
M	Most, Glenn W. 2007. *Hesiod: The Shield; Catalogue of Women; Other Fragments*. Loeb Classical Library. Cambridge, MA.
Montanari	Montanari, Franco. 2015. *The Brill Dictionary of Ancient Greek*. Leiden.
Mot	Thompson, Stith. 1955– 58. *The Motif-Index of Folk-Lore*. 6 vols. Bloomington.
M-W	Merkelbach, Reinhold/M.L. West. 1967. *Fragmenta Hesiodea*. Oxford.
OCD[4]	Hornblower, Simon/Anthony Spawforth, eds. 2012. *The Oxford Classical Dictionary*. 4th ed. Oxford.
OED	OED Online = *Oxford English Dictionary Online*. http://www.oed.com.
PMG	Page, D.L. 1962. *Poetae Melici Graecae*. Oxford.
PMGF	Davies, Malcolm. 1991. *Poetarum Melicorum Graecorum Fragmenta*. Vol. 1 (Alcman, Stesichorus, Ibycus). Oxford.
	Poltera, Orlando. 2008. *Simonides lyricus: Testimonia und Fragmente: Einleitung, kritische Ausgabe, Übersetzung und Kommentar*. Schweizerische Beiträge zur Altertumswissenschaft 35. Basel.
Powell	Powell, John U. 1925. *Collectanea Alexandrina*. Oxford.
Radt	Radt, Stefan. 1985. *Tragicorum Graecorum Fragmenta*. Vol. 5. Gottingen.
Roscher	Roscher, Wilhelm H. 1884–1904. *Ausführliches Lexikon der griechischen und römischen Mythologie*. 4 vols. Leipzig.
Schwyzer	Schwyzer, Eduard. 1939–1971. *Griechische Grammatik auf der Grundlage von Karl Brugmanns Griechischer Grammatik*. Vol. 1 (Allgemeiner Teil; Lautlehre; Wortbildung; Flexion) by Schwyzer (1939). Vol. 2 (Syntax and Syntaktische Stylistik) by Albert Debrunner (1950). Vol. 3 (Register) by Demetrius J. Georgacas (1953). Vol. 4 (Stellenregister) by Fritz Radt and Stefan Radt (1971). Munich.
SE	Freud, Sigmund. 1953–1974. *The Standard Edition of the Complete Psychological Works of Sigmund Freud*. Ed. by James Strachey. London.

Smyth	Smyth, Herbert Weir. 1956. *Greek Grammar*. Rev. by Gordon M. Messing. Cambridge MA.
ThesCRA	Lambrinoudakis, Vassilis/Jean Ch. Balty, eds. 2004–2014. *Thesaurus cultus et rituum antiquorum*. 8 vols.; 2 suppls.; index. Basel.
W	West, M.L. 2013. *The Epic Cycle: A Commentary on the Lost Troy Epics*. Oxford.
West[2]	West, M.L. 1989. *Iambi et elegi Graeci*. Vol. 1. 2nd ed. Oxford.

Introduction

What is a Greek myth?[1] What are the sources for Greek myths? The answer to the first question is determined wholly or in large part by the answer to the second. Many, probably most, scholars consider the poets, from Homer to Callimachus, to be the main sources.[2] Certainly these poets are the main sources *for us*. They have this status, however, partly through lack of other sources, partly through undervaluation of the other sources that we do have, and especially because the principal medium of communication of myths, word of mouth, was ephemeral. This medium was still ongoing in the second century C.E., as the reports of Pausanias show.[3] For earlier times there is no Pausanias. Of undervalued available sources vase paintings and other visual media are the most important. My first chapter uses the Theseus myth to test the truism that "[p]oetry tends to inspire artistic representation, rather than the other way around", and argues that in the case of Theseus visual media inspired poetry.[4] The extensive study of vases from the point of view of ancient markets has drawn attention to the interaction of consumers with images. A certain myth or a scene from a myth would have hoped to attract a certain kind of consumer. This kind of marketing obviously does not work unless the consumer knows or can be reminded of the myth. There were many other visual media besides vases (ch. 1). My second chapter discusses some kinds of casual everyday myth-telling as well as the use of myth in oratory. Chapter 3 discusses the differences between myth, on the one hand, and epic and modern fiction, on the other, with respect to names, stories and characters.

---

[1] In posing this question I am far from assuming that the answer must be ontological, although some of the answers that I will consider are ontological. Delattre 2005, 40 refers to the "tyranny" of this question but there are some, also to be considered, who have certainly escaped.

[2] Cf. Hawes 2014b, 127: "Studies of Greek myth have more commonly focused on the literature and culture of the archaic and classical periods, charting a well-trodden path from Homer to Plato. The most distinctive poetic products of these periods were performed publicly; texts from these periods seemingly capture such communal spectacles in written form." It is as texts in this sense that we study Greek myth, even if, as Hawes go on to observe, we conceive of these texts as an oral phenomenon.

[3] Pretzler 2005 is fundamental for oral tradition in Pausanias.

[4] Mills 1997, 19 and n. 73. See Burgess 2001, 54–59 for a critical survey of scholarly opinion concerning Homer as the inspiration for early Greek art. He goes on to consider several further cases in point.

Only glimpses of everyday myth-telling remain. They are discussed in the Appendix. In Thucydides the myth-tellers are recognized but anonymous.[5] He mentions them alongside the poets as sources to be dismissed. In the "Archaeology" with which Thucydides' work begins, he argues that the Trojan War, though the greatest of all previous wars, was surpassed by the war that he is going to recount. In two passages he refers to word-of-mouth myth as distinguished from poetry. (I discuss Thucydides on history as corrective of *muthos* in the Appendix.) In the first of these two passages he says: "And that Mycenae was small, or if any city of those days seems now inconsiderable—without using valid proof one would be doubting that the expedition was as great as the poets have said and as in the prevailing account (*logos*)."[6] The *logos* here is the oral *logos* that is derived from the poets.[7] In the second passage, Thucydides concludes his argument concerning the scale of the Greek expedition against Troy by saying: "But through poverty both previous (expeditions) and this one itself, more famous than its predecessors, are shown to be inferior to the common report (*phēmē*) of them and to the account (*logos*) of them that now prevails because of the poets."[8] Here Thucydides distinguishes two sources for the Trojan War, one popular and the other poetic. The terms that he uses implicitly contrast these two sources, even if, from the point of view of veracity, they can now, after Thucydides' discussion, be seen to be equally mistaken. Thucydides makes a comparable distinction in the excursus on the population of Sicily at the beginning of Book 6: "The Cyclopes and the Laestrygonians are said to be the oldest ones to inhabit any part of the territory, of whom I can say neither what race they were or whence they came from or where they went. Let it suffice as it has been said by poets and as each person somehow knows about them."[9] What each person knows is presumably what he

---

5 The places that I discuss here should be distinguished for the impressively and, to most, surprisingly longer list of places in which Thuc. refers to myth: for the list see Rood 2019, 337.
6 Καὶ ὅτι μὲν Μυκῆναι μικρὸν ἦν, ἢ εἴ τι τῶν τότε πόλισμα νῦν μὴ ἀξιόχρεων δοκεῖ εἶναι, οὐκ ἀκριβεῖ ἄν τις σημείῳ χρώμενος ἀπιστοίη μὴ γενέσθαι τὸν στόλον τοσοῦτον ὅσον οἵ τε ποιηταὶ εἰρήκασι καὶ ὁ λόγος κατέχει (1.10.2). For the translation "valid proof": Hornblower 1991, 33 on 10.1. Cf. in App. on Thucydides' τεκμήρια "inferences drawn from evidence."
7 Greenwood 2006, 61: Thuc. uses *logos* of his own account only once. She takes *logos* in 1.10.2 to refer to "written works." But the distinction is the same as at 1.11.2.
8 ἀλλὰ δι' ἀχρηματίαν τά τε πρὸ τούτων ἀσθενῆ ἦν καὶ αὐτά γε δὴ ταῦτα, ὀνομαστότατα τῶν πρὶν γενόμενα, δηλοῦται τοῖς ἔργοις ὑποδεέστερα ὄντα τῆς φήμης καὶ τοῦ νῦν περὶ αὐτῶν διὰ τοὺς ποιητὰς λόγου κατεσχηκότος (1.11.2).
9 παλαίτατοι μὲν λέγονται ἐν μέρει τινὶ τῆς χώρας Κύκλωπες καὶ Λαιστρυγόνες οἰκῆσαι, ὧν ἐγὼ οὔτε γένος ἔχω εἰπεῖν οὔτε ὁπόθεν ἐσῆλθον ἢ ὅποι ἀπεχώρησαν· ἀρκείτω δὲ ὡς ποιηταῖς τε εἴρηται καὶ ὡς ἕκαστός πῃ γιγνώσκει περὶ αὐτῶν (6.2.1). See the long valuable note at Hornblower

or she also says about them, on the basis of information that did not come from the poets.[10]

Thucydides is talking in the first two passages about the Trojan War, of Panhellenic renown thanks to Homer and the Cyclic poets. The primary and, for the vast majority of Greeks, the only mode of its communication was, down through the classical period, oral performance. What of those who had never attended a performance? One thinks of another aspect of that vast, now surd, myth-telling. What of the "woman working with her husband in the fields on the island of Chios" or "the Arcadian goatherd tending his flock in the valley of the Neda" or "the slave…toiling in the Laurium silver mines"?[11] Did such persons ever attend a performance of Hesiod or Homer or a tragedy?[12] Although the Arcadian goatherd might have to say that he had not done so, he would have known of the nymph after whom the river Neda was named (Paus. 8.38.3). Local myths, like the ones that Pausanias heard, would have been his "Greek myths."

Another mostly lost source of Greek myth is early mythography. If we had the complete works of Hecataeus, Acusilaus and Pherecydes, we would have a fundamentally different picture of the state of myth at the end of the archaic period and in the fifth century. Although Thucydides saw the attractions of mythography and of poetry as the same, we would probably continue to prefer poetry.[13] But what we think of as Greek myth would be different. Chapter 4 discusses Greek mythography, scholarship on which has been a trend in the last generation and continues strong today. Not only the three "founders" just mentioned and the others in Robert Fowler's *Early Greek Mythographers* but also a second phase, beginning at the end of the fourth century and extending down into Imperial times receive new attention. Apollodorus (2nd c. C.E.?) no longer stands in isolation.

Greek myth in Greek mythography raises the question of what a Greek myth is. Fowler raised this latter question apropos of mythography:

[W]here or what is the "myth" that the mythographer seeks to reduce? The difficulty of locating this elusive entity lies behind the oft-repeated dictum that there is no myth, only

---

2008, 264–66 for i.a. Homeric reference to the Cyclopes and the Laestrygonians. He points out that only Hesiod definitely puts the Laestrygonians in Sicily.

10 See Rood 2019, 339 for a list of the terms with which Thuc. introduces mythical material (from which, as Rood points out, he usually distances himself).

11 I have taken these hypothetical examples from Buxton 1999, 4, who uses them apropos not of myth but of sociological differentiation in knowledge of intellectual developments in the 6th to 4th centuries BCE.

12 For the places of performance in this period: Tsagalis 2018.

13 Thuc. 1.21.1. He uses the word λογογράφοι.

myths: stories told in particular contexts. It is certainly true that myths do not tell themselves. Yet the mythographer must have something in mind—and so do we when we speak, as we cannot stop doing, of "the myth of X."[14]

But the question arises already for the *Iliad*. The throwing of Hephaestus from Olympus is recounted twice, in different places. Once it is Zeus who throws him (1.590–94) and once it is Hera (18.394–99).[15] What is the myth of the throwing of Hephaestus? This kind of question arises again and again, despite our scanty sources, scanty in relation to all the myths told by ancient Greeks or recorded in writing or put in one form or another of verse. Fowler's answer to the question:

> "The" myth is the hypostasis of all the versions the mythographer has heard, and the color and the flavor of the contexts in which he has heard them. His unity, however arbitrarily derived, notionally underlies the inherited multiplicity. Like language, however, myth is a social phenomenon, existing both in the individual and in the group. In some sense myth is indeed "out there." Any individual telling responds to a social nexus, and that is where "the myth" must be.[16]

Fowler's words represent what I call a third way of dealing with the question of what a myth is. I return to this third way after discussing two other ways, one beginning with Walter Burkert, the other with Marcel Detienne. (These beginnings have a history, not to be entered into here, behind them.)

Burkert gave a widely accepted definition of Greek myth is his Sather lectures of 1979.[17] It was the fourth and concluding thesis of his "theses" on Greek myth:

> The specific character of myth seems to lie neither in the structure nor in the content of a tale, but in the use to which it is put; and this would be my final thesis: *myth is a traditional story with secondary, partial reference to something of collective importance.* Myth is traditional tale applied; and its relevance and seriousness stem largely from this application.[18]

---

14 Fowler 2017b, 24. An extreme version of this thought can be found in Delattre 2005, 42 ("[L]e mythe n'existe pas, même pas en tant qu'émanation des versions que le composent", etc.)
15 Discussed by Edmunds 1997, 421–22.
16 Fowler loc. cit. The concept of the "nexus" is well articulated by Gadamer 1993 [1981]a, 177. Delattre 2005, 36–39 has given his own analysis, in his own terms, of what transpires in the communication of a myth to a listener or listeners. In this context (36–38), he also discusses belief in myth, which he describes as a temporary adherence comparable with that of the modern reader to fiction.
17 Cf., e.g., Fowler 2009, 22, who uses the expansion of Burkert's definition by Louden 2006, 9.
18 Burkert 1979, 23 (each of the four theses is italicized). For further discussion of the fourth thesis see below ch. 7.3.

He immediately explains what he means by the qualifications "secondary" and "partial." "The reference is secondary, as the meaning of the tale is not to be derived from it…; and it is partial, since tale and reality will never be quite isomorphic in these applications." The question immediately arises: how does one know what the primary and total meaning of a myth is?

Burkert's definition later became: "Myths are traditional stories with special 'meaningfulness'."[19] The reason for Burkert's quotation marks is unclear. He does not doubt that myths have meaning, as his fuller statement of the same definition shows and as was already clear in the fourth thesis quoted above, although he did not use the word "meaning" in that context.[20] Further, he formulates a dynamic that would account for the variation found in the attestations of Greek myths: "The 'applied story' takes elements of its application into itself and thus brings about secondary crystallizations of a singular kind."[21] Burkert's fundamental notion is that myths verbalize something already in the minds of teller and audience which concerns them because of its social or institutional importance. (Burkert tends to assume that the myth already, before its application, has some meaning that is adapted to the circumstances. I return to this aspect of Burkert's definition in my discussion of Fowler's third way.)

The definition given by Fritz Graf in some ways resembles Burkert's but replaces meaning with another characteristic: "Myths are traditional stories, with transferability into other languages and a claim to be binding".[22] In the English

---

19 Burkert 1993, 17: "Mythen sind traditionelle Erzählungen mit besonderer 'Bedeutsamkeit'." (cf. the following for "significance"). Bremmer 1987, 1–9 is a critique of Burkert's definition, which concludes by revising it: "traditional tales relevant to society" (7). For critical reflection on the two main terms here ("traditional" and "meaningfulness") see Bettini 2012, ii–iii. Bettini's project for an "Atlante antropologico della mitologia greca e romana", a new atlas of Greek and Roman myth to be organized by themes, is directly in line with Burkert's definition of myth, despite his criticism of the concept of tradition (see ch. 7):"Al centro del nostro interesse abbiamo posto non tanto i racconti considerati in sé, quanto alcuni temi di rilevanza culturale che emergono dai miti dei Greci e Romani: proprio quegli elementi, cioè, che la «significatività» del mito è in grado di «far passare» attraverso le maglie del racconto, portandoli in questo modo all'attenzione della comunità a cui questi racconti si rivolgono" (Bettini 2012, v.; note the chaste quotation marks).
20 Burkert 1993, 18: "Nehmen wir Mythen als traditionelle, bedeutsame Erzählungen" etc. (note that here "bedeutsame" is not in quotation marks).
21 Again Burkert 1993, 17.
22 "Mythen sind traditionelle Erzählungen, mit Übertragbarkeit in andere Sprachen und Anspruch auf Verbindlichkeit (in Abgrenzung von Sage, Legende, Märchen, Fabel)" (Graf 1987, 7). I have not discussed the part of this definition in parentheses. (Burkert 1979, 23 says the opposite about the fable.) I have not found this definition as such in Graf 1993, the translation of Graf 1987.

translation of the book from which this sentence has been taken, Graf says that "traditional" means that myths "are transmitted from one generation to another without anyone knowing who created them" (2). If I have understood him, he understands this transmission to go on in the form of something like plot summaries, which are easily translatable from one language into another (the second element in the definition quoted above) (3). He refers to Lévi-Strauss's famous dictum on the translatability of myth.[23] As for the binding aspect, it depends on a certain conception of myth: "A myth makes a valid statement about the origins of the world, of society and its institutions, about the gods and their relationship with mortals, in short about everything on which human existence depends" (3). (Graf does not argue for this definition, which applies only to a fairly small percentage of Greek myths.) The statement that a myth makes is valid, however, only if it has cultural relevance and it can have this relevance only if it can adapt to changing circumstances (3). Thus the oft-observed variability of myth. But there were different kinds of cultural relevance, which varied according to the contexts of narration (4). There were stories told to children by nurses and grandmothers (Pl. *Rep.* 376b11–377c5), whereas "the truly relevant narration of myth, until the time of Euripides, was public and took place at times prescribed by the religious calendar: thus only the 'greater myths' were subject to group control" (4).

The results of Graf's definition seem to be twofold. On the one hand, myth makes a valid statement about matters of the utmost concern. On the other, this statement is always changing according to circumstances and thus the validity of myth must also be always changing. After these results, all that really remains is the traditionality of myth. Graf has probably been led to the validity of myth by his notion of two kinds of myth, one higher and one lower, the former poetry and the lower represented by the nurses and grandmothers (Graf's distinction comes in fact from Pl. *Rep.* 377c6–d5). Although he distinguishes between myth and poetry, Graf holds, to repeat, that "the truly relevant narration" of myth took place

---

[23] Lévi-Strauss 1955, 430: "Myth is the part of language where the formula *traduttore, tradittore* reaches its lowest truth-value. From that point of view, it should be put in the whole gamut of linguistic expressions at the end opposite to that of poetry, in spite of all the claims which have been made to prove the contrary. Poetry is a kind of speech which cannot be translated except at the cost of serious distortions; whereas the mythical value of the myth remains preserved, even through the worst translation. Whatever our ignorance of the language and the culture of the people where it originated, a myth is still felt as a myth by any reader throughout the world. Its substance does not lie in its style, its original music, or its syntax, but in the story which it tells. It is language, functioning on an especially high level where meaning succeeds practically at 'taking off' from the linguistic ground on which it keeps on rolling."

in the public performance of poetry.²⁴ One has to ask, then, how adaptation to changing circumstances could have taken place in the performances of Homer and Hesiod after, say, the middle of the sixth century. (Opinions on the history of their texts in antiquity vary widely. I assume fixation at least of performance texts by the mid-sixth century.) For Homer, Graf at best could appeal to the quotations of Homer in Aeschines' *Against Timarchus*.²⁵ With tragedy he might be on surer ground. In the past generation criticism has emphasized communication to the polis.²⁶

Turning to the other way of dealing with the questions of Greek myth, which I spoke of as starting with Marcel Detienne, I will pursue a faintly discernible filiation that leads back to him. Charles Delattre begins his *Manuel de mythologie grecque* (2005) thus:

> ...myth is fleeting, elusive, it continually escapes investigation and is never more misleading than when one believes that he has grasped it. The proof of this is the multiplication of possible definitions, of affirmations concerning its condition and its status, and of attempts to define its scope.²⁷

Delattre could go, from this observation, in either of two directions, back to antiquity, on the assumption that "myth" is a meaningful word, in order to rethink current definitions, or into the present, in search of an explanation for the impasse that he has described. He chooses the latter course, referring to the need

---

24 Graf 1993 [1987], 2: "A myth...does not coincide with a particular text or literary genre. For example, in all three major genres of Greek poetry, the story of Agamemnon's murder and of Orestes' subsequent revenge is told: in epic (at the beginning of the *Odyssey*), in choral lyric (e.g., Stesichorus' *Oresteia*), and in the works of all three tragedians. A myth is not a specific poetic text. It transcends the text: it is the subject-matter, a plot fixed in broad outline and with characters no less fixed, which the individual poet is free to alter only within limits." Cf. Burkert 1985, 120–21: "Scholars...speak...of early epic art. This art grows up on the foundation of myth, but is not identical with it. If myth is defined as a complex of traditional tales in which significant human situations are united in fantastic combinations...to illuminate reality, then Greek epic is both less than this and more than this. It is less because it concentrates on heroic motifs,...and it is more because it shapes these tales to the highest formal perfection..."
25 On this oration: Dover 1978, ch. 2; Ford 1999.
26 Easterling 2012, 1495 (paragraph beginning "Recent criticism...", which is more or less repeated from the previous edition). See also the bibliography in Dowden and Livingstone 2011, 21 n. 8.
27 Delattre 2005, 6: "...le mythe est fuyant, insaisissable, il se dérobe san cesse a l'enquête et n'est jamais plus trompeur que lorsqu'on croit le tenir. Preuve en est la multiplication des définitions possibles, des affirmations sur son état et son statut et des tentatives pour le circonscrire."

for a Foucauldian "archaeology" of myth, which he proceeds to sketch out.[28] In this spirit, he shows how myth has been created by the discourse about myth.[29] (Delattre also has a positive definition of myth, which I have discussed in ch. 7.3.)

Delattre refers in passing to Suzanne Saïd's description of Greek myth as a "catégorie poubelle" ("trash can category").[30] In the introduction ("Qu'est-ce qu'un mythe?") to her *Approches de la mythologie grecque* Saïd says:

> In short, for the historians as well as for the orators and philosophers of antiquity, myth is first of all a "trash can category," a notion which is defined only negatively by opposition to a narrative which describes a past reality in an exact manner or a discourse that strictly obeys the rules of logic.[31]

She is right that the concept of myth arose from the opposition of one kind of discourse to another. This opposition is already in Pindar (see my App.). She is wrong about the various writers to whom she refers. Negative reflections on myth can be found; they are not the whole story. Myth has its place in Thucydides (ch. 4.2; see also above) and in Herodotus; in Plato and Aristotle (see my App.); and in orators (see ch. 2)[32]

In her introduction she also refers with approval to Detienne's description of myth as a "poisson soluble." Detienne holds that myth is nothing but the construct of mythology, the discourse about myth that began in antiquity and the contemporary history of which he traces from the eighteenth century. Myth dissolves in this construct. Thus "Poisson soluble dans les eaux de la mythologie, le mythe est une forme introuvable", which echoes the title of the book by the surrealist André Breton, *Poisson soluble* (1924).[33] Saïd proceeds to discuss general

---

28 Delattre 2005, 7–15, citing Foucault 1969 (Eng. trans. 1972).
29 "Reste que la mythologie n'est…qu'un discours, qui a peine à se reconnaître elle-même comme instance unifiée d'interprétation" (13).
30 Delattre 2005, 6, citing Saïd 1993, 7 = 2008, 7; also Delattre 2005, 13.
31 Saïd 2008, 9. She puts "catégorie poubelle" in quotes not to distance herself from this expression but to indicate that it is already in use in other fields. "Bref, pour les historiens comme pour les rhéteurs et les philosophes de l'Antiquité, le mythe est d'abord une 'catégorie poubelle', une notion qui ne se définit que de manière négative par opposition à un récit qui décrit de manière exacte une réalité passé ou à un discours qui obéit strictement aux règles de la logique."
32 Thucydides: cf. also Thomas 2019, 75–76. Herodotus: Dewald 2012: "Herodotus has constructed a dense legendary and mythic framework comprised of the genealogies, the various forms of mythic background, and the religious *thômata* ('wonders'), on which the main narrative itself floats" (first sentence). For Herodotus also Baragwanath 2012, 35–38 (cited in ch. 2); Baragwanath 2019.
33 Detienne 1981, 238. Incorrectly translated in Detienne 1986, 131–32.

definitions of myth but, consistently with the view of the matter that she has expressed, she does not propose any definition of Greek myth in particular.

The filiation of the three scholars that I have traced does not include Claude Calame. His views are akin, however, to theirs. In many publications he has said that myth was not an indigenous category among the ancient Greeks.[34] This skepticism concerning the use of the word myth to refer to Greek antiquity is obviously a corollary of Detienne's thesis that myth is a modern construct. The stories (*récits*) that we call myths have, however, a remarkable cultural efficacy that is founded on poetic speech (*mise en discours d'ordre poétique*).[35] These stories, which, to repeat, do not constitute a category that could be studied as such, must be studied in their always singular poetic instantiations. Each so-called "myth" can only be read in the particular version in which it comes to its audience (*déstinataire*) in the particular cultural context in which (alone) it makes sense.[36] To study a Greek "myth" can, then, be only a matter of studying a particular poem. (Several works of Calame are cited in ch. 8 apropos of his Greimasian method.)

To return to what I called the third way, in the second of the quotations of Fowler given above, he referred to a "social nexus" of the teller and the group or addressee as the location of what one calls "myth." He thus answers the question with which he began (the first of the quotations): "[W]here or what is the "myth" that the mythographer seeks to reduce?" The question of where in effect replaces the question of what and the answer to where replaces the answer of what. Fowler's comparison of myth to a language reminds of an essay by Petr Bogatyrev (1893–1971) and Roman Jakobson (1896–1982).[37] They describe the difference between oral folklore and written literature with reference to Ferdinand de Saussure's distinction between *langue* and *parole* as the two components of language.[38] The former is the system of language, possessed by everyone, that

---

[34] Note the title of Calame 1991: "'Mythe' et 'rite' en Grèce: Des catégories indigènes?" In this article the discussion of Homeric *muthos* and *logos* and related words could not take account of Martin 1989. In Calame 1999: 122 n. 4 there is a brief reference to this work. Calame 1999 could not take account of Martin's further reflections on Homeric *muthos* in Martin 2013. My views on these words can be found in App. For a strong statements of his position: Calame 1996, 46: "...pas de mythe...pas de mythologie...pas de mythe comme genre...pas de mythe...come type idéal...pas d'ontologie de mythe"; Calame 2014, 283.
[35] I am paraphrasing and summarizing some sentences in Calame 2015, 10.
[36] I am paraphrasing a sentence in Calame 2015, 76.
[37] Bogatyrev and Jakobson 1966 [1929] = 1982 [1929]. (Bogatyrev and Jakobson 1976 [1931] is a summary.) The following discussion of the essay by Bogatyrev and Jakobson is a summary of Edmunds 2016a: 3–5, with repetition of some footnotes.
[38] Saussure 1972, 37–38 = 1986, 19.

enables the latter, the ephemeral instance of speech. This is *parole*. Folktales correspond to *langue*, because they exist primarily *in potentia*, in their potentiality for retelling. A retelling, in terms of the comparison an act of *parole*, must, in order to be accepted in the first place, conform to the community's norms for this kind of communication.[39] Here is Fowler's "social nexus" of the teller and the group. Another analogy to the "social nexus" can be found in another comparison. Jonathan Ready made a comparative study of the simile in Homer and in the oral epic and other kinds of poetry of several peoples. He defined three elements with which the oral performer works: "elements unique to his performances (idiolectal), elements shared among performers in his region (dialectal), and elements shared among performers in different regions (pan-traditional)."[40] "The knowledgeable tradition-oriented audience member" grasps the performer's, or the poet-performer's "modulation between the idiolectal and the shared."[41] In this way, audiences are able tacitly to maintain their part, even at the level of the verse itself, in the performance, which turns out to be a joint enterprise.

Fowler's comparison of myth to a language, to which I have added the specification of the Saussurean distinction between *langue* and *parole*, provides a way of sorting out Burkert's notion of the secondariness of myth as applied to particular circumstances. While no one would doubt that a myth bears a relation to the occasion of its telling, in whatever form of telling, including verse, the question of myth as a "secondary crystallization" on each occasion remains. Burkert's phrase "secondary, partial reference" (quoted above) suggests that, for him, a myth has some primary meaning in the "tradition" from which it has come. Or, to use his metaphor, there is a primary "crystallization" of meaning lying in the background of the particular retelling of a myth. But in terms of the Saussurean distinction, the retelling of a myth is *parole* and its antecedent state is *langue*,

---

[39] "Should this oral work, created by this individual, be unacceptable to the community for one reason or another, should the other members of the community not appreciate it, it will be condemned to extinction. Only a chance recording by a collector can save it by transporting it from the sphere of oral poetry to that of written literature": Bogatyrev and Jakobson 1966 [1929], 2 = 1982 [1929], 35. But modification must be an alternative to condemnation. Cf. Gayton 1935, 285: "As much a factor in the dissemination and reformation of tales as the narrator, is the listener. He must be satisfied with what he hears; if not, modifications must sooner or later be subtly or overtly demanded."
[40] Ready 2018, 127.
[41] Ready 2018, 79.

which provides not meaning but the potential for meaning. Burkert's implied primary crystallization cannot ever have happened. "The telling is the tale."[42] (For further discussion of Burkert's definition: ch. 7.3; ch. 8.2.1; ch. 9.3.)

A new question now arises: what are myths in the state of *langue*, i.e., in their potential state? How are they remembered and in what form? Cognitive science would give an answer both too specific (parts of the brain) and too general (the workings of memory, as apart from the memory of some kind of thing). Comparison with the performers of epic and other kinds of poetry would only tell us—and in fact has already told us much—about the capacities of specialists. How or in what form ordinary persons, such as the mother of Melanippe (see App.), remembered myths, in her case a cosmogony, remains unclear. Once again folkloristics might provide material for comparison. An enormous amount of research has gone into the study of tale-tellers and tale-telling.[43] (Burkert's answer to the question of how myths are remembered emerges in the theory of myth that he offered in an article published in 1988. See ch. 9.3; Conclusion.)

The definitions that I have discussed and the first of the two quotations of Fowler all presuppose that the word "myth" in "Greek myth" applies to myths from the archaic period onwards. This conventional use of 'myth" does not correspond to the meaning of its etymon, *muthos*, in its earlier uses, when it refers to one kind of speech or another, not necessarily containing a story, and is synonymous with *logos*. In the history of their semantics these two words underwent a change in the fifth century. *Muthos* came to be used of stories about gods and heroes that poets or ordinary people told. *Logos* came to be contrasted with *muthos*, to the discredit of the latter, as new kinds of discourse asserted themselves. (The history of the semantics of these two words is traced in the Appendix.)

When we use "myth" as in the definitions just indicated we are in the first place taking a broader historical perspective than the history of its semantics allows and "myth" is also used in cross-cultural comparisons between Greek and other myths. Our use of "myth" for the whole history of "Greek myth" can be called etic but does not have to be disallowed for that reason.[44] This term and its opposite, emic, were coined by the linguist and anthropologist Kenneth Pike

---

[42] Almost proverbial. In Edmunds 2016a, 33 n. 64 I cited Ben Amos 1971,10.
[43] An overview: Dégh 1984.
[44] See Fowler 2009, 22–23 on our necessarily etic use of "religion" and cf. on terminology in ch. 6. Cf. Graf 2003b, 12: "[O]ften there are compelling reasons for the use of a scholarly non-native term for certain phenomena even where there would be a native word as well, be it to maintain compatibility with other cultures, or more simply just to understand what is going on."

(from "phonetic" and "phonemic") to distinguish between the cross-cultural and the cultural-specific or between the insider's and the outsider's points of view.[45] The distinction is not, however, hard and fast and was not so even in Pike's mind. He said that the two were not a dichotomy and he conceded the possibility of a stereoscopic view of the same phenomena:

> Through the etic "lens" the analyst [i.e., as distinguished from the "untrained person"] views the data in tacit reference to a perspective related to all comparable events...of all peoples, of all parts of the earth; through the other "lens", the emic one, he views the same events, at the same time, in the same context, in reference to a perspective oriented to the particular function of those particular events in that particular culture, as it and it alone is structured. The result is a kind of "tri-dimensional" understanding of human behavior instead of a "flat" etic one.[46]

Pike studied the languages of indigenous peoples, which, once mastered by him, gave him an emic foothold. His nativism and preference for the emic are obvious in his writings. The historically minded philological student of Greek myth would also prefer to recover the emic point of view. But knowledge of ancient Greek does not in itself do more than establish points of reference. Can he or she establish that emic point of view? A larger discussion lies behind Pike's emic and etic. The problem of the commensurability or incommensurability of the modes of thought of different societies is of long standing and is hardly limited to anthropology.[47] (Cf. ch. 3.5 on the cross-cultural study of emotion.) The fact that we use "myth" etically does not mean that we give up on the possibility of emic understanding but, to use Pike's image, that we take a stereoscopic view. This book begins by looking at "myth" in various ancient perspectives (chs. 1–6), without the illusion that the etic can be excluded. The following chapters deal with modern ways of interpreting ancient Greek "myth."

The inevitability of the etic is asserted by Ken Dowden and Niall Livingstone in the introductory chapter of their *A Companion to Greek Mythology*. After a first paragraph in which they affirm what I have called the second way, they then assert the rights of the etic stance:

---

[45] As in Headland, Pike and Harris, eds. 1990. This distinction was referred to by Henrichs 2008 and discussed by Naiden 2013, 316–20.
[46] Pike 1967, 41. Quoted by Edmunds 2016a, 27 in the course of a longer discussion of Pike than the one here.
[47] Lloyd 1979, 1–2. See also Edmunds 2016a, 360 n. 154 for references to discussion of the grounds of the comparability of the ancient and the modern self.

> 'Myth'…refers to a network of Greek stories to which it is conventional to apply the term 'myth'. This is a matter of empirical fact, not philosophy or circular definition. We know a Greek myth when we see one and have no need of definitions, guidance, or codes of practice to identify it as such. It is, however, not a random network, but has a strong core of a system that was on occasion told as a system.[48]

They go on to give the example of Apollodorus' library and to pursue the idea of system and they refer to the pervasive manifestation of this system in ancient Greek life.[49]

Fowler's myth as told provides a definition of myth but one of the two questions posed at the outset still remains unanswered. What are the sources for Greek myths? Or what are the sources for a Greek myth, the one that someone is studying? Fowler faced this question in an article on Apollodorus. Every telling of a myth, he said, "introduces new variants, or new combinations of old ones." Ancient "[m]ythography, the recording of myths, merely reflects this plenitude."[50] If to mythography one adds poetic sources, scholia, papyri and visual media, the number of variants for a given myth is likely to increase.[51] The ancient mythographer, he said, aims at univocality, whereas his modern counterpart sets out all the known variants and tries to make sense of them, to interpret them in one way or another. He thinks that he occupies an Archimedean position but "he succeeds only in adding another variant to the pile."[52]

Nevertheless, not all of the activities of the modern mythographer are in vain. Among these he identifies the determination of "the relationships amongst sources, fixing chronology" and "explaining contexts."[53] These are standard activities of classical philology and would be considered necessary preliminaries. But there remains the question of how a myth is defined in the first place (cf. above on the hypostasis). Claude Lévi-Strauss's expansive Oedipus myth (discussed in ch. 7.3) is an example. It includes the dragon killed by Cadmus, the Spartoi born from the dragon's teeth, and the shadowy Labdacus, the grandfather

---

48 Dowden and Livingston 2011, 3. Cf. Buxton 1994, 14.
49 System was an element of the definition of Greek myth given in Edmunds 1990, 15–16.
50 Fowler 2017a, 158.
51 Variation belongs to the definition of Greek myth: Edmunds 1990, 5–6, 14–15; Edmunds 1997, 420–25; Edmunds 2014, 3, 5–6, 9, 18; Pàmias 2014, 46. Fowler 2017a, 159.
52 Fowler 2017a, 159. For the ancient mythographer he cites Fowler 2017b. Cf. Most 2017, 228: "[M]odern scholars who study the ancient mythographical tradition are themselves part of this very same tradition and cannot suppose that they assume a secure standpoint outside of it from which they could evaluate it objectively."
53 Fowler 2017a, 158.

of Laius. Oedipus' family line is separate from the one descending from the Spartoi. Most scholars would set narrower chronological limits. The premise is also going to include lateral boundaries, violated, one might say, by Lévi-Strauss's Spartoi. But what of other characters who have a better claim to belong to the definition of the myth, such as the informant or informants from whom Oedipus learns of his true parentage? Completely unrecognized in the summary of the myth in the *Odyssey* (11.275), he or they have important roles in tragedy.[54] In Euripides' *Phoenician Women* a horseherder came to Thebes came from Sicyon (a city near Corinth), told Oedipus how he had found him and given him to Merope. He showed Oedipus the swaddling clothes and the pins from his feet and asked for the pins as a reward for saving his life (Eur. *Phoen.* 26–28; schol. Eur. *Phoen* 1760, the Pisander scholium = *FGrH* 16 F 10 = *Oedipodea* Arg. B).[55] In Sophocles' *Oedipus the King* there are two informants, the Corinthian and the Theban shepherds, and the discovery comes about only because of the coincidence of their appearance in Thebes.[56] Someone might want to argue that these characters belong to a separate myth, which has been called "the exposure of the royal child."[57] Then what is "the Oedipus myth"?

In Fowler's list of the activities of the modern mythographer the next is "analysing narratives." This activity begins with the segmentation of a myth into parts. In folktale studies these parts are called motifs, which define types. These types, not individual folktales, are sometimes compared with Greek myths. Stith Thompson's full definition of motif began: "A motif is the smallest element in a tale having the power to persist in tradition."[58] The motif has a paradigmatic and syntagmatic aspect. The former is shown in the recurrence of a particular motif in a great number of texts, which is the basis of Thompson's index (*Mot*). The latter has been defined in this way: "The syntagmatic [i.e., narrativized] integration, different in each case, of the motif in a concrete textual context...is an object of individual interpretation."[59] This sentence, which, with its apparent disjunction between the two aspects of the motif, has pessimistic implications for theory

---

54 *Od.* 11.274: ἄφαρ δ' ἀνάπυστα θεοὶ θέσαν ἀνθρώποισιν ("and the gods soon made these things known among men"). On the semantics of ἄφαρ: Finglass in D-F, p. 360 n. 18.
55 In Androtion horseherders (plural) raised Oedipus themselves (*FGrH* 324 F 62 from schol. *Od.* 11.271).
56 On this coincidence: Edmunds 2006b, 47–48.
57 Cf. Binder 1964.
58 Thompson 1946, 415.
59 Würzbach 1999, col. 948: "Die jeweils unterschiedliche syntagmatische Integration des M.'s in einen konkreten Textzusammenhang...ist Gegenstand der Einzelinterpretation."

and method, applies equally well to the study of Greek myth, an ad libitum business, no matter the name that the units of analysis go under. (I have discussed some examples in chapter 8.2.1).

The terminology for Greek myth that I have used in this Introduction has for the most part been limited to myth in the sense of a particular kind of ancient Greek narrative and to mythology, especially in the quotation of titles, as referring collectively to the Greek myths. Myth also has this collective sense (OED^3 s.v. "myth" 1.b).[60] Mythology can be used for the study of myths.[61] The terms "legend" and "saga" are sometimes used to refer to stories about Greek heroes. These terms can cause difficulties and are avoided in this book.[62] The terms used for the segments of Greek myth vary according to the taste of the scholar (again see ch. 8.2.1).[63]

---

[60] For a brief history of the word "myth" in English: Hansen 2017, 5.
[61] For these two main senses (corpus of myths and study of myths): Bies 1999, col. 1074; OED^3 s.v. "mythology": 3.a–b; 4. Cf. Bremer 2012, 991: Mythology "is the field of scholarship dealing with myth but also a particular body of myths." Both of these senses are a far cry from μυθογραφία, first in Plato, where its two main senses are fiction and story-telling (LSJ and Montanari are in agreement).
[62] For the difficulties see Edmunds 2016a, 1–2. Allen 2011, 342: "To separate myths about gods from legends about humans is unhelpful where gods and humans interact and interbreed". For "legend": Ecker 1996. I once distinguished between "legend" and "myth", as in Edmunds 1985. The words "saga" and "legend" have senses in German somewhat different from their senses in English (Graf 1993 [1987], 6).
[63] "Mythologem" does not have an entry in *EM* and is not common. In the glossary in Dowden and Livingston, eds. it is defined as "[a] fundamental unit or element of a mythic narrative (Greek *mythologēma*, a piece of mythic narrative)" (2011, xxii–xxiv).

1 Myth in Visual Media: The Example of Theseus

Against the wide-spread notion that the performances of Homer, Hesiod and choral lyric were the primary medium in which myths were communicated must be set the fact of day-to-day contact with myths as represented in visual media. As Robert Fowler has said: "In everyday life in Greece reminders of the mythical heritage were ubiquitous in the visual and built environment: in the decoration on domestic furnishings, the images on your coins, the herm at your door, hundreds of landmarks in village, town and country, the shrines, the great temples, the national and panhellenic sanctuaries."[1] Of these media, painted vases literally brought home mythical scenes. The different kinds of vases, including the non-utilitarian kinds, could be "read" by their owners and presumably by others who saw them.[2] This chapter considers the use of vase painting and sculpture in the Athenian appropriation of Theseus as their national hero and compares the evidence for the visual media just mentioned with the evidence for Theseus in verse. The purpose of this comparison is to test the truism that "[p]oetry tends to inspire artistic representation, rather than the other way around."[3]

Two large questions can be safely left in the background. One concerns the older, pre-Trojan War Theseus, a hero in some ways like and in other ways unlike Heracles, without a pronounced Athenian identity.[4] The other concerns the period in which he took on that identity. Of the four periods that have been proposed the earliest is the years of Solon's leadership of Athens (archon 594/3 B.C.E.). The earliest artistic evidence for the Athenian Theseus, the François Vase (see below) comes from these years. For the next period, ca. 540–510, vase paintings, some of them cited below, provide the main evidence. The story that Theseus and the Athenians whom he rescued from the Minotaur stopped on the island of Delos and performed the "Crane Dance" may have been invented to serve as an aition for Peisistratus' "purification" of Delos (Hdt. 1.64.2; Thuc. 3.204.1).[5]

---

1 Fowler 2017c, 9.
2 For the metaphor of reading: Bérard 1983, 2. The relevant statement is quoted in Edmunds 2014d, 353. For somewhat fuller accounts of these trends in scholarship on Greek vases see Edmunds 1990d; Edmunds 2014d.
3 Mills 1997, 19 and n. 73.
4 Mills 1997, 4–5. And also like Jason: see Hansen 2002a, 151–66.
5 Shapiro 1998, 145 and n. 25.

The cults of Theseus in Athens develop along with the myths.[6] In the third period, 510–490 B.C.E., Theseus becomes conspicuous in Athenian art and sculpture. Finally, Cimon's bringing of the bones of Theseus from Skyros (470 B.C.E.) also has an obvious reflex in vase painting.[7] A detailed survey of these periods has concluded that Theseus was already the polis-hero in the first, Solonian period and "each subsequent age, including the Tyranny of Peisistratus, the democracy of Kleisthenes, the oligarchy of Kimon, and the radical democracy of Perikles, could adopt the hero as its own and promote those aspects of his career which best suited its own purposes."[8]

To begin with verse in the seventh and sixth centuries, Theseus does not appear often. In the *Iliad*, mention of his mother, Aethra as the handmaid of Helen is usually taken to be an Athenian interpolation (3.144).[9] (The care-taker of Helen, Aethra, was taken captive by the Dioscouroi when they sacked Aphidna and recovered their sister, whom Theseus had abducted.[10] Having returned to Sparta with them, Aethra then accompanied Helen to Troy.) Another reference to Theseus in the *Iliad*, the line in which Nestor recalls the superior heroes of the preceding generation, is omitted in most manuscripts (*Il.* 1.265 = Hes. *Scut.* 182). Theseus does not fare much better in the *Odyssey*. In the underworld, Odysseus pauses, after the disappearance of Heracles, in the hope of seeing more heroes of the past (11.630–33). He names Theseus and Peirithous (631). The line has been suspected since antiquity.[11] The solidest evidence in Homer for an early association of Theseus with Athens is Odysseus' sight, again in the underworld, of Ariadne "whom Theseus tried to bring to the hill of holy Athens" (*Od.* 11.321–25). (I return below to the question of a Homeric Theseus.) The Homeric references to Theseus, especially if they reflect an Athenian redaction of the *Iliad*, are, as

---

6 Walker 1995a, ch. 1.

7 Zaccarini 2015, 191 concludes that the recovery of the bones of Theseus by Cimon "neither dates to the fifth century nor derives from a single personality. On the contrary, most of its details date to later times and should be largely credited to fourth- and third-century authorities, as well as to later developments up to Plutarch's time." He does not discuss vase painting. Cf. von den Hoff 2002, 334, who regards the recovery of the bones of Theseus as an impulse to sympotic vase paintings showing cycles of the hero's deeds.

8 Shapiro 1998, 146. For a survey of Theseus vase painting: von den Hoff 2002.

9 Kirk 1985, *ad loc.*; cf. Sourvinou-Inwood 2014, 389–90; Krieter-Spiro 2009, *ad loc.* But for sixth-century evidence for the recovery of Aethra at Troy see Edmunds 2016a, 71–72; Bowie 2019, *ad loc.* Finglass 2020 discusses four possible attestations of Phaedra between the *Odyssey* and Sophocles.

10 On the abduction of the young Helen: Edmunds 2016a, 57–68.

11 But for arguments in its favor see Heubeck 1989, *ad loc.*; Finglass 2020, 187–88.

Claude Calame has said, an indication of the secondary character of the Athenian focalization of the Theseus myth.[12]

If there was a Theseus epic (attested in two scholia to Pindar and in Plutarch's *Theseus*), or if even if there was more than one Theseus epic, as Aristotle implies (*Poet.* 1451ᵃ19–21), the absence of any reference to this epic or to these epics in Athenian literature is surprising.[13] In hexameter verse known to us, Theseus appears as the Athenian polis-hero for the first time in a fragment doubtfully attributed by Bernabé to the *Minyas* (Θησεῦ Ἀθην]αίων βουληφόρε θωρηκτάων, fr. 7.26) and to a Hesiodic *Peirithou Catabasis* by Merkelbach and West (fr. 280.26 M-W).[14] This presumably mature Theseus, the one known from fifth-century tragedy, appears only in this poem and in a fragment of Exekias (ca. 540).[15] The surviving fragments of the poem, for which Bernabé suggests an early fifth-century date, have to do with the encounter of Theseus with Meleager in the underworld. Theseus as wise Athenian king, even if this conception of his character was early, seems to have been prominent in neither verse nor visual media before Athenian tragedies in the second half of the fifth century, the *Heracles* and *Suppliants* of Euripides and the *Oedipus at Colonus* of Sophocles.[16] The Theseus who organized the synoecism of Attica, presumably as king, is likely a mythical precedent for Cleisthenes' reforms at the end of the sixth century (see below).

Two of four other early appearances of Theseus in verse refer to episodes following the slaying of the Minotaur, a mission that begins in Athens. Theseus abandons Ariadne (Hes. fr. 298 M-W from Plut. *Thes.* 20). He does so, according to Athenaeus, out of love for Aegle (13.557a–b). In Sappho, according to a report by Servius, Theseus rescues seven youths and seven maidens, surely the Athenians known from many other sources, from the Minotaur (fr. 206 V from Serv. *Aen.*

---

12 Calame 1996, 399–400.
13 It is difficult to agree with Bernabé 1987 when he says: *Plures Theseïdas iam Aristot. cognovit, praeter carmen Atticum saec. VI ut videtur, unde credimus pendere plurimos artifices et poetas posteriores...* (on his *Theseïs* Test. 1). See Walker 1995b, 16–19 for discussion of scholarly opinion concerning a *Theseïd* of Peisistratid date. (Bernabé 1987 uses *Theseïs* as the title. The usual title is *Theseïd*.) Walker 1995a, 20 argues that the "myth of Theseus must have been known to epic tradition."
14 They grant the possibility of attribution to the *Minyas* (see app. crit. init.)
15 An amphora fragment in the University of Lund museum: *ABV*, p. 145, no. 17. (I regret that at the time of this writing I am unable to provide the *LIMC* reference.)
16 But how wise is he in Sophocles *OC*? See Finglass 2012a, 44–47 for doubt.

6.21, which does not specify the place in Sappho).[17] I discuss the other two references, in Alcman and in Theognis, after continuing with the Minotaur in vase painting, in which it was the earliest, and for centuries the favorite, episode concerning this hero.[18]

The first certain appearance of the Minotaur on a vase is on a relief amphora of about 670–60 B.C.E. (*LIMC* "Mi." 33* = "Ar." 36). There are also a stamnos from the same period (*LIMC* "Mi." 6) and gold plaques and a shield band (*LIMC* "Th." 246*–247).[19] Theseus appears in the uppermost band of the *chef d'oeuvre* of black-figure pottery, the François Vase (ca. 570–565 B.C.E.; *LIMC* "Th." 264). Lyre in hand, he leads youths and maidens in a dance. They are next to a ship. Ariadne is present.[20] (This vase also provides the earliest datable evidence for Theseus' fighting against the Centaurs. For *Il.* 1.265 see above.)[21] In the same period or perhaps earlier, Theseus with a lyre and Ariadne holding a crown (στέφανος) appear on the Chest of Cypselus, which has been dated to ca. 600 B.C.E. (Paus. 5.19.1). These accoutrements imply dancing.

A passage in the *Iliad* may bear a relation to the dance seen on the François Vase. On the Shield of Achilles, Hephaestus cunningly wrought youths and maidens dancing on a dancing-floor like the one that Daedalus built for Ariadne in Cnossus (*Il.* 18.590–92).[22] This dancing floor appears neither in the story of Theseus and Ariadne as told in Pherecydes (*EGM* 1, fr. 148) nor in what I would call the major mythographical tradition (Diod. Sic. 4.61.4; Apollod. *epit.* 1.8–9; Hyg. *Fab.* 42) nor in a puzzling variant in the *Odyssey* (11.321–25).[23] Nor is Theseus mentioned apropos of the dancing floor wrought by Hephaestus. A dance, however,

---

17 Only in post-fifth century sources does the reason for sending the youths and maidens appear: Gantz 1993, 262–63.
18 For a bibliography: *LIMC* "Th." VIII init.
19 Gantz 1993, 265–66.
20 For interpretations: Gantz 1993, 267–68; Woodward 1994 in *LIMC*.
21 Walker 1995b, 22.
22 Paus. 9.40.3 refers to a work of Daedalus at Cnossos, Ariadne's dance or dancing floor (ὁ τῆς Ἀριάδνης χορός), carved in relief on white marble. For Daedalus in the myth of Ariadne: Romani 2015, 59–60.
23 Theseus intended to bring Ariadne to Athens but Artemis slew her in Dia through the witness of Dionysus (Διονύσου μαρτυρίῃσι, 11.325). It is unclear why Dionysus brought witness against her and what he alleged. There is a version without Artemis in which Ariadne is abandoned on Naxos and Dionysus falls in love with her. See Heubeck 2003, 286 on lines 324–45. The two versions are combined in schol. MV *Od.* 11.322 = Pherecydes fr. 148 *EGM*: when Theseus and Ariadne land on Dia, Aphrodite tells Theseus to abandon Ariadne, Dionysus comes to her, and finally she is killed by Artemis because of her lost virginity. These are not all the stories. Cf. Plutarch's complaint: Πολλοὶ δὲ λόγοι...καὶ περὶ τῆς Ἀριάδνης, οὐδὲν ὁμολογούμενον ἔχοντες (*Thes.* 20.1).

was said to have been taught by Theseus to the youths and maidens whom he had rescued from the Minotaur. It imitated their path through the labyrinth (Plut. *Thes.* 21; schol. D *Il.*18.590). On their return to Athens they stopped at Delos and performed the dance, referred to at the beginning of this chapter apropos of Peisistratus, which the Delians called "The Crane" (Call. *Hymn* 4.307–15; Lucian *De salt.* 34). This minor mythographical tradition shows the nexus: Theseus-dance-youths and maidens-Delos. Comparison with the other sources is clearest in tabular form:

Tab. 1: Comparison of sources for Theseus, Ariadne and dancing or dancing floor.

Source	Theseus	Ariadne	Dance or dancing floor	Youths and Maidens	Place
François Vase	√	√	√	Ø	Cnossos?[24]
Chest of Cypselus	√ (with lyre)	√ (with στέφανος)	(√)	Ø	Ø
Shield of Achilles	Ø	√	√	Ø	Cnossos
Major mythological tradition	√	√	Ø	Ø	Ø
Minor mythological tradition	√	Ø	√	√	Delos

The reason for Ariadne's omission in the minor mythographical tradition is probably that, in returning to Athens from Cnossos, Theseus would have reached Naxos before Delos and Naxos was where Ariadne was left. Theseus is conspicuous by his absence on the Shield, the reason for which might be the implicit Homeric rule of his exclusion, the rule often assumed by scholars in discussion of the few places in the *Iliad* and the *Odyssey*, in which mention of him is found to be intrusive. In any case, if the puzzling lines in the *Odyssey* referred to above were alluding to a version of the myth established in epic hexameter, reference to this version would have turned up somewhere in the mythographical traditions. The *argumentum ex silentio* seems safe in this case. The conclusion for all the various myths entailing Theseus, Ariadne and dancing must be that visual

---

[24] For the place: Gantz 2003, 267–68 gives various possibilities.

precede verbal sources.[25] Beholders of the myths as represented in one medium or another could easily "read" them and, if they so wished, retell them because these myths belonged to a common oral domain.

Theseus' slaying of the Minotaur continued to be the favorite scene in vase painting of the sixth century and was also depicted on the Amyclae throne in this century (Paus. 3.18.9, 11).[26] The Minotaur received, by Minos' demand, a novennial sacrifice of seven Athenian youths and seven maidens (Plut. *Thes.* 15.1; Diod. Sic. 4.60.4–5–61.1–3).[27] In the version of the myth known from Bacchylides, Minos himself has come to Athens, chooses Theseus amongst the others and accompanies them to Crete (Hellanicus *EGM* 1, fr. 164 from Plut. *Thes.* 17.3). En route, a quarrel arises that leads Minos challenge to Theseus, i.e., recovery of a ring that Minos throws into the sea, and the hero's meeting the challenge (Bacch. *Dith.* 17).[28] Vase paintings from the early fifth century depict this event (*LIMC* "Th." 219–22), of which the earliest is a cup painted by Onesimos (*LIMC* "Am." 75*). The vase paintings probably antedate Bacchylides.[29]

The dithyramb was composed for the Ceans, the poet's fellow-citizens, to be performed by a chorus on Delos and addressed to Apollo, as the last three lines show.[30] If this song is dated to the 470s, as by most scholars, then its theoric purpose will be to express Cean solidarity with the Delian League and with its leader, Athens.[31] Thus the Athenian national hero, Theseus, appears as the son of Poseidon and in the depths of the sea he visits his mother-in-law Amphitrite, who gives

---

25 Cf. Romani 2015, 65: "Il tratto forse più curioso di queste prime narrazioni del mito di Arianna è che, a ben pensarci, è più facile guardarle che leggerle."
26 For an illustrated discussion: http://www.amyklaion.gr/?page_id=1301. von den Hoff 2010, 164 n. 14 for a bibliography of studies of Theseus images in the sixth c.
27 Gantz 2003, 262–63.
28 Bacchylides does not mention the ring, which Theseus ought to display at the end of the story, but cf. Paus. 1.17.2–6; Hyg. *Astr.* 2.5.
29 Contrary to Maehler 2004, 174–75, who argues that Bacchylides is the inspiration for the vase painting, "making this ode one of the earliest extant poems of Bacchylides." Maehler's conclusion concerning the date of the poem is obviously the premise of his argument concerning the sequence of poem and vase painting. Zaccarini 2015, 181 n. 43 doubts that Bacchylides can be dated by the painting by Micon on the wall of the Theseion (Paus. 1.17.3). On the problem of the site and the date of the Theseion: Walker 1995a, 21–22.
30 Maehler 2004, 172. I use "dithyramb" arbitrarily. For the debate over the genre to which this song belongs and for her own thesis, see Pavlou 2012, 510–11 and notes.
31 For the discussion of the date of the dithyramb and its Athenian orientation see Pavlou 2012, 511–13 with notes. Her own purpose: "to scrutinize the ways in which Ode 17 serves to advance on the one hand Delos as the Ionians' (and the Greeks') cultural omphalos and on the other the Athenians as Apollo's favourite minstrels and legitimate ministers" (513).

him gifts, a purple robe and a garland.³² Minos may at the moment be in control of the sea but the victory of the Athenian hero in the incident narrated in the ode prefigures the ultimate Athenian victory over what had been the Cretan maritime empire. The Athenian myth of the early supremacy of Minos is historicized by Thucydides in the "Archaeology." "Minos is the oldest of those whom we know by hearsay to have acquired a fleet and he had power over most of what is now the Hellenic sea" (1.4).³³ Simon Hornblower remarks on this passage that Thucydides "was, like a tragedian, reworking a myth for his own purposes".³⁴ When the historian refers to the sea that is now Hellenic, he avoids using the adjective that he uses elsewhere, "Aegean" (ἐν τῷ Αἰγαίῳ, 1.98.2; τὸ Αἰγαῖον πέλαγος, 4.109.3). In this way, he keeps the mythical version of Minos' loss of his thalassocracy out of the account.³⁵

In that version, various episodes of which have been discussed above, Aegeus, who is the father of Theseus, commits suicide because of an unfortunate lapse of memory on the part of his son. Theseus had said that, when he returned from Crete, if he was successful he would change the black sail under which he left Athens to a white one. He forgot to make the change. In his grief Aegeus threw himself into the sea, which was called "Aegean" after him. As it happens, Hyginus is the first one in whom the sea acquires the eponym for this reason. But a well-attested tradition for the change of sails goes back to Simonides (fr. 550 *PMG* = fr. 248 Poltera). Why would there have been such a story if it had no consequences?

The two other early references to Theseus are in Alcman and in Theognis. Both of these references have to do with his abductions of women, one of which, voluntary on the woman's, Ariadne's, part, was an episode in the mission to and return from Crete. In Alcman, at the time when the Dioscuroi recovered their sister from Aphidna, they sacked Athens in the absence of Theseus (Alc. fr. 21 *PMGF*; cf. *Cypria* fr. 13 Bernabé; *Il.* 3.144 cited above). Theseus, having abducted the

---

32 For the garland as signifying the winner, here a "secondary association": Danek 2008, 79–80. But in the context of the typical heroic combat described by Danek still an important association.
33 Μίνως γὰρ παλαίτατος ὧν ἀκοῇ ἴσμεν ναυτικὸν ἐκτήσατο καὶ τῆς νῦν Ἑλληνικῆς θαλάσσης ἐπὶ πλεῖστον ἐκράτησε... Here τῆς νῦν Ἑ. θ. sc. οὔσης (sic credimus). Cf. K.-G. 2.102 (b), e.g., ὡς ἐμοῦ μόνης πέλας sc. οὔσης (Soph. *OC* 83); Schwyzer 2.404.
34 Hornblower 1991, 19.
35 Calame 2007, 270: "Under the pen of Thucydides, the heroic legend...becomes history...[T]he taking of political and economic control by Athens in the Aegean Sea would be consecrated by the creation of the Delian League just after the Persian Wars, with Delian Apollo's sanctuary serving as its cultic and administrative center".

young Helen, was aiding his comrade Peirithous in his ill-conceived descent to the underworld to abduct Persephone. This story may lie behind the reference to Theseus in Theognis, the fourth of the early sources in verse:

> Σχέτλι' Ἔρως, μανίαι σε τιθηνήσαντο λαβοῦσαι·
> ἐκ σέθεν ὤλετο μὲν Ἰλίου ἀκρόπολις,
> ὤλετο δ' Αἰγείδης Θησεὺς μέγας, ὤλετο δ' Αἴας
> ἐσθλὸς Ὀιλιάδης σῇσιν ἀτασθαλίαις. 1231–34

> Cruel Eros, madness-spirits nursed you from your birth.
> Because of you was Ilios brought low,
> and Aegeus' son, great Theseus, and Oïleus' son,
> the noble Ajax, through his foolishness.[36]

The only story about Theseus in which he died because of Eros is attested in Greek literature in a single author, Diodorus Siculus. When Theseus went with Peirithous to the underworld to aid the latter's quest for Persephone, both of the two heroes were trapped there and did not return to earth (ἔνιοι δὲ τῶν μυθογράφων φασὶν ἀμφοτέρους μὴ τυχεῖν τοῦ νόστου, Diod. 4.63; cf. Verg. *Aen.* 6.617–18). In the better-known version, Theseus is freed by Heracles and Peirithous remains (Apollod. 2.5.12) and Theseus later dies on the island of Scyros (Plut. *Thes.* 35.4).

In this survey of the evidence for Theseus in visual media, mostly vase paintings, and in verse down to the end of the sixth century, the former clearly predominate in our sources and there is no reason to doubt that these sources are a good indication of the historical development of the Theseus myth.[37]

Whatever what one makes of the passage in Theognis, eros is a theme in the stories about Theseus, beginning with his love for Ariadne, whom, in one version of the return from Cnossos, he abandons when he falls in love with Aegle (δεινὸς γάρ μιν ἔτειρεν ἔρως Πανοπηΐδος Αἴγλης, Hes. fr. 298 M-W from Plut. *Thes.* 20.1). Plutarch compiled a list of the women carried off willingly or unwillingly by Theseus (*Thes.* 19.1–2; *Comp. Thes. et Rom.* 6.1). One of them was the Amazon Antiope, for whom the evidence in archaic verse is slight, amounting only to a passing reference to Pindar in Pausanias (7.2.6 = fr. 175 Sn.). Pherecydes (*FGrH* 3 F 151 = *EGM* 1, fr. 151) and Hellanicus (*FGrH* 4 F 166 = *EGM* 1, fr. 166) cited by Plutarch for Theseus' capture of Antiope would be earlier than or contemporary with Pindar

---

[36] West 1993, 151. Arguments for archaic date: Vetta 1980, 38–39.
[37] Calame 1990, 400: "l'extraordinaire développment de la représentation figurée sous toutes ses formes nous donne l'impression que l'imagerie anticipe sur la poésie dans le développment et dans la diffusion de la légende de Thésée."

(Plut. *Thes.* 26.1).[38] In a short period between the end of the sixth century and the middle of the fifth, however, the episode inspired Attic vase painters (and two non-Attic: *LIMC* "An." 14, 15). Pherecydes may also have been the one who reshaped the events of Theseus' life from the time of his arrival in Athens to his expulsion of Medea (on which see below).[39]

Theseus' abduction of the child Helen was a well-known episode, attested early in verse, the *Cypria*, Alcman, and Stesichorus, and also in art.[40] A fifth-century series of Athenian vases reinterprets the episode, which would not have contributed to the image of Theseus as national hero, by representing him as an ephebe, not the older man that he is in literary sources, so that he is pulled into the iconographical schema of "ephebe abducting marriageable girl."[41] So Christiane Sourvinou-Inwood showed.[42] A red-figure cup by Euphronius (ca. 520–505 B.C.E.; *LIMC* "Th." 286) has been interpreted as representing Theseus' acquisition of women in three modes, at three different times of his life—seduction (Ariadne), conquest in war (Antiope), and forcible abduction (Helen). Further, in an inscription in the Ariadne scene, Theseus says ΧΑΙΡΕ ΣΥ, a sympotic greeting. When a real reader speaks Theseus' words he momentarily takes on Theseus' identity. The cup provides images of admirable male exploits.[43] It should be remembered that the abduction of a woman is not in itself reprehensible. In Book 3 of the *Iliad* Hector asks Paris if, when he sailed to Sparta with his comrades and brought back Helen, he was the kind of man that he now appears to be, i.e., a coward (46–53). The implication is that Paris was a better man then and not reprehensible as he is now (46–48). Hector has in mind the typical exploit of bride-capture, of which he does not disapprove in itself.[44] Even if the symposiasts who drink from the Euphronius cup are not expected to go out and abduct women from other cities, they see in Theseus the "ephebe par excellence."[45]

In the versions of the three early Greek mythographers cited earlier Theseus fought the Amazons having gone to their homeland on the southern shore of the

---

[38] Herodorus, cited by Plutarch in the same place, is later (*FGrH* 31 F 26 = *EGM* 1, fr. 25**b).
[39] For this suggestion: Sourvinou-Inwood 2014, 368.
[40] *Cypria* (fr. 13 B); Alcman (fr. 21 *PMG/PMGF*); Stesichorus (fr. 86 F). Kahil 1988, §56.28. See Davies and Finglass for a detailed survey of the sources (2014, 325–26). Theseus' abduction of Helen may also have been a part of Ibycus S151 *PMGF*, on which see Finglass 2017b, 26–27.
[41] The vases: *LIMC* "Hel." 27–53.
[42] For discussion and for references to Sourvinou-Inwood: Edmunds 2016a, 70–71 and 327 n. 31. See also Gantz 2003, 289–90.
[43] I have followed the interpretation of Steiner 2007, 104–106.
[44] Edmunds 2019, 23.
[45] Sourvinou-Inwood 2014, 357, 361, 391.

Black Sea. Vase paintings from the end of the sixth and the beginning of the fifth centuries B.C.E. show him carrying off Antiope.[46] To return to the three modes of Theseus' acquisition of women, the historian Istros distinguished abduction (ἁρπαγή), love (ἔρως), and legal marriage (*FGrH* 334 F 10). Istros does not use Antiope as an example but another Amazon, Hippolyte, who turns up also in other sources as a variant of Antiope.[47] (In Euripides' *Hippolytus*, the eponymous character is the illegitimate son of Hippolyte.)

The date at which the Antiope vases begin to appear suggests the Peisistratid cultivation of the Theseus myth to which scholars have often referred. One can distinguish between a stronger and a softer model. According to the stronger, the striking new phase in the elaboration of the Theseus myth can be attributed to the Peisistratids. According to the softer, this phase should not be so attributed but should be seen as a more pronounced phase in a movement in Athenian visual media, and to a far lesser degree in verse, that began in Solonian times.[48] With Cleisthenes' reforms, however, which included the political-geographical reorganization of Attica, can probably be associated the tradition that Theseus as king of Athens had organized the synoecism by which all the Attic towns were united under a central council in Athens, the people became Athenian citizens, and Attica one polis (Thuc. 2.15).[49]

Whichever of the two models is preferred, in the decade after Cleisthenes' reforms (beginning in 510 B.C.E.), the deeds of the young Theseus when he is en route from Troezen to Athens along the edge of the Saronic Gulf begin to appear in vase paintings.[50] Now his slaying of several murderous sadists (Periphetes, Sinis, Sciron, Cercyon, and Procrustes) and the aggressive Sow of Crommyon come to the fore and also his capture of the Marathonian Bull.[51] The earliest evidence in verse is a dithyramb of Bacchylides, undateable but later than the vases. It was performed in Athens and takes the form of a dialogue between a chorus of Athenians and king Aegeus, who anticipates the arrival of the young Theseus (*Dith.* 18).[52] While this dithyramb cannot be the inspiration for the vase paintings,

---

[46] For these versions in relation to later ones and for the vase paintings: *EGM* 2, 485–86.
[47] *EGM loc. cit.*
[48] This is the thesis of Walker 1995b. For a discussion of phases: Shapiro 1998.
[49] On this passage in Thuc. see Munson 2017, 263–64.
[50] von den Hoff 2010, 164 nn. 12 and 15 for bibliographies of studies of this new series.
[51] Mills 1997, 20–25; Gantz 1993, 256.
[52] Athanassaki 2016 discusses points of contact between the dithyramb and the metopes of the Athenian treasury at Delphi. If, as Maehler suggests, the opening of the song recalls the opening scenes of Aeschylus *Pers.* and *Suppl.* and Sophocles *OT*, then it is likely to be later than the metopes (2004, 18).

the old truism is again asserted: "[T]he vases almost certainly reflect poetry, perhaps an authoritative poem commissioned by either Peisistratus or by one of his sons or by one of their rivals, the Alkmeonids. If it was a poem...could it have been the *Theseid* mentioned by Plutarch...?"[53]

Also in the period between 510 B.C.E. and the Persian Wars, the Athenians erected their treasury at Delphi, with its metopes depicting the deeds of Theseus and of Heracles. Scholars are divided on the date. Von den Hoff argues for the decade after the Cleisthenean reforms.[54] The treasury would thus be further evidence linking the emergence of the Athenian Theseus with these reforms (cf. the introduction to this chapter on the periodization). Scholars are also divided on how the four sets of metopes were arranged.[55] Whatever the answer, clearly the intent is to put Theseus on a par with Heracles.[56] As Calame has said:

> On the threshold of the classical era, the Athenians offer...to the eyes of the faithful, as they converge from their cities on the religious center of the Greek world, the spectacle of the equivalence, established from now on, between Heracles, the Panhellenic hero, and Theseus, the secondary protagonist taken from the myths of other cities to be elevated, in a reinvented narrative framework, to the rank of national hero of the city destined to be the political and cultural leader of classical Greece.[57]

Metope 5, which shows Theseus standing before Athena, epitomizes the hero's new Athenian role. Theseus and Heracles appear in Athens again in the Marathon painting in the Stoa Poikile (perhaps 460s; Paus. 1.15.3) and in the metopes of the Hephaisteion (460–450 B.C.E., although the metopes may be later).[58]

A series of Athenian vases (from ca. 470) show Theseus, the captured Marathonian Bull, Aegeus and an unnamed woman appear (*LIMC* "Th." 163; *LIMC* "Ai." 2*–17). The woman has a jug and libation dish. She is assumed to be Medea.

---

53 Maehler 2004, 191–92.
54 von den Hoff 2009, 96, 98; von den Hoff 2010, 164–65.
55 von den Hoff 2010, 166–167.
56 Neer 2004, 76. Neer's general thesis: "Treasuries convert upper-class ostentation into civic pride—and this appropriation of elitist spending is, I have argued, their real function. A thesauros is not a just a store-room: it is a frame for costly dedications, a way of diverting elite display in the interest of the city-state" (65). On Theseus and Heracles: Finglass 2013, 45.
57 Calame 1996, 404. My translation. "Au seuil de l'époque classique, les Athéniens offrent...au regard des fidèles convergeant des cités hellénes vers le centre religieux du monde grec le spectacle de l'equivalence désormais établie entre Héraclès, le héros panhéllenique, et Thésée, le protagoniste secondaire retiré à la légende d'autres cités pour être élevé, dans un cadre narratif réinventé, au rang de héros national de la cité destinée à être leader politique et culturel de la Grèce classique."
58 von den Hoff 2010, 173–74.

(In Euripides' *Medea* (431), Aegeus promises Medea a refuge in Athens.) Her attempted poisoning of Theseus seems to be presupposed. The vases are often linked to the Aegeus tragedies of Sophocles and of Euripides. For the dating of these tragedies only the *termini post quem* of Sophocles' (468 B.C.E.) and Euripides' first competing at the City Dionysia (455 B.C.E.) are certain. The date for Euripides seems to rule out his *Aegeus* as the inspiration for the vases and the date for Sophocles does not provide a firm evidence that his *Aegeus* preceded them. The fragments of these tragedies are too scanty to permit a conclusion about which of two versions of the attempted poisoning of Theseus they are following. In one version, by far the most common in the mythographical tradition, Medea tries to poison Theseus upon his arrival in Athens and he captures the bull later. In the other version, scantily attested but perhaps seen in Euripides' *Aegeus*, he first captures the bull and Medea later tries to poison him.[59] Someone in this tragedy generalizes about the antipathy of stepmothers to stepsons.[60] (The date of the dithyramb of Bacchylides concerning Theseus' arrival in Athens is likewise uncertain but in any cases sheds no light on the sequence of events under discussion here.) The vase paintings certainly presuppose a story in which Theseus' capture of the Bull and Medea's attempt to poison him are linked. (Another threat faced by the young Theseus after his arrival in Athens came from his uncle Pallas and Pallas' sons, rivals for the throne.[61] This episode cannot be positively identified on vases: see *LIMC* "Th." 172–75.)

In another series, of five vases an unnamed youth, sword in hand, chases an unnamed woman (not included in *LIMC* "Th."). On the basis of detailed iconographic and semantic analyses Christiane Sourvinou-Inwood identified these figures as Theseus and his step-mother Medea.[62] Her interpretation rests on a fully articulated method. The reason for Theseus' pursuit can be assumed to be Medea's two attempts to kill him, by persuading Aegeus to send him to capture the

---

59 On the two different versions of Medea's attempted poisoning, before or after Theseus' capture of the Marathonian Bull: Gantz 1993, 255; Kannicht 2004, 152. In the standard version she attempts to poison him upon his arrival in Athens and he goes after the bull later. Collard and Cropp 2008.1, 4: "In a variant version found only in Apollodorus (*Epit.* 1.5–6...) and the Vatican Mythographer (1.48...), Medea first persuaded Aegeus to send Theseus against the Bull in the hope that it would kill him, and only attempted the poisoning after he had subdued it."
60 fr. 4 Kannicht: πέφυκε γάρ πως παισὶ πολέμιον γυνὴ / τοῖς πρόσθεν ἡ ζυγεῖσα δευτέρῳ πατρί.
61 Gantz 1993, 276–77.
62 Sourvinou-Inwood 2014, 355 for references to her earlier work on this subject; 364–66 for Medea as the bad stepmother.

Marathonian Bull and by attempting to poison him.[63] Medea's son by Aegeus, Medus, was the founder of Media, thus the ancestor of the Medes (Diod. Sic. 10.27).[64] Sourvinou-Inwood speculates on the possible derivation of the pursuit of Medea from the *Aegeus* of Sophocles (on which see above). In any case, her interpretation of the scene can stand on the merits of her semantic analysis and in her view iconography does not depend on verbal myth.[65] Sourvinou-Inwood's interpretation, though accepted by some, was rejected on the grounds that "there is no literary or inscriptional evidence for such an encounter."[66] This statement presupposes the truism quoted in the opening of this chapter in a weaker (we need verbal evidence to confirm the subjects of vase painting) or stronger (vase painting derives from literature) form.

The truism emerges from the history of scholarship on Greek vases. The more recent trend in the study of vase painting to which I have referred was preceded by the classification of vases—of shapes, style, painters, and workshops—and on dating and periodization. The study of iconography remained in the service of these projects. Another project was and is the *Corpus Vasorum Antiquorum*, a catalogue of painted Greek vases divided into fascicles by museum and country. It began to appear in 1922 and is ongoing. The first departures from the historical-aesthetic scholarship were in the direction of the potters and their patrons, the uses of the vases, and the vase trade in economic history. Those scholars, a distinct minority, who addressed themselves to the mythological subject matter of Greek vase painting, typically understood it as illustration of the verbal myths. This tendency is apparent in many articles in the *Lexicon Iconographicum Mythologiae Graecae*, which began publication in the same year (1981) in which Claude Bérard, a professor at the University of Lausanne, began a seminar in which he was to articulate the aims of the new semiotic approach and introduce the metaphor of "reading" the images on vases. This new approach, exemplified in this chapter by Sourvinou-Inwood's interpretation of the vases depicting an ephebe chasing a woman, does not dispense with but builds upon the necessary information provided by the older approaches.

---

[63] The attempted poisoning of Theseus by Medea is attested first in Call. *Hecale* (fr. 232 Pf.). Aegeus calls out not to drink it (fr. 233 Pf.).
[64] Sourvinou-Inwood 2014, 367–68.
[65] Sourvinou-Inwood 2014, 397–98.
[66] LIMC "Th." XII. Gantz 1993, 255, 297 independently arrived at the same interpretation as Sourvinou-Inwood's.

The truism concerning the priority of poetry to art does not hold up in the case of Theseus. Even if it were still true of other myths, the question would remain of how the beholder "reads" the vase painting or the sculpture or an image of the myth in some other medium. Did he or she try to think of a poem? Clearly the women in Euripides' *Ion* who refer to myths that they discern in sculptures at Delphi did so spontaneously and succinctly (for this example see Appendix) and without any apparent reliance on poetry.[67] The next chapter turns to storytelling as a mode of communication of Greek myth. This mode would have been enough for the knowledge of the women at Delphi, who, after all, speak of the story-telling that accompanies their weaving (Eur. *Ion* 196–200). It was enough for Thucydides in the case of Minos, one of the great antagonists of Theseus. Minos, he says, is one of those of whom we know by hearsay (ὧν ἀκοῇ ἴσμεν, cited above).[68]

---

[67] The question of how they know the myths should be distinguished from the question of how they identify the myths as represented in the sculptures, on which see Woodford 2011, 157–60.
[68] Hornblower 1991, 19–20 has a full discussion of this phrase. He observes that "[i]t is rare for Th. thus to appeal to hearsay evidence." For three places in which Thuc. refers dismissively to this kind of evidence (tellers of myths mentioned alongside poets as sources to be dismissed): Introduction pp. XVI–XVII.

2 Greek Myth as Story-Telling and in Oratory

Not only were myths visibly available everywhere in various media, they were also stories that came to mind and were alluded to or retold by whoever it might be (cf. τοὺς ἐπιτυχόντας ὑπὸ τῶν ἐπιτυχόντων μύθους, Pl. *Rep.* 377b1–2) for one purpose or another.[1] This tendency causes one version of a myth to differ from another (2.1–2). A particular use of myth considered in this chapter is in reference to the location in which someone finds herself or himself (2.3). Another use is in oratory, in which myths can be a form of argument (2.4). Contrary to the impression given by epic and tragedy, myths could be short. They become longer not only by poetic elaboration but also by a potentiality for combination with other myths (2.5)

2.1 Story-telling and variation

Myths are stories that can be told, in principle, by anyone, as the circumstances require.[2] Examples appear already in the *Iliad* and the *Odyssey*, in which most non-Iliadic and non-Odyssean stories are told not by the narrator but by the characters. (For the semantics of *muthos* as used of this story-telling in Homer see Appendix.). Each of these epics as a whole tells a story but that story is in both cases shorter than the relevant myth. The *Odyssey* is a long poem but, as Aristotle said, its main story is short and the rest is episodes.[3] The *Iliad* Aristotle called a "unitary part" of the Trojan War (*Poet.* 1459a35) and it is a rather small part, covering fifty-odd days.[4] The *Iliad*'s references to the parts of the Trojan War before and after these fifty-odd days are infrequent.[5] The distinction between epic and myth as

---

[1] Finkelberg 2014 surveys the sources for the myth of Boreas and Oreithyia, distinguishing between literary and non-literary, and concludes that at no point in the transmission of this myth, from its earliest attestation in Athens in 480 B.C.E. to Pausanias' sources in the second century C.E., did a literary text, whether written or oral, play a significant role (98).
[2] Cf. Edmunds 2014a, 1–2. For "story", see Kolesnikoff 1993b.
[3] "[T]he main story of the *Odyssey* is short: a man is abroad for many years, is persecuted by Poseidon, and is left desolate; further, circumstances at home mean that his property is consumed by suitors, and his son is a target for conspiracy; but the man survives shipwreck to reach home again, reveals his identity to certain people, and launches an attack—his own safety is restored, and he destroys his enemies. This much is essential; the rest consists of episodes" (*Poet.* 1455b17–23; Transl. Halliwell 1987, 51).
[4] Latacz 2000, 151–55.
[5] Cf. Létoublon 2011.

https://doi.org/10.1515/9783110696202-002

story-telling is clear. Faith in these two epics as best sources for Greek myth, unless it is a matter of the particular version of a myth recounted by a character, is unfounded.

Still less can tragedy retell the "received myths" that it must use (παρειλημμένους μύθους, *Poet.* 1453^{b}22–23). The tragic action, ideally taking place in a single day (*Poet.* 1449^{b}12–13), can hardly constitute the myth as a whole, whatever it is, which comes out only now and then in analepses by characters or by the chorus. (On tragedy and myth see ch. 3.2). Myths as genealogies could go on at length in verse, as in Hesiod, and perhaps also in the early mythographers, although the fragments that we have do not allow an estimate. If, however, someone recounted his genealogy to someone else, as Aeneas does to Achilles in Book 20 of the *Iliad*, it was going to be much shorter.[6] From the time of the early mythographers myths as stories, taken from verse or oral versions, are concise, as those places show in which we do not depend on a scholiast but seem to have a quotation in a later author (e.g., Pherecydes *EGM* 1, fr. 18a). Paradoxically, the short forms of myth are better sources of myths than the long verse forms.

In the telling and retelling of myths, variation is the norm, the result of the story-teller's particular intention.[7] If, in the case of a particular myth, this intention is not simply entertainment, then it comes under the heading of rhetoric, as in Aristotle's definition (quoted in 2.4 below).[8] The story-teller has some point, implicit or, usually, explicit, to make and the myth seeks to persuade the listener or listeners of this point. His or her story thus comes to differ from previous versions.[9] This observation holds for the ordinary person and also for the mythographer. When Hecataeus opposed his work to the existing multiplicity of stories, he could not really have been making a claim to arrest variation. (Cf. ch. 4.1 for the preface of Hecataeus.) He would have known that someone else could also produce a mythography, a written record of myths, who would implicitly or explicitly make the same claim that he made and then proceed to offer his own new or different versions of the same myths, as in fact other mythographers were doing and

---

6 Even if commentators complain of its length, e.g., Hainsworth 1969, 31: "the rambling genealogical excursuses of Glaucus ... and Aeneas ..., in which we take no interest." Aeneas' speech has, however, a clear rhetorical strategy not harmed by its relative lengthiness.
7 The question of how much one version can differ from another and still be the "same" myth arises also with folktales in relation to folktale types: Edmunds 2016a, 30–37.
8 As for entertainment, Delattre 2005, 39–40 stipulates pleasure as one of two "constitutive principles" of myth, the other being efficacity.
9 Edmunds 1990a, 15; Edmunds 2005, 31–33, with particular reference to myth and epic; Edmunds 2014a, 5. Martin 2013, 48: "Myth-stories *do* something *for* you and against your opponent", if it is a matter of an opponent.

would continue to do. Or someone could make a critique of Hecataeus, as Herodotus did (2.143.1–4).[10]

The modern scholar of myth, who is aware of the shakiness of the mythographical project, tends to go in one or the other of two opposite directions. He or she may choose a best source or sources for the myth to be interpreted and, in effect, establish a new version, in effect continuing the ancient practice of storytelling and of the mythographers. Or the modern scholar may go in the direction of encyclopedism and compile all the ancient versions of myths about a particular hero, without preference for one or another.[11] The first of these approaches tends to simplify the character of the hero—he or she is simply the protagonist. The second avoids the question of what those who told and heard these various myths concluded about the hero, who may differ considerably from one myth to another (ch. 3.1).

2.2 Myths in daily life in the polis

Even in the fifth century B.C.E., despite much growth in literacy, the telling of myths would have remained the primary mode of their communication, even with the advent of mythography. William Harris concluded his survey of the uses of literacy in fifth-century Attica by saying: "For the population of Attica as a whole, it should probably be set in the range between 5% and 10%."[12] Even if other scholars have increased these figures by a factor of two or three or more, one imagines with difficulty an Athenian responding to the representation of a myth on a vase by consulting or referring to a written work. (Such a representation was usually of a single episode and required memory of the story from which it came.) The gradual transition from orality to literacy in Athens and other poleis has been a theme of the books of Rosalind Thomas.[13]

Myths told by citizens of Athens to one another have an ambivalent status. In Plato, women are the ones who tell myths. In particular mothers tell myths to their children.[14] Strabo in the introduction to his *Geography*, implicitly opposing

---

10 Asheri, Lloyd and Corcella 2007, 345 on Hdt. 2.143.1–4 refer to "the demolition of Hecataeus' genealogical pretensions and, *ipso facto*, his concept of early Greek chronology."
11 For these two tendencies of modern scholarship on myth see Fowler 2017, 158–59.
12 Harris 1989, 114. See the reflections of Ford 2002, 152–57.
13 Thomas 1989; Thomas 1992.
14 Surveys of the evidence: Buxton 1994, 19–21; cf. 160–61; Hansen 2002a, 12–13. In the second Book of the *Republic* (376e1–end) Socrates discusses with Adeimantus the education of children. He presupposes that mothers and nurses tell children stories about gods and heroes that come

Plato, gives a lengthy and closely reasoned justification for the use of myths in the education of children and uneducated and half-educated adults. When he says that "we employ" myth for the exhortation and dissuasion of children he must have oral story-telling in mind.[15] He then gives the example of Lamia and other myths that have a deterrent effect. With children and their myths he contrasts "those who live in the cities", i.e., the general population, and their exhortation by pleasing myths that they hear from the poets.

Hippias, who has spent more time in Sparta than anywhere else, tells Socrates that the Spartans like to hear about the genealogies of heroes and men and about the foundations of cities and in sum all ancient lore. Socrates says that he understands why the Spartans enjoy listening to him, knowing as much as he does, and use him as children use old women, for their pleasant telling of *muthoi* (πρὸς τὸ ἡδέως μυθολογῆσαι).[16] The addressees of myths are children, however, even apart from reference to women. The Eleatic Stranger says that everyone who has tried to divide the things that are into three parts—they all seem to me to be telling us a *muthos*, as if we were children (*Soph.* 242c8–9). In the *Stateman*, the sequel to the Sophist, the *Stranger* indicates a change in the kind of argument he is using and tells his addressee to pay complete attention, as children do, to the *muthos* that he is about to introduce (*Polit.* 268e4–5).

Women, when their voices can be heard, do not regard myth-telling in the same light as men do. In Euripides' *Melanippe the Wise,* the heroine recalls a theogony (cum cosmogony) that she heard from her mother but without any indication of disparagement either of the source or of the myth:

κοὐκ ἐμὸς ὁ μῦθος, ἀλλ' ἐμῆς μητρὸς πάρα,
ὡς οὐρανός τε γαῖά τ' ἦν μορφὴ μία·
ἐπεὶ δ' ἐχωρίσθησαν ἀλλήλων δίχα,
τίκτουσι πάντα κἀνέδωκαν εἰς φάος,
δένδρη, πετεινά, θῆρας, οὕς [θ'] ἅλμη τρέφει
γένος τε θνητῶν.

The story is not mine, but from my mother:
Sky and Earth were once a single form.

---

from Hesiod, Homer and "the other poets." When Herodotus says that Homer and Hesiod "created a theogony for the Greeks and gave the gods their epithets and distinguished their honors and arts and indicated their appearances" he cannot be taken to mean that all Greeks acquired this knowledge from these poets by reading or by listening to rhapsodes.
15 τοῖς τε γὰρ παισὶ προσφέρομεν τοὺς ἡδεῖς μύθους εἰς προτροπήν, εἰς ἀποτροπὴν δὲ τοὺς φοβερούς (1.2.8).
16 *Hipp. mai.* 285d6–e1; 285e10–286a2. Cf. Fowler 2011, 63–64.

> When they were split apart from one another
> They created and delivered all things to the light:
> Trees, birds, beasts the sea supports
> And the race of mortal men.[17]
>
> *Melanippe the Wise* fr. 484 Radt[18]

This passage is a fragment but nothing in the fragments of the tragedy taken together suggests that Melanippe does not deserve her epithet. Women also tell myths to one another, again without any negative implication concerning this practice (see the reference to the women at Delphi at the end of the preceding ch. and more fully in Appendix). To take another example, as Medea is killing her children, the chorus of Corinthian women exclaims "I have heard of one, one woman who turned her hand against her own children, Ino". and briefly recalls this deed (Eur. *Med.* 1282–89).[19] Mythological comparanda occur often in tragedy and can be assumed to seem "realistic" to the audience, as corresponding to a use of myth that they knew in their own lives.

The negative view of female myth-telling is the male view. In principle, myths are not told at the male symposium. Xenophanes gives the following admonition:

> ἀνδρῶν δ' αἰνεῖν τοῦτον ὃς ἐσθλὰ πιὼν ἀναφαίνει,
>   ὡς ᾖ μνημοσύνη καὶ τόνος ἀμφ' ἀρετῆς,
> οὔ τι μάχας διέπειν Τιτήνων οὐδὲ Γιγάντων
>   οὐδὲ < > Κενταύρων, πλάσμα<τα> τῶν προτέρων[20]
>
> Applaud the man who, when he drinks, brings out good things,
>   so that attention is attuned to good:
> don't be relating wars of Titans or of Giants
>   or Centaurs, fictions of the men of old.[21]

In both Plato's and Xenophon's *Symposium* the standard of intellectual conversation for gentlemen is avowed, in the former's by Eryximachus (Pl. *Symp.* 176e4–

---

17 Transl. Collard et al. 1995, 252–53, who follow (as Radt does not) Wecklein's bracketing of θ'.
18 The title distinguishes this tragedy from Euripides' *Melanippe the Captive*. Melanippe is "wise" because her mother, Hippe, was the daughter of the wise centaur Chiron. For the kinds of myth: West 1966, 192: "When your gods include the Heaven and the Earth, a theogony entails a cosmogony."
19 And their exemplum is course only one of those known: see Mastronarde 2002, 370 on line 1282.
20 D-K 21 B 1.19–22 = Xenophanes (I) B 1.19–22 West².
21 Transl. West 1993, 157, slightly revised.

10; cf. Socrates at *Protag.* 347b8–348a2), in the latter's by Socrates (Xen. *Symp.* 3.2), in implicit conformity with Xenophanes.

In practice, however, myths were difficult to exclude. In Plato's *Symposium* Phaedrus gives two mythical examples in support of the proposition that no one will die for you but a lover: Alcestis and Eurydice. He also gives the counter-example of Orpheus, who did not dare to die for love's sake but entered living into Hades. Each of these examples is narrated, at least in outline, and not simply referred to by the name of the hero or heroine (Pl. *Symp.* 179b4–180a4). Phaedrus points out each time how the gods rewarded (the two positive examples) or punished (the negative example) the mythical figure. (The punishment of Orpheus: he died at the hands of women.) In Xenophon's *Symposium*, myths are sometimes referred to (cf. 2.3 below for Erechtheus) but never narrated. The symposium concludes, however, with the mime of the marriage of Dionysus and Ariadne, introduced by the Syracusan impresario who has brought his troupe to Athens. He gives a précis of the action before the performance begins (9.2). In *Memorabilia*, apropos of Socrates' conduct at symposia, Xenophon remembers his frugality with respect to eating and his referring, apparently at symposia or a symposium, to the myth of Circe, her turning Odysseus' men into pigs, and Odysseus' self-restraint (*Mem.* 1.3.6–7). Socrates, it seems clear, did not narrate the myth but only referred to it, half joking, half in earnest, in order to encourage others not to overindulge.[22] In *Memorabilia*, however, he also retells at length Prodicus' essay on the choice of Heracles (2.1.21–34). addressing Aristippus. Xenophon does not give an indication of the physical setting. Socrates refers, however, to Prodicus' epideictic delivery of this essay before large numbers of persons (2.1.21). One can compare Hippias' reference to "Spartans" as his audiences. In both cases, and also in the well-known example of Protagoras' myth in the eponymous dialogue (320c8–323a4), myth-telling goes on in everyday life, in public performance, but not in the form of verse. Kathryn Morgan has discussed the performances of Hippias and Prodicus as "mythological role-playing", in which they give advice to young men.

> A mythological youngster is confronted with advice on how he should live his life. The educational situation in the myth parallels that of the sophist and his pupil in real life, and

---

[22] Socrates was giving his own version of the myth. Odysseus has the magic herb given him by Hermes (*Od.* 10.310–22) and he refrains from eating and drinking because of grief for his companions (*Od.* 10.371–87.) See Bevilacqua 2010, 328 n. 24.

thus the sophist/teacher can align himself with figures from the wisdom tradition such as Nestor, or even with the more problematic Odysseus.[23]

Protagoras' myth belongs to the same "genre."[24]

2.3 Myths and places

The mythical geography of the earth as a whole and of large-scale features of the earth such as landscapes and rivers has become a theme of research on Greek myth in the past generation.[25] Cities and places within cities have their own myths, in particular foundation myths, another theme of research.[26] Cities could also use myths to authenticate claims against other cities, as Argos did in its rivalry with Sparta for supremacy in the Peloponnesus.[27] The myths of heroes often have their itineraries, some like the expedition of the Argonauts covering much of the known world, some like those of Heracles and of Theseus continuing into the underworld. Hecataeus (on whom see ch. 4) wrote a *Periodos* or *Periegesis* (both titles are attested) as well as the *Genealogies*. (Sometimes one does not know to which of these two works a fragment should be assigned.)[28] The focus of the present discussion is not myths concerning place on a larger or a smaller scale but the use of such myths by particular persons in particular circumstances.

A well-known example is Phaedrus' reference to Oreithyia as having been carried off by Boreas somewhere in the vicinity of the place where he and Socrates find themselves and Socrates' detailed and dismissive reply (Pl. *Phdr.* 229b4–e4). This example is worth citing once again in order to observe that Socrates does not actually retell the myth (for the myth cf. Appendix §1). If a myth is well known to those present or if the story as a whole would not serve any further purpose, reference to the myth is enough. The people of Eleutherae, on the road from Thebes to Eleusis, said that the common soldiers of the seven contingents of the Seven were buried in their town.[29] The people of another town on the Boeotian border,

---

23 Morgan 2002, 106.
24 Morgan 2002, 132–54.
25 Buxton 1994, 80: beyond every colony was "the setting of mountain, sea, river, cave, meadow and spring" (80), all with their myths. More recently: Cohen 2007 (though also on landscape in art and poetry); Hawes 2017; Clarke 2017.
26 Malkin 1994 was a pioneer. More recently: Hawes 2017, 21–25. Cf. Delattre 2005, 246–63. On Delattre's example, i.e., Aeneas as the founder of Rome, see also Edmunds 2005, 39–43.
27 Hall 2007, 336–38.
28 Patterson 2013, 202.
29 Eur. *Suppl.*: 754–59; Plut. *Thes.* 29.4. For a map see Steinbock 2013, 6 (fig. 1).

Harma (Chariot), said that their town was named after the crash of the chariot of Adrastus, the sole survivor of the campaign of the Seven against Thebes. He then fled on his horse Arion (Strabo 9.2.11). In a variant local tradition, that of Colonus Hippius, a town two kilometers north of Athens, Adrastus arrived there on his chariot when he was fleeing from Thebes (*Etym. Magn.* s.v. Ἱππία).[30] There was also a hero cult of the Seven at Eleusis and one of Adrastus at Colonus Hippius (Paus. 1.30.4).[31] The myth was well known and presumably a townsperson in one of these towns did not have to retell the myth in order to make his or her point about the town's connection with the Seven.[32] Likewise, in Aeschylus' *Suppliants*, the chorus of Danaids, fleeing Egypt and arriving in Argos, only alludes to the myth of Io: "They say that Io was once the priestess of the temple of Hera in this land of Argos" (291–92).[33] Pelasgus, the king, replies: "She was indeed and the report prevails everywhere."[34] To take another example from a tragedy, when Orestes and Pylades arrive in Tauris the former recalls the oracular response that he received at Delphi: he must take the statue of Artemis from her temple to Athens, the statue "which they say fell here from the sky into this temple (Eur. *IT* 87–88).[35] Even Thucydides uses the geographical-mythical allusion. He refers to the strait between Rhegium and Messene as Charybdis, "where Odysseus is said to have sailed through" (ᾗ Ὀδυσσεὺς λέγεται διαπλεῦσαι, 4.24.5).

One of the myths that Pausanias heard required a somewhat fuller telling. Crossing a plain on the way to Mantinea, Pausanias passes a spring called Lamb (Ἄρνη). He recounts a story told by the Arcadians that explains the name:

> When Rhea had given birth to Poseidon, she placed him in a flock to live there with the lambs, and as for the spring it received its name because the lambs pastured around it. She

---

30 Ἐκλήθη οὕτως ἡ Ἀθηνᾶ ("Thus Athena was called") ... Then two explanations for her name and then a third: Ἢ ὅτι Ἄδραστος Θήβηθεν φεύγων, ἐπὶ Κολωνῷ στήσας τοὺς ἵππους, Ποσειδῶνα καὶ Ἀθηνᾶν ἱππίους προσηγόρευσεν ("or because Adrastus, fleeing from Thebes, stopped his horses on [the hill] Colonus and addressed Poseidon and Athena as gods of horses").
31 For the evidence for Eleusis see Steinbock 2013, 160.
32 These examples are taken from Edmunds 2014a, 17 with slight revision.
33 κληδοῦχον Ἥρας φασὶ δωμάτων ποτὲ / Ἰὼ γενέσθαι τῇδ' ἐν Ἀργείᾳ χθονί. Johansen and Whittle 1980.2, 234 ad 291: "not tentative...but indicating that the matter is established...by living tradition". For φασι as a way of introducing such a story see in addition to the n. just cited: Edmunds 2006b.
34 Cf. Sommerstein 2019, 174 on 291–92 and 293.
35 λαβεῖν τ' ἄγαλμα θεᾶς, ὅ φασιν ἐνθάδε / ἐς τούσδε ναοὺς οὐρανοῦ πεσεῖν ἄπο. For φασι see preceding n.

told Kronos that she had borne a horse and she gave him a foal to swallow instead of the child, as she later also gave him a stone wrapped in swaddling clothes instead of Zeus.[36]

This myth is not well known except to local Arcadians (did Pausanias hear it in Mantinea or were there persons, perhaps shepherds, in the unnamed plain when he passed across it?) and is heretofore unknown to Pausanias' readers. Whoever told the story knew the Panhellenic myth of how Rhea saved Zeus (Hes. *Theog.* 468–91) and astutely made the local myth an antecedent of, perhaps a precedent for, the more famous one.

2.4 Myth in oratory

The well-attested use of myth in Athenian oratory has a discernible historical antecedent in the rhetorical use of myth by characters in Homer and even in the unnarrated mythical exempla in elegy and the lyric poets.[37] Aristotle called rhetoric "the capacity to consider, in each matter, the persuasion that is open" to the speaker.[38] In the orators myth is one of the means of persuasion.[39]

To begin with an example from Homer, Agamemnon uses a myth in the speech in which he gives before the Achaean army in the scene of his reconciliation with Achilles. This speech, first of all, follows a typical pattern, which begins and ends with the connection of the myth to the larger narrative. The myth-teller (1) assumes that the audience already knows the story; (2) focuses on a particular point of contact between the story and the situation to which he applies it; (3) uses it as an argument and states the application of the story;[40] (4) because he assumes his audience's prior knowledge he tells the story elliptically, omitting much; (5) the story has a meaning beyond the one intended by the teller.[41]

---

[36] Paus. 8.8.2. Transl. Jones 1933, 381 with revisions by me.
[37] For myth in Greek rhetorical theory, where it remains, so to speak, pre-Herodotean in the absence of a distinction between myth and history: Gotteland 2001, 19–49.
[38] Ἔστω δὴ ἡ ῥητορικὴ δύναμις περὶ ἕκαστον τοῦ θεωρῆσαι τὸ ἐνδεχόμενον πιθανόν, *Rhet.* 1355ᵇ26. Cf. Mackie 2011, 826: "In general, stories in the *Iliad* are intended to persuade the listener to some kind of action". For Herodotus see Baragwanath 2012, who shows the significance of the mythic past to the Greeks of his time and the self-interested application of stories from this past by characters in Herodotus. "[M]yth of its nature exists in varying versions, evolving over time…according to the needs of the particular community that transmits it" (53–54).
[39] For a bibliography of studies of this use of myth: Steinbock 2013, 28 n. 129.
[40] Willcock 1964, 142; Nünlist and de Jong 2000, s.vv. "Argument-Funktion", "Paradeigma."
[41] This typology slightly revises the one given in Edmunds 1997, 419–20.

Agamemnon addresses the assembly first, saying that he will declare his mind to Achilles (19.78–84). He then turns briefly to Achilles (85–86a), then back to the assembly (86b–136) and finally to Achilles again (137–44). Formally, Agamemnon's speech from 86b to 137 can be analyzed as consisting of two parallel parts: his *transfert du mal* to the gods, who cast ἄτη into his mind (86b–94); the example of Zeus overcome by ἄτη (95–133), with a brief conclusion to the example (134–37). The two parts, with their conclusion (ὡς καὶ ἐγών κτλ., 134), amount to an *argumentum a maiore ad minus*: if Zeus, greatest among gods and mortals (95–96), could be blinded by ἄτη, then so could I, a mortal (sc., and I should not be blamed: cf. ἐγὼ δ' οὐκ αἴτιός εἰμι, 86b, the proposition with which Agamemnon began).

His mythical example follows the pattern defined above. (1) Agamemnon assumes that his audience knows that Alcmene was the wife of Amphitryon (*Il.* 14.323–24; *Od.* 11.266–68) and that she was impregnated on the same night by both him and Zeus, giving birth to Iphicles and Heracles—an example of "heteropaternal superfecundation", as in the case of Polydeuces and Castor.[42] (2) The point of contact between Agamemnon's story and his own situation is atē / Atē, which becomes (3) the *argumentum ad minus* already noted.[43] (4) He alludes to the labors imposed by Eurystheus (133; *Od.* 11.620–25; *Hymn. Hom.* 15.4–6) but says nothing about them (cf. 8.362–69; 15.639–40) or about Hera's enmity toward Heracles (*Il.* 15.25–29; 18.117–18) (5) The subordination of Heracles, the son of a god, to the inferior Eurystheus is an implicit, unintended analogy to the subordination of Achilles, the son of a goddess, to the inferior leader of the Achaeans.[44] Further, Agamemnon's comparison of himself with Zeus is an imposture.[45] The larger narrative context of myth-telling in Homer makes it possible for the narrator to show the speaker's self-interested but somewhat inept manipulation of the myth. The narrator's detachment and implicit irony put him at the beginning of the criticism of myth that later emerges explicitly when myth is opposed to other kinds of discourse (see Appendix).

The use of myth was standard in oratory and continued the practice of public story-telling just observed in Homer.[46] (To the speaker and the audience the myth,

---

[42] For the comparison cf. schol. Pind. *Nem.* 10.80–82; Edmunds 2017, 84–85.
[43] For this kind of argument in Homer see Grethlein 2006, 49, who points out that Agamemnon is the only character in Homer who compares himself to a god. For a survey of cases of "the formation of meaning by example" (*exemplarische Sinnbildung*): 43–63 with 43 n. 1 for bibliography.
[44] Davidson 1980, 200; cf. Coray 2009, 95–133n.
[45] Cf. Versnel 2011, 163 n. 28.
[46] Cf. Martin 1989, 45.

no matter how fanciful from our point of view, the remote past was "historical.") Oratorical use of myth required individual (the orator's) memory of the retold myth and also collective memory (his audience's).[47] How these two kinds of memory work has been the subject of much research in several fields.[48] In myth-telling, the orator has to remember the retold myth in the first place in order to make a new or a newly repeated point, inevitably reshaping the myth for this purpose, while the audience does not get the point unless it already knows the myth. The new version that emerges may or may not go into collective memory, but, to repeat, on the occasion the orator is able to give a new sense to the collective memory from which he began.

Three kinds of oratorical use of myth to be discussed here are myth in diplomatic oratory, myth, specifically the myth of autochthony, in Athenian funeral orations, and myths in law courts. Speeches in Xenophon and Herodotus well illustrate the first.[49] A particular kind of myth used in diplomatic oratory, kinship myth, is a large subject here omitted.[50] The opposing speeches of anonymous Athenians and Tegeans before the battle of Plataea are a favorite Herodotean example of the first of the three kinds to be discussed.[51] They argue their cities' claim to hold the left wing in the battle line of Greek allies (9.26–28.1). (It is a given that the Spartans hold the right wing.)

The Tegeans: At the time when the Heraclids attempted to return to the Peloponnesus they were opposed by a Peloponnesian army at the Isthmus. There Hylus proposed to decide the issue by single combat. The Tegean king, Echemus, slew him and, by the terms agreed upon, the Heraclids could not return to the Peloponnesus for a hundred years. From this exploit, say the Tegeans, we have always commanded the right wing on common expeditions (9.26.1–5).

The Athenians then give a list of the deeds that entitle them to hold the contested place in the battle-line. First, they once saved the Tegeans from domination by the Mycenaeans. Second, they led an army against Thebes in order to recover and bury the corpses of the Seven and their comrades. Third, they fought bravely against the Amazons when they invaded Attica. Fourth, they were second to none in the Trojan War (9.27.1–4).

---

[47] For the concept of social memory: Steinbock 2013, 7–8 (What is Social Memory?").
[48] Steinbock 2013, 8–13. In the field of Classics: Small 1997.
[49] Valuable survey by Fowler 2015, 198. See also Baragwanath 2012, 35–38 for general reflections on the use of myth in Herodotus, with references to earlier studies. For the comparable instances in Thuc.: Munson 2017, 259.
[50] For a useful study: Patterson 2010.
[51] For a bibliography: Boedeker 2012, 18 n. 5. Steinbock 2013, 57, 130, 134, 156–57, 196–97, 348 also discusses this example.

The single Tegean example is more copious than any of the Athenian examples, which decrease in length from the first to the last (seven words long). Except perhaps for the first, everyone knows these examples well and to "tell" the myth requires only an allusion, as in other examples discussed above. Deborah Boedeker has pointed out: "Aspects of both Athenian and Tegean accounts of the past are…subtly discredited by their disagreement with the primary narrative, which has the appearance of objectivity, in contrast to the motivated accounts of the past offered by the debating sides."[52] When the debate is concluded, however, the Lacedaemonian army shouts out that the Athenians are more worthy than the Tegeans to hold the right wing (9.28.1). The modern reader does not know if it was the "mythical" or the subsequent part (9.9.27.4–6) of the Athenian speech or both that persuaded the Lacedaemonians but even if, as seems unlikely, they took the first part with a grain of salt, they were not dissuaded.[53] The myths were effective on the occasion. The same point can be made about the speech of Agamemnon discussed above. The ineptitude of the Achaean leader that the narrator's presentation of his speech lets the external audience or the reader see does not count against the speaker. Agamemnon has addressed Achilles (19.83). He concludes with a repeated offer, now in his own voice, of the gifts promised to Achilles by Odysseus (9.260–99) and rejected at the time. Now, however, Achilles concedes that it would be fitting (ἐπιεικές, 19.147) for Agamemnon to give the gifts, even if Achilles is indifferent—give them or keep them. Odysseus intervenes and the reconciliation proceeds. In the context, Agamemnon's speech has been at least adequate.

The myth of Athenian autochthony was a *topos* in the funeral oration.[54] There are six examples, which have been much studied.[55] These examples have brevity and generality in common. Despite myths of at least four Athenian autochthons (Erechtheus, Erichthonius, Cecrops and Cranaos), none is ever referred to by

---

52 Boedeker 2012, 20–21.
53 The particular use of myth to argue for military privilege was now new. At the time of the second Persian invasion, Greek envoys go to Gelon of Syracuse to invite him to join the forces against the barbarian (7.157). Gelon agrees, on condition that he be the general commander of the Greeks (158.5). Syagrus, a Spartan, replies, "Surely the Pelopid Agamemnon would groan aloud if he heard that the command had been taken away from the Spartans by Gelon and the Syracusans" (7.159.1 echoing *Il.* 7.125). For interpretation of Syagrus' reply: Edmunds 2016a, 203–204. The Athenian ambassador then replies to Gelon, granting the command to the Spartans, if they want it, but, if not, demanding it for the Athenians. He refers to their autochthony (!) and to Homer's praise of an Athenian (sc. Menestheus, *Il.* 2.522) as the best commander at Troy (7.161.3).
54 For other myths, a limited set, in funeral orations: Buxton 1994, 37–38.
55 Dem. 60.4; Hyp. 6.7 Jensen; Isoc. 4.24–25; Lys. 2.17; Pl. *Menex.* 237b2–3; Thuc. 2.36.1.

name in a funeral oration nor is any detail of his myth. The references to Athenian autochthony constitute the zero-grade of narrative. For example, in the funeral oration that Socrates recites to Menexenus he says:

> The nobility of these men's origins is rooted in that of their ancestors. The latter were not immigrants and did not, by arriving from elsewhere, make these descendants of theirs live as aliens in the land, but made them children of the soil, really dwelling and having their being in their ancestral home, nourished not, as other peoples are, by a stepmother, but by a mother, the land in which they lived. Now they lie in death among the familiar places of her who gave them birth, suckled them, and received them as her own.[56]

The topos can be elaborated as here and in other examples but not with concrete reference.

One can speculate that the complexity of the relevant myths made them too difficult to use. The sequence of the early Athenian kings and autochthons, often the same persons, is for us notoriously difficult to reconstruct and probably was difficult already in antiquity. The early mythographers might have been the first ones to put this complex story into some kind of order but the fragments that we have do not offer any evidence that they were (with the possible exception of Hellanicus *EGM* 1, fr. 40). These references give what Martin West called a "strangely complex appearance" of the early mythical history of Athens. He referred to a "succession of earthborn figures...developing into a straggly genealogy".[57] Besides this complexity there is also the fact that the Athenians were variously called Ἐρεχθεῖδαι (e.g., Eur. *HF* 1166), Κεκροπίδαι (e.g., Eur. *Ion* 296), Κραναΐδαι (Eur. *Suppl.* 713) and παῖδες Κραναοῦ (Aesch. *Eum.* 1011), and also, in later sources that presuppose classical or archaic use, Ἐριχθονίδαι (e.g., Apollonius Dyscolus 2.2.494).[58] Further, two of the ten Cleisthenian tribes were named after autochthons: Erechtheis and Cecropis. Under these circumstances an orator

---

56 Pl. *Menex.* 237b2–c3: τῆς δ' εὐγενείας πρῶτον ὑπῆρξε τοῖσδε ἡ τῶν προγόνων γένεσις οὐκ ἔπηλυς οὖσα, οὐδὲ τοὺς ἐκγόνους τούτους ἀποφηναμένη μετοικοῦντας ἐν τῇ χώρᾳ ἄλλοθεν σφῶν ἡκόντων, ἀλλ' αὐτόχθονας καὶ τῷ ὄντι ἐν πατρίδι οἰκοῦντας καὶ ζῶντας, καὶ τρεφομένους οὐχ ὑπὸ μητρυιᾶς ὡς οἱ ἄλλοι, ἀλλ' ὑπὸ μητρὸς τῆς χώρας ἐν ᾗ ᾤκουν, καὶ νῦν κεῖσθαι τελευτήσαντας ἐν οἰκείοις τόποις τῆς τεκούσης καὶ θρεψάσης καὶ ὑποδεξαμένης. Transl. Ryan 1997, 953.
57 West 1985, 105. But he constructs a genealogical table: 181. He lists Cekrops, Cranaos, Amphiction, Erichthonius as the Athenian autochthons (103). I have not found evidence for Amphiction as an autochthon. West does not include Erechtheus, probably because West shares the common opinion that Erichthonius and Erechtheus were originally the same figure (West 1985, 104).
58 For the first of these names (Ἐρεχθεῖδαι) cf. Eur. *Hipp.* 151; *Ion* 24, 1060; *Phoen.* 852; *Supp.* 387, 681, 702; Soph. *Ant.* 982; *Aj.* 202. Diaeresis of the diphthong (Ἐρεχεΐδαι) sometimes occurs: Eur. *Med.* 824; *Ion* 1056; Ar. *Eq.* 1015, 1030; Ap. Rhod. 1.101.

might have implied adherence to one myth or another of autochthony if he used one or another of these names.

On the other hand, Demosthenes, for example, outside the context of the topos under discussion, refers to the Athenians as the Erechtheidae and to Erechtheus' sacrifice of his daughters "to save the land."[59] An orator could use an individual autochthon as an example for Athenians to emulate. In Xenophon's *Memorabilia* Socrates advises the son of Pericles on what he should say to the Athenians, who are despondent after their defeat in the battle of Delium (424 B.C.E.). Socrates says that he should remind the Athenians of their earliest ancestors, who were most excellent, and he refers to Erechtheus (3.5.10).[60] Socrates has in mind Erechtheus' defeat of the Eleusinians and their Thracian ally Eumolpus.[61]

Finally, speakers in Athenian law courts used myths. In the agon of Aristophanes' *Wasps*, Philocleon, the passionate juror, who delights in condemning the accused party, defends his way of life against his son, Bdelycleon. One of his pleasures is listening to speakers' attempts to win him over by recounting myths or something funny from Aesop (οἱ δὲ λέγουσιν μύθους ἡμῖν, οἱ δ' Αἰσώπου τι γέλοιον, 566).[62] The same two kinds of stories are referred to at the beginning of *Peace* when Trygaeus' daughter discovers, to her dismay, that he intends to ride up to heaven on the back of a gigantic dung beetle. Trygaeus justifies his plan by saying that in Aesop the beetle is the only winged creature who has reached that realm (129–30) and he refers to a particular fable (133–34). His daughter replies that he ought to have harnessed a Pegasus (135–36), i.e., that he ought to have emulated Bellerophon (although Bellerophon, who fell off his horse and back to earth, is not a promising example). The use of myths to which Philocleon refers might be illustrated by the Unjust Argument's examples of Zeus's binding his father (to show that justice is problematic) and of Zeus's inability to resist adultery (to show that it must be forgivable if even a god could not resist the temptation).[63]

---

[59] ᾔδεσαν πάντες Ἐρεχθεῖδαι τὸν ἐπώνυμον <τὸν> αὐτῶν Ἐρεχθέα, ἕνεκα τοῦ σῶσαι τὴν χώραν τὰς αὐτοῦ παῖδας...εἰς προῦπτον θάνατον δόντ' ἀναλῶσαι (60.27).

[60] ... καὶ τὴν Ἐρεχθέως γε τροφὴν καὶ γένεσιν, καὶ τὸν πόλεμον τὸν ἐπ' ἐκείνου γενόμενον πρὸς τοὺς ἐκ τῆς ἐχομένης ἠπείρου πάσης... For the inspirational value of autochthony cf. Pl. *Rep.* 414d–e. For bibliographies on the much studied topos of Athenian autochthony: Hornblower 1991, 12–13 on Thuc. 1.24; Frangeskou 1999, 319 n. 20. On Thuc. and Hdt.: Pelling 2009.

[61] In this way, Erechtheus was able to open the Eleusinian Mysteries to the Athenians: Xen. *Symp.* 8.40: see Huß 1999 *ad loc*. Also Thuc. 2.15.1; for the Mysteries: Paus. 1.38.3.

[62] Aristot. discusses at length the fable as a kind of παράδειγμα, giving examples of this use of example (*Rhet.* 1393ᵃ28–1394ᵃ5).

[63] *Clouds* 902–907, 1079–82. I am following Biles and Olson 2015, 263 on line 566.

It is the *argumentum ex Iove* seen in the speech of Agamemnon discussed above (compare the reasoning of Euthyphro: ch. 5).

2.5 Longer and shorter myths

Greek myths are known to us in the medium of printed texts but in archaic and classical Greece they were primarily oral even after the writing down of myths began (ch. 4). The performances of epic and of choral lyric might seem to us the primary modes in which myths were told and heard in the archaic and classical periods but much evidence shows their use outside of verse, as they served various purposes in everyday life (2.2–4 above). Their source was memory. How many someone could remember and in what form in his or her memory are unknown. One can assume that most Greeks remembered some myths, but how many? One can also assume that the number and the particular myths differed from one person to another. In the telling, as circumstances required, a myth could be expanded. In any case, each retelling, depending on its purpose, produced a different version and it was this result that mythography aimed to overcome (ch. 4.1). Little by little, writing, called by Prometheus "the worker mother of the Muses" (*PV* 461), also replaced memory. On the side of prose, the main idea of the proem of Herodotus is that he "wants to save from oblivion …what deserves to be remembered" and "in a still predominantly oral culture this task mainly consists in writing down memories and testimonies."[64] The collections of myths that began to be compiled in the Hellenistic period were, amongst other things, aides-mémoire.

Myths may be longer or shorter. What about the Trojan War (of which the *Iliad*, long as it is, convers only fifty-odd days)? In Martin West's retelling the Trojan War amounts to fewer than a hundred words:

> *You all know the story of* the Trojan War: how Helen, the most beautiful woman in the world, was abducted to Troy by Paris; how her husband, King Menelaos of Sparta, and her brother-in-law, King Agamemnon of Mycenae, gathered a *large* army from all of Greece and the Aegean islands and sailed against Troy in over a thousand ships; how they fought there for ten years and at last, after many toils, took and burned the city of Priam and returned *the repentant sinner* Helen to her husband.[65]

---

64 Asheri 2007, 73.
65 West 2011, 97.

If the italicized words were omitted, then this retelling would be eighty words long. Myths of this length could be effective or could be expected to be effective, as by Nestor in the assembly of the Achaeans in *Iliad* Book 1. He recalls that he fought beside Theseus and other heroes of that generation against the centaurs. His comrades listened to his advice then, he says, as they should do now (260–73).

A character in the *Iliad* or the *Odyssey* can also retell a myth at considerable length, as in Phoenix's retelling of the myth of Meleager in order to persuade Achilles to accept the gifts that have been offered him (*Il.* 9.524–605). In the *Odyssey*, Nestor tells Telemachus at some length of the returns of the heroes (3.130–200), events that have taken place in his lifetime but already have exemplary value for the young Telemachus and amount to an epic narrative within the epic.[66] Nestor is also a teller of myths in the *Cypria*. When Menelaus, gathering an army to go to Troy and recover Helen, comes to him, Nestor recounts the stories of Epopeus, Oedipus, and Theseus and Ariadne (arg. 22–29 B = arg. 36–39 D). But how he applied these myths to the situation at hand is unclear from the brief report that we have.[67]

While the expansion of a myth in epic or in Pindar can be understood in relation to the context and to the narrator or the poet, a simple mechanism, independent of verse, was the addition of one myth to another. The great mobility of heroes enables them to enter an ongoing story about others and, in the example to be considered, to complete it. Heracles enters the story of the servitude of Poseidon and Apollo to Laomedon, ordered by Zeus (Poseidon in *Il.* 21.443–45). This was their punishment for participation in a palace revolution (referred to by Achilles in *Il.* 1.396–400).[68] Laomedon was to have paid them wages but reneged. Poseidon then sent a sea monster against Troy. Consulting an oracle Laomedon received the response that he should set out his daughter Hesione as fodder for the monster and that thus he would be freed of the threat. Having set out his

---

[66] As L-N-S 2000, 103 on 1.248–89 and on 1.248 point out, the expressions that characterize Nestor as a speaker have poetological associations.
[67] See West 2013, 98–100.
[68] L-N-S 2000, 139 on 1.400 seem to assume that the three gods named by Achilles in this line are the only ones who revolted against Zeus, thus that Apollo was not one of them. But Achilles, who is addressing Thetis, has already said that she told him that *she alone* (397) sided with Zeus, as against *the others* (399), i.e., all the others. Having framed this contrast between Thetis and all the others, Achilles then names three gods (Ἥρη τ' ἠδὲ Ποσειδάων καὶ Παλλὰς Ἀθήνη, 400). Syntactically this list of three is in apposition to ἄλλοι (399) but in sense it cannot be exhaustive. Why Achilles choose these three examples is not clear. In any case we are dealing with "character speech" as distinguished from "narrator-speech" (on this distinction see introduction to ch. 9).

daughter on the seashore, he proclaimed that he would give the immortal horses to the one who destroyed the monster, the horses that Zeus gave to Tros in recompense for Ganymedes. At this point Heracles enters the story, arriving with the Argonauts, who are on their way to Colchis. Heracles then steps out of the myth of the Argonauts and into the myth of the servitude of Poseidon and Apollo to Laomedon, long enough to kill the monster and rescue Hesione. As for what happens next, the sources give different versions, which do not have to be pursued here.[69] The mobility of Heracles includes, in the first place, his joining the expedition of the Argonauts. Many other heroes, who have what one could call their own myths, also joined the crew, Theseus, the Dioscouroi, and Nestor, for example.

Another example appeared in the preceding chapter but was not discussed as such: the myth in Bacchylides 17, in which Theseus, one of the seven youths and maidens whom Minos is conveying to Cnossos for sacrifice to the Minotaur, opposes Minos when he tries to lay hands on one of the girls. Minos throws his golden ring into the sea and challenges Theseus to fetch it. He succeeds. And the journey to Crete continues. This myth has no consequences for the myth that frames it (the events leading to the Athenian tribute, the story of the labyrinth, Theseus' slaying of the Minotaur, and the ultimate death of the father of Theseus).[70] The shorter, framed myth is an addition.

2.6 Conclusion

Myths as story-telling can be considered a normal experience in the polis, as also in the countryside (cf. the shepherds referred to in 2.3 sub fin. above). Athenian norms concerning the tellers and audiences of myths were hard to maintain in practice. The symposium was clearly a site of ambivalence. Poetry as a source of myth also had an ambivalent status, which was of fundamental importance in the development of the somewhat or sometimes negative concept of myth in the fifth century B.C.E. The history of this development is traced in the Appendix. For ad hoc personal reasons and for political reasons, places were attached to myths. Thales said: "All places are full of gods" (θεῶν πλήρη πάντα, D-K 11 A 22 = L-M D10, R34a). We can say: all places are full of myths. Myths may be longer or shorter, depending on who is telling a story and in what circumstances. If a myth

---

69 For the myth see Finglass 2011, 266–67 on Soph. *Aj.* 434–46; for the myth as told in Mythographus Homericus (schol. D *Il.* 20.145) see Edmunds Forthcoming(1).
70 Danek 2008, 74.

is well-known, it can serve as the frame for the expansion of single incident, as in the *Iliad* the Trojan War serves as the frame for the story of the anger of Achilles.

3 Characters and Names in Myth, Epic and Fiction

A character will usually be self-consistent in any one work in verse but may be inconsistent from one myth about him or her to another (§1). While tragic characters loom large in our minds and tragedies seem to be about characters, Aristotle took another view of the matter, arguing that character was secondary to plot (§2). An argument like Aristotle's can be made concerning character in epic (§3). Comparison of the status of character in tragedy and epic with character in the modern novel helps to elucidate this argument (§4) as does the comparison of emotion in particular in these genres as the inner dimension of character (§5). The names of characters bring out the differences between the ancient and modern genres (§6). The points made in this chapter concerning the relation of names to narrative are borne out by consideration of the function of names in genealogies (§7).

3.1 Inconsistency of character in myth

Study of Theseus has shown that he differs markedly from one myth to another and even in different episodes in the same myth. He kills the Minotaur and releases Athens from the tribute due to Minos but he abandons Ariadne, who made possible his exploit.[1] (And when he returned he forgot to raise the white sail, the sign of success agreed upon with his father, Aegeus, and caused the old man's suicide.) In tragedy, except for the Hippolytus tragedies of Euripides, he is the civilizing hero who fits the Athenian self-conception. (For the relation of Theseus in art and in verbal myth: ch. 1.) His ultimately unsuccessful abduction of the young Helen and his foolhardy attempt to aid Peirithous in the abduction of Kore would not have caused dissonance in the minds of Athenians, as far as we tell. Thus Sophie Mills concludes her study of Theseus in tragedy: "What the Athenians do not like, they either change, or simply ignore...Even if it is possible to interpret Theseus as a rather ambivalent figure between good and bad in the context of the Theseus myth in all its various elements, I doubt that this actually was how he was seen by the Athenians".[2] Socrates is an exception. In his extensive purification of Greek myth in Books 2 and 3 of the *Republic* he rules out the "terrible abductions" of Theseus and Peirithous (391c8–d1).

Study of Medea has likewise shown how she differs from one myth about her to another. She aided Jason in carrying out the tasks imposed by Aeëtes and in

---

1 Mills 1997, 13–17.
2 Mills 1997, 264.

taking the golden fleece from the serpent who guarded it and she sacrificed her brother to ensure Jason's and her escape. So far in her biography she is a barbarian princess, distinctly non-Greek in her possession of magical powers (Jason: σοφὴ πέφυκας καὶ κακῶν πολλῶν ἴδρις, Eur. *Med*. 285) but the helper of a Greek hero. She continues in this role when she causes the death of Pelias, in effect taking vengeance on him for Jason. As such, by a presumable "cultural relativism", she is not reprehensible in the minds of Greek audiences. In Corinth, however, in Euripides' *Medea*, her "otherness" comes up against Greek norms of social behavior to which she cannot adapt and again in Athens, whither she flees from Corinth. She attempts to poison her stepson, Theseus (see ch. 1). As Donald Mastronarde has said apropos of the audience's response to Euripides' tragedy, "Medea had a significant role in a number of famous stories, but in archaic times and in the fifth century each episode was usually treated as relatively self-standing, and there was no compiled life of Medea in which all incidents had to be brought into logical harmony."[3] If, as in Alan Sommerstein words, "Tragedians never felt in the least inhibited about presenting or presupposing different and incompatible versions of a story in different works", one cannot be surprised at Mills' and Mastronarde's observations on the myths of Theseus and of Medea.[4] Athenians, at least those who were able to attend the performances of tragedies, were schooled in inconsistency.

Heracles, in proportion to his greatness as a hero, is the greatest example of ambivalence. He surpasses all the others and yet he performs his civilizing labors as the vassal of Eurystheus. He is harassed throughout his life by Hera. She sends the fit of madness that caused him to kill his wife and children. His death, though unintentional on her part, comes at the hands of his wife, Deianira. Yet many cities claimed him as a protecting hero or deity. Diodorus, when he comes to Heracles in his survey of Greek myth (cf. ch. 4.5), has to face the doubts that he expects from his readers and to make an apology.[5] They tend to disbelieve that Heracles performed the feats that are told of him in the myths. (They do not doubt that there was a Heracles; they doubt that everything that is said of him is true.) But if, Diodorus argues, we are willing to accept Centaurs and Geryons in the theater, even if we think that such creatures never existed, we should accept the myths of Heracles.

---

[3] Mastronarde 2002, 45, with citation of Graf 1997.
[4] Sommerstein 2005, 168.
[5] Cf. Fowler 2019, 36–37.

And strange it would be indeed that Heracles, while yet among mortal men, should by his own labours have brough under cultivation the inhabited world, and that human beings should nevertheless forget the benefactions which he rendered them generally and slander the commendations he receives for the noblest deeds, and strange that our ancestors should have unanimously accorded immortality to him because of his exceedingly great attainments, and that we should nevertheless fail to cherish and maintain for the god the pious devotion which has been handed down to us from our fathers.[6]

When Diodorus speaks of slander (συκοφαντεῖν) he seems to have in mind a strong form of the disapproval to which Theseus and Medea might have seemed to be open. In their cases, there were reasons why they might not in fact have received such disapproval in, say, the fifth century. In Diodorus, writing in the first century B.C.E., a new stage of the reception of Greek myths has been reached.

3.2 Character and action in tragedy

"Tragedy is an imitation not of men but of an action" (*Poet.* 1450^{a}16). Aristotle has no term for the dramatic characters, who are simply the ones on stage "doing something" (*prattontes*).[7] The word in the *Poetics* translated "character", *ēthos*, refers to "the ethical qualities of actions."[8] According to Aristotle what we call dramatic characters come to be of a certain sort (*poioi*), acquire a certain identity, through the manifestation of *ēthos*, which shows moral choice (1454^{a}17–19). In short, action precedes what we would call character. In the famous passage in which Aristotle said that poetry is more philosophical than history because poetry tells the universals (τὰ καθόλου), which he defined as "whatever sorts of things it befalls a certain person to do or say in accordance with probability or necessity", he also said that poetry does so "adding the names that fit (τὰ τυχόντα ὀνόματα) afterwards" (1451^{b}5–10). The point about names is to us counter-intuitive because we imagine the tragedians beginning with the great figures of myth and dramatizing one or another of the stories attaching to them. From this point of view, their names might seem to be primary. What Aristotle has in mind, however, as in the later passage on tragedy as the imitation of an action, is that action

---

6 4.8.5. Transl. Oldfather 1935, 367.
7 He uses *prosopon* of the mask: 1449^{a}36, 1449^{b}4, 1461^{a}13. On πράττειν and related nouns see Halliwell 1986, 140–42.
8 Halliwell 1986, 151.

is technically (i.e., poetically in the radical sense) primary and characters, thus their names, are secondary.[9]

While dramatic characters have a moral character and also have the capacity to argue for something or against something, they become *dramatic* characters, personages, only after the fact.[10] For this reason, the spectator does not perceive the action as arising out of the character but vice versa. This even more profoundly counter-intuitive notion concerning character and story was articulated by Propp, for his own reasons, at the beginning of twentieth-century narratology: "[T]he will of personages, their intentions, cannot be considered...essential...for their definition. The important thing is not what they want to do, nor how they feel, but their deeds as such, evaluated and defined from the viewpoint of their meaning for the hero and for the course of the action".[11] (Propp is discussed in ch. 9.2.)

The priority of story to character means that the same story can be told of two or more different characters.[12] As Walter Burkert said, "Myths...are like formulae with variables for which different names may be substituted".[13] For example, the rescue of Hesione by Heracles bears an obvious resemblance to the rescue of Andromeda by Perseus.[14] These myths belong to the broad type of "The Dragon-Slayer", widely attested in folktales (AT 300; revised in ATU 300) and in other genres. In this type, the hero's reward for slaying the dragon is sometimes the maiden herself (*Mot* T68.1). William Hansen has discussed this type in relation to Greek myth, including the examples of Heracles and Perseus.[15] The character who happens to play the role of dragon-slayer is secondary and who he is will depend upon the particular circumstances of the telling of the story.

---

9 Riu 2017, 47–49 argues that in this place in Aristotle ὄνομα means "character." He compares 1451b22, where Aristotle, saying that the tragedian Agathon invents names, clearly means than Agathon invents characters.
10 There is also *dianoia*, argument for something or against something (1449^{b}37–38). Cf. Halliwell 1986, 154–55.
11 Propp 1968 [1928], 81.
12 And the same story can be told more than once concerning the same character but set in different places, as with some of the deeds of Heracles, for which see Hawes 2017, 7. Cf. the contrasting definition of Graf 1993 [1987], 2: "A myth is not a specific poetic text. It transcends the text: it is the subject-matter, a plot fixed in broad outline *and with characters no less fixed*, which the individual poet is free to alter only within limits" (my emphasis). (For other aspects of Graf's definition see Introduction, pp. XIX–XXI.).
13 Burkert 1985, 120.
14 This example is taken from Edmunds Forthcoming(1), where it is more extensively discussed.
15 Hansen 2002a, 119–30; Hansen 2002b. See now Ogden 2013, 123–29.

3.3 Character and narrative in epic

The same kind of argument concerning the priority of the story can be made also for the *Iliad* and the *Odyssey*. The notion of story applies in the first place to each of these epics itself. The tripartite scheme of Gérard Genette is useful: story (Fr. *histoire*), i.e., narrative content; narrative (Fr. *récit*), narrative "discourse", the organization of the story as narrated; narrating (Fr. *narration*), "narrative situation", e.g., the omniscience of the Homeric narrator. (Genette's scheme is more fully discussed in ch. 9.4). Each of the two epics has a story, the anger of Achilles and the return of Odysseus, which the narrative shapes in various ways.[16] On the largest scale, the *Iliad* consists of two narrative arcs, the first and longer of which begins with Achilles' anger against Agamemnon (Book 1) and extends to his renouncing it (Book 19). A second, shorter arc begins with the death of Patroclus (16.777–867) and terminates in the burial of Hector at the conclusion of the poem.[17] The *Odyssey* has two main narratives, one concerning the return of the hero, the other concerning his son and wife, which ultimately intersect.

With epic as with tragedy characters loom large in our minds and the *Iliad* and the *Odyssey* seem to be about them. This impression is not completely wrong. Probably most scholars would agree with the view expressed by Wolfgang Kullmann, who contrasted characterization in Cyclic Epic and in Homer, minimal in one, fuller in the other.[18] In the *Iliad*, he said, there is extraordinary differentiation in the depiction of persons, who have a new inwardness (*Verinnerlichung*).[19] He gives Helen as an example. "Homer describes ... what is going on with the abducted Helen of the [pre-Iliadic] saga. The recklessness of the woman, who lets herself be seduced, is transformed into disappointment, but disappointment leads in turn to the consolidation of personality. In suffering, Helen has a new life."[20] He points to direct speech in particular as a means of transposing the fact into the psychological (*Psychische*).[21]

---

[16] For a systematic application of this distinction to the *Il.*: Beck 2019.
[17] For these arcs: Latacz 2000, 153–54. What is often called the structure of the *Iliad* (the division of the epic into twenty-four books, or six four-book segments, or three large "movements") is another matter. These arcs traverse the *Il.* no matter how it is segmented.
[18] Kullmann 1960, 382–88.
[19] Taplin 1992: 11 reckons that there are over thirty characters in Homer who are "recognizably individualized ... with consistent attributes and life-stories."
[20] "Homer schildert...was mit der geraubten Helena der [pre-Iliadic] Sage vor sich geht: Der Leichtsinn der Frau, die sich verführen ließ, schlägt in Enttäuschung um, die Enttäuschung führt aber wieder zur Festigung der Persönlichkeit; im Leid wächst Helena wieder."
[21] This paragraph has been taken from Edmunds 2019, 139.

But the stories of the *Iliad* and the *Odyssey* are parts of the larger story of the Trojan War. No matter what the narrative self-substantiality of each of these epics and no matter what the force of character is, the stories of the heroes depend upon the larger one. They had not been born when it began. Achilles will not even live to see the fall of Troy, as he well knows.[22] With Odysseus, although he does not know it, that larger story is coming to an end. Gregory Nagy said of Helen's second speech in the farewell scene in Book 15 of the *Odyssey*, when she interprets the bird omen (170–78): "This meaning of the *Odyssey* is intended not for Menelaus and Helen, characters who are left over from the old world of the tale of Troy; rather, the outcome of the *Odyssey* is meant for the characters of the new world as represented by Telemachus and his companion."[23] Richard Martin takes a further step: "By preposing the Telemachy and thus foregrounding the whole problem of father-son relations, the poet of the *Odyssey* made a conscious attempt to perform a poem about the *end* of tradition."[24] The wily Odysseus knows his own destiny, thanks to the prophecy of Teiresias (11.121–34), and he no doubt imagines that his line continues with his son. According to the *Telegony*, Telegonus, having killed his father by mistake (not the death prophesied by Teiresias), takes Telemachus, still unmarried, and Penelope, to Circe. Telemachus then marries Circe, Telegonus Penelope, and they live on in Aiaia.[25] It is the end of Odysseus' line.[26] No matter what the prophecy and what happened to Odysseus in the end, we know that the story is over. (See Conclusion init. for further comments on the end of the stories of Penelope, Odysseus and Telemachus.)

3.4 Character in the novel

The relation of character to story in myth inverts, one could say, this relation in the novel, by which I mean the realist novel, to the exclusion of non-realist and post-modern fiction.[27] The realism of the realist novel is only, in Roland Barthes's

---

[22] *Il.* 1.351–52 (Ach.), 416–18 (Thetis to Ach.), 505–6 (Thetis to Zeus); 18.59–60 (Thetis to Nereids), 95–96 (Thetis to Ach.), 458 (Thetis to Hephaestus); 21.277–78 (Ach.).
[23] Nagy 2002, 146.
[24] Martin 1993, 240; his emphasis.
[25] *Teleg.* arg. 17–20 B = arg. 22–25 D = h 4a–4b (incl. testimonia) W (pp. 304–306); fr. 5 B = F 6 W (p. 306).
[26] This paragraph has been adapted from Edmunds 2019, 109.
[27] See Fludernik 1996, 37 for the use of "realism" to refer not to the nineteenth-century movement called Realism but to "the novel's mimetic evocation of reality both from a sociological and psychological perspective" (with references to Watt 1957). Cf. 131. The realism of the novel is

well-known formulation, the *effet de réel* but even so, in spite of Barthes, a reader may, and no doubt often does, take the characters in a novel to represent persons in the real world. The idea of realist representation is implicit in words for character such as Germ. *Figur*, Ital. *personaggio*, Fr. *personnage*, and Span. *personaje*.[28] In a representational text, the reader "believes" that the character is a person and the presumed realism of characters is the basis of analysis.[29] Characters are not simply the constructs of language or the functions of texts as in narratology. On the contrary, they represent persons in the real world "out there", independent of the reader's mind, and they drive the story or the plot. Henry James asked: "What is character but the determination of incident? What is incident but the illustration of character? What is either a picture or a novel that is *not* of character? What else do we seek in it and find in it?"[30]

Stephen Halliwell, contrasting Aristotle and Henry James on character observes:

> Psychological inwardness is a major assumption in modern convictions about character, and this in turn leads to typical emphases on the uniqueness of the individual personality and on the potential complexities of access to the characters of others. If character is thought of in strongly psychological terms, then the possibility readily arises that it may remain concealed in the inner life of the mind ... '; but, equally, that it may be glimpsed or intimated in various unintended or unconscious ways. Such ideas and possibilities, which find their quintessential literary embodiment in the novel ... are by their very intricacy and indefiniteness the antithesis of the theory of dramatic character presented in the *Poetics*.[31]

---

something that has been seen through by many sophisticated critics who see something else. Watt retains his prestige in a recent survey of novel criticism: Wild 2020, 4.

28 See the discussion of Fr. *personnage*, *type* and *figure* in Delattre 2005, 119–20 and their relation to narrative.

29 For present purposes, this focus on characters in the novel who are perceived by readers as corresponding to persons in the real world now or in the past is sufficient. Characters in non-literary genres such as film and computer games and of certain characters in non-realist and post-modern fiction can be excluded. Theory of character has been complicated by the need, in order to be systematic, to include monsters, aliens, robots, and animals.

30 James 1884, 511–12.

31 Halliwell 1986, 150.

The modern realist novel, which is probably the primary or at least an influential literary culture for most classical scholars, casts its spell over the reception of character in ancient Greek poetry and myth.[32]

3.5 The inner as emotion

The psychological inwardness of characters in novels consists of what they think and what they feel. Authors tell readers what a character feels or readers draw their own conclusions from what a character does or says. Either way, the reader of an ancient poem faces the question of the correspondence of his or her own terms and concepts to those of the ancient poet. The question arises also for the interpretation of Greek myth, in which emotions run high. In the past generation of classical studies this question has arisen many times as the field has taken an "emotional turn."[33] Classical scholars have been able to draw upon research in psychology and other fields, where they have encountered a double tradition of research, one going back to Charles Darwin, the other to William James.[34] The first views emotions as "natural kinds", the second as socially constructed. If a classical scholar takes the first, evolutionary perspective, then the question of historical difference is diminished or disappears. Identifying one or more of the emotions hypothesized to be natural kinds (typically surprise, anger, fear, sadness, happiness, and disgust), he or she can trust his or her own intuitive understanding of ancient characters.[35] The way they felt and the way we feel under the same or comparable circumstances are the same. If he or she takes the other perspective, then an ancient emotion is specific to the society of the character who feels it. The way that a certain character in a certain ancient poem felt is different from

---

[32] Fantham 1992, 195: "preoccupation with the novel shapes the questions we ask and the expectations with which we approach an ancient text." For the primacy of character cf. Cf. "WITHOUT A HERO, THERE'S NO STORY" (in large, bold-face capitals): adv. for Lee Child, *The Hero*, TLS Books, in *TLS*, Nov. 29, 2019, p. 16.

[33] Lateiner 2016 uses the expression "emotional turn." For a bibliography of major books and collections: Sanders 2014, 1 n. 1. The expression "affective turn" is not synonymous; from the point of view of its practitioners affect theory is a separate field or fields.

[34] Darwin 1998 [1872] (for a brief history of Darwin on emotion: Eidinow 2016, 80–81); James 1884. For an overview and adjudication of the two main lines of research in psychology and contiguous fields: Lindquist et al. 2013. All of these fields taken together are to be distinguished from affect theory, for an overview of which see La Caze and Lloyd 2011. The relation of emotion to affect in affect theory is problematic. That there is a difference between the two is argued against by Leys 2011.

[35] Lindquist et al. 2013, 256 n. 1 for this list.

the way we feel under the same circumstances in reaction to the same stimuli, even if our modern languages seem to have adequate words to translate the text of that poem. This second perspective is sometimes called cultural determinism.[36] It makes engagement with research on emotion in psychology and other fields irrelevant.[37] Such, in an unnuanced description, are the two opposite perspectives. In the "emotional turn" in classical studies scholars have, however, taken up not only characters in poetry but also the concepts of emotion to be found in the orators and in ancient philosophy and, more broadly, the cultural discourse or "emotion talk" of historical groups of persons.[38] Research in psychology and other fields has grounded method.[39]

Research on Greek myth awaits its own "emotional turn." The parameters within which emotions can be understood to operate have been suggested in the preceding discussion in the comparison of ancient myth and the modern realist novel. The reader of a novel, even carefully plotted, as it is likely to be, by the author, has the impression that a character's emotions are, at least partly, driving his or her actions. The reader reads on in order to discover the outcome. The ancient audience of a myth already knows the basic story, no matter what today's variant may be, and thus already has an Aristotelian perspective on the relation of story to character. The characters are going to reenact the story that the audience encounters today. The characters and a fortiori their emotions (as also prophecies, the assignment of tasks and whatever else motivates the action) are secondary to the story.

3.6 Names

In realist fiction names are one of the means of creating characters in the first place and obviously offer the reader a way of identifying characters.[40] They also offer various kinds of information, which depend on what kind of name the author has chosen. Quite apart from theory of character, literary onomastics has studied the semantics of names and has constructed typologies.[41] There are, for

---

[36] As by Cairns 1993, 42 n. 100; Cairns 2003.
[37] Except perhaps for research on the history of emotions. For a bibliography: Cairns and Fulkerson 2015, 8 n. 33.
[38] For "emotion talk": Eidinow 2016, 97–101.
[39] Eidinow 2016, 80–97 is a notable example.
[40] For the creation of characters see in Jannidis 2004 the section "Erzeugung" (129–130) in his chapter on names; Margolin 2007, 66.
[41] Birus 1987 gives an overview and critique of typologies and offers his own.

example, "speaking names" (as in Homer), which give information about characters because they contain elements of the general vocabulary; names indicating social class or religion or nationality; names that are phonetically imitative of one thing or another.

If names in fiction are significant, they fit the theory of real-world names according to which names have semantic value and constitute definite descriptions.[42] This theory, called descriptivist, has long been contested by another, called Millian, after John Stuart Mill, according to which names only denote individuals "and do not indicate or imply any attributes as belonging to those individuals."[43] Discussion of the names of Homeric characters has tended to assume the descriptivist theory.[44] Thus the etymology of a character's name, if it can be discovered, may be the fundamental description of that character. Further, research on archaic hexameter sometimes assumes a sense of tradition, indubitably including characters' names, as a rich source of significance. In John Miles Foley's "traditional referentiality", [t]raditional elements reach out of the immediate instance in which they appear to the fecund totality of the entire tradition …, and they bear meanings as wide and deep as the tradition they encode."[45] Here is descriptivism gone wild.

The discussion of names by philosophers has concerned real-world, not fictional names. The notion that connects the two realms, and thus makes philosophic relevant to literary discussion of names, is possible worlds. In analytical philosophy possible worlds became a tool for resolving problems in the expression of statements involving possibility, impossibility, necessity, and contrafactuality (i.e., the problems of modal logic). Saul Kripke called a possible world a "'possible state (or history) of the world', or 'counterfactual situation'."[46] This definition, an intentional restriction of the scope of possible worlds in the thought of contemporary philosophers, would still allow the application of the notion to the worlds created by fictional texts, as in fact happened in literary theory. Lubomír Doležel, Umberto Eco, Thomas Pavel, and Marie-Laure Ryan were the pioneers.[47] (The ontology of characters, their existence in fictional worlds, also taken up by Kripke, is a separate question.)[48] The account of names which Kripke opposed to the descriptivist one sounds to a classical scholar like a good

---

42 Cumming 2016, §2.3.
43 From *A System of Logic* (1843) book 1, ch. 2.5.
44 Edmunds 2016a, 89–90.
45 Foley 1991, 6.
46 Kripke 1980, 15.
47 See Ryan 2013.
48 Kripke 2013, from lectures given in 1970.

account of names in the minds of the audiences of the oral performances of which our texts are the result. Kripke proposed "initial baptisms" and causal chains:

> Someone, let's say, a baby, is born; his parents call him by a certain name. They talk about him to their friends. Other people meet him. Through various sorts of talk the name is spread from link to link as if by a chain. A speaker who is on the far end of this chain, who has heard about, say Richard Feynman, in the marketplace or elsewhere, may be referring to Richard Feynman even though he can't remember from whom he first heard of Feynman or from whom he ever heard of Feynman.[49]

Kripke called a name in this sense a "rigid designator." Without entering into his elaboration and defense of this still current concept, one can adopt it intuitively as a way of understanding names in ancient Greek poetry and in myth.[50]

This kind of chain is what Antiphanes, a poet of Middle Comedy, was assuming his *Poiēsis*, when he spoke of the great advantage that tragedy has over comedy. The stories (λόγοι) of tragedy are already known and the poet has only to mention Oedipus, for example, and the audience knows all the rest—his father was Laius, his mother Iocasta, who his daughters and sons were, what he will suffer and what he did (fr. 189 K-A). In other words, the name Oedipus in each tragedy about him, or in all possible tragic worlds, will always designate the same character. Each tragedy differed in how the story was told (cf. Sommerstein, quoted at the end of 3.1 above). The crossroads at which Oedipus killed Laius was in Phocis (Soph. *OT* 732–34; Eur. *Phoen.* 38) or in Potniae (Aesch. fr. 387A Radt). Jocasta hung herself after the discovery of the identity of Oedipus (Soph. *OT*) or she lived on to witness the conflict between her sons (Eur. *Phoen.*).[51] Further, the tragedies differed from the Theban epics, as some of the fragments of the latter show. Antiphanes was talking about a basic story attached to the name, which the name always designated, but not about a characterization or description of a set traits. Further, Antiphanes is not assuming knowledge of particular earlier tragedies, whereas, in the case of same-name characters in different modern texts, the author of the later text assumes the reader's knowledge of the earlier one.[52]

---

49 Kripke 1980, 91.
50 For the discussion in philosophy: LaPorte 2018.
51 Finglass argues that in Stesichorus fr. 97 F (the "Lille Stesichorus") the Queen, who is the mother of Polynices and Eteocles, is not Jocasta/Epicaste (pp. 365–66).
52 Cf. Margolin 2007, 69.

3.7 Names in genealogies

Names have a function in genealogies that epitomizes the use of myths to link persons to particular places (cf. Ch. 2.3). Ancestry and place go together, as in the formula τίς πόθεν εἰς ἀνδρῶν (*Il.* 1x; *Od.* 7x). It combines two questions: "Who of men are you and where do you come from?"[53] The overlapping of ancestry and place can be seen in the Hesiodic *Catalogue*. Fowler discusses a place where this poem departs from its usual vertical organization to pursue a genealogy on its horizontal axis.[54] Following West's reconstruction, Fowler points out how

> carefully the poet has accounted for all the places throughout the Aiolian heartland of south Thesssaly, Boiotia, and Korinth, as well as the outlying region of Aitolia, claimed to be Aiolian through a maternal ancestor, and the western Peloponnese, inhabited by two sons of Aiolos, Salmoneus and Perieres, and the Neleid clan, which is affiliated to the Aiolians through Neleus' mother Tyro, daughter of Salmoneus.[55]

Here maternal filiation in effect organizes the geography of large parts of Greece.[56] (The genealogies in the *Catalogue* and in the *Theogony*, it should be added, are basically matrilinear.[57])

Earlier, in a similar vein, Claude Calame, in "Spartan Genealogies: The Mythological Representation of a Spatial Organization", argued that Spartan royal genealogies have a geographical function, pointing out that in the first generation, anthroponyms and toponyms even coincide: Eurotas, Taygete, Sparta, Lacedaemon, and Amyclae. Later generations leave their mark on what Calame called the "Argos-Sparta-Messenia triangle, with Sparta as apex."[58] Calame concluded with remarks on how womanhood, generally "a representation of the exterior", i.e., as coming from outside the sphere into which she marries, comes to be integrated into the center.[59]

---

53 Thus Garvie 1994, 212 on lines 237–38.
54 Fowler 1998, 2–4.
55 Fowler 1998, 9; West 1985, 177.
56 Cf. Fowler 1998, 5–6.
57 West 1966, 34–35. For subsequent discussion: Aguirre Castro 2005, 20 n. 8. She argues that "in general, with regard to the structure and the use of expressions and formulae, there are not apparently very deep differences between the *Catalogue* and the *Theogony*" (24).
58 Calame 1987, 177.
59 Calame 1987, 180–81. Synthesis with Fowler's observations on women would be possible but would lie outside the concerns of the present discussion. There is a larger, ongoing discussion of genealogy (cf. ch. 4.1 for genealogy in mythography). Especially important: Thomas 1992. Good bibliographies in the expected places: Meister 2006b; Thomas 2012.

But genealogy did not have to be political or ideological. Ancient audiences could enjoy listening to long genealogies, even of persons completely unrelated to them. Hecataeus of Miletus, Acusilaus of Argos, Pherecydes of Athens, and Hellanicus of Lesbos could expect readerships for their genealogical works. The Hesiodic *Catalogue* must have had receptive listeners, despite a narrative that seems to us of minimal interest (though we exploit it as a source of information). "What drives the *Catalogue* along is men's inability to resist an attractive woman. Women appear and gods and men fall for them…That is the basic narrative without which there would be nothing to hold the *Catalogue* together".[60] This short repetitive narrative is carried along by the rather bare genealogical scheme and by the names, which had an appeal for the ancient audience that they do not have for us.

This appeal is reflected in Hesiod's *Theogony*, in which the genealogies of the gods sometimes lead to lists of names to which no narrative is attached, as in the case of Night. Her parthenogenic offspring comprise a list that culminates with fifteen abstractions, as we would call them, with a minimum of epithets (two) and explanatory phrases (two, of which one, on Horkos, serves to conclude the list) (226–33).[61] A starker example is the list of thirty-three Nereids in Book Eighteen of the *Iliad* (39–48), explicitly incomplete (49).[62] As commentators have often pointed out, the Nereids have no role to play in the account of Thetis' going to her grieving son. Hesiod's list of Nereids, the offspring of Nereus, contains fifty names, a canonical number (*Theog.* 240–64), and has the same bareness as the list of Night's offspring.[63] In these examples, the names themselves, no matter what the semantic value of their composition, and no matter what the aesthetic effect of the verses in which they appear, have no narrative significance. The list is significant *as such* in its context.

Lists by themselves, without any verbal narrative at all, also had an appeal. The top-most frieze on the neck of the François Vase shows the Calydonian boar hunt and gives the names of twenty hunters.[64] (They are unnamed in Phoenix's

---

[60] Osborne 2005, 13–14; quoted in Edmunds 2019, 136.
[61] On these so-called abstractions see West 1966, 33–34.
[62] For the list of names and its relation to the list of Nereids in Hes. *Theog.* see Edwards 1991 on 18.39–49.
[63] Hom. *Il.* 11x, as of ships (2.509, 556, 685) and rowers (2.719), of a contingent of ambushers (4.393), or of Stentor, who could shout more loudly than fifty other men (5.786). In Hes. *Theog.* those who have fifty heads are Cottus, Briareus, and Gyges (151), Cerberus (312), and the Hundred-Handers (672), who aid Zeus in the Titanomachy.
[64] For the hunting scene in the organization of the iconography of the vase as a whole and its significance: Barringer 2013. For the names of the hunters on the vase and in the mythographical

account of the hunt in *Iliad* 9.529–99.) The names of seven dogs are included, all "speaking names."⁶⁵ In one instance, the sense of the dog's "speaking name" corresponds to its action: Μάρφ[σο]ς has jumped onto the back of the boar and is biting its neck (cf. μάρπτω). But one might not even want to call this and the other names "rigid designators." The name of one of the heroes on the vase, Ἁρπυλέᾱς, and the name of one of the dogs, Λάβρος, turn up as the names of two of Actaeon's dogs (Ov. *Met.* 3.222, 224). Wachter refers to a Chalcidian vase fragment on which there is a Centaur Μάρφσος and refers to "the fact that quite a few names of mythical dogs recur as names of Centaurs".⁶⁶ "Floating signifiers" might be a more appropriate description of these names. The lists of the names of Actaeon's dogs in the mythographical tradition convey an even stronger sense of their fungibility.⁶⁷ For modern reception the names of these dogs in particular mark a high, or a low, point. Albert Henrichs, whose patience was greater than the average scholar's, confessed:

> The close study of mythological names and their transition from the poetic into the mythographical tradition is admittedly tedious. Modern unease over the tedium of the various catalogues itemising the names of Aktaion's dogs provides a measure of the distance which separates epic decorum and the mark it left on ancient mythography from our own aesthetic sensibilities.⁶⁸

A list of dogs' names appears also in Xenophon's *Cynegeticus* (7.5), forty-seven in all, thus approaching the canonical fifty.⁶⁹ The relation of this list to the lists in the mythographical tradition has not been studied. There are no coincidences

---

tradition: Henrichs 1987, 252 and notes. For the list itself and for commentary: Wachter 1991, 87–88, 91–95. For a list of contingents participating in the Calydonian boar hunt: Stesichorus fr.183 F and pp. 515–16, Finglass 2012b.
65 Λάβρος, Μεθέπῶν, Ὄρμενος, Μάρφ[σο]ς (Μάρφ[σα]ς Pugliese Carratelli), Qόραχς, Ἐγέρτες, Ἔ(ν)βολος (Pugliese Carratelli; alii: Ε(ὔ)βολος). The reading Ε(ὔ)βολος is not implausible: cf. Νόης and Γνώμη in Xenophon's list, quoted below.
66 Wachter 1991, 93.
67 See Van Rossum-Steenbeek 1997, 133–34 for a commented list of these lists of Actaeon's dogs, with n. 36 for bibliography.
68 Henrichs 1987, 254.
69 Τὰ δ' ὀνόματα αὐταῖς τίθεσθαι βραχέα, ἵνα εὐανάκλητα ᾖ. εἶναι δὲ χρὴ τοιάδε· Ψυχή, Θυμός, Πόρπαξ, Στύραξ, Λογχή, Λόχος, Φρουρά, Φύλαξ, Τάξις, Ξίφων, Φόναξ, Φλέγων, Ἀλκή, Τεύχων, Ὑλεύς, Μήδας, Πόρθων, Σπέρχων, Ὀργή, Βρέμων, Ὕβρις, Θάλλων, Ῥώμη, Ἀνθεύς, Ἥβα, Γηθεύς, Χαρά, Λεύσων, Αὐγώ, Πολεύς, Βία, Στίχων, Σπουδή, Βρύας, Οἰνάς, Στέρρος, Κραυγή, Καίνων, Τύρβας, Σθένων, Αἰθήρ, Ἀκτίς, Αἰχμή, Νόης, Γνώμη, Στίβων, Ὀρμή.

with the list of dogs' names on the François Vase but semantic similarities appear.[70] Although all of Xenophon's names are "speaking", he recommends them as short (they are all of two syllables) and thus convenient for calling the dog. He says nothing of a connection between the sense of the name and the characteristics, physical or behavioral, of the dog, although these vary to a degree that surprises the non-hunter or non-dog fancier (3.4–4.8). Xenophon may have assumed that the hunter assigned the name when the dog was still a pup, so that, as in the case of human "speaking names", the name expressed a hope or was honorific. In the case of the infant Astyanax, this was the name that the Trojans gave him in honor of his father, who defended the city (*Il.* 3.399–403; cf. 24.506–507).[71]

3.8 Conclusion

The names of characters in myths are secondary to the stories. The priority of action to character, formulated by Aristotle as a rule for tragic plots, applies to myths in general. Thus, as Burkert said, the variants of a particular myth may show different names, while the myth remains fundamentally the same. This view of the relation between name and story is articulated in the preface of Palaephatus, probably independently of Aristotle:

> οὐ γὰρ ὀνόματα μόνον ἐγένοντο, λόγος δὲ περὶ αὐτῶν οὐδεὶς ὑπῆρξεν· ἀλλὰ πρότερον ἐγένετο τὸ ἔργον, εἶθ' οὕτως ὁ λόγος ὁ περὶ αὐτῶν. Festa 1902

> For names by themselves did not come into existence, without there being any account of them, but the deed came first, and then accordingly the account concerning them (i.e., those named).

For his own purposes, Palaephatus argues for the sequence: deed, account thereof, names of the characters in the account. (For further discussion of his preface see ch. 4.3).

The contrast with modern realist fiction makes the secondariness of names all the clearer. The storyteller, for his or her part, and in Aristotle's conception the tragedian, has a store of remembered myths, probably in the abstract form as given by Antiphanes in the case of Oedipus or perhaps some particular variant. In this mental state myths are short (as they seem to be when the mythographers write them down) and may not be attached to a particular hero—someone rescued

---

70 With Xen.'s Ὁρμή cf. Ὅρμενος. See *DELG* s.v. ὅρμενος.
71 The love of lists of all kinds persisted down into Roman times: Fowler 2017, 22–23.

a maiden who was going to be devoured by a monster. As the discussion in chapter 9 of the typology or classification of Greek myths suggests, the girl in Burkert's "girl's tragedy", under different names plays the same role in several myths.

It also happens that a certain character, bearing the same name each time, turns up in more than one story and the stories may even give contradictory impressions of the same character, as in the cases of Theseus and Medea. The extension of Kripke's "rigid designator" to the names in the possible worlds of Greek poetry and myth helps to explain this phenomenon. In genealogies names appear in minimal narrative contexts and sometimes lists of names appear, without any narratives except the ones in which the lists are embedded. Names in these lists have not become primary. The lists are significant in themselves. If any of the names is known from some other context, then it is a "rigid designator", indicating only that the identity of the figure is the same.

4 Mythography

The word μυθογράφος "mythographer" is first attested in the pseudo-Aristotelian *On the Flooding of the Nile*.[1] It occurs also in Palaephatus, who, concluding his rationalization of a story about Glaucus, uses the opposition, by his time familiar, between fabricated myth and truth or reality (ἀφ' οὗ οἱ μυθογράφοι τὸν μῦθον ἔπλασαν, 26.18).[2] (For Palaephatus see 4.6 below.) The word μυθογραφία "mythography" first occurs in Strabo, in a pejorative sense (1.2.35; 8.3.9).[3] Despite these unpromising beginnings, "mythographers" and "mythography" are now standard terms.

Those called mythographers have in the past generation come into their own as a fundamental resource for the study of Greek myth.[4] They complement archaic and classical poetry, long taken to be the principal sources.[5] In the second edition of *Approaches to Greek Myth* I spoke of the scholarly activities of what could be called "the Barcelona school" of mythography, centred in the Universitat Autònoma.[6] There is also Polymnia (Réseau de recherche sur les mythographes anciens et modernes), under the direction of Jacqueline Fabre-Serris (Lille) and Françoise Graziani (Corsica). Robert Fowler alone, with his edition of early mythographers (on which see below) and his many writings on mythography, stands next to the groups just mentioned. A digital database, based in the School of Literature, Languages and Linguistics at Australian National University, is currently under construction, "Mapping Ancient Narratives, Territories, Objects" (MANTO), of which Greta Hawes and R. Scott Smith are co-directors. This project includes a database of mythical names.[7]

---

[1] This work survives only in a medieval Latin Transl. See *EGM* 1, xxvii and n. 1 for discussion.
[2] On the relative dates of the work by ps.-Aristotle and Palaephatus: *EGM* 2, xiv n. 3.
[3] For the history of "mythography" from the nineteenth century on: Bremmer 2013, 55–56.
[4] Trzaskoma 2013, xx speaks of Cameron 2004 as the "watershed moment." For a brief history of scholarship leading to the present reevaluation of mythography: Hawes 2014b, 127–29. For a succinct and useful welcome to mythography: Marincola and Romano 2019, 1.
[5] Burkert 1993, 13 lists five literary corpora of Greek myth (Hesiod, Homeric Hymns, Stesichorus, tragedy) and also Apollodorus. Homer is not included. The only mythographer whom Burkert lists is Apollodorus. He adds: "Gewiß kommt dann noch Wichtiges dazu, vor allem was bei Plutarch und Pausanias steht." In sum, however, he omits most of mythography.
[6] Edmunds 2014a, 24–25.
[7] See his blog post "The Ontology of Mythical Entities: Part 2" (https://www.manto-myth.org/blog/the-ontology-of-mythical-entities-part-2, accessed June 29, 2020) for the theoretical basis of this project.

An obvious use of mythography is the supplementing of myths only partially retold in an epic or in a tragedy but belonging to the background knowledge of their first audiences. It contributes both to an understanding of their horizon of expectation and also to the study of the myths as such.[8] Euripides' *Medea*, for example, alludes to the events that took place in Colchis and then in Iolcus, before the dramatic time of the tragedy, but for us the stories remain lacunose, even after the *Argonautica* of Apollonius of Rhodes.[9] (On Medea see 4.5 below.) In order to reconstruct them, and also to become aware of variants in Euripides, such as the place where Medea murdered her brother, one relies on mythographers.[10]

The following discussion is not another survey of the mythographers, which is unnecessary, but concentrates on differences between the two distinct periods of mythography (4.1), on instances of mythography in writers not considered mythographers (4.2), on the early mythographers' goals in the writing down of myths (4.3), on the taste for collections in the second period (4.4), some main characteristics of Hellenistic and Imperial mythography (4.5), and finally on some particular aspects of Palaephatus (4.6).[11]

4.1 The two periods

Mythographical works, great in number and heterogeneous, can be divided into two periods. The first begins with Hecataeus of Miletus, who wrote at the end of the sixth century, and continues to the end of the fourth B.C.E. Fowler's *Early Greek Mythography*, for the foreseeable future the standard collection and commentary, covers this period. The writers included by Fowler are sometimes called "historians" and sometimes "historians/mythographers" because they typically continue from what we can rightly call "myth" to what would come to be called history.[12] A well-known subset of these writers consists of the Atthidographers, of

---

8 For the audiences: Mastronarde 2002, 45.
9 Graf 1997; Mastronarde 2002, 45–49.
10 Burkert 1987, 255 refers, apropos of the approach of scholars "in recent decades", to a "shared concern for the whole of the mythical narrative in relation to its constituent parts." But, he says, the practitioners of this approach "do not always seem to realise that it is impossible to determine the overall structure of a particular myth, let alone its presumed meaning, without acquiring first as complete and clear an understanding of its transmission in antiquity as possible. This is where mythography comes in."
11 For a survey see Pàmias Forthcoming(1), with a bibliography; Pàmias Forthcoming(2); Trzaskoma and Smith 2011.
12 *EGM* 1, xxviii–xxix.

whom Hellanicus of Lesbos, one of Fowler's early Greek mythographers, is considered the first and the founder of Atthidography.¹³ Hellanicus also counts as a "logographer," along with others who, from another perspective, are "mythographers."¹⁴ Herodotus is considered the first to make the distinction between myth and history or between a *spatium mythicum* and a *spatium historicum*, to use favorite modern terms, and, in doing so, to be distinguishing himself from the mythographers (3.122.2).¹⁵ In the oral culture from which Herodotus emerges there is a "floating gap" between the present and the mythical past.¹⁶

The two-part chronology that I am proposing thus in the first part combines genres usually distinguished by modern scholars, who use the various names just surveyed. Fowler is an exception. He in effect reassembles a corpus within which Felix Jacoby made a distinction between older writers of genealogies and later writers on individual cities and lands.¹⁷ Within his new corpus Fowler has put the kind of books, or the parts of books, that "concentrated on the 'mythical' period", and not recent history.¹⁸ Toward the end of this first period, a new approach receives systematic and extensive expression for the first time in the Περὶ ἀπίστων (*On Incredible Things*) of Palaephatus (a pseudonym for an unidentified person; 4.6 below).¹⁹ In the epitome that we have, he rationalizes forty-five myths

---

13 Meister 2006a. For the modern terms: first Pohlenz 1937, 7.
14 Rowe 2012, 856. On these terms: *EGM* 2, 658 n. 3. The Atthidographers belong to the large group of writers of polis or local histories. For this category: Thomas 2019, ch. 1. For *muthoi* in these writers see Thomas 2019, 76–77.
15 Asheri, Lloyd and Corcella 2007, 30. But it is an argument from silence. The remains of the early mythographers are so scanty that one cannot be certain that none of them made the distinction.
16 Vansina 1985, 23.
17 "A. Alte Genealogie (saec. V–IV)", *FGrH* vol. 1, part A; "Autoren über einzelne Städte (Länder)", *FGrH* vol. 3.B. Of the writers listed under the first of these headings nine are included in Fowler's edition (Acusilaus of Argos; Anaximander of Miletus; Andron of Halicarnassus; Damastes of Sigeion; Hecataeus of Miletus; Hellanicus of Lesbos; Pherecydes of Athens; Polus of Acragas; Simonides of Ceos. In *FGrH* vol. 1, part C ("Monographien. Romane. Schwindelliteratur"), Jacoby has 42 texts or authors, of whom two are included in Fowler (Herodorus of Heracleia; Metrodorus of Chios). Of the remaining eighteen mythographers in Fowler, twelve appear in *FGrH* vol. 3 B (see the beginning of this n.) and the remaining six in other vols. For the rationale of Jacoby's divisions: a brief statement in *FGrH* vol. 1, VII–X; see *EGM* 1, xxix n. 4 for Jacoby's earlier statement of the matter.
18 *EGM* 2, xiv.
19 For the *Zeitwende* marked by Palaephatus: Pàmias Forthcoming(1)§2.4; Hawes 2014a, 39. The treatise of Palaephatus is the first of its kind of which we know. But rationalization clearly predates Palaephatus, as in Socrates' interpretation of the myth of the abduction of Oreithyia by

4.2 Mythography outside mythographers

Writers who would not come under the heading of mythography dealt with myth from a critical perspective. Fowler refers to Herodotus' many points of contact with the mythographers and to Thucydides' excursuses on myths.[21] Andrew Ford has recently, building on a suggestion of Greta Hawes, proposed that "already in the late archaic period mythography had developed a distinctive discursive style, an authoritative rhetoric favouring a set of terms and topoi, that was imitated or parodied by non-mythographers."[22] He discusses Socrates on the myth of Oreithyia in Plato's *Phaedrus*, Pindar on Pelops in *Olympian* 1 and Callimachus' *Hymn to Zeus*. The source of the authority of the speaker in each of these places remains a question. As for Hecataeus, with reference to whom Ford defines this rhetorical stance, writing itself gave fixity to his versions of received myths (cf. 4.3 below) and his detailed research would have conferred *bona fides* on his words.[23] One has also to reckon with his social position in Miletus. A passage in Herodotus shows that he was one of the leaders at the time of the Ionian revolt, when he opposed the policy of the foolhardy Aristagoras (Hdt. 5.124–25).[24] His prestige in his city might have given his words authority among his fellow-citizens. Socrates gives a rationalizing interpretation of the myth of Oreithyia and then turns his back on this kind of intellectual activity, calling it a boorish kind of cleverness (ἀγροίκῳ τινὶ σοφίᾳ, 229e3). Socrates has another intellectual project, to know himself, in accordance with the Delphic oracle (230a1–6), which, as readers of other dialogues well know, entails the elenchos (cf. the conversation with Alcibiades in *Alc.* 1 127d9–129a9, with reference to the oracle). Pindar has

---

Boreas (discussed below in this ch.). Cf. Teiresias' rationalization of Dionysus' birth from the thigh of Zeus (Eur. *Bacch*. 286–97).
20 For the extant Palaephatus as an epitome and for the distinction between the first forty-five myths and the remaining seven see Stern 1996, 4–5.
21 *EGM* 2, xvii. Fowler cites Thuc. 1.1–21, 2.15–16, 6.1–5.
22 Ford 2019, 6, referring to Hawes 2014a, 13–17.
23 Hawes 2014a, 7 of Hecataeus: "Authority is no longer the preserve of established tradition, but answerable to the mental calculations of the individual." For the superiority of written accounts over oral ones she cites Bertelli 1996, 67–68 and Bertelli 2001, 83–84. Cf. Hawes 2014b, 130.
24 For a skeptical interpretation of this passage: S. West 1991b, 154–58.

the authority of the inspiration that an Olympic victory inspires (*Ol.* 1.5–9). One can compare another poet's correction of a myth, Stesichorus' of the myth that Helen went to Troy (fr. 91a F, from Pl. *Phaedr.* 243a2– b3).[25] Callimachus turns the standard hymnal opening ("How shall we sing of him?") into a parade of allusion to variants of the myth of Zeus. For his sophisticated audience his authority comes from his learning and cleverness. "I sing nothing that is not attested" (ἀμάρτυρον οὐδὲν ἀείδω, fr. 612 Pf.). It is true, then, that the style of mythography can be found outside the mythographers but the impulse and the implicit justification are relative to the kind of work in which it appears.

Even Aeschylus and Euripides might be included among imitators or adapters of mythography. Andrea Rodighiero has shown that, within the limits of tragic conventions, the chorus in the parodos of *Agamemnon* and in the first stasimon of *Trojan Women* is able to transpose Homeric narrative into song.[26] Rodighiero concentrates on the reflexes of this transposition in meter and style. In the present context, the tragic poets' narrating in song appears as another venture in mythography by non-mythographers. These mythographic choral songs begin, as might be expected, with an indication of authority. The chorus of old men in Agamemnon, in a section of the parodos on the portent sent to the Atreids at Aulis, begin "I have authority to tell out" (κύριός εἰμι θροεῖν, 104), claiming that still at their age they are inspired with persuasion by the gods (ἔτι γὰρ θεόθεν καταπνεύει /πειθώ, 105–106). The chorus of Trojan women invoke the Muse at the beginning of their song on the fall of Troy: "Of Ilium, Muse, sing for me with tears a funeral lament (made of) new song" (ἀμφί μοι Ἴλιον, ὦ / Μοῦσα, καινῶν ὕμνων / ᾆσον σὺν δακρύοις ᾠδὰν ἐπικήδειον, 511–13). It is an epic beginning that, in the same breath, asks for a new kind of song.[27] The women of the chorus were also eye-witnesses (551–55).

To give a last example, even Thucydides offers an example of mythography when he briefly retells the myth of Procne and Philomela in order to distinguish the Tereus of this myth from the Thracian Teres, of whom Thucydides is speaking at this point (2.29).[28] Tereus dwelt in Daulia, in Phocis in central Greece. The his-

---

25 Cf. Edmunds 2016a, 137–38 for this interpretation.
26 Rodighiero 2018.
27 See the n. of Barlow 1986 *ad loc.* for the chorus' rather complex rhetoric.
28 Τηρεῖ δὲ τῷ Πρόκνην τὴν Πανδίονος ἀπ' Ἀθηνῶν σχόντι γυναῖκα προσήκει ὁ Τήρης οὗτος οὐδέν, οὐδὲ τῆς αὐτῆς Θρᾴκης ἐγένοντο, ἀλλ' ὁ μὲν ἐν Δαυλίᾳ τῆς Φωκίδος νῦν καλουμένης γῆς [ὁ Τηρεὺς] ᾤκει, τότε ὑπὸ Θρᾳκῶν οἰκουμένης, καὶ τὸ ἔργον τὸ περὶ τὸν Ἴτυν αἱ γυναῖκες ἐν τῇ γῇ ταύτῃ ἔπραξαν (πολλοῖς δὲ καὶ τῶν ποιητῶν ἐν ἀηδόνος μνήμῃ Δαυλιὰς ἡ ὄρνις ἐπωνόμασται),

torian uses three kinds of argument. One is the poets' use of "Daulian" as an epithet for the nightingale into which Philomela was transformed. The second is that Pandion, the father of Procne and Philomela, would not have married the former to someone in distant Thrace but for strategic reasons to someone among his neighbors. (This Tereus would have been one of the Thracians dwelling in Daulia whom Thuydides has mentioned.) Third, Teres and Tereus are not even the same name. (For the second argument, from τὸ εἰκός, see Appendix.)

4.3 Hecataeus, Acusilaus, and the goals of writing down the myths

Hecataeus' *Genealogies* begins:

> Ἑκαταῖος Μιλήσιος ὧδε μυθεῖται· τάδε γράφω, ὥς μοι δοκεῖ ἀληθέα εἶναι· οἱ γὰρ Ἑλλήνων λόγοι πολλοί τε καὶ γελοῖοι, ὡς ἐμοὶ φαίνονται, εἰσίν. *FGrH* F 1a = *EGM* 1, fr. 1
>
> Thus speaks Hecataeus of Miletus: I write following things as they seem true to me; for the stories of the Greeks, as they seem to me, are many and foolish.[29]

What he hoped to achieve in the medium of written prose is the true, authoritative version (though with a qualification).[30] This version is by implication single, as against the multiplicity of stories to which he refers, which as such renders them foolish.[31] These stories are known to Hecataeus and his contemporaries in oral tellings, in performances of epic and lyric verse, in choral performances in which a myth was part of the song, and in poems already written down.[32] Clearly "the Greeks" were not going to turn their backs on the many stories known to them in many versions.[33] Hecataeus' distinction between what seems true to him, on the

---

εἰκός τε καὶ τὸ κῆδος Πανδίονα ξυνάψασθαι τῆς θυγατρὸς διὰ τοσούτου ἐπ' ὠφελίᾳ τῇ πρὸς ἀλλήλους μᾶλλον ἢ διὰ πολλῶν ἡμερῶν ἐς Ὀδρύσας ὁδοῦ (2.29). Cf. Apollod. 3.14.8.
29 For a commentary on this fr.: *EGM* 2, 677–80.
30 *EGM* 2, 678–79. For the connotation of authoritativeness in μυθεῖται: Martin 2013, 57–58.
31 In A τε καὶ B the second element may heighten the first, as in e.g. πολλά τε καὶ ὄλβια (Hdt. 1.31) or A may stand to B as the general to the particular (K-G 2.250).
32 *EGM* 2, xii: "...[W]e have their [the poets'] texts because they wrote them down, and by Hekataios' time the number of verses of all kinds, epic, lyric including citharody, elegy and iambus, oracles) numbered at least two hundred thousand."
33 In a passage often compared with Hecataeus fr. 1 Herodotus says: Λέγουσι δὲ πολλὰ καὶ ἄλλα ἀνεπισκέπτως οἱ Ἕλληνες· εὐήθης δὲ αὐτῶν καὶ ὅδε ὁ μῦθός ἐστι τὸν περὶ τοῦ Ἡρακλέος λέγουσι, 2.45.1 ("The Greeks tell many other things without due attention, and this story, too, that they tell about Heracles is foolish").

one hand, and Greek gullibility, on the other, implies that he is addressing a readership much smaller than "the Greeks", one which would share his critical perspective.[34]

Hecataeus is, after all, in competition with received and ongoing myth. His genealogy proceeds from those of Hesiod and presumably from other genealogical traditions. The chances of his version depend on their fixity in writing. Other versions of the same myths have come and gone or can be expected to go while his remain. This importance of the written medium appears clearly in a testimonium concerning the *Genealogies* of Acusilaus of Argos:

> Ἀκουσίλαος· Κάβα υἱός· Ἀργεῖος ἀπὸ Κερκάδος πόλεως οὔσης Αὐλίδος πλησίον. ἱστορικὸς πρεσβύτατος. ἔγραψε δὲ Γενεαλογίας ἐκ δέλτων χαλκῶν, ἃς λόγος εὑρεῖν τὸν πατέρα αὐτοῦ ὀρύξαντά τινα τόπον τῆς οἰκίας αὐτοῦ. *FGrH* 2 T 2 = *EGM* Test. 1 (from Suda s.v. Ἀκουσίλαος)

> Acusilaus: the son of Kabas. He was an Argive from Kerkas, a city near Aulis. He is the oldest historian. He wrote Genealogies from bronze tablets which, his logos says, his father found when he dug up a certain place in his house.[35]

Acusilaus' authentication of his writing is an earlier writing down of the material.[36] Likewise Pherecydes was said not to have had a teacher but to have trained himself from recondite Phoenician books that he had acquired.[37]

4.4 The taste for collections

Toward the end of the fourth century, mythography goes in a new direction, leaving behind genealogy, an inheritance from oral myth, and the genealogical organization of myths. The writing down of myths now exploits the possibility of collections of myths organized by subject-matter or, in one case, by a theory of myth, to be discussed below (4.6).[38] Whether or not oral sources have been left behind is a question that would probably receive different answers for different myths in different collections.

---

34 Cf. Asper 2007, 87–88. *EGM* 2, 679 speaks, less plausibly, of a "pan-Hellenic stance" (cf. xiii).
35 For the translation of ἃς λόγος εὑρεῖν: Pàmias 2015, 55–56. As for Acusilaus as "the oldest historian", ... see *EGM* 2, 660. See now Andolfi 2019 ad loc.
36 The device of authentication took various forms: see *EGM* 2, 624 ad n. 7.
37 Pherecydes T 1 *EGM*, from the Suda: αὐτὸν δὲ οὐκ ἐσχηκέναι καθηγητήν, ἀλλ' ἑαυτὸν ἀσκῆσαι, κτησάμενον τὰ Φοινίκων ἀπόκρυφα βιβλία. For the questions surrounding this testimonium: Martin 2013, 63 n. 65.
38 In these collections the myths appear as items belonging to a category, without internal connections between them: cf. Hawes 2014b, 134.

In the Lyceum, the making of collections of various kinds was a normal kind of preparation for philosophic inquiry. The *Constitution of the Athenians* is the sole example of "the collections of constitutions" and "the collected constitutions" referred to at the end of the *Nicomachean Ethics* (1181^{b}7, ^{b}17). In *Topics*, on the collecting of reputable opinions (*endoxa*), Aristotle distinguishes between oral and written sources of collecting or listing and, of the two, seems to assume that the latter may be less apparent to his addressees. He says: "We should select also from the written handbooks of arguments, and should draw up sketch-lists of them upon each several kind of subject, putting them under a separate heading".[39]

The mythographical collections seem to begin with the *Tragodoumena* of Asclepiades of Tragilus, a pupil of Isocrates. He may have compared the myths in the tragedians with other versions.[40] If so, his project presupposes a readership that was losing contact with, but was curious about, the multiplicity of myths of which the first mythographers complained. Scholarly uptake is reflected in the citations of Asclepiades in the scholia to tragedy.

4.5 Hellenistic and Imperial mythography

In the second of the two main periods of mythography,[41] collections become the norm, which are of two general kinds. One consists of the myths lying behind the works of the poets. (The distinction between the poem and the myth is presupposed.) The ancient scholia to Pindar, Euripides, Theocritus, Apollonius of Rhodes and Lycophron provide evidence of this kind of collection.

Dicaearchus, a student of Aristotle, wrote hypotheses to the tragedies of Euripides and Sophocles, probably scholarly and not the ones found in most manuscripts of these tragedians.[42] These hypotheses, the "Tales from Euripides" (Zuntz's name has stuck), are simply plot summaries, which some might have read instead of reading the plays (cf. the anonymous epigram on Apollodorus'

---

39 105^{b}12–14. Transl. Pickard-Cambridge 1984: 175 (ἐκλέγειν δὲ χρὴ καὶ ἐκ τῶν γεγραμμένων λόγων, τὰς δὲ διαγραφὰς ποιεῖσθαι περὶ ἑκάστου γένους ὑποτιθέντας χωρίς…).
40 For an overview of Asclepiades of Tragilus: Villagra 2012. For a possibly comparative approach: Villagra 2008 (2009).
41 For mythography in the context of the Second Sophistic: Trzaskoma 2017.
42 Verhasselt 2015 argues that neither the "learned" hypotheses which a few tragedies have (list on p. 612) nor the narrative hypotheses should be attributed to the Peripatetic Dicaearchus. Cf. Mastronarde 2017, p. 15 and n. 56. For other collections of tragic plots: Fowler 2019, 45. For Dicaearchus' book *The Life of Greece* and his methods: Fowler 2019, 47–50.

Library, referred to in the Conclusion of this chapter).[43] In the manuscripts in which they are found these hypotheses sometimes have mythographical addenda. The hypothesis to *Medea*, for example, provides information on parts of her story only alluded to or left unmentioned in the play, with citation of sources. Medea refers rather obliquely to her murdering the usurper Pelias when she and Jason returned from Colchis to Iolcus (*Med.* 9–10, 486–87, 505). Neither she nor anyone else refers to her deception of Pelias' daughters, prepared for by her rejuvenation of a ram or of Jason himself (Hypoth. 11–18).[44] She killed Jason having persuaded him to sleep under the prow of the Argo. (How and when she did so is not explained but it was clearly in Corinth.) Jason complied, and the prow, rotten with time, fell on and killed him (Hypoth. 20–24). In the play Aegeus the king of Athens happens to pay a visit to Corinth. Medea secures from him the promise of hospitality in his city (*Med.* 663–823). From the hypothesis one learns that Medea married Aegeus there (Hypoth. 10–11).

The other general kind of collection is organized by theme. Such are the *Catasterisms* of Eratosthenes of Cyrene (3rd c. B.C.E.) and the *Erotica Pathemata* of Parthenius of Nicaea or Myrleia (1st c. B.C.E.).[45] A favorite theme was metamorphosis, which may have been another of Parthenius' projects.[46] Ovid could draw on Hellenistic collections, of which none survives, for his *Metamorphoses*. A book of excerpts by Antoninus Liberalis (prob. 2nd c. B.C.E.) is the first extant example of its kind. The *Diegeseis* of Conon of Cappadocia were apparently more miscellaneous (1st c. B.C.E–1st c. C.E.).[47]

Another favorite kind of collection consisted of incredible stories (ἄπιστα).[48] The writing down of myth now makes possible the recording of stories that cannot be believed simply because they are self-evidently unbelievable. The writers, called paradoxographers, are usually distinguished from mythographers, but they do not constitute a separate class.[49] Myths may enter the account of a paradox, as fairly often in the pseudo-Aristotelian "On Marvellous Things Heard"

---

43 Zuntz 1955, 135–36; readership: Rusten 1982, 358. For a typology of thee "Tales": Van Rossum-Steenbeek 1997, 2–3.
44 Lines numbers to the Hypothesis as in Diggle 1984.
45 For the history of the text of Eratosthenes that we have: Pàmias 2008, 20–26; Hawes 2014a, 233–38.
46 See *OCD*[4] s.v. "metamorphosis."
47 Henrichs 1987 speaks of Conon's *Diegeseis* as the most interesting and at the same time the most neglected of the smaller mythographical collections" (244–47). There are now Brown 2002 (text, English translation, commentary); Hawes 2014a, ch. 4.
48 Giannini 1965, in the standard edition, establishes a canon of twenty paradoxographers.
49 For the usual distinction: Higbie 2007, 238–41. For an overview: Rusten 2012.

(830ᵃ5–847b10).⁵⁰ *Incredibilia* are only another multifarious kind of story, like metamorphosis or catasterism.

Two landmarks in the second period are the work of Mythographus Homericus (hereafter MH) and the *Bibliotheca* of Apollodorus. The second has a name but his identity is no more certain than that of the first. The dates of both are also uncertain.⁵¹ Apollodorus is often assigned to the second century C.E. MH is known mainly from two hundred or so scholia in the D manuscript of the *Iliad* and eleven papyri (nine for the *Iliad* and two for the *Odyssey*).⁵² Again thanks to the "Barcelona school" and to Joan Pàges in particular, MH has become a mythographer among the others (although he does not have an article in *OCD⁴*).⁵³ Long ago Albert Henrichs spoke of the mythographical scholia attributed to MH as the most important collection of its kind and lamented its inaccessibility.⁵⁴ Pàges' edition will be superseded by the edition of the complete MH, for both the *Iliad* and the *Odyssey*, with translation and commentary, on which he and Nereida Villagra are working. Opinions differ widely concerning the purpose of the work of MH. The papyri show that he organized his work by lemmata. A didactic purpose might thus be inferred. His readership certainly had expectations different from Apollodorus'.⁵⁵ These two mythographical works are, however, equally different from the orators of the Second Sophistic and both presuppose readerships less sophisticated than the orators'.

Two authors whose works have recently, at least in certain respects, been brought within the fold of mythography are Diodorus Siculus and Strabo. The *Library* of Diodorus (first c. B.C.E.) begins with a survey of the mythology of the known world, divided between east (Books 1–3) and west (Books 4–6), after which comes the history of Greece from the Trojan War to the death of Alexander (Books 7–17) and so forth. Those interested in Greek myth focus on Book 4, in which Diodorus surveys the "Greek heroes and demi-gods of ancient times"

---

50 But not in the paradoxographical work (title uncertain) of Callimachus (frs. 407–411 Pf.).
51 Finglass, in D-F, p. 83, dates MH to the first century B.C.E. ("he cites no-one later than Didymos, and the oldest papyri of his work are from the late first century AD").
52 The D scholia were at last edited by van Thiel 2014.
53 Edition: Pàges 2007.
54 Henrichs 1987, 243, unknowingly bearing witness to its inaccessibility when he refers to "several hundred 'mythical narratives' (*historiai*)." There are about two hundred for the *Il.* and fewer for the *Od.*
55 On the readership of MH: Van Rossum-Steenbeek 1997, 117–18. She speaks of "Greek Readers' Digests." Pàges 2017, 77–78 does not distinguish between the audiences of the two mythographers. He refers to them as "parallel examples" and connects them especially with the Greek and Hellenized populations of Egypt. For the readership of Apollodorus: Edmunds 2017, 96–97.

(4.1.5). In the prooemium to this Book, Diodorus justifies his inclusion of myths with reference to the honor that the heroes and demigods still receive.[56] In practice, he often shows skepticism about or rationalizes the myths that he reports.[57] Strabo (first c. B.C.E.–first c. C.E.) distinguishes between myth and history: "For the things that are ancient and false and marvelous are called myths, but history intends the truth, whether ancient or recent, and contains little or none of the marvelous."[58] He is critical of myths again and again, applying, like Diodorus, the rationalizations of a mythographer. And yet, with apology, he includes myths. Of certain historians (συγγραφεῖς) he says that they have introduced many fabrications concerning the coast of Libya, on which he has commented earlier, but "now too I am speaking of them, asking pardon for the telling of marvels, if it happens that I am compelled to digress into such a thing, in order to avoid dismissing them all in silence and in a way crippling my history."[59]

Fowler reflects on myth in the historians:

> It is clear that historians could not bring themselves to throw myth over; the power of tradition, and the conviction that there might just be something in it, were too strong to dismiss. At some level they *wanted* to believe in these myths. Given this commitment, they must choose from the same limited menu of methods of dealing with these myths...: ignore them; rationalise them in some manner; or tell them straight and leave the reader to decide.[60]

Even Thucydides would come under this description (see 4.2 sub fin. above). Rosalind Thomas discusses tales in Herodotus "commonly seen as oral traditions and 'traditional tales', implying that they had a longer life as separate tales before Herodotus heard and retold them, or as 'folktales'." She gives as examples Arion and the dolphin (1.23–4), Solon's visit to Croesus, the story of Harpagos (1.108–

---

56 For discussion of 4.1.1–4: Fowler 2019, 35–37.
57 Rationalization: Saïd 2014, 79–82. Sulimani 2011, ch. 5 has stressed the influence of Diodorus' own times on his reporting of myths, in particular the deeds of kings and rulers such as the foundation of cities and advancing the life of mankind in various ways. For other studies of Diodorus' treatment of myth see Fowler 2019, 37 n. 23.
58 τὰ γὰρ παλαιὰ καὶ ψευδῆ καὶ τερατώδη μῦθοι καλοῦνται, ἡ δ' ἱστορία βούλεται τἀληθές, ἄν τε παλαιὸν ἄν τε νέον, καὶ τὸ τερατῶδες ἢ οὐκ ἔχει ἢ σπάνιον, 11.5.3.
59 καὶ νῦν δὲ λέγομεν, συγγνώμην αἰτούμενοι τῆς τερατολογίας, ἐάν που βιασθῶμεν ἐκπεσεῖν εἴς τι τοιοῦτο, φεύγοντες τὸ πάντα σιγῇ παραπέμπειν καὶ τρόπον τινὰ πηροῦν τὴν ἱστορίαν, 17.3.3. See Patterson 2013, 209–11 for the two passages that I have quoted. Patterson's article well explains the kind of concerns that bring the geographer and historian close to the mythographer Hecataeus.
60 Fowler 2019, 33–34 (his emphasis), citing Marincola 1997, 118. Cf. Stern 1999, 220: even in Palaephatus myth does not disappear but is made "prosaically credible."

19), Polycrates and the ring (3.40–43), and the story of Pactyes the Lydian and the people of Cyme (1.157–60), among others.[61]

4.6 The example of Palaephatus

Palaephatus (end of 4th c. B.C.E.), the first collector of *incredibilia* of whom we know, was like Asclepiades of Tragilus and Dicaearchus in taking his myths from written texts and in his presupposition of a literate culture.[62] He rationalized the myths he reported, showing that they could, with fantastic elements removed, be explained as ordinary events.[63] He had a theoretical basis for his procedure and in his preface offered the first theory of myth. At this point I digress for a moment on theory as applied to myth. On a common-sense view of the matter, a theory abstracts a model from a set of phenomena, in the present case a set of myths, a process that requires the repeated application and refinement of a set of rules or methods.[64]

Palaephatus' theory is found in his preface, in which, having announced the theme of ἄπιστα, he proceeds to argue as follows:

> ἐμοὶ δὲ δοκεῖ γενέσθαι πάντα τὰ λεγόμενα (οὐ γὰρ ὀνόματα μόνον ἐγένοντο, λόγος δὲ περὶ αὐτῶν οὐδεὶς ὑπῆρξεν· ἀλλὰ πρότερον ἐγένετο τὸ ἔργον, εἶθ' οὕτως ὁ λόγος ὁ περὶ αὐτῶν)· ὅσα δὲ εἴδη καὶ μορφαί εἰσι λεγόμεναι καὶ γενόμεναι τότε, αἳ νῦν οὐκ εἰσί, τὰ τοιαῦτα οὐκ ἐγένοντο. εἰ γάρ <τί> ποτε καὶ ἄλλοτε ἐγένετο, καὶ νῦν τε γίνεται καὶ αὖθις ἔσται. Festa 1902

In the following translation, the stages of his argument are indicated by letters in parentheses:

> (a) I think that everything that is said (i.e., the ἄπιστα) happened. (b) For names by themselves did not come into existence, without there being any account of them, but the deed

---

61 Thomas 2019, 75–76.
62 For the fourth-century date: Hawes 2014a, 38, 227–33. For Palaephatus' sources of his myths (Homer, Hesiod, tragedy): Hawes 2014a, 70.
63 Stern 1996, 7.
64 Cf. the first sentence of Kant's *On the Proverb: That May Be True in Theory, But Is of No Practical Use* (1793): "An aggregation of rules, even of practical rules, is called a *theory*, as long as these rules are thought of as principles possessing a certain generality and, consequently, as being abstracted from a multitude of conditions that nonetheless necessarily influence their application" (Transl. Ted Humphrey in Kant 1983 [1793], 61). "Man nennt einen Inbegriff selbst von praktischen Regeln alsdann Theorie, wenn diese Regeln als Principien in einer gewissen Allgemeinheit gedacht werden, und dabei von einer Menge Bedingungen abstrahirt wird, die doch auf ihre Ausübung nothwendig Einfluß haben": Kant 1923 [1793], 275.

came first, and then accordingly the account concerning them (i.e., those named). (c) The forms and shapes that are spoken of as existing then, which now do not exist, such did not exist (then). (d) For if something happened once in the past, it happens now, too, and will be again.

Palaephatus then aligns himself with the Eleatic denial of the possibility of change, invoking the authority of Melissus of Samos and the obscure Lamiscus of Samos. The sentences that I have quoted contain the nucleus of Palaephatus' theory. (a) He states his premise concerning ἄπιστα. His reader might find the premise itself incredible and Palaephatus proceeds to argue for it, beginning, however, with a parenthetical observation. (b) The deeds are primary and the names of the characters and the account of the deeds are secondary. Festa has correctly put this observation in parentheses. Palaephatus' argument takes the form of the two ensuing categorical propositions, the first negative and the second positive. (c) If "forms and shapes" said to exist then do not exist now, they did not exist then. With the unusual phrase εἴδη καὶ μορφαί, he indicates the poetic elaboration that he intends to remove. (d) If something happened in the past, it happens now and will happen again (cf. Melissus D-K 30 B 1 = L-M 21 D2a: ἀεὶ ἦν ὅ τι ἦν καὶ ἀεὶ ἔσται).[65] In short Palaephatus can take the present as the criterion for whatever myths allege to have happened in the past.[66]

As for Palaephatus' methods (cf. the rules for application in Kant's definition of theory), Jacob Stern identified five: he demonstrated (1) onomastic puns, (2) other puns, (3) misunderstood metaphors, (4) "first inventors", i.e., persons in the past whose inventions were incomprehensible to their contemporaries and thus mythicized, and (5) miscellaneous other methods.[67] Palaephatus thus has a complete theory of myth.

His own statement of his method, at the end of his preface, bears no relation to the methods just enumerated and could not have led to his results:

---

[65] With ἐγένετο and γίνεται Palaephatus "perverts a central tenet" of Melissus "by substituting 'coming into being'...for 'being'": Hawes 2014a, 44. Hawes sees superficiality of understanding of Melissus and she may be right but one might argue for a deliberate adaptation of Melissus to Palaephatus' own theory. One also has to consider the use of γίγνεσθαι in Melissus D-K 30 B 1 (3x) and B 2 (4x).

[66] Hunter 2016 interprets the tone of Palaephatus' preface as ludic, whereas, as he says, it "is almost universally taken as a serious justification for the practice of myth rationalization" (246).

[67] Stern 1996, 18, with n. 47 for earlier scholars' definitions of these methods. Cf. Hawes 2014a, 48–52 on Palaephatus' "hermeneutic consistency." Hawes takes the view that Palaephatus' methods can be reduced to his demonstration of "problems created by ambiguous language" (59–64) and in particular by oracle-like *adunata*, in which an impossible scenario is ultimately seen to have predicted an actual event (64–68).

ἐπελθὼν δὲ καὶ πλείστας χώρας ἐπυνθανόμην τῶν πρεσβυτέρων ὡς ἀκούοιεν περὶ ἑκάστου αὐτῶν, συγγράφω δὲ ἃ ἐπυθόμην παρ' αὐτῶν. καὶ τὰ χωρία αὐτὸς εἶδον ὡς ἔστιν ἕκαστον ἔχον, καὶ γέγραφα ταῦτα οὐχ οἷα ἦν λεγόμενα, ἀλλ' αὐτὸς ἐπελθὼν καὶ ἱστορήσας.

> I traveled through many lands and enquired of the older persons what they knew about each of them (the myths in my collection). I am recording what I learned from them. And I myself saw the lands, the condition of each of them, and I have written the following not as they were told (to me) but having myself gone and made inquiry.

The style and the method are distinctly Herodotean.[68] The claim to Herodotean *historia* (ἱστορήσας) seems absurd.[69] In fact, Palaephatus never refers to this kind of fieldwork in his analyses of individual myths. These concluding sentences must have been tacked on to the preface at some point in the long history of the text.

Besides rationalization, there are two other kinds of ancient myth interpretation, Euhemerism and allegoresis, that are often discussed with Palaephatus. Neither of these two comes under the heading of mythography. The allegoresis of Theagenes of Rhegium is discussed in ch. 5. Euhemerus (not the first to practice what would be called Euhemerism) wrote a travelogue concerning his voyage to an island in the Indian Ocean, where he discovered the historical origin of the Greek gods. The three kinds of ancient myth interpretation have been distinguished thus: "Each of these traditions was concerned with a particular facet of myth: rationalization was concerned with historicism, Euhemerism with cultic origins, and allegoresis with the philosophical truths of poetry."[70]

4.7 Conclusion

From the time of the first of the mythographers surveyed in this chapter, the writing down of myths presupposes that they have a kind of audience, in the first place literate, probably urban, that is open to a new attitude toward these myths. The older myth-telling continued simultaneously, as Pausanias' *Description of*

---

68 With, for example, ἐπυνθανόμην, ἐπυθόμην cf. Hdt. 2.18.1, 2.29.1, 6.117.3, 7.224.1; with εἶδον cf. Hdt. 2.44.2, 3, 2.75.1, 2.148.1, etc. See Hawes 2014a, 46 for the Herodotean aspect of Palaephatus' methodological conclusion.
69 Hawes 2014a, 45–48, 69; Hawes 2014b, 137–38. Hunter 2016, however, integrates a Herodotean strain into his interpretation of the preface. "…Palaephatus placed himself in the Herodotean tradition of the traveling enquirer…" (254).
70 Hawes 2014a, 35.

Greece shows (for Pausanias see ch. 2.1, ch. 5, ch. 6.2). His account does not suggest that the places that he visited were at all affected by mythography, which would certainly have been known to him at least in part. For that matter, he himself is in effect a mythographer. The kinds of collection that begin at the end of the fourth century B.C.E. put myths in new contexts, tending to remove them from their roles in daily life, in verse, and in visual media. Apollodorus' *Bibliotheca*, while its organization continues the old genealogy, sums up the entire corpus of Greek myth for readers who might have little contact with it otherwise but want to acquire some knowledge of this inheritance. The epigram that Photius found in his copy of the *Bibliotheca* says that one no longer has to read the poets: everything can be found here.[71]

---

[71] Edmunds 2017, 96, with n. 51 for textual problems in the epigram.

5 The Question of Belief in Myth

Did the Greeks believe in their myths? This question, thus articulated in the title of a book by Paul Veyne, is still unsettled.[1] His answer and others' are discussed in this chapter. An obstacle to clarity has been the ambiguity of the words "believe" and "belief" in the English language, as of the corresponding words in other languages of scholarship. "Believe" in the theological sense that may come first to mind means to "rely on or trust to a person or…a god or the name of a god" (*OED* s.v. 1) or "to have confidence in or be convinced of the actual existence or occurrence of a thing" (7). For this definition "believe in God" is an example (7.b). "Believe" in this sense includes belief in documents and doctrines (2). But "believe" can have another sense. It can mean "to give intellectual assent to, accept the truth or accuracy of (a statement, doctrine, etc.), give credence to" (3.a). These two meanings of "believe" can be related to two different concepts of belief, which H.H. Price distinguished as belief "in", of which belief in a person or god is the important type, and belief "that", which, as in the dictionary definition just given, is assent to a proposition.[2] He referred to "evaluative" belief-in and "factual" belief-that. He was entering a philosophic discussion in which the reducibility of belief-in to belief-that was the prevailing view and he argued for that view.[3] It continues to prevail, although not in Price's terms. Belief-that is now generally a "propositional attitude" much discussed in Anglophone philosophy of mind.[4]

Veyne's question might, as such, refer to either of these two kinds of belief. The following discussion keeps open the distinction between them, not in order to enter the philosophic discussion but as a way of sorting out the Greek evidence and evaluating Veyne's answer to his question. The distinction is just that and not a binarism awaiting post-structuralist dissolution into some less distinct version of belief that might seem to rescue the kind that is denied with respect to Greek myth.

---

[1] Veyne 1983; Transl. Veyne 1988.
[2] Price 1969. I follow Price in using "belief-in" and "belief-that" to refer to these concepts.
[3] Price does not give references to this discussion. At the end of this lecture he briefly discusses belief in God (i.e., apparently the Christian God), "the most important of all the varieties of evaluative belief", and concludes that it is irreducible to an existential proposition (452–53).
[4] Schwitzgebel 2019 init.

5.1 Belief and the gods in Homer and Hesiod

As for the myths of the Trojan and the Theban Wars, the Greeks certainly believed *that* in substance they were true.[5] Both Herodotus and Thucydides, despite cavils, assumed the veracity of the myth of the Trojan War (cf. App. §1 for the places in these historians).[6] Pherecydes' genealogy made Miltiades a descendant of Ajax (frs. 2, 149 *EGM*).[7] Pindar set the victory of Theron, tyrant of Acragas, against the backdrop of the alternating fortunes of the Labdacids, of whom Theron was a descendant (*Ol.* 2.35–45).[8] This continuity from the heroic age to the present is provided for in Hesiod's large-scale scheme in *Works and Days*. The heroes who died fighting at Troy and at Thebes are the fourth of five distinct races (*Op.* 156–73) and we are the fifth.[9]

As for the gods of epic and of Hesiod's *Theogony*, they met with a well-known challenge from Xenophanes of Colophon, who in the sixth century composed hexameters on their immorality:

πάντα θεοῖς ἀνέθηκαν Ὅμηρός θ' Ἡσίοδός τε,
ὅσσα παρ' ἀνθρώποισιν ὀνείδεα καὶ ψόγος ἐστίν,
κλέπτειν μοιχεύειν τε καὶ ἀλλήλους ἀπατεύειν D-K 21 B 11 = L-M 8D8

Homer and Hesiod attributed to the gods everything that among men is matter for shame and rebuke—stealing, committing adultery and deceiving.

Xenophanes clearly did not believe *in* these gods. He was a monotheist (frs. 23–26). Whether his monotheism entailed belief-in or belief-that is a question that cannot be answered from the fragments that we have. In a somewhat less dogmatic fragment he says that in the matter of the gods "opinion clings to everything" (fr. 34) but in this fragment he is concerned with knowledge of the gods, something probably closer to belief-that. The sixth-century Homeric scholar, The-

---

[5] Cf. Hansen 2017, 6–7 on "credence narratives" ("stories…shaped in such a way as to present, or imply, a claim to historicity"); 423–29.
[6] For this reason myth cannot be called a "catégorie poubelle" for them, despite Saïd 2008, 9.
[7] See *EGM* 2, 474–77. Cf. Thomas 2012.
[8] Edmunds 2006b, 29–30, with Fig. 1.
[9] Stern 1996, 8–9 argues that the rationalizing of myths, as by Palaephatus, did not aim to create disbelief but rather "to remove impediments to belief—belief in the historicity of the legendary heroes." In other words, it is the same kind of rationalizing, which was to some extent practiced also by some of the early Greek mythographers (Stern 1996, 11), and also by Herodotus and Thucydides.

agenes of Rhegium took another approach to the unseemliness of the gods' behavior. He saved the appearances by means of allegorical interpretation. For example, the strife of the gods in Book 20 of the *Iliad* stands for the strife of the elements, the dry against the moist, the hot against the cold, and fire against water (schol. B Hom. *Il.* 20.67; D-K 8 A 2).[10]

In his criticism of the Homeric gods Xenophanes explicitly takes human morality as his standard and his point of view is theological. But the behavior of the gods, no matter how unseemly, can be, and has often been, regarded as internal to the epics, as an aspect of their poetic imaginary.[11] In particular, they can be regarded as serving the purposes of the narrative. In a book published in 1986, Helmut Erbse argued that

> The epic poets…permit the gods to act in such a way that they serve the context of the narrative (*Erzählung*). But that is possible only because the course of the action willed by the poet determines the decisions of the gods and stamps their intention. Only then are they in a position to influence humans. It is not possible to speak of Homer's gods if one leaves out of consideration the goal of the action that is taking place at any given time.

The gods become visible only in the given context.[12] Erbse's premise, taken over from Bruno Snell, was that the epic poet needed the gods in order to render human action comprehensible, because men were unfree, especially in crucial situations, to make their own decisions.[13] The human mind remained to be discovered. Erbse's position on the gods met immediate criticism.[14] His interpretation of the Homeric gods as specific to epic continues, however, in new formulation's, to be discussed below.

To turn to Hesiod's gods in particular, they are presumably the ones whom Socrates and Euthyphro have in mind in Plato's *Euthyphro*. To justify his prosecution of his father on a capital charge, Euthyphro has appealed, against human law, to customary acceptance of the succession myth that begins with the separation of Sky and Earth. In this myth, known to us and presumably to many ancient Greeks from Hesiod, although Euthyphro does not refer to a source or authority, Sky is castrated by Cronus and then Cronus and his fellow Titans are overthrown by Zeus (*Theog.* 630–720). This story is accepted by the very humans,

---

10 Domaradzki 2011 argues that Theagenes' apparently naïve allegorizing was at the service of a rationalized Homer who could be accommodated in Milesian philosophy.
11 Most recently: Martin 2015, 152. For the history of this interpretation: Bremer 1987, 32.
12 Erbse 1986, 295. Quoted in Edmunds 2016b, 114.
13 Snell 1975. Eng. Transl. of an earlier ed.: Snell 1953.
14 Bremer 1987, 43–44.

i.e., Athenians, who might oppose what he is doing, Euthyphro has said, using the verb νομίζω (governing an accusative and infinitive) to express this acceptance of the story.[15] It sounds as if Euthyphro is talking about "belief in" the gods and the standard dictionaries of ancient Greek tend to translate νομίζω in this construction with "believe" despite the basic meaning of this verb, "to make x one's *nomos*."[16] Socrates' reaction to Euthyphro's acceptance of the story shows how νομίζω should be understood. He asks him if he "really considers that these things happened" as he says that they did (σὺ ὡς ἀληθῶς ἡγῇ ταῦτα οὕτως γεγονέναι; 6b3; cf. *Rep.* 377e6–378a6).[17] Socrates' criterion for acceptance or non-acceptance is the truth: "Are we to say that these things are true?" (ταῦτα <u>ἀληθῆ</u> φῶμεν εἶναι, 6c3–4). The point of difference between Socrates and Euthyphro lies in "belief that", not "belief in." Socrates' "do you consider that" and "shall we say that" hardly imply that he is asking Euthyphro to give up a belief in the sense of an "inner psychological state of pious commitment."[18]

An oft-quoted passage of Herodotus gives the impression that the gods of Hesiod and Homer and the myths about them were canonical.[19] Herodotus speaks of these poets as having created a theogony for the Greeks and the story concerning Sky and his descendants that comes up in the *Euthyphro* seems to corroborate this view of Hesiod in particular, even if Euthyphro does not refer to Hesiod. The *Theogony* did indeed have Panhellenic currency, as, for example, numerous references to Hesiod in other dialogues of Plato show.[20] But for the question of belief, the account of theogony cannot end here. First, in the archaic period, there was a plethora of poems in this genre and there was also at least one theogony in lyric,

---

15 αὐτοὶ γὰρ οἱ ἄνθρωποι τυγχάνουσι νομίζοντες τὸν Δία τῶν θεῶν ἄριστον καὶ δικαιότατον, κτλ. *Euthyphr.* 5e5–6.
16 Montanari s.v. νομίζω 1.b "giudicare, considerare, stimare" but for Pl. *Leg.* 886a (πάντες νομίζουσι κτλ.): "tutti *credono nell*'esistenza degli dèi" (my emphasis) The same drift can be seen in LSJ s.v. νομίζω II "own, acknowledge, consider as" but in sub-divisions under this heading some examples are translated by "believe."
17 For the too facile assumption that Socrates is asking about belief the translation by Grube 1997: 5 is an example: "[D]o you really believe". Grube may, however, be using "believe" in the sense of "belief that."
18 Stewart and North 2012.
19 "Whence each of the gods came and whether they all existed always and of what sort they were in appearance, they [the Greeks] did not know until yesterday or the day before, so to speak. For I think that Homer and Hesiod lived four hundred years before my time. These are the ones who created a theogony for the Greeks and gave the gods their epithets and distinguished their honors and arts and indicated their appearances" (2.53).
20 On the Panhellenic Hesiod: Nagy 1990, 36–37.

as Alcman fr. 5 *PMG* attests—presumably a Laconian theogony.²¹ The best known of these other theogonies, thanks to the discovery of the Derveni papyrus in 1962, is the Orphic, of which there were several versions, composed at different times.²² The most obscure of the archaic composers of theogonies, both in his identity and in his date, is Epimenides.²³ Second, theogonies in prose begin at the turn of the sixth century with Acusilaus of Argos and in the fifth century with Pherecydes of Athens.²⁴ Acusilaus agreed with Hesiod on Chaos as the primordial entity (Hes. *Theog.* 116; Acus. frs. 6a–d *EGM*). In Hesiod, Gaia, Tartarus and Eros belong to the first, created generation (*Theog.* 116–22). A line in Theocritus, however, shows both that Eros was thought to have had parents and that it was uncertain who they were. (ᾧτινι τοῦτο θεῶν ποκα τέκνον ἔγεντο, *Id.* 13.2). A scholiast on this line finds different parents in different sources and says that Acusilaus made him the son of Night and Aether (= fr. 6c *EGM*). The variation that the scholiast found in his sources is in itself hardly surprising and in principle there is no reason to doubt that Acusilaus differed from Hesiod on this point. The mother of Euripides' Melanippe, for her part, had sky and Gaia as the two primordial beings (quoted in ch. 2.2).

Even if Hesiod's theogony was the most popular in the domain of performance, whether or not its particular version was canonical for "the Greeks", as Herodotus said, is another matter. A Greek might enjoy hearing a rhapsodic performance of Hesiod more than of any other theognony that was on offer. At the same time, this Greek might have held that a particular local theogony or a particular local genealogy within a Panhellenic theogony was the true one. He might have seen some third version in sculpture or in a vase painting.²⁵ Goethe called myth "luxe de croyance", a definition that well fits Greek myth.²⁶ The Greek that I have been imagining availed himself of this luxury.

5.2 A word for belief-that: πείθεσθαι

Another word that expresses belief-that is πείθεσθαι and its compound ἀναπείθεσθαι (e.g., Pl. *Rep.* 381e2). Herodotus, whose skeptical references to stories that

---

21 West 1966, 12–13.
22 Survey in Meisner 2018.
23 His genealogical fragments: *EGM* 1, frs. 1, 6–18.
24 But in general theogony is "weakly attested" in the sources for mythography: *EGM* 2, 3.
25 See Buxton 1994, 162–63 on plurality of belief in Greek religion. There is no reason—perhaps more reason—to think that the same is true of Greek myth.
26 Goethe 1842, 161: "Mythologie. – Luxe de croyance."

he calls *muthoi* were pointed out in the first chapter, states as his working principle: "I am bound to tell what I am told, but not in every case to believe it" (ἐμοὶ μὲν οὖν λέγειν μὲν τὰ ὑπὸ Ἑλλήνων λεγόμενα ἀνάγκη, πείθεσθαι δὲ πᾶσιν οὐκέτι ἀνάγκη, 7.152).[27] Pausanias remembered Herodotus and adopted the same principle: "I must say what is said by the Hellenes say but I do not have to go so far as to believe everything (or everyone)" (ἐμοὶ μὲν οὖν λέγειν μὲν τὰ ὑπὸ Ἑλλήνων λεγόμενα ἀνάγκη, πείθεσθαι δὲ πᾶσιν οὐκέτι ἀνάγκη, 6.3.8). Finally in Arcadia Pausanias hears a myth that he is willing to believe, one concerning Lycaon, a contemporary of Cecrops, who sacrificed a human baby on the altar of Lycaean Zeus and was changed into a wolf (*lykos*). He says: καὶ ἐμέ γε ὁ λόγος οὗτος πείθει (8.2.4). Here the active form of the verb is Pausanias' way of expressing his willingness to believe-that. Pausanias' criteria for this belief are the age of the story and its probability, owing to the fact that the pious men in the days of the story's origin dined with the gods and some mortals, Heracles, Aphiaraus and the Dioscouroi, were changed into gods. He concludes: "So someone might persuade (us) of Lycaon's turning into a wolf and Niobe's into a stone" (οὕτω πείθοιτο ἄν τις καὶ Λυκάονα θηρίον καὶ τὴν Ταντάλου Νιόβην γενέσθαι λίθον.) The so-called "conversion" of Pausanias emerges in his comments on a spring called "Lamb" that he passes on his way to Mantinea.[28] The spring got its name from the lambs that pastured around it. Rhea, having given birth to Poseidon, put him among the lambs and gave Cronus a foal to swallow in place of Poseidon, as she gave him a stone to swallow in place of Zeus (Hes. *Theog.* 468–91). Pausanias says that when he began to write his history he considered such stories foolishness (εὐηθία) but when he reached Arcadia he changed his mind. His reason is that the wise Greeks of old spoke in riddles and so the stories about Cronus must be a form of wisdom (8.8.3). He does not offer an explanation of these stories as riddles. The words for belief that I have considered do not appear in Pausanias' account of his "conversion."[29]

---

27 Cf. Ξεῖνε, ὅ τι δεῖ γενέσθαι ἐκ τοῦ θεοῦ, ἀμήχανον ἀποτρέψαι ἀνθρώπῳ· οὐδὲ γὰρ πιστὰ λέγουσι ἐθέλει πείθεσθαι οὐδείς, 9.16. Cf. also Socrates, apropos of the abduction of Oreithyia by Boreas: ... πειθόμενος δὲ τῷ νομιζομένῳ..., Pl. *Phdr.* 230a2.
28 First so-called by Oliver 1972, whose concern was not the "conversion" as such but its relation to the *Panathenaic Discourse* of Aristeides.
29 For discussion of these passages in Pausanias see Pirenne-Delforge 2008, 71–72, 345–46; Pirenne-Delforge 2009, 41–42.

5.3 Belief and Cult

Veyne's question gets a positive answer, then, on the evidence considered so far, only in the sense "belief that." What, however, of Greek religion? The gods of Hesiod and Homer were also worshipped in cult. The question then becomes: did the Greeks believe in the gods of cult? The answer might seem obvious and might imply that the conclusion just reached should be rethought, on the hypothesis that the gods of Homer and Hesiod and the gods of cult cannot be absolutely distinguished. The cult is the central institution of Greek religion, about which the question of belief can be raised again. Many cults were linked to myths that explained how the divinity or divinities came to be worshipped in this place or that or how a temple, an altar, a tomb or a statue came to be constructed. It might seem that participation in the rituals or observances attaching to a cult entailed belief in the relevant myth or myths. On the contrary, these myths did not have the status of doctrine, nor was there any doctrinal basis of any kind for obligation toward a cult.[30] Its sanctuary, its personnel and its rituals, particularly those involving sacrifice and purification, are governed by a set of rules. Many of these so-called "sacred laws" have survived in inscriptions on stone.[31] The concerns that they show are anything but doctrinal (see ch. 6 on myth and religion).[32]

For the question of belief in the gods of cult, Socrates again provides an example. The first item in the indictment against him is impiety toward the gods of the city.[33] On the standard English translation: "he commits injustice not believing in the gods in which the city believes."— It is the same verb (νομίζω) used by Euthyphro concerning Athenian acceptance of a certain myth (cf. above).—In Xenophon's *Apology*, Socrates makes a common sense defense against the charge of impiety: "anyone else who happened to be there...used to see me sacrificing in the communal festivals and on the public altars" (11). He does not speak of an inner disposition toward the city's gods but to his observance of the practices, in

---

[30] Cf. Delattre 2005, 67: "L'individu grec n'est pas un croyant ni un fidèle, il ne fait pas à proprement parler acte de foi, et sa croyance n'est pas du même ordre que celle exigée dans le cadre des religions juives, chrétiennes et musulmanes."
[31] Parker 2012b. For the problems of categorization to which Parker refers see Carbon and Pirenne-Delforge 2012.
[32] As Graf 1993 [1987] says in the conclusion of his discussion of the mythical etiologies attaching to cults, "Myth and ritual are...autonomous phenomena" (116).
[33] Pl. *Apol.* 24b8–c1, 27a5–6; Xen. *Apol.* 10; Diog. Laert. 2.40. Socrates paraphrases the *antomosia*: Σωκράτη φησὶν ἀδικεῖν τούς τε νέους διαφθείροντα καὶ θεοὺς <u>οὓς ἡ πόλις</u> νομίζει οὐ νομίζοντα, ἕτερα δὲ δαιμόνια καινά (24b8c1).

particular sacrifice, of civic cults.[34] Likewise in Plato's *Apology*, when Socrates paraphrases the first part of the indictment against him, using the verb νομίζω, he means "observe customary practices regarding."[35] But his self-defense takes a form that might be considered more characteristic of the Platonic Socrates. In his cross-examination of Meletus, his main accuser, he leads him to clarify the indictment as complete non-belief in the city's gods (τὸ παράπαν οὐ νομίζεις θεούς, 26c7). Socrates is able to show that, if he believes concerning *daimonia* then he must believe concerning *daimones* and if he believes concerning *daimones* then he must believe concerning gods (27c8–9). From this point, continuing to the end of the cross-examination, Socrates ceases to use the verb νομίζω and uses ἡγέομαι (27d1–28a1: 7x; cf. *Euthyphr*. 6b3, quoted above). For this verb, as for νομίζω, the translation "believe" is given (LSJ s.v. III.1) but it can only mean "belief that." In Plato's *Apology*, Socrates has, then, restated the part of the indictment concerning the gods in order to make it matter of their existence but when he uses these verbs he is not talking about "belief in."

What is true of νομίζω is also true of ὅσιος and εὐσεβής, words that occur often in the *Euthyphro*. The first of these words, when used of persons, means "pious, devout, religious" (LSJ s.v. II). In her detailed semantic study Saskia Peels concluded: "*Hosios* is what humans do to please the gods and give them the *timē* they deserve..."[36] εὐσεβής is a synonym.[37] The fundamental idea of the verb σέβομαι, from which the adjective comes, is "to withdraw."[38]

The distinction implicit in the Xenophontic Socrates' self-defense, which is in our terms one between observance and belief, has been for a century or more a central tenet in the history of ancient Greek religion. Fritz Graf speaks of "the absolute predominance in pagan Greek and Roman religion of ritual actions over

---

[34] Cf. Edmunds 2014a, 18, from which some of the sentences in this paragraph are taken.
[35] Burnet 1924, 184 (in a long valuable note on Pl. *Apol* 24c1): "The charge is one of nonconformity in religious practice, not of unorthodoxy in religious belief." Cf. De Strycker and Slings 1994, 87. Cf. Seckler 1962, 528 on the meaning of belief in the Old Testament: "Was das NT am AT als Glaube bezeichnet, trifft dort auf keinen begrifflich eindeutig formulierten Sachverhalt. Israel begründet seine Existenz im Jahwe-Bund. Der glaubende Mensch ist Glied der durch den Bund erstellten Gemeinschaft, der Glaube zeigt primär kollektive Struktur." ("What the NT refers to in the OT as belief has to do with no state of things there that is clearly formulated as a concept. Israel bases its existence on the Yahweh covenant. The believer is a member of the community created by the covenant, belief shows primarily a collective structure.")
[36] Peels 2015, 255.
[37] Hare 1981, 11: "εὐσεβές and ὅσιον are not distinguished in the dialogue."
[38] *DELG* s.v.: "la diversité remarquable des emplois se réduit à la signification unique 'se retirer', ou 'faire se retirer' confirmée par l'étymologie".

faith."[39] In a study of "literary religion", as distinct from other kinds of evidence for cult and ritual, Thomas Harrison takes a contrary view, challenging "principle tenets of modern scholarship on Greek religion." One of these tenets, predictably, after Graf and others, is: "What mattered in Greek religion was ritual, not belief or dogma."[40] He surveys the history of this distinction, which he brings up to the 1990s.[41]

5.4 The scholarly debate on belief

The question thus arises: how does belief enter the picture?[42] As for myth, Richard Buxton appealed to Veyne's invocation of Michel Foucault's "plurality of programs of truth."[43] Lee Paterson's extensive discussion of degrees of credulity in kinship myth in diplomatic contexts is a useful case in point.[44] Buxton gave examples of persons who express belief and non-belief at different times.[45] But these are all expressions of belief-that or non-belief-that, credence or non-credence, credulity or incredulity. Likewise, refinements on the distinction between "high-intensity" and "low-intensity" belief that look for a home for the latter in ancient Greece still presuppose the belief-in which the distinction was intended to surpass.[46] No matter how variously "low-intensity" belief is expressed it remains belief-that.

---

39 Graf 2003, 980. Cf. Buxton 1994, 159 with n. 35. Versnel 2011, 544–45 provides a list (consisting of quotations from eight different authors, not including Graf) of those who maintain the distinction between ritual practice and belief.
40 Harrison 2007, 382–84; italicized by him.
41 Harrison 2015 (online).
42 Harrison does not answer this question. His way of avoiding it requires a rather long quotation: "This is not the place to discuss the relative merits of the term belief (or of alternatives such as religious 'knowledge') and its anachronistic overtones (see, e.g., Harrison 2000, 1–30, and especially Feeney 1998, 12–46). It is fair to say, in Denis Feeney's words, that 'not all religions place as high a value on belief in key dogmas as does modern Christianity' (1998,13). Such stark contrasts, however, as between dogma and ritual offer us little more than a choice of caricatures. It is the area of religious experience that falls between these two poles, of "beliefs" that fall short of dogma, that literature – so long as it is read as not merely literature – can illuminate" (384).
43 Veyne 1988, 27: "Throughout the ages a plurality of programs of truth has existed, and it is these programs, involving different distributions of knowledge, that explain the subjective degrees of intensity of beliefs...that coexist in the same individual."
44 See his program: Patterson 2010, 21 and discussion.
45 Buxton 1994, 156–57.
46 Harrison 2015 (online).

Denis Feeney, in a book on Roman religion, also appeals to the Foucauldian Veyne.⁴⁷ In a short section on the Greeks he restates Veyne's plurality of modes of belief, which he applies also to cult.⁴⁸ Veyne extended pluralism, however, to the position that "The plurality of modalities of belief is in reality the plurality of the criteria for truth."⁴⁹ The classical scholars who have been discussed did not follow him along this further path. At the level of generality reached by Veyne we seem to enter a "night in which all cows are black" or cannot even be discerned in the first place.⁵⁰ What could be gotten from Veyne, as this brief survey has shown, was the notion of the plurality of beliefs. What is still lacking is the demonstration that the Greeks had a concept of belief-in.

H.S. Versnel entered the discussion on the side of those who held the view that belief-in, in some form, could be found in the Greeks.⁵¹ He begins with a scathing review of scholars, especially Simon Price, who hold the opposite view.⁵² In the course of this review he discusses the use of νομίζειν in the charge against Socrates and in the works of Plato discussed above, without, as far as I can see, any consequences for the view that he is attacking.⁵³ He then turns to his own view of the matter.⁵⁴ He begins with the proposition that "The most general and comprehensive meaning of 'to believe', to be found in modern dictionaries…is: 'to hold a thing for true without being able to prove it'." With this report of modern dictionaries must be compared the citations of the *Oxford English Dictionary* (*OED*) given at the beginning of this chapter, which is surely a modern dictionary. (Versnel might have had dictionaries in other modern languages in mind.) The main premise of Versnel's lengthy discussion is: "Scholarly discourse is always

---

47 Feeney 1998, 14–15, with a survey of related approaches "which stress the contingent and contextual nature of belief systems."
48 Feeney 1998, 22–25, with a critique of Mikalson 1983 and Mikalson 1991. "[W]hat we label 'real religion' is itself a mobile set of discourses with varying degrees of overlaps and competition" (25).
49 Veyne 1988, 113.
50 For critiques see Brillante 1990, 116–17; Buxton 1994, 158–59 (the lengthy n. 31).
51 Versnel 2011, 539–59 (App. 4: "Did the Greeks Believe in Their Gods?").
52 Versnel 2011, 539–46.
53 Following Fahr 1969, Versnel 2011, 542–44 concludes his discussion of νομίζειν in the charge against Socrates: "After his arguments it can no longer be questioned that the latter part of the fifth century witnessed a gradual shifting from 'die Götter nicht nach Brauch ehren' ['not to honor the gods according to custom'] towards 'die Existenz der Götter nicht für wirklich halten' ['not to believe that the gods exist']." But (1) how else would one interpret νομίζειν θεούς (cf. my discussion) and (2) what does Fahr's finding have to do with belief-in, which is what Price and others denied?
54 Versnel 2011, 546–59.

etic and should therefore be conducted in etic terms. This means that the person who engages in this type of research must clarify that (s)he will use the term 'believe' in its broad 'low intensity' meaning and not in its Christian 'high intensity' application with all its well-known implications."[55] As I pointed out above, there is a *petitio principii* in the invocation of "low-intensity" belief in the argument for something like belief-in.

In the history of the Greek language it would be the words πιστεύω and πίστος that in their Christian usage would come to express belief-in. The two dictionaries of ancient Greek that are standard for Anglophones are not equally useful in their entries on the relevant words, which are πιστεύω and πίστις. The Liddell-Scott-Jones dictionary gives as the first meaning of the first of these words "*trust, put faith in, rely on* a person, thing, or statement" (1), adding "later with Preps.", where the examples are biblical. This entry does not make it clear that the change in construction corresponds to a change in meaning. Montanari's definition, "to have faith" is recognized, however, as "later", and the examples are again biblical. For πιστεύω, the standard Anglophone dictionary of New Testament Greek is, not unexpectedly, much clearer: "*believe (in), trust*, of religious belief in a special sense, as faith in the Divinity that lays special emphasis on trust in his power and his nearness to help, in addition to being convinced that he exists and that his revelations or disclosures are true. In our lit. God and Christ are the objects of this faith" (2 init.).[56] In this meaning, the verb is used especially with εἰς (2.a.γ). An example familiar to Christians is: "For God so loved the world that he gave his one and only Son, that whoever believes in (πιστεύων εἰς) him shall not perish but have eternal life" (*Ev. Jo.* 3.13; King James Transl.).[57] Seckler comments: "Johannine belief refers to the mysterium of salvation manifested in Jesus, in which to believe "in" and to believe "someone" coincide".[58] Further, that which the Christian believes in supersedes the object or objects of antecedent belief of whatever kind, in particular Greek myth.[59]

---

[55] Versnel 2011, 548: "Our conclusion...must be that while θεοὺς ἡγεῖσθαι is prevalent in the sense of 'believe (in the existence of) gods', θεοὺς νομίζειν, too, is frequently used in the same cognitive meaning. It is only at this point that we now may safely conclude that the question "did the Greeks believe in gods" is intrinsically absurd, but if for the sake of argument taken seriously (and taken in its 'low intensity' sense), should be answered in the positive" (559).
[56] Arndt and Ginrich 1979.
[57] For John's preference for the verb πιστεύειν over the noun πίστις see Seckler 1962, 532–33 (β).
[58] Seckler 1962, *loc. cit.*
[59] Gadamer 1993 [1981], 178–79. "Alles, was nicht im geschichtlichen Zusammenhang der Heilsgeschichte seinen Platz hat, verliert vom Glauben her die Verbindlichkeit, und die mythologische Vermittlung wird zur heidnischen Verirrung." ("Everything that does not have its place in

This brief discussion of a vast subject is enough to show the distance between any kind of ancient Greek belief, of whatever degree of "intensity", and Christian belief-in. The two kinds of belief, -in and -that, have often been conflated, sometimes unconsciously and sometimes deliberately, as in Versnel's etic interpretation. While Versnel is right that scholarly discourse is always etic, it does not follow that an etic, or "outsider's" point of view supersedes the emic, the insider's or the "native's." The etic emerges only from the emic and everyone who has thought about these matters, beginning with the originator of the etic-emic distinction, Kenneth Pike, has had to face the problem of connecting the two points of view.[60] In the matter of ancient Greek belief-in, the connection remains to be made.

5.5 The Erythraean Paean

The discussion of belief and cult (5.3 above) did not include what some might consider an obvious counter-example to my negative conclusion concerning belief, viz., the use of myth in cults songs or hymns. How could those who performed these hymns and their audiences not have believed in the gods to whom they were addressed? To answer this question, one leaves out compositions such as the hymns of Callimachus that envisage a reception, whatever it might have been, other than cultic. There remain many possibilities, from which I have chosen the *Erythraean Paean*. As a paean, it belongs to the larger category of cult song or hymn.[61]

This paean is so called after an inscription discovered at Erythrae (on a peninsula opposite the island of Chios). It is attested also in inscriptions from Athens, Dion (Macedonia), and Ptolemais (Egypt). The Erythraean, after which the paean is named, is from the fourth century, the others from the second-third centuries B.C.E. Each of these versions was clearly intended for performance and thus the mythical component, standard in cult hymns, should be understood in the first place as itself performative.[62] The variations in this component from text to another are a function of the context of performance, as might be expected.

---

the historical context of salvation history loses its binding force in terms of faith, and mythological report becomes pagan aberration.").
60 For the etic-emic distinction: Edmunds 2016a, 26–29.
61 Furley and Bremer 2001.1, 10–14. The word ὕμνος is an exacerbated case of the terminological difficulty presented by Greek religion. See introduction to ch. 6 sub fin.
62 The discussion of this paean by LeVen 2014, 296–302 emphasizes the performative and ritual function of the paean.

The Erythraean inscription:

[Παιᾶνα κλυτό]μητιν ἀείσατε
[κοῦροι Λατοΐδαν Ἕκ]ατον,
    ἰὲ Παιάν,
ὃς μέγα χάρ[μα βροτοῖς]ιν ἐγείνατο
μιχθεὶς ἐμ φι[λότητι Κορ]ωνίδι   5
ἐν γᾷ τᾷ Φλεγυείαι,
[ἰὴ Παι]άν, Ἀσκληπιὸν
δαίμονα κλεινό[τατ]ον,
    ἰὲ Παιάν·
[το]ῦ δὲ καὶ ἐξεγένοντο Μαχάων   10
καὶ Πο[δα]λείριος ἠδ' Ἰασώ,
    ἰὲ Παιάν,
Αἴγλα [τ'] εὐῶπις Πανάκειά τε
Ἠπιόνας παῖδες σὺν ἀγακλυτῶι
εὐαγεῖ Ὑγιείαι·   15
ἰὴ Παιάν, Ἀσκληπιὸν
δαίμονα κλεινότατον,
    ἰὲ Παιάν.
χαῖρέ μοι, ἵλαος δ' ἐπινίσεο
τὰν ἁμὰν πόλιν εὐρύχορον,   20
    ἰὲ Παιάν,
δὸς δ' ἡμᾶς χαίροντας ὁρᾶν φάος
ἀελίου δοκίμους σὺν ἀγακλυτῶι
εὐαγεῖ Ὑγιείαι·
ἰὴ Παιάν, Ἀσκληπιὸν   25
δαίμονα κλεινότατον,
    ἰὲ Παιάν.

Sing, lads, of Paian famed for his cleverness, the farshooting son of Leto, Ie Paian!, who fathered a great delight for mortals, after he had lain in love with Koronis in the Phlegyeian land, Iē Paian! Asclepius, a god most famous, Ie Paian!

From him (i.e. Asclepius) were also born Machaon, Podaleirios, Iaso, Ie Paian!, beautiful-faced Aigla, Panakeia, the children of Epione, with glorious, bright Hygieia, Iē Paian! Asclepius, a god most famous, Ie Paian!

Be pleased with me and approach our spacious city with gladness, Ie Paian!, and grant that we in delight see the welcome light of the sun with glorious, bright Hygieia, Iē Paian! Asclepius, a god most famous, Ie Paian![63]

Powell p. 136; cf. Lyr. Adesp. fr. 934 *PMG*

---

[63] Transl. Faraone 2011, 208–209. The spaces in this translation indicate not a division into strophes (the paean is monostrophic on his account) but the paean's three primarily dactylic segments.

The paean is in three parts, invocation of Apollo in the third person (1–3), genealogy (5–18), and prayer in the second person (19–27). Here the genealogy does the work of the myth typical in cult hymns.[64] Apollo, addressed as Paian, begot Asclepius from Coronis. Asclepius begot from Epione six children: Machaon and Podaleirios (heroic healers: *Il.* 2. 732), Iaso (cf. ἴασις "cure"), Aigla, Panakeia ("Cure-All"), and Hygieia ("Health"). The only name here that has no immediate connection with health is Aigla (αἴγλη "gleam" of the sun or moon).[65] In the inscription from Dion the off-spring of Asclepius receive an addition: καὶ Πο[δα]λείριος ἠδ' Ἰασώ Ἀκεσώ τε πολλύλιτος (11).[66] Also ἐν γᾷ (6) has been omitted and Φλεγυείαι has become Φλεγύαο, so that Koronis is the daughter of Phlegyas, king of the Lapiths.[67]

As the genealogical variants in the Dion inscription show, the myth varies according to location. The people of Dion appropriate Koronis by making her the daughter of Phlegyas, a king in their region.[68] No doubt the obscure Akeso has also entered the genealogy for local reasons. While the belief that Asclepius is the son of Apollo is central, there are different beliefs in different places about who the progeny of Asclepius were. Here, then, is yet another example of the local variation attested many times in Greek myth.

The use of myth in the *Erythraean Paean* is not an affirmation of belief but has a particular functional value, as identifying the Apollo with whom the Paean begins. In the genealogy attached to his name, the presence of his son Aclepius

---

64 Furley and Bremer 2001, 6: "What is seldom adequately realized...is that myth is the substance of hymns, and that the stories told about the gods in myths were in fact the stories sung *to* the gods in worship in order to flatter, remind, praise and cajole a recalcitrant stone image into beneficial action" (their emphasis).
65 The Erythraean inscription reads Αγλαια. Editors print Αἴγλα, from the Ptolemais and Dion inscriptions.
66 Akeso (cf. ἀκέω "heal"). For the hiatus Faraone 2011, 213 n. 20.
67 For these differences in the inscriptions: LeVen 2014, 293 and nn. 24–25. A textual history can be found already in Powell, p. 137. Faraone 2011 opposes the stemmatic conception of the relation of the four inscriptions, which he regards as "witnesses to a hitherto unappreciated genre of paean to Apollo and Asclepius composed almost entirely in dactyls and exhibiting the vocabulary, prosody and metrical flexibility usually associated with hexametrical verse rather than lyric" (207). The four might stand in a stemmatic relation and at the same time, as an ensemble, come under Faraone's generic description.
68 Powell, p. 137: Usus adjectivi patrii notus est tanquam Thessaliae maxime propius, ubi Aesculapii cultus antiqua sedes, velut Triccae... But it has also been argued that all four inscriptions go back to a fourth-century Athenian "rescension" of the original, an argument that entails Athenian motivation for Akeso and the omission of ἐν γᾷ. See the discussion by Furley/Bremer 2001.1, 213–14.

becomes more certain. The performance proceeds to enact its success by bringing Asclepius, who appears first in the genealogy, as the son of Apollo, into the refrain. The genealogy thus leads to the celebration of the god, which aims to secure his goodwill and culminates in the prayer to him at the end.[69] As Furley and Bremer say, the celebrants aim to draw "a recalcitrant stone image into beneficial action."[70]

On the front of the stone on which the paean is inscribed, there are instructions for the ritual:

παιωνίζειν πρῶτον περὶ τὸμ βωμὸν τοῦ Ἀπόλλωνος τόνδε τὸμ παιῶνα ἐστρίς· ἰὴ Παιών, ὤ, ἰὴ Παιών (ter) [ὤ] ἄναξ Ἄπολλον φείδεο κούρων φείδ[εο...

First sing this paean three times around the altar of Apollo: Iē Paian! O! Iē Paian! (three times) O, Lord Apollo, save the lads, save...

How these instructions should be interpreted in relation to the paean is uncertain.[71] The lads who are directed to sing this paean must, however, be the same as the ones addressed in the second line of the paean on the other side of the stone. The instructions to the lads put great weight on the cry of "Iē Paian!", which is inscribed three times. The inscription obeys its own injunction (ἐστρίς) and dramatizes (if this word can be used of an inscription) the summoning of the god. In sum, what the celebrants believe in is not the myth but its ritual efficacy and their performance of the Paean on any particular occasion expresses this belief.

The performance is tantamount to an offering and the concluding prayer of the paean wells fits Simon Pulleyn's general thesis concerning *charis* as the primary characteristic of the relationship between the ancient Greeks and their gods and thus of prayer in particular. He explains *charis* thus:

[I]t refers to a whole nexus of related ideas that we would call reciprocity. When one gives something to a god, one is giving χάρις in the sense that the offering is pleasing; but equally

---

[69] Lozynsky 2014, 61: "The genealogy of the Erythraean paean—which includes Hygieia in the list of Asclepius' children—may be designed as a basis for the request to grant 'Health' to the worshippers."

[70] See n. 64 above.

[71] See Furley and Bremer 2001, 212–13 and notes. The cult of Asclepius and Apollo at Erythrae also had the typical kind of regulations concerning sacrifice, which turned up in an inscription close in time to the paean (*CGRN* 76).

one is storing up for oneself a feeling of gratitude on the part of the god, which is also χάρις The whole two-way relationship can be called one of χάρις.⁷²

Christian prayer is not the path to understanding prayer in this sense.⁷³

5.6 Conclusion

Two concepts of belief, which correspond to a lexical distinction between two meanings of the word, are belief in someone or something and belief that someone or something is or does such and such. Discussion of Veyne's well-known question concerning Greek myth has not taken sufficient account of the two kinds of belief. Ancient Greeks believed that the Trojan and Theban Wars had taken place. The gods of Homer and Hesiod were another matter. When Socrates raises the question of belief with respect to these gods, he uses the verb νομίζω, which does not refer to belief-in. From the sixth century, these gods could expect at best belief-that (§2). The gods of cult did not command belief-in any more than the gods of myth. Worship of the gods of cult was a matter of ritual and did not depend on belief-in (§3). Scholarly discussion oscillates between denials and affirmations of belief-in, swinging toward the latter in recent discussion (§4). Even if cult observance is primarily a matter of ritual, the use of myth in cult songs or hymns might seem, despite everything that has been said in this chapter, to reflect belief-in. Study of the *Erythraean Paean* fails to confirm this notion (§5).

---

72 Pulleyn 1997, 4.
73 Graf 2020 (IV): "A feature...unfamiliar in the Graeco-Roman world is the dominance of a single prayer, the Lord's Prayer...This set the pattern for the departure of Christian prayer from the Graeco-Roman attitude of a mutual give and take, and allowed for the possibility of communicating with God in prayer, directly and independently of any ritual structure."

6 Myth and Religion, Myth and Cult, Myth and Ritual

The gods of Greek myth and the gods of Greek religion have the same names but are otherwise different from one another.[1] The point of contact of these two separate domains is the cult and in particular the cult image, in which the god is assumed to be present, while the worshipper is well aware of the god's other life in stories having nothing to do with the cult (6.1). The function of the myth is to explain the origin of the cult (6.2). Myths also explain rituals. The most famous of these myths explains not a particular ritual but the reason for humans' consumption of the best parts of the sacrificial victim while the other parts are burnt for the gods (6.3). A smaller group of myths tells of the movements of cult images from one place to another (6.4).

What is obvious to the historian of Greek religion may not be so obvious to the scholar of Greek myth and is briefly repeated here.[2] The most conspicuous public place of a cult was the precinct (*temenos*) of the god, with his or her temple, cult image(s), and altar. A cult might include two or more divinities—"the cult of ill-assorted divinities", it has been called.[3] This, the center of the cult, might also include the shrine of a hero or heroine.[4] Or this kind of shrine, of which there were many, might have its own location. Likewise, the nymphs, again numerous, were worshipped along with a god or goddess or independently.[5] The main forms of worship were animal sacrifice, votives, and prayer.[6] Civic cults of the gods were regulated by various rules, called "sacred laws", of which much

---

[1] Delattre 2005, 67–69.
[2] For a more detailed overview, see Kearns 2012a.
[3] Gordon 2012.
[4] For other structures and for a survey: Sinn 2004.
[5] See Malkin 2012a.
[6] For a discussion of the three kinds of prayer (εὐχή / εὔχομαι, λιτή / λίσσομαι, ἀρά / ἀράομαι): *ThesCRA* vol. 3, pp. 108–109. For votive offerings: Malkin 2012b. Animal sacrifice is an unsettled matter. The distinction, in particular, between sacrifice to a god and to a hero has become problematical. See Edmunds 2016a, 181–82. The orthodoxies represented by Burkert, Vernant and Detienne are challenged by Naiden 2013.

inscriptional evidence survives.[7] The central form of worship of the god or goddess of the cult was the sacrifice of a large animal.[8] Some sacrifices were parts of larger so-called festivals, recurring on certain dates in conjunction with other ritual observances. In contrast with the civic cult, the mystery cult offered the initiate the chance of personal transcendence of quotidian existence or, in the case of the Eleusinian Mysteries, better hopes for the afterlife. All the forms of worship in the various cults go under the name "ritual", a conspicuous example of the general terminological difficulty in discussion of Greek religion.[9] This difficulty begins with the word "religion" itself, which does not have a corresponding word in Greek.

6.1 Double existence

Whereas a particular god is embodied in his or her cult statue and worshipped as present in that form, that same god leads a separate existence in myth. The *Iliad* provides a clear example. After a string of Achaean successes on the battlefield, Hector enters the city and tells his mother Hecabe to place a robe on the knees of Athena in her temple on the acropolis and to promise her twelve oxen if she takes pity and keeps Diomedes away from the walls of the city (6.237–311). It is clearly the cult of a city-goddess. Not only does Athena have a temple at which oxen might be sacrificed, she has a cult image. (The only one mentioned in Homer.) She has also a cult epithet (ῥυσίπτολι, 305). She has a priestess, who has been chosen by the Trojans (6.298, 302). Hecabe, accompanied by other women, takes her most beautiful robe to the temple. The women lift their hands and make a ritual shriek (301). Theano, the priestess, places the robe on the knees of the image of Athena (302–303) and offers the prayer (304–10). She asks that Athena cast Diomedes into the dust (306–307). But Athena, the omniscient narrator says, refuses the prayer (6.311). Athena seems to be present in her cult image. Her refusal is no surprise. She has already appeared in the narrative several times, in support of the Achaeans. In particular, she has assisted Diomedes in his aristeia in Book 5. Precisely with respect to Diomedes, the prayer of Theano is futile. The Athena

---

[7] Analyzed in *CGRN* by themes under the headings "Sacrificial Performance" and "Purity and Purification."
[8] Described in memorable pages in Burkert 1985, 56–57. And more extensively in Burkert 1983, 3–7. See also Parker 2012a. (I cite Burkert 1985, to some extent a second ed. of Burkert 1977, and not Burkert 2011, the second German edition, which is for the most part the same as the first.)
[9] On terminology: Kearns 2012b; cf. Parker 2012a init. On ritual: Graf 2012a.

who has appeared in the action at Troy decides, in effect, for the cult goddess Athena.[10]

The temple of Apollo in Troy is also part of the narrative of the *Iliad*, which knows of the temple of Athena in Athens (2.549–51) and of the temple of Apollo at Delphi (9.404–405). These gods are in their temples; they are also on Olympus or wherever in the world they may happen to be. Clearly the day of the double existence or multi-existence of the gods has arrived. "The gods can traverse vast distances, but they are not omnipresent; they will come to visit their temples, but are not confined within the cult image."[11] Further, if necessary, myths can be adjusted to conform to the situation "on the ground", in cult. In Hesiod's *Theogony*, Heracles kills the eagle that is tormenting Prometheus; then leaves him (523–33). In *Prometheus Bound*, however, Heracles also releases him (872). "This was a natural development at Athens, where Prometheus was actually worshipped and could not be regarded as still a prisoner and enemy of Zeus."[12]

Location is one of three criteria by which the gods of cult and the gods of myth can be distinguished, not only in Homer but also generally in the practice of Greek religion.[13] The second is the name of the god. In cult, the god has his or name, as in myth, and also a surname that designates the god's function in the particular cult. In Athens, in different places, Athena is worshipped as Polias, Promachos and Ergane. The name of the god in myth (to which in the form of verse an epithet may attached, to be distinguished from the cult surname just mentioned) tends, unlike the surname of cult, to be impenetrable, perhaps, as Burkert has suggested, because at most only semi-intelligibility was wanted. The name, striking in its very opacity, causes the one who is named to stand out all the more memorably.[14] The origin of the divine name, like the origin of the names of heroes, i.e., how they got these names, as distinguished from etymologies of the names, is irrecoverable from the tradition from which it has come but the same relation of name to narrative sketched in chapter 4 would apply.

The third criterion is identity. The god or goddess of cult has a particular attribute and his or her identity is implicitly limited to the function indicated by this attribute. Athena is the guardian of the city (Polias), the one who fights in the

---

10 This discussion of Athena in the *Il.* is adapted from Edmunds 2016b, 112–14. Footnotes have been omitted.
11 Burkert 1985, 183.
12 West 1966, 313 on *Theog.* 523–33. West goes on to say: "There are other cases of gods being forced by their coexistence in cult to make up their differences in mythology" and gives examples.
13 I have taken these three criteria from Delattre 2005, 67–69.
14 Burkert 1985, 182.

forefront (Promachos), and the worker (Ergane).—Athens (Ἀθῆναι) is probably named after Athena (Ἀθήνη), a name found in Mycenaean Greek but not etymologized and thought to be of pre-Greek origin.—The god or goddess of myth, with his or her name, has an identity on the human model. He or she has, in the first place, parents and, if it so happens, a child or children. The gods of myth lead a notoriously anthropomorphic life, best known in Homer and Hesiod, already scandalous early on. To repeat Xenophanes from chapter 5, "Homer and Hesiod attributed to the gods everything that among men is matter for shame and rebuke—stealing, committing adultery and deceiving" (D-K 21 B 11 = L-M 8D8).

This scandal is often discussed in the isolation of scholarship on the *Iliad*, in which the justice of Zeus in particular has been a central question.[15] The exchange between Euthyphro and Socrates shows that the frame of reference was much larger (again cf. ch. 5). Euthyphro wants to use Kronos' and Zeus's treatment of their fathers as the justification for his prosecution of his own father in an Athenian court. Socrates, who takes a different view of the gods, asks if Euthyphro believes what the poets (presumably Homer and Hesiod in particular) have said and then he adds: and what other such stories, which are represented on the robe annually presented to Athena at the Panathenaic festival (*Euthyphr.* 6b6–c4), tell. Euthyphro himself refers to similar stories, which are unknown to most people (6b5–6; 6c5–7).

6.2 Myths explain origin of cults

Myths account for the origins of cults, although once a cult is established its functions are independent of the myth. In Athenian history the myth of Erechtheus twice accounts for cult devoted to him, although in neither case to him alone. He was one of the early autochthonous kings.[16] His great achievement was the defeat of the Eleusinians and their Thracian ally Eumolpus.[17] When he killed Eumolpus

---

15 The negative view, stated many times, already in Nägelsbach 1861, A.II.3.b "Sittliche Gebundenheit." The positive view is variously argued in Lloyd-Jones 1983; Griffin 1980, 144–204; Janko 1992, 4–5. The question of justice includes the other gods; but it can be posed concerning Zeus in particular. On this question: Allan 2006. Cf. Edmunds 2016b, 117–18.
16 γηγενής, Hdt. 8.55; cf. *Il.* 2.547–8; *Od.* 7.81. Erechtheus is also given various human and divine parents: Roscher vol. 1, cols. 1296–97. (I say nothing of the old, often-repeated idea that Erechtheus and Erichthonius were "originally identical." For a bibliography on this matter: *EGM* 2, 449 n. 6.)
17 In this way, Erechtheus was able to open the Eleusinian Mysteries to the Athenians: Xen. *Symp.* 8.40: see Huß 1999, *ad loc.* Cf. Thuc. 2.15.1.

he provoked the vengeance of Eumolpus's father, Poseidon, who in turn killed Erechtheus. Either he struck him with his trident and drove him into the earth (Eur. *Ion* 281–82) or hid him beneath the earth.[18] In his temple Erechtheus was then worshipped as Poseidon-Erechtheus.[19] This temple is mentioned twice in Homer.[20] The second cult is the one included in the fifth-century Erechtheum (see below).

This postmortem reconciliation of a hero and his divine antagonist is well known from the story of Neoptolemus at Delphi. Neoptolemus is killed by Apollo or by attendants of Apollo at Delphi as punishment for Neoptolemus' killing of Priam when Troy was sacked (Pind. *Paean* 6.105–22).[21] The hero then after his death receives a hero cult in the precinct of the god, with whom the hero now cooperates.[22] (In the case of Erechtheus the situation is reversed. He already has a temple.)

In the fifth century, an altar of Poseidon and Erechtheus was one of several sacred places in the Erechtheum (421–407 B.C.E.).[23] There is some evidence from this period that the myth of Erechtheus had particular inspirational value.[24] In Xenophon's *Memorabilia* Socrates advises the son of Pericles on what he should say to the Athenians, who are despondent after their loss at the battle of Delium (424 B.C.E.). Socrates says that he should remind the Athenians of their earliest ancestors, who were most excellent, and he refers to Erechtheus (3.5.10).[25] Euripides' *Erechtheus* (422 B.C.E.?) dramatizes the king's decision to sacrifice his daughter in compliance with the response that he received at Delphi and his setting out for the battle with the Eleusinians and Eumolpus. In Euripides *Ion* (414–

---

18 Cf. *Erechth.* fr. 370.59–60 Kannicht, which may refer to the incident more graphically described in the *Ion*.
19 Eur. *Erechtheus* fr. 370.93–94 Kannicht. See Collard-Cropp-Lee, *ad loc.*
20 *Il.* 2.546–552; *Od.* 7.78–81. μιν at *Il.* 2.550 = "him", i.e., not Athena, although Athena reared him (Eur. *Ion* 269–70).
21 Cf. Simonides fr. 11.7–9 W². Apollo is responsible for the death of Neoptolemus also in Eur. *Andr.* 1161–65 (the messenger who has come from Delphi with the corpse, censuring Apollo). Cf. Paus. 10.24.4 θεάσαιο δ' ἂν ἐνταῦθα καὶ ἑστίαν, ἐφ' ᾗ Νεοπτόλεμον τὸν Ἀχιλλέως ὁ ἱερεὺς ἀπέκτεινε τοῦ Ἀπόλλωνος.
22 See Burkert 1985, 202–203; Nagy 1999 [1979], ch. 7 (on the death of Neoptolemus); Visser 1982, 409–10; *EGM* 2, 559–60; for further bibliography see Kurke 2005, 100 n. 59.
23 Extensive records of the construction: IG^3 474–79.
24 IG^3 873, a dedication to Poseidon Erechtheus, is dated to ca. 450 B.C.E. but, if the script is archaizing, could be later.
25 ... καὶ τὴν Ἐρεχθέως γε τροφὴν καὶ γένεσιν, καὶ τὸν πόλεμον τὸν ἐπ' ἐκείνου γενόμενον πρὸς τοὺς ἐκ τῆς ἐχομένης ἠπείρου πάσης... For the inspirational value of autochthony cf. Pl. *Rep.* 414d–e. When Socrates refers to his τροφή he must have Athena in mind.

412), Creusa, one of the daughters of Erechtheus, at Delphi recovers her son by Apollo, abandoned in a cave when he was an infant. Some of the old king's story is remembered (277–83).[26]

Cults still have their explanations in myths many centuries later, as Pausanias found again and again.[27] Different people whom he encountered might have somewhat different stories for honoring the same god or goddess. The Megarians say that the body of Ino washed up on their coast and was buried by the granddaughters of Lelex and that they were the first to call her Leucothea, to whom they sacrifice every year (1.42.7). In Messenia, however, the people of Corone say that a place on the coast, on the road leading to their city, is sacred to Leucothea because there, already so named and a divinity, she appeared from the sea (4.34.4).[28] (Pausanias does not refer to a cult in the place near Corone or to any other use of the place, probably because he had no further information.) Pausanias assumes, as his informants already assumed, that the story of Ino is well known—how as a mortal woman fleeing from her husband she cast herself, along with her son, Melicertes, into the sea, where she became the goddess Leucothea (cf. *Od.* 5.333–35).[29] Likewise, on the Isthmus of Corinth, in the precinct of Poseidon, Pausanias saw a temple of Palaemon, in which there was a statue of Leucothea (2.2.1). Again he does not have to comment. As Ino left her mortal name and existence behind her, so her son Melicertes became the god Palaemon, the protector of ships.[30]

6.3 The myth of the sacrifice at Mecone

The famous origin myth referred to in the introduction to this chapter concerns Prometheus' deceptive division, as between gods and men, of the sacrificial animal. In Hesiod's *Theogony*, at a banquet of gods and men, in the days when they

---

26 Also in a passage corrupt and probably also lacunose: 721–24.
27 See Petropoulou 2008, 103–104 for arguments for accepting the cults described by Pausanias as old and inherited, not of recent invention.
28 For discussion of these passages and others in Paus. on humans who attain divinity see Pirenne-Delforge 2010, 378–80.
29 In ch. 2 I cited the use of Ino as an example by the chorus of Corinthian women in Eur. *Med.* 1282–89. For the new papyrus fragment of Eur. *Ion* (W. Luppe and W.B. Henry, *P. Oxy.* LXXVIII 5131) see Finglass 2014; Kovacs 2016; Finglass 2016; Chong-Gossard 2016, 41–42; Finglass 2017a.
30 Pausanias' references to Leucothea are consistent. But he also refers to a sanctuary and an oracle of Ino in Laconia (3.26.1), without any reference to a myth. Ino had an existence in myth independent of Leucothea.

were still living together, Prometheus divides the parts of the sacrificial victim unequally and tricks Zeus into choosing the inferior share (535–61). (The unstated assumption is that Zeus's decision will be binding forever. The gods will always get the part chosen by Zeus and men will always get the other, preferable part.) Zeus perceives the trick but, because he foresees ills for mankind, he chooses that part. (His choice prepares for those ills.) At the same time, he is enraged at the result. (He sees that the trick will justify his future negative dealings with mankind but he is angry with Prometheus for playing this trick in the first place.) Ever since then, mortals have burnt for the gods the bones of the sacrificial animal wrapped in fat. Thereafter Zeus, "mindful of his wrath", deprived men of fire. Prometheus then stole (from an unspecified source) fire and gave it to men (562–69). In retaliation Zeus created and adorned Pandora, the first woman, a "beautiful evil" (καλὸν κακόν, 585), and gave her to men (570–612). The moral of this set of stories is that it is impossible to evade or deceive the mind of Zeus (613–16). Hesiod tells these stories also in *Works and Days* (42–105), where Pandora has a jar, from which she removes the cover and out come death, illness and other evils (*Op.* 90–105).

The story of the deceptive sacrifice is set in Mecone, said in ancient sources to be the ancient name of Sicyon. This setting presumably goes back to the Sicyonians.[31] The story has the look, however, of one that has been retold many times and is already known to Hesiod's audience. So telescoping and other features suggest. Prometheus's siding with mortals is unexplained. He was, after all, a god. Behind Zeus's perception of the trick and willing deception must lie a version in which he was thoroughly deceived. But such a Zeus would not be the Hesiodic one.[32] What would have been of interest to Hesiod's audience was the present application of the story.

In his interpretation, Jean-Pierre Vernant regards the three stories (the deceptive sacrifice, the theft of fire, and the creation of Pandora) as constituting a single myth. He speaks of "a rigorously articulated whole" and of "a flawless logic from beginning to end." "The myth must be taken for what it is...a single story."[33] On this premise the apparent meaning of the deceptive sacrifice, which might have seemed to alleviate human guilt concerning their selfish consumption of the desirable parts of the victim, is reversed.[34] According to Vernant,

---

31 West 1966, 318 on 536. For the appropriateness of Sicyon: Vernant 1989, 43–44.
32 West 1966, 321 on 551.
33 Vernant 1989, 22–23.
34 As West 1966, 305 points out, frequently used by Attic comedians as "evidence of the irreligious meanness of men."

> It is necessary...for the "trap" of woman to have appeared in order for the true nature of the "trap" set for Zeus at the outset by Prometheus, when the Titan "fixes" the portions of the sacrificial victim so that men benefit from all the meat, to be revealed in all its ramifications. The good portion, over which mortals congratulate themselves...is revealed in reality as the bad.[35]

Vernant ultimately finds a positive, or at least not entirely negative, aspect of the "cuisine of sacrifice":

> The difference between diets found at the very heart of the ritual seeks...to establish a kind of contact and communication between the two separated races, a bond that leads, as much as possible, to building a bridge between earth and heaven.[36]

But is this an interpretation of the "myth" as the putative single story or is the "flawless logic" Hesiod's own? The same question can be asked of his interpretation (an impressive tour de force) of Prometheus in the frameworks of the *Theogony* and of the *Works and Days*.[37]

As for the question about the three stories that are linked in *Theogony*, the logic would be Hesiod's if it could be shown that these stories were told separately and first combined in his poems. If, on the other hand, the combination of the three was traditional and already known to Hesiod and his audience, then Vernant would be right: what we find in Hesiod would be a myth. West held that "[i]t is useless to assert that Hesiod did or did not reshape them [the stories]; we have no means of telling."[38] West also pointed out, however, that the myths of the theft of fire and the creation of woman are found in many places.[39] In principle, then, there is no reason why they could not have been told separately in Hesiod's time. The first of the myths is another matter. On the one hand, the introduction of Prometheus at this point will complete Hesiod's account of the Titans. The notion of a time when men and gods dined together, as at the marriages of Peleus and Thetis and of Cadmus and Harmonia, is traditional (cf. Hes. fr. 1.6–7 M-W = fr. 1.6–7 H = fr. 1.6–7 M). The Hesiodic feast takes place at a moment in which gods and men are "reaching a settlement" (ὅτ' ἐκρίνοντο θεοὶ θνητοί τ' ἄνθρωποι, 535). The happy period is about to end. In historical times the *theoxenia* might be

---

[35] Vernant 1989, 23.
[36] Vernant 1989, 24.
[37] Vernant 1989, 26–35.
[38] West 1966, 307.
[39] For the theft of fire: Dalgat 1984. For the creation of woman: West 1966, 306–307, citing *Mot* A1275. See now Hansen 2020, 269–70, 271–72 for these stories as particular kinds of aetiological myths and for analogues.

seen as a recollection of this happy period.⁴⁰ On the other hand, the myth of the deceitful sacrifice, in itself an aition for the way we sacrifice now, has a particular function in relation to the succeeding aition (which explains why men have fire). If gods and men are now "reaching a settlement", this may be Prometheus' last chance to change the rules for the division of the parts of the sacrificial victim. The choice that he offers Zeus will be binding on the gods forever.⁴¹ Zeus's choosing of the inferior parts, though deliberate, causes his anger. In this way, he is motivated to deprive men of fire, the fire that they would need to cook the sacrificial meat that is now theirs.⁴² Hesiod has, then, within the traditional commensality of gods and men and its inevitable end, set the stage for the much better established myth of Prometheus' theft of fire. He has used the aition for our sacrificial practice as a way of motivating the second aition, in which Prometheus' theft explains our possession of fire. The narrative causality that links these two aitia begins to look like Hesiod's invention, while each of the aitia has some degree or other of basis in tradition. The same point could be made about the third aition. The three stories taken together undoubtedly have the "flawless logic" that Vernant asserted but it seems to be Hesiod's.⁴³

Walter Burkert referred to Prometheus in his theory of sacrifice but only in passing. Burkert began with Paleolithic Siberian hunting ritual, as reported by Karl Meuli in "Griechische Opferbräuche" ("Greek Sacrificial Customs") (who begins with reference to Prometheus).⁴⁴ "Killing can become sacrificial even among hunters."⁴⁵ This primitive sacrifice is the result of the guilt that the hunters feel over the killing of the animal. With sacrifice religion comes into existence. Yet sacrifice as killing remains primary: "*Homo religiosus* acts and attains self-awareness as *homo necans*."⁴⁶ The myth of Prometheus' deceptive sacrifice serves Burkert as an example of the "objectionable" aspect of the ritual, which seems to

---

40 On the theoxenia: Kearns 2014c.
41 West 1966, 322 on 556.
42 West 1966, 323 on 562.
43 Hansen 2007, 92–114 demonstrates parallels between the myths of Prometheus and the Scandinavian Loki. The causal connections, so marked in Hesiod, between the deception of Zeus, his withholding of fire, and Prometheus' theft are not paralleled in the Scandinavian narrative even if grosso modo the Greek and the Scandinavian myths have a common structure.
44 Burkert 1983, 13–14. Transl. of Burkert 1972, of which the second ed., Burkert 1997, is a reprint of the first with a new preface. More specifically Meuli 1975 (orig. pub. 1946) begins with reference to the article on Prometheus by Thomsen 1909, to which he returns toward the end of his article (990).
45 Burkert 1983, 15.
46 Burkert 1983, 3.

express not piety but human selfishness. This myth, Burkert points out, is the first of a series of examples, including Pythagorean and Orphic prohibitions, of attempts to impugn or prohibit sacrifice. These attempts did not, however, prevent the sacrificial death of Jesus, repeated in the communion, or the persistence of sacrifice in folk custom.[47] Burkert expanded his theory of sacrifice into a general theory. He looked to a phase of human history before the hunt, when men are bound to women and the family must be supported and the danger of aggressiveness threatened the community necessary for the continuation of life. Relying on the work of Konrad Lorenz, he referred to "redirection" outwards:

> [I]t is...group demonstration of aggression toward outsiders that creates a sense of close personal community. The *Männerbund* becomes a closed, conspiratorial group through the explosive potential of aggression stored internally. This aggression was released in the dangerous and bloody hunt.[48]

And also in war, on which Burkert has less to say, although he is led to pessimistic reflection on contemporary society.[49]

These two theories, two of the three which were dominant in the second half of the twentieth century, both in very different ways explain the Promethean sacrifice.[50] For Burkert, comparison with other sacrificial rituals, notably the Athenian Buphonia "Ox-Sacrifice", were more useful than the myth concerning Prometheus. At the Buphonia the bull provokes its own slaying by eating grain on the altar. The sacrificer then flees and the sacrificial knife is tried for murder. (The Buphonia had its own myth of origin: an angry farmer killed a bull that disrupted the grain sacrifice.)[51] Burkert can see "old hunting instincts breaking through the thin crust of civilization."[52] Vernant, for his part, relies entirely on the myth of Prometheus in Hesiod although the tripartite myth that he stipulates may not be traditional but a Hesiodic construct. (Or, if one prefers, a construct of the textual fixation that we happen to have, which in this respect does not necessarily reflect many antecedent generations of transmission.)

---

47 Burkert 1983, 7–9. Cf. 1–2.
48 Burkert 1983, 20; cf. 35.
49 Burkert 1983, 47–48.
50 The third was that of Girard 1972; Eng. Transl. 1977. Girard did not refer to Prometheus. The three theories, those of Burkert, Girard and Vernant, are discussed by Graf 2012b.
51 For the sources: Burkert 1983, 138 n. 11. See further Parker 2005, 187–91.
52 For the sources: Burkert 1983, 138 n. 11. See further Parker 2005, 187–91.

6.4 Myths of transportable cult images

Cult images have a propensity to move on their own, even showing up at battles.[53] A few myths concern the movements of cult images that were small enough to be stolen and transported.[54] The best known is the Palladion, an image of Athena in her temple in Troy but probably not the one on which Theano places a robe (cf. above on *Il.* 6.303).[55] The myths concerning the Palladion are many and various.[56] Another attempt to survey them is not proposed here. They constitute an extreme example of the tendencies of myth to variation observed already in this and in some of the preceding chapters and they also illustrate the tendency, observed in the cases of Theseus and Medea (ch. 3), to inconsistency with respect to the same subject between one myth and another.[57] The mobility of the Palladion as an object seems to have been a realistic basis for the myths. All these myths presuppose the efficacy of the cult image and its consequent desirability.[58]

Odysseus and Diomedes stole the Palladion after the Greeks had learned from Helenus that Troy could not be captured as long as it remained in the temple of Athena.[59] This story is obviously contradicted by the story that, at the fall of Troy, Ajax dragged Cassandra away along with the Palladion to which she was clinging

---

53 For references: *EGM* 2, 67 n. 255. Statues of the Virgin Mary have for centuries had the same propensity. Polinskaya 2013, 459 n. 34: The mobility of Greek cult images is "relatively infrequent" by comparison with other cultures.

54 The survey by Burkert 1985, 88–92 ("Temple and Cult Image") suggests that the small wooden images to which myths were attached were principally those to be discussed here. For the surviving physical evidence for small, mobile cult images see Beck-Schachter 2018, ch. 1. I am distinguishing these small transportable cult images from the much larger class of talismanic statues (see Edmunds 2016a, 144).

55 But *EGM* 2, 66: "Palladion of Troy…It is this statue to which the women…present the peplos".

56 Survey in Gantz 1993, 642–46; Icard-Gianolio 2004, B.3.

57 "[C]ultic myths, the *aitia* of rituals and the aspects of mythological figures that are directly relevant to their persona as cult recipients, focus on particular segments of those figures' mythological nexuses and also particular segments of the polis's history; they are not usually, and certainly not necessarily, placed precisely inside a coherent chronological system of linearly perceived history": Sourvinou-Inwood 2011, ch. 2.1.

58 For the identification of cult image and deity see Bulloch 1985 on Callim. *Hymn* 5.1 with the comments of Renehan 1987, 241. Add Soph. *Aj.* 91–93 (I am grateful to Patrick Finglass for this reference). Steiner 2011 in a discussion of the chaining of cult images: "Incapacitating the statue disarms its subject precisely because the idol re-presents or houses the divinity and exists in a 'persuasive' relationship to the numinous power on which its efficacy depends" (161).

59 The sources: *Il. parv.* arg. 17–18 B = arg. 23–24 D = arg. 4e W (pp. 199–202); Apollod. *Epit.* 5.13. These two sources do not give a clear picture of the relation of this theft to Odysseus' solo entry into Troy in the guise of a beggar (recounted by Helen, *Od.* 4.235–64).

and raped her.⁶⁰ There was also the story of Aeneas' taking the Palladion to Italy, attested for the first time in Dionysius of Halicarnassus but thought to be earlier (*Ant. Rom.* 1.69).⁶¹ Dionysius reconciles this story with the Greek theft of the Palladion by referring to the one in the Greeks' possession as a copy of the original. This doubling of the Palladion occurs already in the myths concerning Odysseus's and Diomedes's theft and is attested in a series of vase paintings beginning with a cup by Macron (LIMC "Ak. and Dem." 6*; 490–480 B.C.E.).⁶² Again the small-scale cult statue as known in real life lies behind the myths.⁶³ The particular etiological value of the myth depends on the variant.

In Euripides' *Iphigenia in Tauris*, Orestes comes with his companion Pylades to the land of the Taurians to fulfill the task imposed by Apollo as the condition of release from the Furies, who have continued to haunt him, it turns out, after his trial and acquittal in Athens (Aeschylus' *Eumenides*). He must steal the statue of Artemis from her temple and take it to Attica. He and Pylades are captured by the Taurians. His long-lost sister, the priestess of Artemis, has the duty of sacrificing foreigners, in accordance with Taurian law. After she and Orestes have recognized each other, they resolve to steal the statue and escape. Iphigenia devises a scheme that will allow them to reach the ship on which Orestes and Pylades arrived. They almost succeed in sailing away but are driven by wind and wave back to the shore. Thoas, the king of the Taurians, resolves to destroy them. Athena now appears as the goddess-from-the-machine and ordains the release of the captives. Orestes must take the statue to Halai on the east coast of Attica and found a sanctuary there of Artemis Tauropolos. Iphigenia will be the priestess of Artemis at Brauron. Thoas desists.⁶⁴

Euripides has put this plot together from already existing myths.⁶⁵ He "corrects" the myth in which Iphigenia died in Aulis and Orestes' pursuit by the Furies ended in Athens in the trial before Athena and a jury of Athenians, the myth

---

60 *Ilioupersis* arg. 15–16 B = arg. 23–24 D = Arg. 3a W (pp. 235–37); Apollod. *Epit.* 5.22.
61 For the sources for the Roman Palladium: Linderski 2012.
62 For discussion of these vases: Sourvinou-Inwood 2011, 232–43. For the myths of the origins of the various cult statues: Bettinetti 2001, 71–75.
63 Beck-Schachter 2018, 15 argues that "even with the development of monumental sculpture and temple architecture in the seventh and sixth centuries BCE, small-scale spaces, which housed multiple small-scale images, were the rule, not the exception." Cf. Paus. 2.17.4–5 on the various images of Hera in the Heraion in Argos. For further examples and discussion: Beck-Schachter 2018, 28–30.
64 Cf. Sommerstein 2005, 173 on these particular etiologies, in the context of a survey of the etiologies, of various kinds, with which Euripidean tragedies typically end.
65 Compare the conglomerate in folktale studies: Kvideland 1996.

as known from Aeschylus' *Oresteia*.⁶⁶ The stories of Iphigenia and Orestes now continue and come together. Euripides did not invent the presence of Iphigenia among the Taurians, which is attested in a scholium to the *Iliad* and also in Apollodorus, neither place apparently deriving from the tragedian. Artemis has taken her to Tauris to be her priestess (schol. b *Il.* 1.108–109; Apollod. *Epit.* 3.21). The mobility of the cult statue is a given. Euripides invents, then, not a myth but a plot, reconfiguring, in the spirit of the old impulse of myth to variation, already available materials.⁶⁷

In a myth attributed by one of the Athenaeus' deipnosophists to Menodotos of Samos, Tyrrhenian pirates, for reasons that are not central to the story as here enucleated, steal the image of Hera from her temple in Samos.⁶⁸ They put it on their ship and attempted to row away but the ship does not move. In fear of this portent, they put the image on the shore, set barley-cakes beside it, and sail away. The Carian inhabitants of Samos found the image, surmised that it had run away, and propped it against a "shield" of withes (πρός τι λύγου θωράκιον ἀπερεισάμενοι), the longest of which they tied tightly around it. The statue was then restored to its temple and annually thereafter carried to the sea, washed and given barley-cakes.

In Book 5 of Herodotus the account of the enmity between the Aeginetans and the Athenians begins with the Epidaurians' carving statues of Damia and Auxesia out of Athenian olivewood (82). Then the Aeginetans revolt from the Epidaurians, whose subjects they had been, and steal the statues (83). The Epidaurians ask the Athenians to recover the statues (84). The Athenians attempt to do so and fail (85–86). Herodotus gives two accounts of their failure, one the Athenian (85), the other the Aeginetan (86). According to the latter, the Athenians, not being able to wrench the statues from their pedestals, threw cords around them, causing them to fall to their knees. The statues have remained in this posture ever since (86.3). This account includes some details of the rites performed by the Aeginetans before the statues (83.3). Another, obvious etiological detail is the posture of the statues. Their intractability, however, is a trait of the statue in the myth about the Tyrrhenian pirates and may lie behind the storm that prevents Iphigenia, Orestes and Pylades from sailing away from Tauris (cf. the storm in the Athenian version of their attempt to recover the statues of Damia and

---

66 On "myth correction": Edmunds 2014, 9–10.
67 Cf. Edmunds 2014, 13–14 on Eur. *Andr.*
68 Athen. 672a–e = *FGrH* 541 F 1. The other source: Nicaenetus 2703–10 Gow-Page. Discussed by Burkert 1979, 129–32 in connection with evidence for the appearance of the statue and its relation to a series of Greek-Anatolian cult statues.

Auxesia: Hdt. 5.85). This trait appears also in a version of the theft of the Palladion, in which, as Diomedes and Odysseus carry it away from Troy, it is moved by some divine agency, thus revealing to Odysseus, whom Diomedes left outside the wall of Troy, that it is the real Palladion and not the substitute that Diomedes pretends that it is.[69]

6.5 Conclusion

That myth and cult, myth and ritual are fundamentally separate is a received truth.[70] In the *Iliad* temples and cult images first appear and, as the example of Athena shows, the same god has a double existence, in cult and in myth. (The same point could be made apropos of other gods in the *Iliad*.) Myths explain the origin of cults or cult practices, as in the case of Hera of Samos, and the general rule of variation applies: if the same god receives cult in different places, then the myth will vary in accordance with local traditions.[71] In the examples discussed in this chapter the myth of Prometheus' sacrifice is exceptional. It explains not a particular cult or ritual but a general practice in the division of the sacrificial animal. This myth inspired one of the three "grand theories" of sacrifice, that of Vernant, that emerged in the twentieth century and are now in abeyance. The centrality of animal sacrifice in Greek cult is, however, hardly in doubt. The future of interpretation may or may not include a rethinking of the Prometheus myth.[72] Myths also explain how certain cult images came to be where they are. The small number of these myths is in inverse proportion to the variations of each of them, which seems to reflect the unfixed, movable nature of the images themselves.

---

[69] Conon *FGrH* 26 F 1 [XXXIV.4] = *Il. Parv.* 25 B. Not included in D or W but cited in W p. 201 n. 48.
[70] Graf 1993 [1987], 116: "Myth and ritual are...autonomous phenomena." Cf. Delattre n. 1 above.
[71] On myth and aetiology: Delattre 2005, 187–91.
[72] Not if the future follows the suggestion of Graf at the end of the article cited above: sacrifice should be understood as a Neolithic invention, in which hunting techniques had "symbolic use" (2012b, 49).

7 Three Great Theories of Myth

One can ask about Greek myth the same question that Fritz Graf asked about Greek ritual: Where are the great theories that used to guide thought? In the case of myth, these were the myth-ritual (§1), the psychoanalytic (principally in the work of Freud and Jung) (§2), and the structuralist theories (§3).[1] For the last of last of the three the plural is appropriate. From 1945, structuralism was the name given to the linguistics of Swiss linguist Ferdinand de Saussure (1857–1913) and of Roman Jakobson (1896–1982).[2] In cultural anthropology, however, it is associated especially with Claude Lévi-Strauss (1908–2009), whose structuralism is discussed in this chapter (7.3 below). His seminal article of 1955 bears the title: "The Structural Study of Myth."[3] Two major figures in the history of classical scholarship, Walter Burkert (1931–2015) and Jean-Pierre Vernant (1914–2007) defined their own conceptions of myth in relation to Lévi-Strauss and come into the following discussion. (I return to the term "structuralism" at the beginning of §3 in the text below.)

Is any of these theories thriving today? The answer differs for each of the three theories.

7.1 The myth-ritual school

The so-called myth-ritual school or the "Cambridge school" became a finished chapter in the history of classical scholarship toward the end of the last century.[4]

---

[1] Cf. Schmitt 2014, 84–85. Cf. Kirk 1970, 42: "There have been three major developments in the modern study of myths. The first was the realization, associated especially with Tylor, Frazer, and Durkheim, that the myths of primitive societies are highly relevant to the subject as a whole. The second was Freud's discovery of the unconscious and its relation to myths and dreams. The third is the structural study of myth propounded by…Claude Lévi-Strauss." The first of these developments could have been described more precisely.
[2] See *OED* s.v. "structuralism" 3.a. Cf. Dammann 2007, col. 1407: "Der entscheidende Transfer der linguistichen S. auf andere Disziplinen der Kulturwissenschaften ist auf der gemeinsame Lehrtätigkeit von Jakobson und C. Lévi-Strauss in New York während der 1940er Jahre zu datieren."
[3] I refer below also to the French revision published in 1958 (the English translation of which is found in Lévi-Strauss 1963).
[4] E.g., Ackerman 1987; Werber 1987; Calder 1989; Arlen 1990 (a book-length bibliography); Edmunds 1990b, 23; Ackerman 1991. I have said "finished", but Delattre 2005, 203–22 calls for renewal of study of the relations between myth and ritual and illustrates the approach that he proposes.

The purpose of the present discussion is not to write that chapter again but to discuss the relation of myth and ritual in two of the ritualists whose work has to some extent lived on and has left traces in a kind of interpretation of myth still current in classical studies. These two are James George Frazer (1854–1941) and Jane Ellen Harrison (1850–1928).

Frazer's massive *The Golden Bough* (twelve volumes in its final edition) is the most famous of the myth-ritualist books but now seems to have few merits, except for enormous learning, and to be of interest only for the intellectual history of its times.[5] Frazer studied the annual rituals of the dying-and-rising god that assure the rebirth of vegetation. In myth he pointed to Osiris, Tammuz, Adonis, Dionysus and Jesus Christ, among others. These myths are not generated by the rituals, however, but arise after the fact in order to explain them. H.S. Versnel has described in Frazer's thought "an almost ideal parallelism of myth and ritual."[6] Frazer did not, however, limit the function of myth to its relation to ritual. He was at heart a Euhemerist and he saw in myths "mistaken explanations of phenomena, whether of human life or of external phenomena", with subjects "as numerous as the objects which present themselves to the mind of man. "[T]he range of myths is as wide as the world, being coextensive with the curiosity and the ignorance of man."[7]

Frazer's notion of myth as a stage in the progress of human rationality now appears as a kind of evolutionary thinking that drew breath from Darwin's *Origin of Species* (1859). Likewise, Freud's theory of the id, the ego and the super-ego can be seen as an evolution of the mind from unconscious to conscious, from uncontrolled or uncontrollable to controlled. (Freud is discussed more fully in the next section of this chapter.) "Wo Es war soll Ich werden." "Where it (the id) was, should I (the ego) be."[8] Although this theory is usually discussed under the heading of the topography of the mind, and not in temporal terms, the superego could be thought of as the final stage of a movement that started in the id.[9] Freud's *Totem and Taboo: Resemblances Between the Mental Lives of Savages and Neurotics*

---

[5] Frazer 1911–1915. Criticism: Von Hendy 2002, 92–97; Werber 1987, 223–24, with some redemption.
[6] Versnel 2014, 91. (Versnel 2014 is a reprint, with slight modifications, of Versnel 1990a.)
[7] 1921, xxvi–xxviii.
[8] In one of the New Introductory Lectures on Psychoanalysis: *SE* 22, 80. (I am citing Freud's works in *SE*. For the corresponding places in Gesammelte Werke see Laplanche and Pontalis 1973, 491–97 ("Bibliography") for a chronological listing of these and other collections.
[9] Laplanche and Pontalis 1973, s.v. "Typography; Topographical." For Freud's *The Ego and the Id* (SE 19) and Frazer's evolutionism: Csapo 2005, 124.

(1913) explicitly adopts the model of cultural evolution.[10] Frazer's *Totemism and Exogamy* (1887) and William Robertson Smith's *Lectures on the Religion of the Semites* (1889) inspire Freud to use psychoanalysis to explain the customs and beliefs indicated by the two terms of his title, totem and taboo. In his final chapter, he postulates their origin in an original patricide committed by a band of brothers excluded from the tribe by the primal father. Their guilt is the origin of the Oedipus complex and Freud says in conclusion that "the beginnings of religion, ethics, society, and art meet in the Oedipus complex."

The massive learning of *The Golden Bough* referred to above lies in the breadth and detail of its social anthropology. Frazer is first and foremost a comparativist. He assumes that "the cultural development of all races and peoples follows the same fundamental course,…one can juxtapose and compare procedures, usages, and beliefs of human societies in different times" and in this way explain something that one does not understand in one culture by comparison with another or other cultures in which its meaning is clear.[11] His comparativism is the basis of his cultural evolutionism and returns later in this discussion.

The other myth-ritualist to be discussed here is Jane Harrison (1850–1928). Her *Themis: A Study of the Social Origins of Greek Religion* (1912), emphasizes ritual.[12] Her book begins with an interpretation of the hymn to Dictaean Zeus recently discovered at Palaikastro on Crete. The opening of the Hymn is preserved:

Ἰώ, μέγιστε Κοῦρε, χαῖρέ μοι, Κρό-
νειε, πανκρατὲς γάνους, βέβακες
δαιμόνων ἀγόμενος· Δίκταν ἐς
ἐνιαυτὸν ἕρπε καὶ γέγαθε μολπᾶ(ι),
τάν τοι κρέκομεν πακτίσι μείξ-
τες ἄμ' αὐλοῖσι καὶ στάντες ἀείδομεν
τεὸν ἀμφὶ βωμὸν (ε)ὐερκῆ.[13]

O supreme son of Kronos, salutations! All-powerful over refreshment, you stand at the head of the gods. Come to Dicte at the turn of the year and take pleasure in our song.
We weave it for you with lyres, having blended it with pipes, and we sing having taken our places around your well-walled altar.[14]

---

10 *SE* 13. For discussion of this book and its intellectual-historical context: Csapo 2005, 113–22
11 Werber 1987, 222. For the importance of W. Robertson Smith (1846–1894) and E.B. Tylor (1832–1917): Versnel 2014, 89–90.
12 For this book in its historical-intellectual context: Von Hendy 2002, 106–11.
13 The text is that of Bosanquet 1908–1909, 343.
14 Transl. Allonge 2005 (in an article challenging the existence of a Cretan Zeus).

Zeus is here the Megistos Kouros and the Kouretes, Harrison says, "are found to represent the initiated young men of a matrilinear group. The Daimon they invoke is, not the Father of Gods and Men, but the Greatest Kouros. He springs from the social emphasis of the rite of initiation, the central ceremony of which was a *dromenon* or enaction of the New Birth into the tribe."[15] The words "initiated" and "initiation" indicate the theme of her book.[16] To expand the concept of initiation to include every kind of annual renewal of the cycles of both life and vegetation, she introduced the term "Eniautos-Daimon", to refer to the god embodied in the rituals and implicitly to contest Frazer's annual dying-and-rising god.[17]

She soon states her thesis on the relation of the myth of the birth of Zeus and his tendance by the Kouretes (which she plausibly assumes was in a lacuna in the surviving text), on the one hand, to the ritual, on the other: "The myth is obviously 'aetiological.' The worshippers of the Kouros say they invoke the Kouros because of the myth...We may of course safely invert the order of things, the myth arose out of or rather together with the ritual, not the ritual out of the myth." This thesis appears again several times, in slightly different forms.[18]

In the history of classical scholarship initiation was to prevail over the dying-and-rising god. "Instead of the 'dying and rising' complex of gods and kings around the New Year festival, the frame of reference is now the initiation candidate, banished, sorely tried, sometimes doomed to death, coming off triumphant, returning."[19] Thus H.S. Versnel, who traces the history of initiation studies.[20] He calls attention in particular to an article by Burkert on the myth of the daughters of Cecrops and the Arrephoria festival.[21] In this article Burkert introduces the comparative dimension only in a *praeteritio* but cites the whole history of the relevant

---

15 Harrison 1912, x.
16 The Greek words translated "initiation" have to do with initiation into mystery cults and there is no word for adolescent initiation. Once again (cf. introduction to ch. 6) we use an etic term. Cf. Graf 2003, 9.
17 Cf. Graf 2003, 5–6. She cites Frazer respectfully several times, however. E.g., for her interpretation of initiation as underlying the myth of Zagreus, she thanks "a paper kindly sent to me by Dr Frazer containing an account of certain initiation ceremonies among the Wiradthuri tribe of New South Wales" (Harrison 1912, 17–18).
18 Versnel 2014, 95 finds three distinctions in the basic proposition.
19 Versnel 2014, 105–11. Quotation from last of these pages.
20 Cf. Versnel 1990b, 51–60 ("From Harrison to Burkert"), a somewhat fuller version of Versnel 1990a.
21 See Graf 2003, 12–14 for the wider context of discussion of the Arrephoria. Burkert's article should be seen in the context of revival of interest in initiation in the late 1960s: Graf 2003, 6. For a useful survey of the most important works on initiation in the twentieth century see Dowden 2011, 503.

scholarship.[22] Burkert, whose comparativism in the interpretation of ritual has already been noticed (ch. 6), is thus the heir of Robertson Smith and Frazer and in the matter of ritual he is the continuator of Harrison (see Conclusion). The difference between Frazer and Harrison as regards the relation of myth and ritual has already been pointed out. One could also peak of a French tradition of initiation studies, not that it was exclusive, beginning with Arnold van Gennep (adoptively French from a young age) and continuing with Émile Durkheim and Henri Jeanmaire and culminating in Pierre Vidal-Naquet.[23] The story continues down into the twenty-first century. A notable example is Ken Dowden's article on Greek myths of initiation.[24]

7.2 Psychoanalytic interpretation of myth

The apostasy, as Sigmund Freud perceived it, of Carl Jung led to a major division within the psychoanalytic movement and thus to a major division in the psychoanalytic interpretation of myth. Although Freud often referred to myths, he rarely interpreted them.[25] Even in the canonic statements of the Oedipus complex, his emphasis alternates between the form of the Sophoclean tragedy and the myth.[26] Even when they were still on good terms he was skeptical of Jung's interest in myth.[27] Jung, however, who turned to the notions of "collective unconscious" and inherited, instinctual "archetypes", believed that myths had therapeutic value.

---

[22] Burkert 1966, 13: "Es kommt…hier nicht darauf an, Vergleichsmaterial zu haufen, sondern nur darauf, anzuerkennen, dass es Riten der Jugendweihe auf der ganzen Welt gibt, und sich klarzumachen, was sie bedeuten".

[23] Van Gennep 1909. Durkheim 1912; cf. Bellah 2005. Jeanmaire 1939. Dodd 2003, xiii puts Vernant and Vidal-Naquet in the center of a revival of initiation studies in the 1960s. For Vidal-Naquet, cf. Pellizer 2011. The picture should include Italy, in particular Brelich 1969.

[24] Dowden 2011. Cf. n. 21 above. But one could hardly say that initiation is the prevailing orthodoxy. Cf. Buxton 2013; *EGM* 2, xx–xxi.

[25] Freud left interpretations of only three myths, those of Oedipus, Prometheus, Perseus, and some jottings, published posthumously, on Medusa. Survey: Csapo 2005, 95–110. It is not the case that "Freud…bekanntlich immer wieder auf das Repertoire des griechischen Mythos zurückgriff, um seine Entdeckungen zu benennen, zu veranschaulichen und zu rechtfertigen" (Most 2002, 117). ("Freud…, as is well known, repeatedly resorted to the repertoire of Greek myth in order to name, illustrate and justify his discoveries.")

[26] Edmunds 1985.

[27] Roazen 1971, 231; 261.

Some of his best-known followers became scholars of and retellers of myths—Eric Neumann, Carl Kerényi, and Joseph Campbell.[28]

Freud's discovery of the Oedipus complex, which he would come to regard as the "nucleus of the neuroses", can be dated to the 1890s.[29] His first publication of his discovery came in *The Interpretation of Dreams* in 1900.[30] Here is the first of Freud's three main discussions of the complex, in each of which he uses Sophocles' *Oedipus the King*. He finds that the complex "is confirmed by a legend that has come down to us from classical antiquity", that is, the legend of Oedipus.[31] Although *Oedipus the King* is the only ancient source for this myth that he uses, he was well aware of the distinction between myth and tragedy.[32] In fact, the psychoanalytic interpretation of both begins in the foundational book of 1900. Freud's reference to Hamlet was taken up by Ernest Jones in 1910, in the article "The Oedipus-Complex as an Explanation of Hamlet's Mystery: A Study in Motive."[33] Although Freud was not much interested in interpreting myth, his followers soon pursued his suggestions. Karl Abraham and Otto Rank both undertook interpretations of myth in books published in 1909.[34]

Jung opposed to Freud's individual unconscious a collective unconscious comprised of archetypes.[35] These never appear as such but as images in the dreams and fantasies of the individual. In order to perceive these images as such the analyst should have a knowledge of myths and religions, in which the archetypes have been enshrined.[36] Myths thus, apart from their diagnostic value in par-

---

28 This paragraph is taken from Edmunds 1990c, 342.
29 On the basis of letters, notably one to Wilhelm Fliess (Oct. 15, 1897; *SE* 1, 265). The following paragraph is adapted from Edmunds 2014e, 407.
30 *SE* 4–5.
31 *SE* 4, 261.
32 Condello 2009, CXXVIII–CXXXVI.
33 Jones 1910. Thirty-nine years later, it became a book: Jones 1949.
34 Abraham 1909; Rank 1909.
35 For "archetype" and the sometimes apparently synonymous "symbol": Von Hendy 2002, 129–32. My summary of Jung's theory follows Segal 1999, 66–97 ("Jung on Mythology").
36 Isler 1993, col. 745: "Nach J.'s Auffassung ist der wesentliche Inhalt aller Mythen und Religionen archetypischer Natur. 'In Mythen und Märchen wie im Traume sagt die Seele über sich in ihrem natürlichen Zusammenspiel, als "Gestaltung, Umgestaltung, des ewigen Sinnes ewige Unterhaltung"'. The quotation is from Jung 1976, 233. The embedded quotation is from Goethe, *Faust*, Part 2, Act 1. The speaker is Mephistopheles. Jung puts himself in the realm of German romanticism. For another example: Von Hendy 2002, 122.

ticular cases, invite the search for the archetypes that they contain. A considerable body of mid-twentieth writings on myth carried on this search.[37] The fortunes of Jungian psychoanalysis in the study of Greek myth have since dwindled.

Freudian psychoanalysis and the Oedipus complex in the history of psychoanalysis have to be distinguished, in the first place, from the history of their reception in classical studies. In the first of these two histories, opposition to Freud came early.[38] Already in 1914 he published *The History of the Psychoanalytic Movement*, a polemic against the rival theories of Jung and of Alfred Adler.[39] Such a book would have had to be written several times, and was sometimes written, to bring the story up to the present.[40] As for psychoanalysis in classical studies, on the other hand, while it persists in work on tragedy, it has dwindled in interpretation of myth.[41] Kirk recognized psychoanalysis as one of the three great theories but considered it unconvincing.[42] Burkert politely turned his back on Freud in his Sather Lectures of 1977.[43] In an essay well-known in its day, Vernant rejected Freud's interpretation of Sophocles' *Oedipus the King*.[44]

The question with which Vernant began was whether or not Sophocles' Oedipus had an Oedipus Complex. The answer was no. Oedipus in fact attempted to avoid committing the crimes of parricide and incest. Freud's interpretation was thus, on Vernant's reasoning, shown to be wrong. As Glenn Most has argued, the relation of the tragedy to the Complex does not admit of a yes or no answer. He describes this relation as chiastic. The deeds of Oedipus in the tragedy correspond to the wishes of the Complex. These wishes, successfully repressed by everyman, correspond to the deeds of Oedipus. Freud's Oedipus ought to be understood, Most concludes, as a case of the reception of Sophocles' tragedy.[45]

Study of reception may look in either (or both) of two opposite directions, from the later to the earlier text, or from the earlier to the later. If from the Oedipus

---

[37] Von Hendy 2002, 122–23; Johnston 2017, 145–46, who takes the story on to Jungian reflexes in popular culture. See also Segal 1999, 95–97 and, for mid-twentieth century as a Jungian culmination, see the survey in Segal 2014, 442–44.
[38] For criticism and revision of the Oedipus complex: Armstrong 2011, 479–80 and for contemporary Freudian revisionism and its reflexes in a revised concept of myth: Segal 2014, 438–42.
[39] *SE* 14.
[40] E.g., Robinson 1993, a defence of Freud.
[41] Wohl 2008 speaks of the "romance of psychoanalysis and tragedy."
[42] Kirk 1970, 279. Recognition of importance: see n. 1 above.
[43] Burkert 1979, 17–18. He preferred explanations coming from "the outward, observable details" (136).
[44] Vernant 1972.
[45] Most 2002, 117–21.

Complex one looks back to the tragedy some meanings appear that might not have appeared otherwise. For the examples that I will give, the "text" of the Complex has first to be completed. In an essay called "The Dissolution of the Oedipus Complex", Freud says that the threat of castration in particular is the "determining factor in the renunciation of the incestuous object."[46] If the theory of the Oedipus Complex includes its dissolution, then, returning to the tragedy, one can say that the Complex brings to light a possible new significance of some elements of the Sophoclean biography of Oedipus. There are two elements that can be interpreted as signifying castration: the mutilation of the feet of Oedipus, when he was exposed as an infant, before the dramatic time of the tragedy, and his self-blinding at the end of the tragedy.

As for his feet, in Athenian slang, "foot" meant "penis".[47] "Foot" in this sense could also be used in a higher linguistic register, as in Euripides' *Medea* (679). The mutilation of feet can thus signify the mutilation of genitals, i.e., castration, and the action of Laius against his new-born son, clearly an over-determination of the common motif of exposure, can be seen as a specific remedy for incest.[48] As for his eyes, these organs, equally with or perhaps more than feet, stand for genitals in Greek myth and also in Greek art. Greek vase-paintings show phalluses with eyes.[49] Blinding is thus a suitable punishment for a sexual crime, and there are many examples in Greek myth.[50] In short, returning to the Sophoclean tragedy from the Complex, one might even say that Freud's interpretation of the tragedy was not Freudian enough.

Despite these authoritative turnings away from Freud noted above, interest never disappeared. Richard Caldwell applied the Freudian interpretation of dreams, in particular the expression of unconscious ideas by displacement, to

---

46 This paper, written in the early months of 1924, was an elaboration of a passage in *The Ego and the Id*. The words I have quoted: *SE* 19, 175.
47 For the evidence in comedy: Henderson 1991, 126 (82), 129–30 (104), 138 (146).
48 While the oracle received by Laius, as reported by Sophocles, did not include incest (711–14), the oracle received by Oedipus prophesied both parricide and incest, and in the same scene and later Oedipus is haunted by the fear of incest with his mother (787–93, 825–26, 976). For the motif of exposure: Binder 1964.
49 I am here following Edmunds 1988, 53–54. (This article is a revision of Edmunds 1986, from a conference paper of 1982.)
50 Devereux 1973.

myth. The three principle mechanisms of displacement are symbolism, decomposition, and projection.[51] One of Caldwell's examples of decomposition, discussed only briefly, is the split identity of Jocasta and the Sphinx.[52] Lévi-Strauss had already made this observation on the basis of comparative anthropological evidence.[53] Here already is a rapprochement of structuralism and psychoanalysis, for which Caldwell argues at length.

Freud's use of the Oedipus myth continued to be discussed by classical scholars and in the past decade psychoanalytic interpretation of Greek poetry and myth has remained alive and well.[54] With Lacan as with Freud a distinction between the thinker's interest in antiquity, on the one hand, and, on the other, the application of his thought to Greek myth should be made. Research on both aspects of Lacan has continued.[55] The case of Jung, discussed above, is somewhat different. In general, however, many would agree that "As a paradoxical 'rational theory of the irrational', psychoanalysis becomes the space where myth re-enters modern culture".[56] Or at least one of the spaces.

7.3 Structuralism

Structuralism and semiology are often used as synonyms.[57] The present discussion observes their separate histories and starts with Claude Lévi-Strauss's article of 1955 "The Structural Study of Myth." Some comments on the structuralist studies of the "Paris School", as it is sometimes called, of Jean-Pierre Vernant and others follow.[58] The synonymy begins, although it probably would not have oc-

---

51 Caldwell 1990, 350.
52 Caldwell 1990, 353.
53 Lévi-Strauss 1973, 4.
54 As shown, e.g., by Zajko/O'Gorman 2013, by Lauwers/Opsomer/Schwall 2018, and by the 2015 issue of *Psychoanalytic Inquiry: A Topical Journal for Mental Health Professionals* devoted to psychoanalysis and tragedy (which includes an article on the Homeric hero): vol. 35.
55 For Lacan's "return to antiquity": Harris 2017. The papers from a conference on Lacan and classical antiquity are published in *Helios* 31. See Porter/Buchan 2004 (the introduction to the papers) for the case for a Lacanian approach.
56 Armstrong 2011, 483.
57 See Culler 1975, 5–6 on these terms. For semiology, see also Greimas/Courtés 1982, 282–84 on the term "semiological." Burkert 1979, 5: "[S]tructuralism is termed the science of signs, to coincide with 'semiology', while at the same time the concept of 'sign' and 'language' has been expanded to cover nearly every aspect of civilization." He does not give any references.
58 For "Paris School", e.g., Strijdom 2007.

curred to Lévi-Strauss, in the article of 1955. He referred, in passages to be discussed below, to Ferdinand de Saussure. As a result, the word "structuralism" came to be retrojected onto Saussure's linguistics, even though Saussure used the word "structural" only of the structure of words.[59] Saussure did, however, use the word "semiology."[60] His definition of this concept, which reached far beyond linguistics, shows why it came to be used as a synonym of structuralism:

> A language is a system of signs, and hence comparable to writing, the deaf-and-dumb alphabet, symbolic rites, forms of politeness, military signals, and so on. ...It is...possible to conceive of a science *which studies the role of signs as part of social life*. It would form part of social psychology. We shall call it semiology...It would investigate the nature of signs and the laws governing them.[61]

Lévi-Strauss cultural-anthropological structuralism was later seen as resembling semiology and thus the synonymy indicated at the beginning of this paragraph came about.[62]

Lévi-Strauss's "The Structural Study of Myth" interprets two myths, the Greek Oedipus myth and an origin myth, in many variants, told by the Zuni. His interpretation of the Greek myth hardly needs another summary. An aspect of his theory and an aspect of his method are both, however, relevant to problems that I have raised. His theory is in three parts, the first two Saussurean. He begins with the observation that the same myths have both a local, contingent presence and appear also in other places in the world. He explained this antinomy with reference to the "arbitrary character of the linguistic sign", by which Saussure had accounted for the capacity of the same phonemes to express different things in different languages.[63] But if, as spoken, myth is language, then one has only said that myth is like language in general. "Myth will become confused with any other kind of speech." Lévi-Strauss appeals to another Saussurean concept, *langue* and *parole* as the two components of language. The former refers to its supra-individual, social dimension, the latter to the particular instance of speech.[64] In this way,

---

59 E.g., Saussure 1986, 32. For the retrojection: *OED* s.v. "structuralism" 3a: "Structuralism in linguistics is considered to begin with the work of Swiss linguist Ferdinand de Saussure" and note the first three attestations. Cf. Dammann 2007, col. 1406: Roman Jakobson is said to have introduced the term (1929).
60 *OED* s.v. "semiology" 3.
61 Saussure 1986, 33.
62 Cf. *OED* s.v. "structuralism" 3b.
63 Lévi-Strauss 1955, 429–30 (2.0–2.2).
64 For this distinction: Edmunds 2016a, 3 and nn.

the analogy of myth to language is saved. Myth is both of these things.[65] The third part of his theory starts begins by observing that myth, although it is ostensibly or in the first place about the past refers also to the present and the future. It is an "absolute object on a third level which, though it remains linguistic by nature, is nevertheless distinct from the other two." After an aside on the difference between myth and poetry (quoted in the Introduction, p. XX n. 23), he returns to this point: myth "is language, functioning on an especially high level where meaning succeeds practically at 'taking off' from the linguistic ground on which it keeps on rolling."[66]

Here meaning enters the theory and recalls meaning in some of the definitions of myth discussed in the Introduction (pp. XIX–XXI). Leaving language behind, except in the sense that myth is spoken ("linguistic by nature"), he uses a metaphor ("taking off") to describe the special status of meaning. Floating in the air, it seems to have, even in this closely reasoned, highly self-conscious article, the same problematic character as in those definitions. Although Lévi-Strauss concludes his interpretation of the Oedipus myth by saying what it means, he could have done so without having brought meaning into his theory.[67] No one would have felt a lack. Further, he intends ultimately to explain not meaning but something else. After his discussion of the Zuni myths in the second stage of his article, he says that structural analysis "enables us to perceive some basic logical processes which are at the root of mythical thought."[68] These processes are prior to meaning.

Having completed his theory, Lévi-Strauss introduces his method. He begins by referring to the linguistic model that he has evoked. Like language myth is made up of constituent units, the smallest of which, corresponding to phonemes, he calls "mythemes."[69] At higher level units they form "gross constituent units." He then somewhat apologetically ("only method we can suggest at this stage") describes a trial-and-error approach to isolating these units.[70] In what I called Kant's common-sense definition of theory, he referred to the application of theory, which he allowed might be influenced by the conditions from which the theory came in the first place (ch. 4.3). (In other words, the application, or method, is not here aprioristic.) Lévi-Strauss method has this same practical character.

---

[65] Lévi-Strauss 1955, 430 (2.3).
[66] Lévi-Strauss 1955, 430–31 (2.4–2.5).
[67] Lévi-Strauss 1955, 434 (4.10): "Turning back to the Oedipus myth, we may now see what it means."
[68] Lévi-Strauss 1955, 440 (7.0).
[69] I.e., in Lévi-Strauss 1958, the French revision of the article I am discussing.
[70] Lévi-Strauss 1955, 431 (2.6–3.2).

But Kant also said: "Between theory and practice, no matter how complete the theory may be, a middle term that provides a connection and transition is necessary. For to the concept of the understanding that contains the rule must be added an act of judgment by means of which the practitioner decides whether or not something is an instance of the rule."[71] A tacit act of judgment comes into Lévi-Strauss's article at the point at which he turns from his method to the Oedipus myth. "The time has come to give a concrete example of the method we propose. We will use the Oedipus myth which has the advantage of being well-known to everybody and for which no preliminary explanation is therefore needed."[72] The reader expects to see and does see the "gross constituent units" of this myth—as Lévi-Strauss implicitly has defined the myth. How did he arrive at this definition? This question points to a problematic aspect of his method. His theory has explained what a myth is in general. His method might have been expected to provide for the determination of the myth that is constituted by the units. In practice, what Lévi-Strauss calls the Oedipus myth includes the dragon killed by Cadmus and the Spartoi who were born from the dragon's teeth. Even the fullest of ancient Greek variants of the Oedipus myth, the four-generations that extend from Laius to Oedipus to his sons and to their sons, as told in three archaic epics, does not include the shadowy Labdacus, the father of Laius.[73] But the main objection to Lévi-Strauss's Oedipus myth is that the family line of Oedipus is separate from that of the Spartoi, who are the founders of the noble families of Thebes.[74] Having analyzed the Oedipus myth, Lévi-Strauss takes up the methodological question: "[O]ur method eliminates a problem which has been so far one of the main obstacles to the progress of mythological studies, namely, the quest for the true version, or the earlier one. On the contrary, we define the myth as consisting of all its versions; to put it otherwise: a myth remains the same as long as it is felt as such."[75]

---

[71] "Daß zwischen der Theorie und Praxis noch ein Mittelglied der Verknüpfung und des Überganges von der einen zur anderen erfordert werde, die Theorie mag auch so vollständig sein, wie sie wolle, fällt in die Augen; denn zu dem Verstandsbegriffe, welcher die Regel enthält, muß ein Actus der Urtheilskraft hinzukommen, wodurch der Praktiker unterscheidet, ob etwas der Fall der Regel sei oder nicht " (Kant 1923 [1793], 275). Transl.: Kant 1983 [1793], 61.
[72] Lévi-Strauss 1955, 432 (4.3).
[73] Edmunds 2006b, 13–14.
[74] Vian 1963, 199.
[75] Lévi-Strauss 1955, 435 (4.11.2).

In his Sather lectures of 1977 Burkert made a critique of Lévi-Strauss in the course of setting out his own theory of myth, consisting of four theses.[76] The first thesis is that *"myth belongs to the more general class of traditional tale"* (1).[77] The second: "the identity of a traditional tale…is to be found in a *structure of sense* within the tale itself" (5). He distinguishes between two kinds of structural analysis, that of Vladimir Propp (1895–1970) and that of Lévi-Strauss. Here I point out only that the title of the relevant work by Propp was *Morfologija skazki* (*The Morphology of the Folktale*) (1928). (For further discussion of Propp see ch. 9.2.) He abstracted from folktales of a certain type a sequence of thirty-one "functions." Burkert applied this method to seven myths concerning the mothers of important Greek heroes and showed a sequence of five functions, which he called "the girl's tragedy" (5–7). Burkert does not like the high number of functions but he vastly prefers Propp's method to Lévi-Strauss', which he criticizes at some length (10–14). His main point is that the latter's is a kind of idealism, not touching reality. "Maybe I am too clumsy to join the absolutism of semiology and get rid of objective reality" (13–14, using "semiology" as a synonym of "structuralism"). Burkert argues for a "structure of sense" or "program of action" in the Proppian functions and says that it must be derived from "the reality of life, nay, from biology" (15). Returning to "the girls' tragedy" he observes that it reflects initiation rituals, which in turn are "determined by the natural sequence of puberty, defloration, pregnancy, and delivery" (16). His third thesis is indeed: *"tale structures…are founded on basic biological or cultural programs of action"* (18). His fourth thesis comes under the heading "The Tale Applied" (22). The specific character of myth lies neither in structure nor in content but "in the use to which it is put." Thus *"myth is a traditional tale with secondary, partial reference to something of collective importance"* (22–23).[78] Burkert explains: "The reference is secondary, as the meaning of the tale is not to be derived from it". Like Lévi-Strauss, Burkert completes his theory with the meaning of myth and like Lévi-Strauss he gives meaning a special status. Not only is meaning not to be found in whatever a myth refers to, in someone's application of it on some occasion (whereas, he says, a fable is invented for the sake of its application), but meaning is also partial because myth and reality "will never be quite isomorphic in these applications" (23). The meaning of myth is thus apparently always held in reserve, perhaps up in the air, as in Lévi-Strauss's theory. But Burkert quickly returns to earth: "And still the tale is

---

[76] Burkert 1979, 1: "I shall try to formulate some theses which may add up to form a tentative theory of myth, without Hellenocentric bias".
[77] In this and the following quotations from Burkert, the emphasis is his.
[78] For a critique of "traditional" in this definition: Bettini 2012, iii.

often the first and fundamental verbalization of complex reality" and "[t]he phenomena of collective importance which are verbalized by applying traditional tales are to be found, first of all, in social life" (23). Myth thus does not and also does have meaning in the instances of its application.

In 1969 Vernant avowed himself a structuralist but not a Lévi-Straussian. He associated himself as structuralist with Dumézil (ch. 9.1), who did not in fact wish to be called by this name.[79] Vernant criticizes Lévi-Strauss at length in the magisterial "The Reason of Myth."[80] He challenges Lévi-Strauss's interpretation of the Oedipus myth in particular.[81] He objects to the intrusion by a non-Hellenist into ancient Greece and prefers the "rigorous demonstration of his methods" in *La geste d'Asdiwal*.[82] (He questions Lévi-Strauss's segmentation of the myth, as I have done, but without giving examples. On the problem of segmentation, which is more complex than Vernant seems to assume, see ch. 9.) Vernant's concludes his critique of Lévi-Strauss by acknowledging that with him a turning-point in the study of myth has come:

> Nevertheless, one must recognize that following Lévi-Strauss the situation is no longer the same either from a theoretical point of view or so far as the concrete work of decipherment is concerned; his work marks a turning point and a new departure. For his adversaries as for his disciples and those working along parallel lines, mythological research now not only confronts new questions; it is no longer possible to pose even the old problems in the same terms.[83]

The central point of difference between Vernant and Lévi-Strauss was the relation of myth, as interpreted structurally, to society. Vernant's title, *Myth and Society in Ancient Greece*, sums up the relation. For Burkert myth also has to do with "social life" and thus with history (the title of the book that I discussed was *Structure and History in Greek Mythology and Ritual*) but extends much farther, even into the biological. While the concepts of the social or of society and of history differ greatly between Burkert and Vernant, they have in common the grounding of myth in lived reality, as against the mentalism of Lévi-Strauss's structuralism.

Charles Delattre sums up what I referred to in the Introduction as his "positive" definition of myth in this way:

---

79 Dosse 1997.1, 32 (Dumézil); Dosse 1997.2, 224 (Vernant). Vernant is introducing his structuralist analysis of the myth of the races (1983 [1969]).
80 Vernant 1988 [1974], 246–52.
81 Vernant 1980c, 249–50.
82 Lévi-Strauss 1957.
83 Vernant 1980c, 253.

> We have defined myth, in the tradition of structural analysis, as an autonomous act of expression and of speech, which amounts to making myth a practice, a rhetorical device that falls within the field of communication.[84]

This definition does not differ substantially from my own.[85] The source of this definition, i.e., "structural analysis", calls for comment. What Delattre has in mind is the structuralisms of Lévi Strauss, of Dumézil, and of the "school of Paris."[86] The question remains of the point at which any of these structuralisms returns from structure to particular instance, to myth as *parole*. What example would Delattre give of the importance of that instance in the thought of these structualists? A more fundamental difficulty is his implicit definition of structuralism as French. Burkert said that "there are...two prominent names which stand for two types of structural analysis, Vladimir Propp and Claude Lévi-Strauss."[87] Burkert takes his cue from Propp, whose morphology was the starting-point of Greimas. His main exponents in the study of Greek myth have been Claude Calame and Ezio Pellizer (ch. 9.2.1). The difficulty that I have indicated is not simply a matter of intellectual history. The more fundamental question is how to grasp that particular instance, the myth "out there", the question that I posed in the Introduction (p. XXIII) and have returned to at various points in this book.

7.4 Conclusion

The two main influences that went into Harrison's theory were the study of rituals and comparative anthropology. Her relation to Frazer in this respect is clear in *Themis*. Three other forebears were Wilhelm Mannhardt (1831–1880), E.B. Tylor (1832–1917), and William Robertson Smith (1846–1894), in particular those parts of their works on ritual.[88] Harrison's book, written by a classicist, brought anthropological or ethnographic comparison and initiation into the field of classics,

---

[84] Delattre 2005, 34 "Nous avons défini le mythe, dans la lignée de l'analyse structurale, come un acte d'expression autonome et de parole, ce qui revient à faire du mythe une pratique, un dispositif rhétorique qui ressortit au champ de la communication".
[85] I call attention to the word "pratique." The title of my introduction to Edmunds 1990 was "The Practice of Greek Mythology" (Edmunds 1990a).
[86] Thus the tripartite division of his bibliography (33). For the "school of Paris": 29 n. 11 (Vernant, Vidal-Naquet, Detienne, *et al.*)
[87] Lévi-Strauss 1979, 5.
[88] See Harrison 1912, 136 on Tylor and Robertson Smith. She considered Mannhardt the most important of the three, praising his *Wald- und Feldkulte* (321). On Mannhardt as a pioneer in the study of ritual see Tybjerg 1993. Harrison also cites, in passing, Van Gennep 1909 (1912, 19, 510).

where their history continues. In the preface to the English edition of *Homo Necans*, looking back to the first, German edition published eleven years earlier (1972), Burkert says, amongst other things, that "it introduced, after Harrison's *Themis*, functionalism to the study of Greek religion."[89] The story continues into the present century (see §1 above sub fin.)

Psychoanalysis was already at the time of *Themis* a radical alternative to the functional or ritual basis of myth. In Freud's *The Interpretation of Dreams* the Oedipus myth served in the first place as confirmation of the Oedipus complex but contrariwise the complex also explained the myth. In other words, the myth had a mentalistic, as opposed to a ritual, basis, which Freud discovered in working with his patients. Such was the work that corresponded, or that one might now see as corresponding, to the fieldwork of the anthropologists.

In Lévi-Strauss's structuralism the two bases of myth defined apropos of Harrison and Freud are combined. Lévi-Strauss was an anthropologist and did fieldwork in Brazil (although the thoroughness and depth of this work have been questioned). He regarded myth as having a practical purpose for the people who tell the myth. For the ancient Greeks, the Oedipus myth, as interpreted by him, solved a problem: "The myth has to do with the inability, for a culture which holds the belief that mankind is autochthonous…, to find a satisfactory transition between this theory and the knowledge that human beings are actually born from the union of man and woman." The myth "provides a kind of logical tool."[90] As such, however, myth is mentalistic. His *Mythologiques* aims to reduce a vast collection of myths from North and South America to mathematical formulas.[91]

---

89 Burkert 1983, xiii. The functionalism of ritual is certainly central in Themis.
90 1955, 434 (4.10).
91 Lévi-Strauss 1964–1971.

8 Three Comparative Approaches

In current study of Greek myth, the three main fields of comparison are Indo-European myth, ancient Near Eastern myth, and folklore. The first two are often discussed together because they sometimes meet (a Hurrian-Hittite example is discussed below) but are distinguished in this chapter. The three comparisons have different aims, each different, however, from those of the Cambridge school (ch. 7.1). The three can be compared in the first place with respect to method, each of them, as it happens, illustrating one of the three methods distinguished by Gregory Nagy apropos of epic poetry: genealogical, historical and typological.[1] Whereas Nagy referred specifically to the study of languages, his distinctions can be extended to myths. The first method is that of the Indo-Europeanist, who studies "structures related to each other by way of a common source", "cognate structures", that indicate a "family" of languages, descended from a proto-language spoken by an Indo-European people. The second is the method of the scholar who compares Greek and ancient Near Eastern myths other than Indo-European. These are "structures related to each other by way of...historically ...intercultural contact", usually studied from the point of view of movement from east to west.[2] The goal of comparison is not to ascertain origins (see below on this point). The third method is typological, studying "parallels between structures that are not necessarily related to each other." Folktales are now usually understood to be structures of this kind, even if, in the history of folktale studies, typology once served the purposes of the "geographical-historical school", which sought to establish the geographical origin and diffusion and history of folktales.[3] This approach, which applied to delimited geographical areas, has been abandoned, even if most folklorists are still "diffusionists", holding that folktales turn up wherever they turn up because they have come from somewhere else, not because of the autogenesis or the polygenesis of similar folktales.[4]

---

[1] Nagy 2005, 71–72.
[2] Though sometimes movement in the opposite direction has been discovered: Rutherford 2009, 20 and n. 47.
[3] Röhrich 1987. See Hansen 2002a, 5–6 for a history of folktale studies.
[4] Cf. Edmunds 2016a, 9.

8.1 Indo-European

The field of Indo-European studies, now two centuries old, began with the comparison of languages.[5] Calvert Watkins has summed up the results:

> It has been rightly said that the comparatist has one fact and one hypothesis. The one fact is that certain languages present similarities among themselves...so numerous and so precise that they cannot be attributed to chance and which are such that they cannot be explained as borrowings or as universal features. The one hypothesis is that these languages then must be the result of descent from a common original.[6]

This original language is called Indo-European or proto-Indo-European. If there was such a language, there must have been a people who spoke it and this people must have had a culture. This culture included myth and poetry. There is thus a comparative Indo-European poetics and a comparative Indo-European study of myth, as in West's survey, *Indo-European Poetry and Myth*.[7] The following discussion concentrates on the latter, which entered Greek studies around 1950.[8]

West establishes three historical levels. The oldest is proto-Indo-European (PIE), which splits at the next level into Mature Indo-European (MIE) and Hittite, the earliest attested dialect, with Luwian and Palaic (all together "Anatolian"). At the third and most recent level, MIE has branched into a western (Italic, Celtic) and an eastern (Greek, Armenian, Indo-Iranian) group. He gives a chronology in centuries, Anatolian diverging from PIE by 2900 at the latest, and so forth (10). He surveys the sources for each branch (12–19). He states his method, beginning with the principle that "the comparative method can take us back to different levels, depending on the location of the materials compared" (19–24). Thus a Homeric-Vedic or an Italic-Celtic parallel takes one back only to the third level, a Celtic-Iranian one to the second. "To get back to the deepest level, to PIE, we shall require a comparison involving Anatolian" (20).

If one accepts this chronology and proceeds to a particular comparison at a particular level, there still remains the question of method. Nicholas Allen finds a main divide between "(i) those who reject or ignore the theories of Georges Dumézil (1898–1986) and (ii) those who try to use them."[9] West rejected Dumézil

---

5 For a survey of the history: West 2007, 1–5.
6 Watkins 1995, 4; Watkins 2011, vi.
7 For comparative Indo-European poetics: Watkins 1995, 5–6. West 2007.
8 See Burkert 1987, 19 for a brief history of scholarship.
9 Allen 2011, 343.

(4).¹⁰ Allen himself is a Dumézilian revisionist, as will be seen in the following discussion. First, however, an example of (i) not considered by West.

Bilingual Hurrian-Hittite tablets discovered in 1983 and 1985 contain a text called "The Song of Release."¹¹ West did not use texts in the Anatolian languages. He said, apropos the surviving texts in these languages: "The myths...seem to be taken over from other, non-Indo-European peoples of the region...and have little to offer for the present enterprise."¹² In the case to be considered, the Hittite is a translation of the Hurrian and another objection might arise: the Hittite version is only a borrowing. But one can argue that a synthesis has taken place, as in the case of other such adaptations.¹³ Specialists compare its plot with that of the *Iliad*.¹⁴ For present purposes, what is of interest is the relation of the plot of the "Song" to the myth of the Trojan War, which is the larger context for the fifty-odd days narrated in the *Iliad*—the account of the anger of Achilles, the death of Patroclus, and Achilles' vengeance on Hector.

The fragments of the song concern the causes of the destruction of Ebla (identified with modern Tell Mardikh in northern Syria, thirty-four miles south of Aleppo, on the river Orontes). The destruction is predicted in a conversation between the Storm God (Hurrian Teshub, Hittite Tarhun) and Ishara, a Syrian goddess, on the obverse of the first tablet. (The Storm God is well known from the "Kumarbi Cycle", in which, like Zeus, he becomes the king of the gods.)¹⁵ In a fragment that belong to the first tablet, Tarhun talks with his brother, whom he sends to discuss something with Ishara. Across the ensuing tablets and fragments a narrative can be vaguely perceived. The Storm God goes to the underworld to discuss something with the Sun Goddess of the Earth. The scene then shifts to Ebla, where the Storm God threatens destruction of the city if the people of the town of Inkalis, who are the Eblaites' servants, are not released. The king of Ebla refuses.¹⁶

The myth thus extrapolated from these difficult fragments corresponds partly to the standard version of the Trojan War (as in West's summary, quoted in ch. 4.4) and partly to another version. Of the three sources for this other version two

---

10 For criticism of Dumézil: Colpe 1981, cols. 925–26.
11 The standard edition is that of Neu 1996. I have relied on the translation of Bachvarova 2017.
12 West 2007.
13 For another example, to which he refers as a synthesis: Woodard 2020.
14 As by Bachvarova 2016; Bachvarova 2017.
15 Woodard 2007, 95–96.
16 The division of the tablets and the summary of the story in Livingstone and Haskamp 2011, 376 give me pause. But they conclude: "the end of the story is...lost, but might have contained an explanation for the (historical) destruction of Ebla."

are found in a scholium to *Iliad* 1.5, containing a short prose narrative and the proem to the *Cypria*.[17] In the prose narrative, Zeus begot Helen to be one of two agents of the destruction of the heroes, which was the first step in his plan to relieve Earth of the burden of mortals of which she complained.[18] The other agent was Achilles. In the proem to the *Cypria*, quoted in the scholium, the poet says: "And the heroes were killed at Troy and the plan of Zeus was fulfilled."[19] Zeus's plan in this version of the Trojan War myth would correspond to the prior decision of the gods, at least tentative, concerning the destruction of Ebla. (Differences between the two versions in the scholium are discussed in 8.2 below.)

The divine discussions that takes place in the first and also in the second groups of fragments would correspond to the non-Iliadic version of the Trojan War found in the Hesiodic *Catalogue*.[20] At the end of the passage in this poem on the wooing of Helen, the poet moves directly from Menelaus's winning of Helen to the birth of Hermione to, abruptly, "All the gods were divided in spirit" (Hes. *Cat.* 204.95 M-W = 110.95 H = 155.95 M). This otherwise unexplained Olympian division is the point of correspondence with the Hittite-Hurrian fragments. In the *Catalogue*, there follow at least a hundred lines (many very fragmentary) on Zeus's epochal decision to destroy much of the human race and to end the age of heroes, with their removal to habitations apart from mortals.

The Inkalis people who are held in Ebla must have been somehow captured and correspond to Helen in Troy. The refusal of the Eblaites to return these people to their home-city would corresponds to the Trojan refusal, in Book 7 of the *Iliad*, to return Helen. Such a refusal turns up on the Shield of Achilles. The city at war is besieged by two armies, which have resolved either to sack the city or to divide its possessions, an alternative that the besieged would not accept (*Il.* 18.509–40).

In both the non-Iliadic Greek and the Hittite-Hurrian myths, the abductions (to extend this word to the case of the people of Inkalis) are only the proximate causes of a city's destruction. The remote cause is a divine decision. In the Hittite-Hurrian it is this destruction that is the climax of the story. The fate of the ones who have been abducted, whatever it may have been, is secondary. In what is for

---

17 See Christopoulos 2011 on this scholium.
18 From Eustathius' comment on the same line it seems that the scholiast has conflated another tradition with the *Cypria*; and a passage in Codex Baroccianus 162 in the Bodleian Library (from a commentary on Homer, *Iliad* Book 1 by Andreas Donus (?) (15th c.)) tends to strengthen the hypothesis of a version of the tradition different from the one in the *Cypria*. On the *Cypria* see Davies 1989, 33–34; Currie 2015, 281–305; Davies 2016, 13–35.
19 *Cypria* fr. 1.6–7 B/D = West F 1 (p. 65); cf. Eur. *Hel.* 39–41; *El.* 1282–83; *Or.* 1639–42.
20 On this version see Edmunds 2016a, 117–18, from which some sentences have been taken here.

us the primary Greek tradition, the abducted wife, Helen, is recovered by her cuckolded husband and returns with him to her former home. She is central in the story. But Greek tradition also has a version of the Trojan War myth in which the sack of the city is the climax, the Cyclic *Iliupersis* or *Iliou Persis*. This poem can no longer be regarded as ancillary to the *Iliad*. It has its own raison d'être and represents an independent version, different from the standard (for us) Iliadic one.[21]

To turn now to Dumézil, Allen makes another distinction, this time between (i) "those who accept Dumézil's 'trifunctional' theory as it stands" and (ii) "those who think it needs expansion", amongst whom he includes himself. In the theory, a proto-culture discernible in myths of the speakers of Indo-European languages reflects a social organization and ideology having three hierarchical "functions": the kingly and priestly, the martial, and the agricultural and life-fostering.[22] Dumézil said that he found Greek myth recalcitrant and, after 1938, left it to others.[23] Nevertheless, in a collection of his major articles published in 1968, one finds an interpretation of the Judgment of Paris as a choice among goddesses who represent the three functions (Hera the sovereign, Athena the martial, and Aphrodite the sexual).[24] He observed the consistency of the three goddesses in their three functions throughout the *Iliad*. Further, he showed reflexes of trifunctionality in the descendants of Tros, most conspicuously in the sons of Priam, Helenus the seer (first function), Hector the warrior (second), and again Paris (third).

Allen followed the expansion of Dumézil's trifunctional scheme by Alwyn Rees and Brinley Rees, who proposed a fourth function, "which pertains to what, relative to the core functions, is other, outside or beyond."[25] This fourth function is divided into a positive and a negative aspect, as pertaining to what is valued and transcendent, on the one hand, and, on the other, to what is devalued (hated, feared, excluded). Allen assigns the symbols F1, F2 and F3 to Dumézil's scheme and F4+ and F4- to its pentadic expansion.

---

21 For this conception of the Cyclic poems see Burgess 2001, 148. For the fall of cities: cf. Bachvarova/Dutsch/Suter 2016.
22 For an introduction to the three functions: J. Nagy 2014, 202–204.
23 Edmunds 2014b, 200; Edmunds 2016a, 99.
24 Dumézil 1995, 579–601. (I cite the later single-volume selection.) For a discussion of Dumézil's analysis of the aition of the Trojan War as illustrating key principles of his method: J. Nagy 2014, 204–206.
25 Allen 2011, 344, referring to Rees/Rees 1961. For extensive explorations of the fourth function: Sauzeau/Sauzeau 2012.

This split fourth function in effect broadens the possibilities of Dumézilian analysis of myth because in a particular tradition in which F1 is missing (for example, because it has been lost) F4+, F2, F3 might be the result. The fourth function also helps to complete the description of F1 (kingly and priestly) and F3 (agricultural and life-fostering) when they are ambiguous. An example of the ambiguity of F1 would be a conflict between a king or leader and a priest or prophet, as between Hector and Polydamas in Book 18 of the *Iliad* (245–314). An ambiguous representative of F3 would be Helen, who obviously has both positive and negative aspects. As Joseph Nagy has said, Paris' choice of the prize offered him by Aphrodite has the effect of "setting the tripartite social model on its head."[26]

The difficulties of description in terms of F1, F2 and F3 become all the greater in the version of the Trojan War found in a fragment of Acusilaus:

Ἀφροδίτη χρησμοῦ ἐκπεσόντος, ὅτι τῆς τῶν Πριαμιδῶν ἀρχῆς καταλυθείσης οἱ ἀπ' Ἀγχίσου Τρώων βασιλεύσουσιν, Ἀγχίσῃ ἤδη παρηκμακότι συνῆλθεν, τεκοῦσα δ' Αἰνείαν καὶ βουλομένη πρόφασιν κατασκευάσαι τῆς τῶν Πριαμιδῶν καταλύσεως Ἀλεξάνδρῳ πόθον Ἑλένης ἐνέβαλε καὶ μετὰ τὴν ἁρπαγὴν τῷ μὲν δοκεῖν συνεμάχει τοῖς Τρωσί, ταῖς δὲ ἀληθείαις παρηγόρει τὴν ἧτταν αὐτῶν, ἵνα μὴ παντελῶς ἀπελπίσαντες ἀποδῶσι τὴν Ἑλένην.

When an oracle issued forth that those descended from Anchises would rule as kings over the Trojans after the dissolution of the rule of the Priamids, Aphrodite had intercourse with Anchises, who was already well past his prime. She bore Aeneas and, wishing to furnish a cause for the dissolution of the Priamids, she threw into Alexander a longing for Helen. After Helen's abduction, she appeared to be an ally to the Trojans, but in truth she was consoling them in defeat lest they completely despair and deliver over Helen.[27]

Acusilaus *FGrH* 2 F 39 = *EMG* 2, fr. 39, from schol. *Il.* 20.307

Here the oracle is a first-function beginning and it concerns the first-function future, namely the kingship, of Troy. A third-function goddess intervenes, however, precisely through third-function reproduction, in order to contravene the oracle. Thus F1 followed by F4-. Paris' abduction of Helen as such is appropriate to a warrior and to this extent represents F2.[28] Helen as the most beautiful woman in the world is F3 par excellence but as a captive in Troy, in Acusilaus' version, she

---

26 J. Nagy 2014, 204.
27 Toye 2009 modified.
28 Hector reminds his brother of the strength that he displayed at the time of that predatory expedition to Sparta (*Il.* 3.46–51). Cf. de Jong 2012, 90 on 22.116 citing van Wees 1992, 172–73 on Paris' expedition.

is Aphrodite's agent and so the sign changes and she becomes F4-. The siege of Troy presupposes an army (F2) and a commander (F1). The result:
- F1 (oracle concerning kingship and [commander of army])
- F4 (third function goddess Aphrodite)
- F2 (Paris as abductor and [besieging army])
- F3 (Helen)
- F4- (Helen)

Thus the pentadic scheme refines and preserves the triadic Dumézilian description.

8.2 Near East

Comparison of Greek with Indo-European myth preceded by a century or more comparison with ancient Near Eastern myth, which was long resisted.[29] This resistance came under criticism of varying degrees of vehemence.[30] Little by little, the Near Eastern side won out. Scholars could now "see ancient and prehistoric European culture not as the exclusive product of a mythical Indo-European tribe, but as the result of multi-cultural activity along land and sea trade routes (which...cover much the same region as the Indo-European descendants, but without the hole in the Middle East)."[31] For obvious reasons the comparisons that went on were at the level of stories or myths and not at the level of poetic composition. In recent years, however, the neoanalytic interpretation of the death of Patroclus as modelled on the death of Achilles in the *Aethiopis*, and an anticipation of his often anticipated post-Iliadic death, has been extended to the death of Enkidu in *Gilgamesh*. This death of the hero's friend in *Gilgamesh* has, it is argued, been modelled on the death of Gilgamesh (Bilgames) himself in the earlier Sumerian poem, "The Death of Bilgamesh." Further, the *Iliad* is imitating not only the death of Enkidu but the very way in which Gilgamesh imitates "The Death of Bilgamesh."[32]

---

[29] For rejection of the label "Near Eastern" and preference for specific regional names, Egyptian, Levantine, etc.: López-Ruiz 2010, 17. The frequent inclusion of Egyptian parallels under the heading "Near Eastern" is especially notable.
[30] See López-Ruiz 2014, 156–58.
[31] Goldberg 1998, 251 n. 7.
[32] Currie 2012, 552–54. Cf. Rutherford 2009, 33 of the "Kingship in Heaven Cycle": "The idea that the myth passes from the Near East to Greece in a non-poetic form and is subsequently set to verse by Greek poets, so that we end up with songs in the two traditions is surely less likely

This kind of intertextual relation between an ancient Near Eastern text and the *Iliad* is possible if the Greek epic is conceived of as a written composition.³³ The date of the written *Iliad* that is presupposed remains controversial, however. As for written texts of *Gilgamesh*, certainly they existed from the end of the third millenium B.C.E. This epic underwent many changes in its long history, which culminates in the Standard Version, found in the excavation of the library of Ashurbanipal (668–627 B.C.E.).³⁴ Another example of Near Eastern-Greek intertextual relation, not discussed here, is between the Old Testament and the Bible.³⁵

The following discussion concerns the comparison of Near Eastern and Greek myths, whether literate or oral.³⁶ The Near Eastern background of this kind of contact has a long history, beginning in the third millennium, of myths written on clay tablets. The prestige of this medium appears in an Akkadian myth in which the monster bird Anzu or Zu steals the tablet of destinies from Enlil (one of the three supreme deities). Chaos ensues. Enlil's son Ninurta (god of war and agriculture) defeats Anzu and recovers the tablet.³⁷ Here the medium (a tablet) is the message (the crucial importance of a tablet for world-order). In the history of the *Epic of Gilgamesh* not only did a canonical text evolve but it came to be written on eleven tablets, with the tablets of each exemplar beginning and ending in exactly the same place.³⁸ The medium is part of the message.

Certainly the contexts in which these and other tablets could have become known to Greeks were numerous.³⁹ In those same contexts, myths might more often have gone by word of mouth from one language to another. Neither the storyteller nor a listener had to be bilingual. Both had only to share only a "contact language" (a pidgin, a creole, or mixed language).⁴⁰ As Lévi-Strauss said, "the

---

than that bilingual singers, used to a performance tradition in one culture, gave rise to a similar form of theogonic song for Greece." Also López-Ruiz 2014, 169–70. (For an overview of the difficulties surrounding the Bilgamesh poem see Veldhuis 2001.)

33 For a survey of the three main schools of thought concerning the history of the text of Homer in antiquity: Edmunds 2016c, 2–6.
34 For an outsider's conception of the history of the text of Gilgamesh: Edmunds 2005, 33–34.
35 Most recently Louden 2019.
36 For the word "myth" as including stories of both gods and heroes: Livingstone/Haskamp 2011, 361.
37 *ANET* 111–13 (Akkadian and Assyrian versions).
38 Livingstone/Haskamp 2011, 359.
39 See López-Ruiz 2010, 43–47 and López-Ruiz 2014, 185–86 on contexts and kinds of transmission.
40 Edmunds 2016a, 101.

mythical value of the myth remains preserved, even through the worst translation."[41]

Comparison of non-Indo-European myths from the Near East with Greek myths became a regular approach, although not widely practiced, with the publication of two books in 1966, West's commentary on Hesiod's *Theogony* and Peter Walcot's *Hesiod and the Near East*.[42] They were anticipated by Jacqueline Duchemin, who averred that "we will collect a number of important indications to shed light on the problem of hesiodic sources, if we push our research outside the Hellenic world, in the light of recent discoveries made in the soil of Asia Minor."[43] Geoffrey Kirk's two books on Greek myth (1970 and 1974) both contain sections on Western Asian influences.[44] In the years since then, the *Theogony* has remained a focal point.[45] But *Works and Days* now comes in for the same kind of comparison.[46] So also Orphic theogony, after the discovery of the Derveni papyrus in 1962.[47] On the Near Eastern side, the *Book of Daniel* (Hebrew and Aramaic) has been compared with the Myth of the Ages in Hesiod's Works and Days.[48] There have been new discoveries, the "Song of the Sea" and "Ea and the Beast."[49] Such has been the success of ancient Near Eastern comparison that some Indo-Europeanists have sought to put their side of Hesiod into balance with the Near Eastern side.[50]

The history that has just been sketched leads to the question of the meaning of the numerous parallels that have turned up. Rutherford's answer takes into

---

41 Cf. Lévi-Strauss 1955, 430. He was imagining someone reading the transcription of a myth but his point applies equally well to oral transmission. Cf. López-Ruiz 2014, 161: "Myths are not texts, but they are in texts."
42 Walcot 1966; West 1966, 19: "The Succession Myth has parallels in oriental mythology which are so striking that a connexion is incontestable. They occur principally in Hittite and Akkadian texts, and in Herennius Philo's translation of the *Phoenician History* of Sanchuniathon." He proceeds to a discussion of these parallels (20–28). Livingstone/Haskamp 2011, 381 date the beginning of the Near Eastern sub-field of the study of Greek myth to an article of Lambert and Walcot published in 1965.
43 "[N]ous recueillerons nombre d'indications importantes pour éclairer le problème des sources hésiodiques, si nous poussons notre recherche en dehors du monde hellénique, à la lumière des decouvertes récemment faites dans le sol de l'Asie Mineure" : Duchemin 1995, 6. This article is reprinted from Duchemin 1952. She cites earlier work (nn. 7, 9).
44 Kirk 1970; Kirk 1974.
45 E.g., Rutherford 2009, 9–14; 22– 24; 25–29; 31–35.
46 West 1997, 28, 174; Woodard 2007, 112–15; Rutherford 2009, 16–19.
47 E.g., López-Ruiz 2010, 130–70; López-Ruiz 2014, 180–81.
48 Woodard 2007, 113–14.
49 Rutherford 2009, 24–25.
50 Woodard 2007; Katz 2009.

account three possibilities: a Late Bronze Age cultural *koine*, in which "borrowing or diffusion would have gone from the old centres of Mesopotamia to the periphery of Anatolia and the Aegean", and so forth; "reflections of underlying similarities in the political and social structures", i.e., what I have called autogenesis; "transmission of literary forms, narratives or motifs did indeed take place between one culture to another." (He does not consider the possibility of oral transmission.) He is skeptical concerning all of these possibilities and says that the only strong case for borrowing is that of the *Theogony* from the Kingship in Heaven myth.[51]

The question concerning parallels can be distinguished from the question of the significance of the comparison of a Greek with a Near Eastern myth, no matter what the basis of the comparison, which may, after all, be simply typological (cf. the first paragraph of this chapter). The question of significance will find an answer not at the level of the parallel but at the level of the Greek myth in a particular comparison. Assuming a parallel, of a certain kind and of a certain depth (cf. West's chronological distinctions for Indo-European parallels), what does it show about the Greek myth?

A case in point is Burkert's comparison of the Akkadian "Atrahasis" or the "Atrahasis Epic" with the Greek myth, discussed above, concerning Zeus's decision to destroy the human race or most of it.[52] "Atrahasis" (the name means "Exceeding Wise") begins with the noisiness of humans, which disturbs Enlil, who decides to send a famine, then a plague (in one of the two Neo-Assyrian versions), and then a flood in order to destroy them. Atrahasis apparently intervenes on behalf of humanity and Enlil commands him to build ship.—The flood-story has obvious parallels in the Biblical Flood (*Genesis* 6:11–9:19) and the one in *Gilgamesh* (eleventh tablet).—The three variants of the Greek myth were discussed above apropos of an Indo-European comparandum (§1). These are the prooemium to the *Cypria*, the prose narrative found in the same scholium with the prooemium, and the passage in the Hesiodic *Catalogue*. Burkert emphasizes details that distinguish these variants from each other but concedes that they are "three variations on the concept of a catastrophe affecting mankind through the decision of the ruling god."[53]

---

51 Rutherford 2009, 19–22.
52 For the translation of "Atrahasis" Burkert 1992, 206 n. 3 cites "Lambert and Millard." In his Bibliography he cites Lambert 1960. His summary of "Atrahasis" (1992, 100–101) does not correspond exactly to the text used in *ANET*.
53 Burkert 1992, 102.

This comparison merits further thought. The three Greek sources have in common with each other and with "Atrahasis" the earth's distress, caused by humans, and the highest god's determination to alleviate the earth by destroying humans. In the Hesiodic *Catalogue* and in "Atrahasis", other gods are concerned in the decision and one can perhaps compare the role of Themis in the *Cypria*. What the comparison shows about the Greek myth is that Zeus's plan of destruction is the fundamental story and that the wars (the Theban war is in the Momus version: again §1 above) are specifically Greek and the roles of Helen and Achilles are instrumental and secondary. (The flood, which is Enlil's culminating act against humans, turns up in the Greek myth of Deucalion.)

In the other Greek version of the Trojan War myth, the one lying behind the *Iliad*, the object of Zeus's destruction is not mankind as a whole but the city of Troy. At the same time, the Judgment of Paris and the ensuing abduction of Helen are pushed into the background and the anger of Achilles comes to the fore. This anger initially causes the intervention of Thetis with Zeus and his ensuing plan to honor her son's anger by giving a short-term advantage to the Trojans. In this way he provokes Hera, who hates Troy. They reach a compromise. Zeus concedes to her the ultimate destruction of the city in return for Trojan success during the absence of Achilles from the battlefield. Further, the role of other gods in the fulfillment of the decision is played up, as Zeus must again and again assert his plan against them and their various machinations. In these respects the plot of the *Iliad* resembles the Cyclic (etc.) and "Atrahasis" versions.

Tab. 2: Tabular comparison of Near Eastern myths with Greek Trojan War myths.

Supreme god will destroy:	"Song of Release"	Trojan War 1: *Iliad*	Trojan War 2: *Cypria* etc.	"Atrahasis"
City	√	√		
Mankind			√	√
Roles of other gods	√	√	√	

In the Dumézilian interpretation of the Trojan War myth, contrary to the results of the comparisons just discussed, the role of Helen looms large. The Judgment of Paris, which leads to the abduction of Helen, is the distal cause of the War, and the presence of Helen in Troy is the proximate cause. As Joseph Nagy said, the tripartite Dumézilian model is turned upside down, as a third function figure, Helen, intrudes with dire consequences into the realm of the first function.

8.3 Folklore

Wilhelm Grimm (1786–1859), in a paper read before the Royal Academy of Sciences in Berlin in 1857, presented a set of nine folktales about the blinded ogre, and compared them with the Polyphemus episode in the *Odyssey*.[54] He pointed out consistent differences between his set and that episode. These included the absence of the ogre's inebriation and of the No Man or Nobody ruse (*Mot* K602) and the inclusion of a magic ring given the hero by the ogre. Grimm argued that it would be difficult to explain the folktale version of the story as a borrowing from the *Odyssey*. A much more plausible hypothesis was the descent of both the Polyphemus story and the folktale analogues from what we would now call the same international type, the one described as AT/ATU 1137.[55] Grimm's paper, long preceded by the study of Greek myth in Germany, laid the foundation for comparative study of Greek myths and folktales.[56]

Although Grimm was engaged in what we would call typology, his goal was not the definition of a type but the discovery of the original lying behind the examples that he had assembled.[57] (But the first type indexes did not lie far in the future.) He was engaged in segmentation but not systematically. He had no term for the units that his summaries revealed.[58] For the future, Grimm's most important insight was the independence of the Polyphemus folktale and of its Homeric expression. In other words, neither derived from the other; each was the expression of a shared tradition (a word that he did not use). He left implicit the principle that would be called "genre variance", the phenomenon "in which a story is told by one narrator as a folktale and by another as a legend or myth."[59]

---

54 Published the same year: Grimm 1857. (Of the nine, he omitted to discuss one because he thought that it was derived from the *Od*.) For Grimm's work in the category of "Stoff- und Motivgeschichte": Denecke 1990, col. 188.
55 Up to this point this paragraph is a revision, with new footnotes, of Edmunds 2016a, 39. For discussion of the relation of the Homeric version to the folktales see the discussion of Hansen 2002a, 292–94, with critique of Fehling, who held that folktales have come into existence only in modern times (Fehling 1977; Fehling 1984). Cf. Edmunds 2016a, 37–41 (§10 "How Old Are Folktales?").
56 Hansen 2002a, 7–8 points out an earlier beginning in the work of Wilhelm Grimm's brother, Jacob. For a survey of the study of Greek myth in Germany in the eighteenth and the first half of the nineteenth centuries: Graf 1993 [1987], 13–24 and 24–27 for Wilhelm Grimm and his brother Jacob and their contemporaries in Germany. Grimm's lecture also inspired much further study of the Polyphemus type by both folklorists and classicists: see Conrad 2002; Hansen 2002a, 291.
57 Grimm 1857, 23.
58 *Zug*, plur. *Züge* "trait" is a word that he uses (e.g., 19–20).
59 Hansen 2002a, 8; Hansen 1997a.

Johann Georg von Hahn (1811–1869) published his index of Greek and Albanian folktales in 1864. He refers in his introduction to the Grimm brothers and their followers, who, he said, had shown that "in these unimposing stories there is preserved a mass of traits that accord with the so-called myths of the Hellenic and Germanic sagas (*Sagkreise*) and on the other hand that the same folktales are told among the most different peoples."[60] Von Hahn refers to "formulas" (*Formel*, plur. *Formeln*) and under each heading gives a list of its narrative components, usually two or three in number, for which he has no name (the gap that "motif" would later fill), and then a list of places in the several regional and national collections that were already available. By the end of the nineteenth century, Russia and practically every European country had its folktale index. The Finn Antti Aarne (1867–1925) published in 1910 his *Verzeichnis der Märchentypen*, which proved to be a turning point.[61] Aarne combined a system of classification by kind with a numbered typology, in this way including a large number of the international folktales known at the time.[62] Aarne's index was revised by the American folklorist Stith Thompson in 1928, with a second edition in 1961 (AT).[63] This index was in turn revised by Hans-Jörg Uther in 2004 (ATU). Thompson published in 1955–1958 his six-volume motif index (*Mot*). The type index and the motif index remain the basic tools of typology and comparative typological studies, even if the field of folklore studies has turned to investigation of performance and the situations of tale-telling.[64]

Types and motifs have come into classical scholarship on Greek myth in two ways. One is the definition of types within the corpus of Greek myths, even if they are not called types (see ch. 9.1). The other is the use of a type as already established in AT or ATU to identify a Greek myth as an example of that type and to study it as such. Hansen's *Ariadne's Thread* discusses a hundred correspondences between stories found in Greek and Roman literature, defining six kinds of correspondence, and compares "the ancient stories with the larger tradition with

---

60 von Hahn 1864, 1. For von Hahn's place in the history of type indexes: Uther 2010a, cols. 1073–74; also Uther 2010b, cols. 1084–85.
61 Aarne 1910.
62 Rausmaa 1977, col. 2; Voigt 1977, cols. 565–66; Edmunds 2016a, 20.
63 For the history of AT and the nature of Thompson's revisions: Hansen 2002a, 20–22.
64 A distinction should be made between simple assertions of a preference, with presentation of one's results, and arguments for one approach or the other. Edmunds 2016a: ch. 1 contains arguments. A striking case of the mere assertion of the emic is discussed. Ch. 9.3 discusses Dundes' revelation of the etic nature of AT and *Mot* and his supposed return to the emic. For the turn in folklore studies and for the earlier history of performance studies: Braid 2002, cols. 730, 732–34.

regard to features such as structure, content, and genre."[65] Study of a particular correspondence may show, in a Greek myth, how it has been adapted so that it becomes specifically Greek. (Genre variance was referred to earlier in this section.) Because this approach is not widely known or if known not understood I add some further points. First, the purpose of comparison is not to ascertain origins.[66] Second, comparison is not between a particular folktale text and a Greek myth but between a folktale type and a Greek myth (with Hansen's qualifications as indicated above). Types are defined by motifs and not every motif in the type is in each folktale of that type. A Greek myth compared with a certain type may lack a certain motif belonging to that type, just as the body of folktales on which the type is based will not always have exactly the same motifs. Finally, whatever the theoretical uncertainties concerning the concepts of type and motif and whatever the frustrations of ATU and *Mot*, folklorists, and classicists who wish to do comparative work in this field, have the great advantage of large, widely shared reference works, which were methodologically self-conscious in their preparation.[67]

Folktales have also come into the study of early Greek art, in particular of the relation of this art to Homer. Robert Cook argued that those who found allusions to epic in Greek art down to 530 B.C.E. were mistaken. He concluded a survey of these supposed allusions by saying: "Greek artists did not regularly or often make deliberate use of epic poetry for their subjects, but preferred folk tales <sic> that they knew, probably from childhood."[68] He did not discuss any folktale. Jonathan Burgess made a detailed survey of scholarship after Cook on the question of Iliadic images in art, for the most part siding with Cook's thesis, but observing that interpretation of the art depends on a scholar's approach to the Homeric question.[69] His own is neoanalytic. He takes a somewhat different approach in his discussion of the archaic vase paintings that show Odysseus and Polyphemus. He makes what he calls a "triangular" comparison of the folktale, the Homeric version, and the representations of the Cyclops episode in the vase paintings.[70] He

---

[65] Hansen 2002a, 25. For theoretical uncertainties and for what I am calling methodological self-consciousness: Edmunds 2016a, ch. 1§§1–10.
[66] Cf. López-Ruiz 2014, 160, who makes this point concerning the comparison of Greek and Near Eastern myth.
[67] For the frustrations: Hansen 2002a, 20, 23; Edmunds 2016a, 9.
[68] Cook 1983, 6.
[69] Burgess 2001, 53–61.
[70] Burgess 2001, 94–114.

reaches what he calls "mixed results."⁷¹ The results for an Odyssean source, however, are negative.⁷²

8.4 Conclusion

Each of the three kinds of comparison that have been discussed has some degree of currency in the field of classics. Allen spoke pessimistically of the state of Indo-European comparative mythology. It is, he said,

> at present a somewhat marginal endeavour within academe, enjoying little institutional support. Its new recruits are mostly individuals trained and employed in some other field, often Classics, who sense the excitement of comparativism and accept the risks.[73]

He eloquently describes the risks. What he says is true or truer of folktale comparativism.

The description of the study of Near Eastern by Livingstone and Haskamp is pessimistic in another way:

> The study of ancient Near Eastern mythology reflects the relative youth of Assyriology and the related disciplines. A start has been made but there is still much work to do both in the task of recovering the actual mythology and in its interpretation.[74]

In any case, comparison of Greek with Near Eastern myth seems to have proceeded at the same pace, especially if Anatolia is included. And yet those classicists who have learned one or more of the relevant languages are few.

The three great theories of myth discussed in the preceding chapter were all comparative, even including the psychoanalytic, because the Oedipus myth served Freud as a probative comparison with the Oedipus Complex. Whether the newer comparativisms discussed in this chapter will ever come to have the status of the older ones remains to be seen. The outcome will not, unfortunately, depend on the merits of the particular cases, of which this chapter has attempted to give a sense, but on academic-institutional priorities, which will themselves depend upon forces coming from outside academe.

---

71 Burgess 2001, 110. The results are, however, clearly articulated and important.
72 Burgess 2001, 111.
73 Allen 2011, 342.
74 Livingstone/Haskamp 2011, 381.

9 Typology, Morphology and Segmentation

Scholars sometimes discuss classes of myths, such as myths of metamorphosis or all the myths attributed to a certain god or hero, such as Dionysus or Theseus, or some aspect of myths, such as onomastics (cf. Preface). Scholars also, for various purposes, divide the corpus of Greek myths into large classes, as in introductions and handbooks, such as accounts of the origin of the world as it now is, adventures of the gods and deeds of the heroes. Other, smaller classes are sometimes defined, such as myths concerning the same god in which the settings and other characters differ but the story is the same, or myths attaching to different heroes who do or suffer the same things. Examples are the myths of Dionysus' arrival in particular places, human resistance to him and ultimate acceptance and the often-discussed myth of the hero's life.[1]

The definition of these smaller classes depends on the segmentation of each of the relevant myths into its smallest narrative units and the demonstration of a shared story-pattern consisting of these units. The field of Classics has standard terms for neither the units nor the story pattern.[2] In folktale studies the first are called motifs and the second types (9.1 below; cf. ch. 8.3). Morphology was introduced into the study of folktales in reaction to typology and has to some extent influenced the study of Greek myth (9.2). Both typology and morphology are to be distinguished from the informal classification that has been going on from the time when the mythographers began to make collections organized by subject-matter (ch. 3.2) and also from the large classes mentioned above that sometimes organize modern surveys of Greek myth.

The word "structure" is sometimes used of the story patterns revealed in classification. "Structure" is so used by Burkert in an analysis of a set of Greek myths that proceeds from Proppian "functions" (9.2 below). "Narratology" is a separate concept or set of concepts and is not discussed in this chapter.[3] So-called "structural narratology" comes in briefly, however, apropos of Propp's morphology, with which it shares a conceptual ancestor, and parenthetically, and again briefly, because of its influence in contemporary Homeric studies. The now

---

1 Dionysus: as in Otto 1933.
2 Cf. Delattre 2005, 27: "La délimitation des variations entre les versions permet corrélativement de définir les invariations, que l'on pourra appeler *mythèmes, cellules, thèmes, stéréotypes*, suivant le courant d'analyse auquel on se rattache."
3 For an overview of narratology: Ryan/van Alphen 1993. But the authors incorrectly say that Propp pioneered the study of plot, whereas, distinguishing between plot and fabula or story, Propp concentrated on the latter.

widely accepted distinction between narrator-speech and character-speech in Homer is owing to a particular branch of narratology.[4] This distinction affects interpretation of the telling of myths by characters in Homer.

9.1 Typology

To return briefly to study of the folktale, classification was the beginning of the field (see ch. 8.3) and continued for a long time as its main business. The result was the successive editions of *The Types of the Folktale* and also many specialized type-indexes, so many that indices of indices became necessary.[5] The use of "type" for the result of classification and the use of "motif" for the smallest narrative units became standard. The difficulties, theoretical and practical, of the motif and type indexes, are well known to folklorists; the advantages outweigh the difficulties (ch. 8.3 sub fin.).

In his definition of motif Thompson distinguished three classes: the actors in a tale; certain items in the background of the action—magic objects, unusual customs, strange beliefs and the like; single incidents. The last of these comprises, he said, the great majority of motifs. "It is this last class that can have an independent existence and that may therefore serve as a true tale-type. By far the largest number of traditional types consist of these single motifs."[6] Thompson defined the type as "a traditional tale that has an independent existence. It may be told as a complete narrative and does not depend for its existence on any other tale. It may indeed happen to be told with another tale, but the fact that it may appear alone attests to its independence. It may consist of only one motif or of many."[7] From the time of von Hahn's index (ch. 8.3), folktale types were assigned a name and a number.

In scholarship on Greek myth, classification, corresponding to typology in folklore studies, usually goes on without reference to any concept or definition of type, relying on self-evident similarities among a set of myths.[8] Burkert's discovery of "the girl's tragedy", with its terminological and conceptual peculiarities, is an example (ch. 7.3; 9.3 below). Burkert has the merit, however, of having given

---

4 On this distinction see Edmunds 2014a, 5–8.
5 *The Types of the Folktale*: AT; in its latest edition: ATU. For the antecedents of history of this type-index and Voigt 1977, cols. 565–66. Indices of indices: Azzolina 1987; Uther 1996.
6 Thompson 1946, 415. The definition is quoted in full by Edmunds 2016a, 22–23.
7 Thompson 1977 [1946], 416.
8 Cf. Hansen 1997b.

his discovery the name just quoted. Most such discoveries in the field of Classics go unnamed and thus without a convenient means of reference.

9.2 Morphology

Morphology can be distinguished from folktale typology and indeed Vladimir Propp's *The Morphology of the Folktale* (*Morfologija skazki*) was a reaction to what he saw as the deficiencies of the typological classification of folktales in the work of Aarne (his type-index of 1910) and others folklorists.[9] He challenged Aarne's method of segmentation by motif and he held that the division of tales into types was fundamentally impossible. He replaced the motif, the basic unit of segmentation in Aarne's index, with what he called the "function", that is, with action as independent of character and modality. (Propp's morphology as a prompt for Burkert was discussed in ch. 7.3.) He showed that his "fairy-tales" could all be described as having the same sequence of thirty-one functions or some subset thereof. This pattern is the "morphology" of his title, a metaphor that he took from botany.[10] For example, the first seven functions are:

1. Absentation: A member of a family absents himself.
2. Interdiction: An interdiction is addressed to the hero.
3. Violation: The interdiction is violated.
4. Reconnaissance: The villain makes an attempt at reconnaissance.
5. Delivery: The villain receives information receives information about his victim.
6. Trickery: Villain attempts to deceive his victim in order to take possession of him or of his belongings.
7. Complicity: The victim submits to deception and thereby helps his enemy.[11]

Because of the title *Morphology of the Folktale* (1927) Propp is thought to have invented the kind of classification of folktales called morphology. He emerged,

---

[9] On the word *skazki* in the title see Propp 1968 [1928], ix (preface to the second ed. by Louis A. Wagner). For a short history of type-indexes, beginning in the second half of the nineteenth century: Uther 2010, cols. 1073–74; also Voigt 1977, cols. 565–66.
[10] Propp 1968 [1928], xxv (first sentence of his foreword). Cf. "[A]t a time when minerals, plants, and animals are described and classified precisely according to their structure, at a time when a whole range of literary genres…have been described, the tale continues to be studied without such a description" (13).
[11] Propp 1968 [1928], 25–30.

however, from the so-called "morphological schools" of the 1920s and 1930s.[12] His intellectual affiliations were with the Russian Formalists and the third and final edition of the work under discussion appeared in the Formalist series *Voprosy poétiki* (*Questions of Poetics*).[13] The word "structuralism" is retrojected onto Propp, as onto the linguistics of Saussure (ch. 7.3).[14] Propp worked on a hundred folktales in A.N. Afanás'ev's collection of Russian folktales.[15] He called them, in the English translation, "fairy-tales." Propp's achieved a kind of classification that was seen to clarify the material on which it was based and that could be applied by other folklorists to other material.[16] Propp did not underestimate his achievement. He quoted Viktor Shklovsky: "The tale is ... laid out according to laws still unknown." Then he said: "This law has now been determined."[17]

Propp's kind of segmentation has remained useful in the field of classics. His functions were a prompt to Burkert (9.3 below). Other scholars have used them in analyzing Greek myths.[18] The teaching of Greek myth to undergraduates may include the assignment of using the functions for the analysis of a myth.[19]

9.2.1 After Propp

Of the heirs of Propp, it was not Lévi-Strauss (who, as observed in ch. 7, would not have wished to be seen as an heir) but Claude Bremond (1929–) and Algirdas

---

[12] Voigt 1977, cols. 566–67.
[13] Voigt 1999, col. 922.
[14] Csapo 2005, 189–99 discusses Propp under the heading "Syntagmatic Structuralism." For the relation of Propp to structuralism: Dammann 2007, cols. 1407–1408.
[15] The numeration of the tales in Propp 1968 [1928] has been made to correspond to the numeration in the fifth and sixth edition of Afanas'ev's edition: Propp 1968 [1928], ix (in preface by Louis A. Wagner).
[16] For the slowly unfolding fortune of this book outside Russia: Voigt 2002, cols. 1435–36.
[17] Propp 1968 [1928], 116 n. 6. Propp cites only the name of Shklovsky, not a work, which was his *O teorii prozy* (1925). For a bibliography of the series of Shklovsky's works on prose beginning in 1919 see Kolesnikoff 1993a, 472. This bibliography omits the translation of *O teorii prozy* (Shklovsky 1990).
[18] E.g., Davies, sometimes with explicit reference to Propp: Davies 2002; Davies 2003a; Davies 2003b; Davies 2004; Davies 2005; Davies 2009; Davies 2011a; Davies 2011b; Ruiz-Montero/Sánchez Alacid 2005.
[19] Pedagogy: e.g., Peter T. Struck's course on Greek myth at the University of Pennsylvania (http://www.classics.upenn.edu/myth/php/info/index.php?page=propp).

Julien Greimas (1917–92) (through collaborators and students) who would influence the study of folktales and myths.[20] Bremond, continuing in Propp's direction, abstracted further to a logical model of narrative. He reduced Propp's functions to three and constructed a model of the logical possibilities of narrative development that flowed from the three functions.[21] Greimas likewise started from Propp, to whom he refers again and again in his definition of the "canonical narrative schema."[22] Greimas held that he had taken a decisive step beyond Propp in recognizing the polemical structure underlying Propp's morphology. "The folktale is not only the story of the hero/ine and his/her quest, it is in a more or less hidden way the story of the villain as well. Two narrative trajectories, of the subject and of the anti- subject, unfold in two opposite directions, characterized however by the fact that both subjects seek one and the same object of value. Thus an elementary narrative schema becomes apparent, grounded upon a polemical structure."[23] As the preceding quotation implies, the particular identities of the hero and the heroine are of no interest to the theory.

Greimas abstracted from these identities to the "actant", "which can be thought of as the one who accomplishes or undergoes an act, independently of all other determinations."[24] He established a general "narrative schema", which he defined with constant reference to the "Proppian schema."[25] In the study of Greek myth, one of the two main exponents of Greimasian analysis, and the better known, has been Claude Calame. He uses the term "semionarrative" to refer to the two main aspects of this analysis, the syntax of the narrative and its "semantics" (what the narrative is saying as distinguished from what it is telling).[26] Calame adds performance, which he refers to as the "pragmatic" dimension, without reference to which syntactic and semantic analysis cannot go on.[27]

---

[20] Greek myth: Calame 1985; Calame 1986; Calame 1990; Calame 2014 (revision of Calame 1990); Pellizer 1984; Pellizer 1987 (Transl. of 1984); 1988.
[21] Bremond 1964; Bremond 1966; Bremond 1973. For a sketch of Bremond's relation to Propp see Dammann 2007, cols. 1409–10.
[22] Greimas and Cortès 1982 [1979], 203–6 (s.v. "narrative schema").
[23] Greimas and Cortès 1982 [1979], 205 (6).
[24] Greimas and Cortès 1982 [1979], 5 (s.v. "actant").
[25] Greimas and Cortès 1982 [1979], 203 (s.v. "narrative schema").
[26] Greimas and Cortès 1982 [1979], 272–74 (s.v. "semantics"). They use "semantico-syntactic" (274) but also "semio-narrative" (210). Cf. Edmunds 2014c, 280 for Calame's relation to Greimas in this matter.
[27] Calame 2014, 285–87, in a short methodological statement, departing somewhat from Greimas' definition of "pragmatic(s)" (see Greimas and Cortès 1982 [1979], 240–41 s.v.), states: "The values that a text sets into play, and that a semionarrative analysis attempts to track down, are

Calame takes the view, repeated many times in his writings, that "'myth' collapses into its poetics" in the ritualized circumstances in which poems are performed.[28]

The other exponent was Ezio Pellizer (1943–2018), whose books would probably have been better known if they had been translated into English.[29] In an article on the myth of the Labdacids, Pellizer proposes a Greimasian interpretation and then makes some observations on the heterogeneity of the sources, of which, he says, poetry is only one.

> One will attempt to bring together all the variations at our disposal and to account for all the different versions of the story under examination, in the attempt to reconstruct, if it exists, the logic that governs its manifestations and to put in evidence the deep structures that organize its articulation.[30]

Pellizer's avowal concerning all the variations anticipates a statement that Albert Henrichs was to make a year later. Referring to the dominant schools of myth studies (he names Burkert, Vernant and "narratologists", followers of Propp) and goes on to say that the

> practitioners do not always seem to realize that it is impossible to determine the overall structure of a particular myth, let alone its presumed meaning, without acquiring first as complete and clear an understanding of its transmission in antiquity as possible.[31]

Henrichs calls in particular for the use of mythographical sources. "[S]heer ignorance of the whole range of ancient mythography has never been more rampant than it is today."[32] He gives the example of Callisto. "The complex transmission of the Kallisto myth in the catasterismographic tradition must be the starting point for any attempt to reconstruct the pre-Hellenistic versions of the myth and

---

pertinent only in relation to the interpretive community to which the narrative was originally and practically addressed."

28 Calame 2011b, 521.

29 Pellizer 1982; Pellizer 1991.

30 Pellizer 1986, 549: "[S]i cercherà...di integrare tutte le varianti a nostra disposizione, e di render conto di tutte le diverse versioni del racconto in esame, nel tentativo di ricostruire—se mai esiste—la logica che presiede alle sue manifestazioni, e di mettere in evidenza quale sono le strutture profonde che ne organizzano l'articolazione."

31 Henrichs 1987, 255. With Henrichs' "narratologists" (his quotation marks) compare Pellizer's "analisi narratologica" apropos of the method of Greimas (Pellizer 1986, 549). For the various senses of "narratology": Ryan/van Alphen 1993. For a particular sense of "structural narratology" see 9.4 below in the text.

32 Henrichs 1987, 258.

to interpret their meaning."³³ He presents a chart of the "recurrent elements of the myth which constitute its story pattern."³⁴

Pellizer, however, one of those neglectful "narratologists", saw the need for mythographical research. (Neither Henrichs nor Pellizer could have anticipated the coming "mythographical turn" in the study of Greek myth that is discussed in my ch. 4). In Pellizer's terms, the Greimasian impulse meant the discovery, in a particular myth, of traits that could be discerned in a series of other myths as "homologous elements" reflecting a "common narrative model."³⁵ In a chapter called "Black Hunters and Virgin Bears" ("Cacciatori neri e vergini orse") he begins with Teiresias and analyzes eleven more myths, which are all shown to conform to a certain model.³⁶ The last of these is the myth of Callisto.³⁷ Having shown its affinities with the other myths, he concludes that again there is a close connection between the myth and rituals of initiation that seem to express analogous preoccupations. "It is a matter ultimately of establishing a normative model for the comportment to which young men and women ought to conform in order to complete in 'normal' fashion the passage from their starting condition to their successive integration within organized society."³⁸ I return to Pellizer in the following section.

9.3 Segmentation

Whereas the ancient mythographer tended to present a hypostasis of all the versions he knew, the modern scholar goes in the opposite direction and sets out all the known variants of a myth, in order then to make sense of them as he or she will.³⁹ In order to set out the variants, he or she has to break them down into their smallest narrative units.⁴⁰ The examples of Henrichs, Calame and Pellizer have been discussed. Segmentation may have a theoretical model, as in the case of the

---

33 Henrichs 1987, 260.
34 Henrichs 1987, 258.
35 Pellizer 1982, 12.
36 "Black Hunters": cf. Vidal-Naquet 1981, for obvious reasons not cited by Pellizer 1982 but he does cite Vidal-Naquet's preliminary article on the Black Hunter and its Italian translation (Pellizer 1982, 170).
37 Pellizer 1982, 34–35.
38 Pellizer 1982, 36–37. Before Pellizer there was the article by Vidal-Naquet cited in n. 36 above; also the copious material in Brelich 1969.
39 Fowler 2017a.
40 Fowler 2017a, 158–59; Fowler 2017b, 24.

two Greimasians just named, or it may assume that the "recurrent elements", to use Henrich's term, are self-evident.[41] If so, the question, "comment segmenter un texte", does not have to be raised.[42] The assumption of self-evidence lies behind Dowden's demonstration of what he called the "common structure" of a set of myths: an animal is killed; Artemis is angry; an oracle prescribes a remedy; a girl is to be sacrificed by her father; but she is not sacrificed and an animal is substituted; the prospect of marriage. (He proceeds to interpret the set of myths as an expression of initiation ceremony.)[43] He does not have any term for the elements just listed and his use of "structure" does not seem to have any theoretical affiliation.

Richard Buxton not only does not use but explicitly rejects the various terms that others have used. He refers to what he calls "cross-contextual recurrences" and asks how they are to be described. His answer: "The terms used—theme, pattern, motif, structure, narrative programme, programme of action, mytheme (to confine oneself to English)—carry bulky methodological luggage deriving from earlier scholarship." He proceeds to a critique of these terms. The starting-point of his critique is the proposition that "[g]iving a name to a recurrence involves making a judgement about what is significant." As Buxton's discussion shows, he takes significance to attach to recurring elements, to what they have in common. For example, in the myth of Iphigenia at Aulis the offense of Agamemnon against Artemis is different in two different versions. "[I]n both cases", Buxton says, "Agamemnon infringes on the goddess's territory."[44] But none of the schools of thought rejected by Buxton would look for significance at the level of the smallest definable component of the narrative. The narrative that they define is what is significant. Even in the structuralism of Lévi-Strauss the smallest components (his "mythemes" and also his larger "gross constitutent units", which are groups of mythemes) do not have meaning in themselves but only when the groups into which they fall are shown to stand in a certain algebraic relation to each other (for Lévi-Strauss cf. ch. 7.3).

The following discussion returns to Burkert's "the girl's tragedy" (cf. ch. 7.3) in order to compare his segmentation of a group of myth, his terminology and one of his conclusions with three other groups, as defined by other scholars, which intersect with the stories of two of the girls in Burkert's group. He proposed to

---

[41] Henrichs 1987, 258.
[42] This phrase comes from the title of Calame 1985.
[43] Dowden 2011.
[44] Buxton 1994, 72–74. At this point the myth incorporates the folktale figure called "The Boastful Deerslayer" (AT/ATU 830A), for which see Hansen 2002a, 54–56.

show "how a set of apparently unrelated myths can be analyzed as covering the same basic structure." They "adapt themselves neatly to a sequence of five 'functions,'...which I would call 'the girl's tragedy'", he said, taking "functions" from Propp's *The Morphology of the Folktale*.[45] (His use of quotation marks, by which he distances himself from the concept should be noted. For quotation marks in his definition of myth, see Introduction.)

The functions are:
1. leaving home: the girl is separated from childhood and family life
2. the idyl of seclusion...
3. rape...
4. tribulation: the girl is severely punished and threatened with death by parents or relatives...
5. rescue: the mother, having given birth to a boy, is saved from death and grief...

These are summarized as a "fixed sequence" of "departure, seclusion, rape, tribulation, and rescue as a prelude to the emergence of the hero."[46] (He has introduced these stories as stories about the mothers of heroes.)

Although he does not use the word "type" in this context, it appears in a general reflection on myth published several years after the Sather lectures, in which he had defined "the girl's tragedy":

> There are two main dimensions of myth...: there is a narrative structure that can be analysed as a syntagmatic chain of 'motifemes', and there is some reference, which often may be secondary and tentative, to phenomena of common reality...The narrative structures are based on a very few general human or even pre-human programmes of action, and thus are quite easily understood and encoded in memory...This is the fascination of a tale to which we are all sensitive. One favourite tale type is the 'quest'—the subject of Vladimir Propp's *Morphology of the Folktale*.[47]

The passage from which these sentences are taken is Burkert's most theoretical statement on Greek myth and conforms to Kant's definition of theory (ch. 4.3). His "syntagmatic chain" is a folkloristic rule having the generality for which Kant called and it has been "abstracted from a multitude of conditions." Burkert as usual wished to distance himself from the terminology of folklore (cf. on Burkert in the Introduction) but he did not offer his own. The prior condition of myth is

---

45 Burkert 1979, 6–7.
46 Burkert 1979, 7.
47 Burkert 1987, 11.

its maintenance in human memory, the possibility of which Burkert explains by adding the description "general human or even pre-human programmes of action" to narrative structure.

To continue with "the girl's tragedy", having defined the "structure", Burkert observed that one function (4), the punishment of the girl after her rape by a god and impregnation, was chronologically out of place in the cases of Io and Callisto. (The punishment is metamorphosis into an animal, one of them into a cow and the other into a bear.) His terminology calls for attention. He says: "We must... state that the metamorphosis and sexual union are not in a fixed motifeme sequence. In fact metamorphosis is not a 'motifeme' in this series or elsewhere, let alone an independent tale type, but a widely applicable motif to mark a change of roles".[48] What were "functions" are now referred to as not in a "motifeme sequence" and metamorphosis is said not be a "motifeme" (in distancing quotation marks) but a motif. The question arises of the difference, in Burkert's mind, between a motifeme and a motif and in the first place of what a motifeme is.[49] Earlier in the chapter from which I have just quoted he has observed that Alan Dundes prefers to call functions "motifemes" and proceeds to explain Propp's functions. Dundes is then forgotten except for the observation that he has applied Propp's method to the study of North American Indian folktales.[50] To understand motifeme, one has to go back to the works of Dundes that Burkert cites and in particular to an article that he does not cite.[51]

In this article Dundes observed that all the nineteenth- and twentieth schools of myth were comparative but deficient in method. He held that in folktale studies the motif-index (*Mot*) and the Aarne-Thompson tale-type index (now ATU), also based on comparison, failed to produce genuinely comparable units. Referring to Kenneth Pike's distinction between the etic and the emic, which was discussed in my Introduction, he argued that both the tale type and the motif were etic constructs. He found in the Proppian "function", which was located in a particular place in the sequence of the narration, the emic unit that he desiderated. He translated "function" into Pike's "motifeme." (As will be seen, it is the "motifeme" in this sense that affects Burkert's account of "the girl's tragedy.") This

---

[48] Burkert 1979, 7. For motifeme (in quotation marks): Burkert 1987, 11.
[49] See Conrad 1999.
[50] Burkert 1979, 5–6.
[51] Dundes 1964; Dundes 1976, which has been reprinted with a postscript as Dundes 2007d. The one not cited by Burkert: Dundes 1962, which has been reprinted with an appendix as Dundes 2007b.

word is a combination of "motif" and "emic."[52] Dundes coined the term "allomotif", by analogy with "allomorph", for "those motifs which occur in any given motifemic context", in other words, more than one motif can fill the same slot in a story.[53] As its postscript makes all the clearer, the gravamen of the article on which I am commenting is a critique of the motif-index and the type index. Burkert, then, appears to be relying on Dundes' distinction between motif and motifeme and in particular on Dundes' notion of the motifeme as having a fixed place in a narrative sequence.

One can observe parenthetically that Dundes' rejection of types and motifs (i.e., as in AT and *Mot*) as etic constructs and his preference for Propp's morphology as emic somewhat misconstrues Propp's own relation to the Aarne-Thomson index. Despite Propp's misgivings concerning this index, he accepted from it a certain sequence of tales, which he stipulated a unit, and he formulated his law on the basis of these tales. In terms of Dundes' binarism, the etic classification is presupposed in Propp's emic analysis. In fact, Propp did not reject Aarne altogether but acknowledged the importance of his index "as a *practical reference.*"[54] Further, in 1958 he published an edition of A.N. Afanas'ev's Russian folktales, to which he added a type index following that of Aarne (the one later revised by Thompson, i.e., AT).[55]

To return to Burkert's "motif", he applied this term to Callisto and to Io apropos of the fourth of his sequence of "motifemes" (the relevant sentences were quoted above). The following discussion concentrates on the example of Callisto. Her myth was the example chosen by Henrichs to illustrate the importance of mythographical research as preparatory to interpretation. (Burkert was named as one of those who tended to omit this step.) Henrichs' survey of the sources for the Callisto myth resulted in this summary:

> A virgin nymph and fellow huntress of Artemis, Kallisto, was seduced by Zeus. While pregnant she was transformed into a bear. After she had given birth to Arkas, she was shot to death by Artemis and placed among the stars by Zeus.[56]

In order to compare this story with Burkert's "girl's tragedy" as a whole, I list the five "functions" or "motifemes" of which it consists in his analysis, with his numbering:

---

[52] Pike 1967, 150.
[53] Dundes 2007b, 96. Cf. Dundes 2007c.
[54] Propp 1968 [1928], 11 (his emphasis).
[55] Voigt 2002, col. 1437 and n. 16.
[56] Henrichs 1987, 258.

1. leaving home: the girl is separated from childhood and family life;
2. the idyl of seclusion…;
3. rape…;
4. tribulation: the girl is severely punished and threatened with death by parents or relatives…;
5. rescue: the mother, having given birth to a boy, is saved from death and grief…[57]

In a summary he refers to it as a "fixed sequence" of "departure, seclusion, rape, tribulation, and rescue as a prelude to the emergence of the hero."[58] Callisto appears in items 2–4 in this list and could as well have appeared in the first item. Callisto must have left her home in Arcadia in order to become a huntress in the mountains (cf. Eratosth. *Cat.* 1 Pàmias = Hes. fr. 163 M-W: ἐν Ἀρκαδίᾳ δὲ κατοικοῦσαν ἑλέσθαι μετὰ τῆς Ἀρτέμιδος τὴν περὶ τὰς θήρας ἀγωγὴν ἐν τοῖς ὄρεσι ποιεῖσθαι). Whereas Burkert regards Callisto as intrusive in the fourth item, this item could just as well be considered the conclusion of her myth, i.e., of a separate myth that one could call "Callisto." If so, then she might appear in some other classification of myths concerning young women and does in fact so appear.

Forbes Irving discusses a "group" of stories of young women "distinguished to some extent by common themes and a common pattern." These are Io, Callisto, Atalanta, Taygete, Hippo, the Proitides, Leto (who becomes a wolf to bear Apollo), and Philyra (who becomes a horse to bear Cheiron). All these heroines have as the central action of their stories (1) some illicit sexual experience, usually the loss of virginity. (2) This is usually followed by a taking to the wilds and transformation (these two are closely linked), (3) birth of a child, and either (4a) a final marriage or (4b) an end of all relations with men or animals (i.e., in death or catasterism, as in the case of Callisto, who becomes Arktos).[59]

The story "Callisto" has all of these "themes", although not in the sequence in which they are set out by Forbes Irving. In his sequence, "Callisto" would consist of (2), (1), (3), and (4). Pellizer also included Callisto in a sub-set of myths illustrating his "common narrative model", referred to earlier, that began with Teiresias. Pellizer gave seven more examples of the "black hunter" class of myths (0–7 in his numeration). He then turned to corresponding female figures and discussed Atalanta (8), Polyphonte (9), Daphne (10), Leucippus (i.e., the girl going

---

[57] Burkert 1979, 7.
[58] Burkert 1979, 7.
[59] Forbes Irving 1990, 63–64. (I have added numbers in order to facilitate comparison with Burkert.)

under this name) (11), and Callisto (12). (He considered Leucippus extraneous to the class but observed some common points.) What this group of stories have in common is the girl's flight from city life, hunting in the wilds, refusal of sexuality, a stream or a spring in which she bathes, and the inevitable attempt of the god who desires her, with outcomes that vary considerably. Once again "Callisto" turns up as one of a set of myths having a common story pattern. Dowden, though with less conviction than Forbes Irving or Pellizer, includes Callisto in a "category" of girls who are "slaughtered or sacrificed" by their fathers. His main examples are Iphigeneia,[60] the myths attaching to the Arkteia (he does not specify),[61] and the deceptive (goat for daughter) sacrifice by Embaros at Mounychia.[62] He adds: "It is possible that there is also an outlier in Arkadia, where the nymph Kallisto…is also turned into a bear and shot, this time maybe by Artemis."[63] Finally, Callisto belongs to the list of Zeus's unions with mortal women and thus to yet another class of stories.[64]

From consideration of "Callisto" by itself (as in Henrichs' summary) one would conclude that this myth happens to coincide with "the girl's tragedy" in its first four "functions" or "motifemes", *including the fourth*, which is the end of the story of Callisto. In other words, "Callisto", despite or because of the inconsistency to which Burkert calls attention, as a whole is included in "the girl's tragedy." Further, the inclusion of "Callisto" in the other classes of myths defined by other scholars shows the fungibility of this myth, and the same point could made of most of the other myths mentioned in that survey, as well as those referred to by Burkert apropos of "the girl's tragedy." As Burkert said in another context: "Myths…are like formulae with variables for which different names may be substituted".[65] Burkert regard Callisto as intrusive probably because, despite the

---

60 Cf. Dowden 1992, 76–77.
61 For a survey of the very complex tradition: Gantz 1993, 725–29. His summary of the two main, apparently distinct strands of narrative: "In the first, Artemis' anger includes (when she does not shoot the girl on the spot) the metamorphosis of Kallisto into a bear after her pregnancy is discovered; subsequently the bear is threatened by an unwitting son, or both are threatened by the Arcadians…and Zeus must intervene to take her/them up to heaven…In the second, Artemis merely expels Kallisto from her company, and Hera enters as jealous wife to accomplish the metamorphosis and then deceive (or perhaps order) Artemis to kill the animal, which she does. In this latter account no catasterism is strictly necessary (although always possible) and the child Arkas is seemingly not involved" (727–28).
62 Cf. Dowden 1992, 73–74, 76.
63 Cf. Dowden 1992, 76 for bear myths and Callisto.
64 For the list: Buxton 2009, 159.
65 Burkert 1985, 120.

statement just quoted, he hypostatized "the girl's tragedy" and regarded it as having fixity (as defined by him) and exclusivity.

Calame, in one part of his critique of "the girl's tragedy", mistakes the starting point for the conclusion. "[T]his type of exercise in structural narratology can only be pulled off at the cost of extreme simplifications that reduce narratives, in their different versions and values, to a learned mythographic compendium." On the contrary, from mythography (and archaic and classical poetry) Burkert elicits a shared pattern, which has to be judged in relation to the sources and Burkert's use of them. Burkert's goal as such escapes this part of Calame's critique. (I have commented on his use of sources with respect to his fourth "function" or "motifeme.") The second part this critique concerns Burkert's "ethological" and evolutionist approach, in which the pattern (Calame does not use this word) that Burkert has discovered is "placed side by side with the ritual format found in rites of passage".[66] Indeed Burkert would ground "the girl's tragedy" as defined by him as grounded in biological reality, whatever the immediate inspiration for the telling of the myth might have been and whatever its point on that occasion (cf. my comments in ch. 7.3).

9.4 Structural narratology

The term "narratology" is said to have been coined by Tzvetan Todorov.[67] "Structural narratology" is now often used, inappropriately, however, when it refers to theorists who would not have called themselves structuralists and to structuralists who in fact opposed narratology.[68] The adjective "structural" reflects a Francocentric view of the matter, in which narratology is subsumed under structuralism.[69] Classical scholarship has made use of more than one of the twentieth-

---

66 Calame 2011b, 510. For ritual he gives a cross-reference to Dowden 2011.
67 Prince 1995, 110, citing Todorov 1969, 10.
68 Jannidis 2004, 7: "die immer noch weitgehend prägende strukturale Narratologie." For a history of the antecedents of narratology, Prince 1995, 112–21, including Todorov 1969 and Barthes 1970.
69 Cf. Ryan and Van Alphen 1993, 110: "The history of narratology can be divided into three periods: pre-structuralist (until 1960); structuralist (1960–80); and poststructuralist (including not only further developments of structuralist ideas such as deconstruction but also the recent development of narratology into an interdisciplinary pursuit)." Also Prince 1995: "As for the theory [narratology], it falls historically into the tradition of French structuralism."

century narratologies.⁷⁰ That of Gérard Genette has been the most successful. Genette adapted the tripartite division of narrative of Tzvetan Todorov (French-Bulgarian), in effect putting himself in the Russian formalist tradition.⁷¹ (With his *Théorie de la littérature* [1966], a translation of important Russian formalist texts, with a preface by Roman Jakobson, Todorov was a representative of this tradition in France.⁷²) In Genette's terms narrative was divided into:

A. story (Fr. *histoire*), narrative content
B. narrative (Fr. *récit*), narrative "discourse"
C. narrating (Fr. *narration*), "narrative situation".⁷³

Genette used more than one term for C. He spoke of "the narrative situation or its instance", borrowing Benveniste's term and citing an article of Benveniste, well-known to classicists who study deixis, on the nature of pronouns.⁷⁴ (Benveniste had used the expression "instance of discourse.") Genette also repeatedly used another of Benveniste's terms, *énonciation*, to refer to the actualization of the narrative.⁷⁵ This last term causes difficulties in the English translations "enunciation" and "utterance." The normal meaning of the first of these words is the articulating of a sound and of the second the process, as distinguished from the result, of speaking. Compare the more perspicuous pairs in Spanish (*enunciación* and *enunciado*), Italian (*enunciazione* and *enunciato*), and German (*das Aussagen* and *das Ausgesagte*). The distinction between A. and B. comes from Russian Formalism.

Genette's success in the field of Classical studies is owing in large part to Irene de Jong.⁷⁶ She was a student of Mieke Bal, and she refers to Bal and Genette in the same breath in her *Narratological Commentary on the Odyssey*: "the meth-

---

70 Lowe 2000, a study of the classical plot as a narrative practice antedating Aristotle and persisting up to the present, takes a narratological approach, adopting the scheme of Bal 1997 (he cites the ed. of 1985). On Bal see below in the text.
71 Todorov 1966b, discussed by Genette 1980 [1972], 29–30 = 1972.3, 74.
72 Todorov 1966a.
73 There is a somewhat fuller discussion of these terms in Edmunds 2008, 76–77 apropos of the history of the concept of deixis.
74 Genette 1980 [1972], 31 and n. 10.
75 Benveniste distinguished between *énonciation* ("enunciation") and *énoncé* ("utterance"): Benveniste 1970, 12. The first of these terms referred to the individual act of language use. "L'énonciation est cette mise en fonctionnement de la langue par un acte individuel d'utilisation." The second referred to the product of this act.
76 See Latacz 2000, 150(16) on de Jong.

odological pillars on which this commentary rests include studies by narratologists like Genette and Bal."⁷⁷ Bal, a pluridisciplinary scholar who was interested in narratology earlier in her career, wrote *Narratology: Introduction to the Theory of Narrative*.⁷⁸ She disappears, however, from the chapter on keywords for Homeric poetics ("Homerische Poetik in Stichwörtern") that de Jong and René Nünlist contributed to the prolegomena volume of the new Basel commentary on the *Iliad*.⁷⁹ This chapter amounts to the outline of a Homeric narratology. Genette is not the authors' only source but he is cited thirteen times or roughly once per page.

The most successful of Genette's narratological concepts in classical studies is focalization, with its division into primary (the narrator is the focalizer) and secondary (the character is the focalizer).⁸⁰ The secondary is further divided into someone presented indirectly by the narrator in "embedded focalization" (Bal's term) and someone presented directly in his or her speeches.⁸¹ "Embedded focalization means that the narrative 'embeds' in the narrator-text a character's focalization, that is, his perceptions, thoughts, feelings, or words (indirect speech)."⁸² This concept has an obvious counterpart in the concept of free indirect style or free indirect speech.⁸³

To return finally to the study of Greek myth, a particular importance of Genette's structural narratology has been the application of his distinction between narrator-speech and character-speech. This distinction has been followed in the Basel Commentary on the *Iliad*.⁸⁴ Story-tellers in the *Iliad* and in the *Odyssey* are, on the one hand, like all others, with a point to make that bears on the immediate context (cf. ch. 2.1), and, on the other, to be understood in relation to the narrative (cf. ch. 2.3 on the speech of Agamemnon in *Il*. 19.78–137).

---

77 de Jong 2001a, vii; likewise de Jong 2014, 6.
78 Bal 1997.
79 Nünlist and de Jong 2000, 159–71.
80 Bal 1997 made a critique and revision of Genette's focalization. See Niederhoff 2011, §3 for a survey of critiques of Bal's critique.
81 Nünlist and de Jong 2000, 163 ("Fokalisator"); 169 ("Sekundare Fokalisation"). Cf. de Jong 2001b, 71: "events are not presented by a narrator, but mirrored in the consciousness of a character (a reflector), who is not aware that she is the mediator of the story."
82 de Jong 1997, 296.
83 The origin of these expressions (or of Fr. *discours indirect libre*, which is probably earlier and may have arisen from the controversy over *Madame Bovary*) has been difficult to determine. "Free indirect speech" occurs in the title of Pascal 1977.
84 See in Nünlist and de Jong 2000 lemmata for "Argument-Funktion" (with many cross-references), "Paradeigma", "Erzähler", "Erzählung", "Figuren-Sprache", etc.

9.5 Conclusion

Classics, like folktale studies, is often in the business of typology but does not use this term or any other standard term. Each scholar uses his own. Another approach to folktales has had a limited influence on the study of Greek myth. Vladimir Propp reduced a large set of folktales to a common pattern, consisting of "functions." This pattern he called their "morphology." As in examples discussed above, his functions and morphology have been used by some classical scholars. The principal heir of Propp, Algirdas Julien Greimas, established a still more abstract "narrative schema." His main living exponent is Claude Calame. The majority of those who study Greek myth and for one reason or another wish to determine a common pattern in a particular set of myths do not rely on Propp's morphology or Greimas' "narrative scheme" as their starting-point but define their own patterns. Their procedure is necessarily the segmentation of the myths in question. Classical scholarship lacks, perhaps even avoids, standard terms for the segments, the segmentation, and the results.

10 Conclusion

The question of the sources of Greek myth, one of the two questions posed in the introduction to this book, has usually depended on the verbal sources that are available to us now and these are above all the poets. Already in Plato's *Republic* poetry is the prime source of harmful myths, specifically the myths of Homer, that are disallowed in the polis that Socrates and his interlocutors are founding (*Rep.* 379a–353c).[1] Socrates refers to "an old dispute between poetry and philosophy" (παλαιά ... διαφορὰ φιλοσοφίᾳ τε καὶ ποιητικῇ, *Rep.* 607b5), a dispute between two kinds of first-order thinking (cf. App. §2 for the distinction between first- and second-order thinking). Even if much else remained we would still probably, and not unreasonably, prefer poetry as a source for myth to the others that we have (except for genealogical poetry: cf. ch. 3.7).

My first three chapters attempted to put this preference in a broader perspective including visual media and myth as oral story-telling. In daily life someone tells a story chosen to appeal to a certain taste or for its application to present circumstances. Enough remains for us to see that variation is going to be the result of the re-telling of a myth. It was going on also in poetry, despite its relative fixity, beginning with epic hexameter, and despite the implication of Herodotus' famous statement to the effect that Hesiod and Homer established a canon for the Greeks.[2] When Hesiod's Muses say that they know how to utter both the true and the false (ἴδμεν ψεύδεα πολλὰ λέγειν ἐτύμοισιν ὁμοῖα, / ἴδμεν δ' εὖτ' ἐθέλωμεν ἀληθέα γηρύσασθαι, *Theog.* 27–28), they may be referring to different versions of the same myth.[3] "In a world of multiform oral traditions, conflicts between rival versions were bound to occur. But in these early, formative periods they were aired not by accusations that a singer had interpolated extraneous material of doubtful authorship but branding him a liar who for the sake of his belly would readily produce whatever the audience wished to hear."[4]

Pausanias knew of two versions of the fortunes of Penelope after the return of Odysseus to Ithaca (8.12.5–6). He speaks of two roads leading from Mantinea

---

1 Cf. Fowler 2011, 49–50.
2 Scodel 2005, 182: "No single narrative ever told the whole story of a traditional character, and no single version, even the Homeric epics, had absolute authority."
3 West 1966, 161–62 on lines 26–28 took them to be referring to contradictions, which could be an extreme form of variation. Heiden 2007 on the basis of a detailed study of ὁμοῖα concludes that it means lies that are "as good as truth", so that logically the Muses speak only truth. This interpretation is reconcilable with West's.
4 González 2013, 642.

to Orchomenus, by one of which there is a mound said to be the grave of Penelope. According to what he calls the Mantinean story (*logos*), Odysseus charged her with having brought the suitors into his house and sent her away. She went first to Sparta and then to Mantinea, where she died. He also knows a poem called *Thresprotis*, in which Odysseus, after his return, had a son, Ptoliporthes, by Penelope. The fortunes of Odysseus were also known in versions differing from the ultimately happy ending of the *Odyssey*. The *Telegony* combined two narratives (arg. 1 B = p. 72 D = pp. 292–306 W). In one, Odysseus founds a new kingdom in Thesprotia (the poem known to Pausanias seems to be unrelated), marries and has a son. In the other, he hears that Ithaca is being wasted by someone, and returns to his native island. He is then killed in combat with the invader, who, unbeknownst to either of them, is Telegonus, his son by Circe. Telegonus then takes Penelope and Telemachus to the island of Circe. He marries Penelope and Telemachus marries Circe.[5]

What then is the ending of the myth concerning Odysseus' return? This kind of question can be asked of any myth attested in differing versions. As Fowler asked apropos of mythographical research: "[W]here or what is the 'myth' that the mythographer seeks to reduce?" (fuller quotation in Introduction, p. XVII). A common-sense reaction to a set of variants is to look for a common story-pattern and to call that pattern the myth. This result has a certain plausibility, even if the procedure necessarily abstracts from the circumstances (which may or may not be discernible in any variation as attested in our sources) that generated the variants.

The story-pattern of a myth is defined in terms of its smallest narrative units. The same story-pattern may be discernible in other myths, with the result that a class of myths can be defined and interpreted as such. As pointed out in chapter 9, the field of Classics has standard terms for neither the units nor the story-pattern. Usually the class of myths that has been defined has no name. Burkert's "girl's tragedy" is an exception (ch. 9.1 sub fin.). As discussion of Burkert's example showed, the same minimal narrative unit of a myth, like the foot-loose motifs of folktales, may turn up in some other myth and that myth may belong to some other common story-pattern.[6] Discussion of this phenomenon among classicists has been rare. (Burkert's Auge is one of Heracles' many sexual conquests, which no doubt have a common story-pattern which could be interpreted, beyond its

---

[5] On the *Telegony*: Tsagalis 2015, 380–401. According to Aristophanes and Aristarchus, the *Od.* ended at 23.296. The notion that the ending of the *Od.* itself could have been in play still in Alexandrian times has been very disturbing. Cf. Heubeck in Russo/Fernández-Galian/Heubeck 1989, 342–45 (on 23.297).

[6] For the concept of motif in folklore studies: Edmunds 2016a, 22–25.

simple biological basis. Further, their son was Telephus, who belongs to the very common story-pattern of the exposed child.) A first desideratum is a definition of the minimal narrative unit, with a standard term for the unit. A second desideratum is a standard name, such as "girl's tragedy", for each of the results of the segmentation that yields the story-patterns. Comparison of the results reached by different scholars in research on the same or related myths would be facilitated.

Electronic databases, such as the database of mythical names under development as part of the MANTO project at Australian National University (ch. 4 init.) will have a role to play. Further comparisons are already possible. The Thompson index of folktale motifs (*Mot*) is available online and the classicist's smallest units can be compared with these motifs.[7] The story-patterns of Greek myths often correspond to folktale types, as William Hansen showed in the cases of 113 Greek myths.[8] These are the types as defined in the standard index (ATU, not yet available online), which also provide points of reference for the classical scholar's story-patterns, however they may be designated. A classicist's reliance on the concepts and terminology of folklore could be seen in Burkert's use of "functions", from Propp, "motifemes", from Dundes, and "motif" in his presentation of the "girl's tragedy" (ch. 7.3; ch. 9.3).

In short, myth as oral story-telling produces variation, which leads to the methodological questions just discussed. As such, a myth presents itself in the first place, however, as a performance and, with respect to communication, does not differ fundamentally from myth as heard in the performance of verse. In either mode, in story-telling or in song, a myth entails what Fowler called a "social nexus" between performer and listener or audience (cf. Fowler on the "social nexus" and Ready quoted in the Introduction, pp. XXIV). This social dimension of performance has been much studied by folklorists.[9] The classical scholar, for his or her part, usually finds a myth already decontextualized and inevitably proceeds to put it in a new context. The "social nexus" from which it emerged is unrecoverable, except to some extent in the use of myth in oratory and in the cult hymn.[10] While the research on South Slavic heroic epic by Milman Parry (1902–1935) might come to mind as a comparative approach to the interaction of singer and audience, his work in the former Yugoslavia concentrated on the former to

---

[7] *Mot* is incorporated in "Tales Online" (https://www.talesunlimited.com/).
[8] Hansen 2002a, 539–41 for the list.
[9] Braid 2002.
[10] Cf., in Homeric studies, the concept of an accommodation, in the performance tradition, of the past to the present of the audience. The result is a homeostasis or equilibrium of past and present. Briefly discussed in Edmunds 2019, 12–13, where n. 52 should be corrected to: Cantilena 2012b, 155.

the exclusion of the latter.[11] His purpose was to record and transcribe the performances of certain *guslars* for the purpose of comparison with Homer.[12] (He did not live to complete the comparison, which was elaborated over the years by Albert Lord (1912–91), who had been his research assistant on his second trip to Yugoslavia in 1934–35.)[13]

Sometimes, as in the case of certain hymns, the text in which a myth has been preserved gives evidence of its performance and thus invites speculation on the fugitive "nexus." Sappho's hymn to Hera is a good example (fr. 17 V). The hymn summons the goddess to the present festival (1–2) in the sanctuary known also from Alcaeus (fr. 129 V) and recalls its apparent foundation by the Atreids, who could not accomplish their return voyages until they had come here and invoked Hera, Zeus and Dionysus (3–11). (In Alcaeus fr. 129 the Lesbians established the temenos in Messa with its altars to the three divinities and there is no mention of the Atreids.)[14] The myth of the foundation of the cult is the local variant of an episode in the return of the Atreids from Troy to Greece.[15] The hymn has a clearly delineated deictic framework, spatial and temporal, inscribing the myth in the context of its performance.[16] The myth has an instrumental purpose as part of the summoning of the gods.[17] In the very poorly preserved conclusion, the singer calls upon Hera to come now as she did before (12–20). Does Sappho summon Hera on behalf of the girls and women who can be dimly discerned (14) and are they thus coinvolved? Is the hymn sung by a group of women?[18] If so, one has at least a glimpse of a "nexus."[19]

---

[11] I base this statement on the quotation of Parry's description of his fieldwork in Lord 1971 [1948], 469–73.
[12] Russo 2011.
[13] Nagy 2011.
[14] The opinion of Robert 1960, 300, according to whom the place of exile was modern Messa (the Messon mentioned in two second-century inscriptions), 5 km north of the town of Pyrrha, is now generally accepted.
[15] The myth of the Atreids, in particular the presence of Agamemnon (implied in 3) with Menelaus, on Lesbos is a variant. In Homer the two Atreids return separately to Greece (cf. *Od.* 3.165–72). See Page 1955, 59–60.
[16] Aloni 1997, 29 n. 2.
[17] Cf. quotation of Furley and Bremer 2001, 6 in ch. 5.5.
[18] Commentators have been divided or indecisive on this matter. West 2014, 3: "There was apparently no reference to her personal affairs." Neri/Cinti 2017, 299 consider the possibility that Sappho "intendesse dare una coloritura per così dire 'nostica' all'inno intero, e che ciò potesse avere un significato particolare per il suo gruppo e per la sua eteria."
[19] Calame uses this hymn to illustrate "pragmatic" interpretation of myth, in which myth has a privileged status in the here and now of the ritual context. Calame 2011b, 518–20. Cf. Calame

The embedding of the myth in the ritual song does not *ipso facto* cancel the larger Lesbian context. The local variant may be part of an Aeolic epic that would have had its own story of the Trojan War to tell.[20] The main evidence for this Aeolic epic is Sappho's "Marriage of Hector and Andromache" (fr. 44 V).[21] A first question, then, for interpretation of the myth of fr. 17 V is: what are the boundaries of the myth that one is going to interpret? (The further question of what kind of interpretation is discussed below.) This question has already arisen apropos of Vernant's Prometheus myth (ch. 6.3) and Lévi-Strauss's Oedipus myth (ch. 7.3). Where does the story begin and where does it end? The myth of Callisto, I pointed out, comes to an end before the other examples of the "girl's tragedy" not because of the peculiar characteristics of its concluding motif but simply because this motif concludes Callisto's story. In other words, a larger common pattern may include a shorter example that is complete in itself. One might argue either way about the foundation myth concerning the Atreids, either that the myth as in Sappho's hymn is complete in itself or that it can only be understood as part of the larger myth of the heroes' returns from Troy to Greece.

If, in the case of Sappho fr. 17 V, one decides that the myth is the episode located in the temenos at Messa, then one seems to have a good example of Burkert's application of a story: "The 'applied story' takes elements of its application into itself and thus brings about secondary crystallizations of a singular kind."[22] (I discussed Burkert's notion of secondariness in ch. 7.3, where I pointed out that for him the real meaning of a myth is held in reserve.) Sappho has taken an episode from the story of the Atreids' return from Troy to Greece and has applied it to present circumstances (obscured, to repeat, because of the state of preservation of the conclusion of the song). Sappho's episode would be a "secondary crystallization." Then what is primary? Burkert distinguished between the "syntagmatic chain" of which the secondary application consists, on the one

---

2007, 281. "Considered as religious practices, the stories that we identify and place under the rubric of 'myth' thus reveal themselves to exist only in particular poetic forms." Calame's preference for myth as poetry and ritual is found also in Calame 2011a, 2. Calame is not alone in the privileging of ritual in the communication of myth. In Edmunds 2014a, 19–21 I made a critique of this notion. As I pointed out, the same myth could be retold the next day outside the ritual context and it would be no less the myth that was performed in the sanctuary.

20 For Aeolic epic: West 2002, 406–407. Jones 2012, 65: "The evidence for an Aeolic branch of epic poetry is strong. The evidence that this Aeolic branch preceded Ionian epic is not." Tribulato 2010, 394 is an agnostic. For a bibliography on Aeolic epic (pro and con): Yatromanolakis 2008, 207 n. 7.

21 On the non-Homeric aspects of this fragment: Bowie 2010, 73–74.

22 Burkert 1993, 17. Quoted in Introduction, p. XIX.

hand, and "narrative structures", on the other, such presumably as the "girl's tragedy, that are "based on a very few general human or even pre-human programmes of action, and thus are quite easily understood and encoded in memory".[23] These narrative structures are, then, primary.

In the case of the "girl's tragedy", Burkert spoke of initiation rituals, with their basis in "the natural sequence of puberty, defloration, pregnancy, and delivery" (quoted more fully in ch. 7.3), as programs of action. Apparently the program of action facilitates recollection of the myth or myths. To take another example, marriage and the begetting of children is a program of action based in human biology, a program easily remembered. Because of the incest taboo, whether it is biological or cultural, the marriages of the children are exogamous, and this program may continue for many generations. The result is genealogies such as the ones found in the Hesiodic *Catalogue*. As a specialist, the poet could remember such genealogies (and presumably sorted them out according to his own lights) and they were transmitted by other specialists, rhapsodes. Could the ordinary person have duplicated these feats of memory? The underlying program of action would have been of little use. How did the early mythographers, for their part, specialists of another kind, arrive at their genealogies? Even if one cannot point to their sources, their elaboration of stemmata, sometimes with accompanying detail, seems to go beyond the capacity of individual recall.

The question of how many myths, in what form and of what length an ordinary person remembered is unanswerable. Study of social memory or collective memory, as these terms show, is concerned with myths (and also, in the first place, with events that we would call historical) that everyone in whatever the context remembers or can be reminded of.[24] But the question concerning the ordinary person remains (cf. ch. 2.5). The kinds of answer that would come from cognitive studies may not be useful (cf. Introduction, p. XXV). As often, comparative study might be a path to take.[25] But one can ask: how much of the corpus of myths does anyone have to remember? The linguistics of Saussure suggests an answer to this question. His distinction between *langue* and *parole* as it was applied by Bogatyrev and Jakobson to folktales was discussed in the Introduction (pp. XXIII–XXV). The point was, to repeat, that folktales correspond to *langue*, because they exist primarily *in potentia*, in their potentiality for retelling. (Lévi-

---

23 Burkert 1987, 11. Quoted more fully in ch. 9.3.
24 The terms "social memory" and "collective memory" are not equivalent: Steinbock 2013, 8.
25 See Lehmann 2011, cols. 5–8, with notes, for indications.

Strauss's use of Saussure was discussed in ch. 7.3.)[26] As for memory, Saussure's concept of *langue* as a system is relevant. He said that "... la langue est un système dont tous les termes sont solidaires".[27] Further, it is synchronic and supra-individual, possessed by every user of a particular natural language.[28] At the same time, no one would say that every adult speaker of the same language knows the same number of words. Whatever his or her active vocabulary is, his passive vocabulary is much larger. Analogously, if the corpus of Greek myths, like folklore in Bogatyrev' and Jakobson's conception, is a *langue*, then one can expect that different persons will know different myths, one person more of them, another less, and that someone hearing a myth for the first time will recognize it as such and grasp at least intuitively its place in the system.

The myth constituting the "girl's tragedy", as a shared pattern, has been at the service of an anthropology of ancient Greek initiation and continues a long history of thought (cf. ch. 7.1). Burkert is probably the best known but hardly the only advocate of this interpretation. Once an orthodoxy, it now has many challengers.[29] However the matter is decided, the question of the interpretation of the individual myths remains. If a myth is a particular instance of its expression, in whatever mode, in story-telling, verse, or a visual medium, and if, as the phenomenon of variation implies, its expression bears a relation to present circumstances, then interpretation would in the first place concentrate on the myth in these circumstances. For myths known only or mainly in the mythographic tradition this approach is impossible but for some myths their expression in verse or in visual media offers a chance. To some extent, as study of Greek tragedy in the past generation has shown, the audience's involvement can be inferred.[30] Likewise, in the study of vase painting, the possibility of "reading" mythical scenes

---

26 For a later application of Saussure to Greek myth: Calame 2011b, 507–508. Cf. also Steinbock 2013, 12 for a related application of the distinction: "A good analogy for the relationship between collective and individual memory is the relation between language (*langue*) and speech (*parole*)".

27 Saussure 1972, 159 = 1986, 113. Antoine Meillet 1915, 463 famously said, "[C]haque langue forme un système où tout se tient" ("Each language forms a system where everything fits"). The statement appears in slightly different forms in several of Meillet's writings. For the complex history of this idea see Koerner 1998.

28 Cf. Edmunds 2016a, 3 and nn. 17–18 for further references (to notes by Saussure's students) for the possession of *langue* by every user of a particular language.

29 See the essays in Dodd and Faraone 2003. Cf. Buxton 2013, 45. But this view is hardly dead. See Dowden 2011b.

30 Cf. Buxton 2013, 146–48.

through ancient eyes has been pursued (ch. 1). From the side of the one telling the myth, in whatever mode, myth often has an explicit instructive function.[31]

The lure of higher-order descriptions of myths remains strong, as the discussion of three comparative approaches to Greek myth has shown (ch. 8). In these approaches the primary question is: Is the myth, i.e., usually the hypostasis as described by Fowler (Introduction, p. XVIII), an example of the kind of structure that has been posited on the basis of comparison? If the answer is yes, then the myth is in the first place evidence for the structure. A return from the structure to the myth in order to observe the myth's peculiarities in its own context is not in principle ruled out and sometimes happens. One could, for example, attempt to return from the pattern shared by "Atrahasis", the "Song of Release", and two versions of the Trojan War, to the specificity of the Greek myth (ch. 8.2). But usually the examples or examples are at the service of the structure.

Structure as the description of a myth inevitably has an etic and thus always contestable basis. As pointed out in chapter 7.3 (sub fin.) Lévi-Strauss and Burkert posited vastly different bases for the structures that they discovered. Burkert's "program of action" for the myth that has been discussed is one of what he calls "the antecedent, dynamic structures of experience which have formed human life and molded the human psyche in the vast realm of the past."[32] What I referred to as the mentalism of Lévi-Strauss's structuralism has been described more specifically as Kantian, especially in the "determination to tie all social systems to constituent categories that operate like noumenal categories."[33] This determination is clear in Lévi-Strauss's comparison of the Oedipus and the Zuni myths in the famous article of 1955, which showed what he called the "basic logical processes which are at the root of mythical thought."[34] Vernant occupies a middle position between Lévi-Strauss and Burkert, grounding myth in society. In method, he follows Lévi-Strauss but not into the realm of abstract thought.

The three interpreters of Greek myth just reviewed all see something that can be linked to some ancient Greek mental or social reality. (Psychoanalytic interpretation, whether Freudian or Jungian, looks to universal aspects of the human mind.) Another kind of interpretation proceeds from the notion of a Greek myth as part of a corpus of first-order mythical thinking, in which the gods are central. This notion has some plausibility. In the matter of the gods, Xenophanes already shows the opposition of another kind of first-order thinking to Greek myth.

---

[31] Livingstone 2011.
[32] Burkert 1979, 142.
[33] Dosse 1997, 30.
[34] Lévi-Strauss 1955, 440 (7.0).

Plato's "an old dispute", cited above, between poetry, on the one hand, as a source of harmful myths about the gods, and, on the other, philosophy, is a dispute between two kinds of first-order thinking. In this perspective myth is numinous, perniciously from Plato's point of view.[35] The numinosity of myth, its sign reversed, persists in the thought of Wilamowitz, although for him myth is already pale in comparison with belief. In *Der Glaube der Hellenen* he proposes to trace a three-stage history, from belief in the Greek gods to the passing of belief into myth to its ultimate demise. He would like to see the gods "as genuine belief saw them, if possible, as this belief sprang up in the hearts of men." "Then", he adds, "it is a matter of grasping not mythology but religion."[36] The gods in this scheme are a given, as in his oft-quoted apothegm: "Die Götter da sind" ("The gods are there").[37] Wilamowitz's premise, or the premise behind his premise, is that religion is belief—thus the title of his book.[38] In the discussion of religion in the present book religion is a matter of cult and ritual, which are for the most part separate from myth (ch. 6). Even in cult hymns, the myth is instrumental or practical, as in the case of Sappho's hymn discussed above. As for myth, the question is no longer, for most scholars, whether the Greeks believed in the gods in myths but whether they believed in the myths. This contemporary question was discussed with reference to the distinction between belief-in and belief-that (ch. 5).

Even if belief-in the gods is insisted upon, the fact of mythical burlesque remains. As Carl Shaw has argued, nearly all fifth-century satyr plays include satyrs in traditional myths. Many of these plays treat the birth of a hero or god.[39] He emphasizes the contribution, in this respect, of the satyr play to Middle Comedy.[40] (Satyrs are present also in the Return of Hephaestus, a traditional scene in vase

---

35 Bies 1999, cols. 1077–78.
36 von Wilamowitz-Moellendorff 1931–1932.1, 5: "...die Götter so zu sehen, wie sie der echte Glaube gesehen hat, womöglich, wie dieser Glaube in den Herzen der Menschen erwachsen ist. Dann gilt es nicht Mythologie, sondern Religion zu begreifen" ("to see the gods as they were seen by genuine belief, if possible as this belief has grown up in the hearts of men. Then the important thing is to grasp not mythology but religion").
37 Stated twice in his first chapter: von Wilamowitz-Moellendorff 1931–1932.1, 17, 41.
38 Gadamer 1993 [1981]b, 186: "Hier wird in voller Selbstverständlichkeit ein am Christentum gewonnener Begriff des Glaubens in die Frühe der mythischen Erfahrungen zurückprojiziert" ("Here, completely as a matter of course, a concept of belief gained from Christianity is projected back into the early days of the experience of myths").
39 Shaw 2014, 110. He acknowledges the precedence of Nesselrath 1995 in this line of thought.
40 Nesselrath 1995 discusses the births of gods in fourteen plays of Middle Comedy, a theme deriving from the satyr play.

painting dating from the early sixth century.)[41] Images of a comical Zeus, inspired by Middle Comedy, can be seen in south Italian vases.[42] But the gods were always, so to speak, good for a laugh, apart from any ritual sanction or *parodia sacra*.[43] Already in the *Iliad*, the conflict of the gods in Book 21 (383–513) has the air of burlesque.[44] Richard Janko in his introduction to the Deception of Zeus in Book 14 (153–353) remarked: "Few Greeks ever took their gods wholly seriously; this is, perhaps, the Greeks' greatest gift to civilization."[45] Non-divine myth could also be burlesqued. The birth of Helen from an egg as treated in Cratinus' *Nemesis* has been so interpreted.[46] A South Italian bell-crater showing the same episode, but not Cratinus' version, has been plausibly interpreted as comic by Alan Shapiro.[47]

Another kind of interpretation goes on in reception studies. To take the example of women in ancient Greece, myth is both a supplement to historical documentation, which is frustrating in its limitations, and also offers the possibility of reimagining these women. As for the supplement,

> myth becomes a haven of plenitude, a place where women thrive and behave in provocative and interesting ways; myth helps fulfill the fantasies of those who are unwilling to face the prospect of a past inhabited by cowed and sequestered women and allows the possibility that women then, in their imaginations at least, participated in more contemporary kinds of defiance.[48]

The reimagining of women in fiction and other media has dramatized this defiance and has made "flat" characters "round", to use E.M. Forster's terms.[49] A well-known example is the novel *Kassandra* of Christa Wolf.[50] The novel consists of the memories of Cassandra as she awaits execution in Agamemnon's palace. She remembers a non-heroic Troy in which Helen is not present (she is only an excuse) and economic interests and male egotism motivate the war. Female characters little known or, like Polyxena, unknown in the *Iliad* come to the fore. At

---

41 Mitchell 2004, 28–29. Discussed also in Mitchell 2009. Cf. *LIMC*, "Hephaestus", 636–45 (section III "Le retour d'Héphaïstos dans l'Olympe"); 653–54 (discussion).
42 For images: Rusten 2011, 436–38. Walsh 2008 concentrates on these "Phlyax" vases.
43 Cf. Bakhtin 1984, 127.
44 Rutherford 1993, 85: "One can, if one wishes, speak here of 'comic relief'", but he tries to take the scene as seriously as possible.
45 Janko 1992, 170. Cf. Heath 2019.
46 Taplin 1995, 79–83.
47 Shapiro 2014.
48 Zajko 2007, 390. Cf. Lewis 2011, 444–45.
49 Forster 1927, 67–78.
50 Wolf 1983. See Zajko 1998, 114–19 for a survey of feminist reception of Cassandra.

the capture of Troy, Cassandra could have left with her lover Aeneas but chose to remain (and was thus taken prisoner). Her reason for remaining is a clue to the dynamic of the work as a whole: Aeneas will become a hero; she cannot love a hero, a statue. Stephanie West describes her thus:

> Demythologized, secularized, sexually experienced, neither troubled nor comforted by religious belief, this late-twentieth-century Cassandra has been designed as a representative woman, clever, independent-minded and, like Christa T. and Caroline von Günderrode, possessed of unrealised talents; but she has moved as far from her classical forerunners as she could without becoming completely unrecognizable.[51]

As West's reference to "forerunners" implies, Homer is hardly the only source for Wolf's Cassandra. But the story that Cassandra tells concerns her life before and during the Trojan War and thus reimagines a fuller story than can be found in all of the sources taken together, in which, through her recollections of her past and her expressions of her feelings and thoughts, her character looms large. Cassandra offers a good lesson in the difference as regards characterization between novel and myth (cf. ch. 3.4).

Something like this kind of reception of myth was going on already in ancient Greece. At the end of Plato's *Republic* Socrates recounts a new myth, the Myth of Er, in which souls in the underworld sooner or later draw lots to determine the sequence in which they will choose the kind of life into which they would like to be reborn. Odysseus drew the last lot of all in his cohort and, remembering the toils that went with his love of honor, he sought to find the soul of a private man who minded his own business (βίον ἀνδρὸς ἰδιώτου ἀπράγμονος, 620c5–7). He managed to find such a soul, which, he says, he would have chosen even if he had been eligible to choose first. Odysseus thus rejects the life of a hero, the life that he had led. Socrates, with his reimagined Odysseus, is a Christa Wolf *avant la lettre*.

Claude Calame has served as an anthropologist of contemporary Europe, preserving an example of the reception of a Greek myth in popular culture:

> The "myth of Helen" is still active. A few years ago, it achieved a remarkable success in a French soap opera entitled *Hélène et les garçons* ("Helen and the Boys"). In a new narrative metamorphosis, the Helen of this television series became a girl who, despite arousing passionate and sometimes exotic adolescent love, resists all attempts to seduce her; in her loving fidelity and against an anti-racist background, she becomes a kind of anti-Helen. Each episode of the student life of this Helen, now just "a girl like any other", was put together

---

[51] S. West 1991a, 184–85. Christa T. is the protagonist of a novel by Wolf (1968); Caroline von Günderrode and Heinrich von Kleist are the two main characters in another novel (1979).

on the basis of the reactions to previous episodes of those, both female and male, who were watching the TV series.[52]

This Helen seems to have been completely demythologized, although one would have to have seen the series to be certain. But with the involvement of the audience in the telling of the story one has returned to the "nexus" assumed for ancient myth but usually unrecoverable.

The supplementing of the myths has gone on also, for example, in the cases of Penelope and Eurydice.[53] In reception, characters, male as well as female, often have fuller stories than in the ancient myths about them and acquire a roundness that they lacked, in particular through a typically modern exploration of their feelings (cf. ch. 3.4–5). Character becomes the ground of the new narrative. Freud's apothegm concerning the id applies to the growth of character from its rudimentary state in ancient myth to its modern reception: "Wo Es war soll Ich werden" ("Where it (the id) was, should I (the ego) be"; cf. ch.7.1).

The ancient myths, which could not use character as the basis of expansion, could be expanded in two ways (cf. ch. 2.5). One was to attach a new story to a hero, whether or not the story was consistent with the character in already known stories (ch. 3.1) and whether or not the story bore any narrative connection to these other stories. (We are usually ignorant of when such additions happened, though in some cases, such as some of the similar stories about Heracles and Theseus, we can assume that the ones about Theseus are imitative and later.) The other was agglomeration, the collection of disparate stories within the frame of a larger-scale story (ch. 2.5).[54] Such stories are the quest for the Golden Fleece and, in the next generation of heroes, the expedition of the Greeks to Troy to recover Helen. The accomplishment of the objective may take a longer (Helen) or a shorter (Golden Fleece) time but in both stories the outward journey includes episodes only loosely related to the main stories. The returns are even more open to new adventures and misfortunes, especially the returns of some of the heroes from Troy to their home cities (a preliminary episode was seen in the hymn of Sappho discussed above). Some returned directly to their home cities with favoring winds, others were driven off-course by various adversities over many years (cf. in *Od.* 3.130–85 Nestor on the varying returns). The stories of these unfortunate ones, of which the return of Odysseus is best known to us, illustrate the

---

52 Calame 2009, 659. For a study of the series he cites Pasquier 1993.
53 Penelope: Doherty 2017, 161–63; Eurydice: Lively 2017, 291–97.
54 As I have said in ch. 6.3, the linking of the stories of the deceptive sacrifice, the theft of fire and the creation of Pandora seems to be specifically Hesiodic and not an already existing agglomeration.

mode of agglomeration. The return of the Argonauts from Colchis to Iolcus took them to the edges of the earth.

Genealogies were the most easily expandable kind of myth. Beside every figure there was a virtual space for an addition. The motives for expansions were always there. Genealogies were entertaining in themselves (for the Spartan taste for: ch. 2.2). They also had practical purposes. Thus a family tree could be extended to meet the needs of geographical claims, supplying significant place names (cf. ch. 3.7). Fowler has described the situation that confronted the early Greek mythographers:

> Changing relationships in a traditional society result in constantly revised genealogies. The inevitable contradictions, unexplained links, and chronological problems resulting from these revisions are gaily tolerated. Indeed people are usually unaware of them, since they know only that small fragment of their society's total genealogical lore which concerns them.[55]

The genealogical variants in different texts of the *Erythraean Paean* are a good example (ch. 5.5). When the writing down of myths began, the possibility of correcting genealogies presented itself. Their multiplicity, no doubt including different versions of the same family-trees, could be reduced and the mythographer could present his new rationalized version as the authoritative one. The fact that Hecataeus wrote a book called *Genealogies* suggests that this kind of myth in particular was included in his blanket disparagement of the Greeks' myths as λόγοι πολλοί τε καὶ γελοῖοι (ch. 4.3). The multitude of the genealogical *logoi* demanded reduction and system. He would have corrected Hesiod in the first place, as Acusilaus did (see Hellanicus test. 18 *EGM*, which also refers to differences between Acusilaus and Hellanicus).[56] Besides the fixed genealogies of Hesiod there were all the local ones.

Genealogies on the small scale of, say, two generations, are especially good examples of the ad hoc character of myth. They can be effective, as in diplomacy, because those who hear them intuit or assume the system of which they are parts (and they thus illustrate the Saussurean analogy invoked above).[57] A genealogy as a whole, as in Hecataeus and others, has no significance as such but its assumed existence may confer authority on its parts. All Greek myths, this book has argued, have this immediacy, for the simple reason that they always, even in a

---

55 *EGM* 2, 125.
56 Cf. Dowden 2011a, 55–56.
57 As in diplomacy: Patterson 2010.

rhapsodic performance of Homer, have some bearing on the present situation.[58] Their significance is not partial or secondary, a percentage of some larger significance of the corpus from which they came, but their whole significance as far as teller and addressee(s) are concerned. The number of myths that can be interpreted in this way, in their immediate historical context, is relatively few. Myths in vase paintings are, on the one hand, exactly what the ancient beholder saw; on the other, they are the most difficult to interpret (probably requiring in many cases the cooperative efforts of art historians and philologists or literary scholars).[59] For the rest, scholars will have to define the myth or myths to be interpreted according to their own lights. No Archimedean position is available (Introduction, p. XXVII).

As for interpretation, the etic is inevitable, whether one is Jane Harrison or the user of a new database, no matter what its data structure is and what the searching algorithms are. The etic perspective begins with terminology, as also in the history of ancient Greek religion. This inevitability is not final, however, and does not exclude a stereoscopic view that includes the emic. Interpretation proceeds from the myth that the scholar has defined, either as a single myth, which will be a hypostasis, or the shared story-pattern of a set of myths. The main kinds of interpretation, which have been surveyed in chapters seven and eight, differ widely. They all differ from the interpretation of the text of a poem in proceeding from the assumption that much larger or deeper sources of, or frames of reference for, myths are the goal. Comparison of results is difficult when, as pointed out earlier in this conclusion, a common terminology is lacking.

---

58 The audience of Homer consists of men "such as men now are", as distinguished from the heroes, and times have changed in social and material aspects from heroic times but "according to a view held by many, the process of oral composition in performance, precisely because it had to accommodate its audiences, tended to homeostasis or equilibrium of past and present" (Edmunds 2019, 13).

59 On the relation of the image to its material basis, vase, statue, or as the case may be, and on problems of interpretation, see, in addition to studies already cited, Delattre 2005, 165–84.

11 Appendix: *Muthos* and Myth. From Homer to Plato and Aristotle

The English word "myth" comes into English by way of post-classical Latin from Greek μῦθος (*muthos*).[1] The etymology of this word is obscure.[2] In its earliest attestations, in Homer and the rest of archaic verse, a *muthos* is always a speech or the thought contained in a speech. Martin classified the principal kinds of *muthoi* in Homer as prayer, lament, supplication, commanding, and narrating from memory, of which the last is the one relevant to the present discussion.[3] Further, this word is a synonym of *logos* already in Homer. The two words have to be studied together. In the fifth century, they begin to be opposed as a concept of *muthos* begins to be formed.

Here, however, *muthos* is first discussed as a lexical concept, of the kind "that tend[s] to be associated with individual words in natural language."[4] I then discuss the formation of a concept of myth. By concept, I mean simply a principle of classification that can tell us whether something belongs in a certain class or not.[5] The new concept of myth is anticipated in Pindar *Nemean* 7 and first articulated or at least adumbrated in Herodotus and Thucydides, when myth is opposed to another kind of narrative about the past. This new concept is negative. Myth in the estimate of these historians is something exaggerated or simply incredible. (See below in 11.1 on the formation of this concept.) In Plato, this new concept appears again, this time on the basis of another opposition, of *logos* to *muthos*.[6] This emergence of new forms of thought and discourse is summed up in the book-title, *From Mythos to Logos*.[7] But, as will be seen, neither in Plato nor in Aristotle is myth completely excluded from philosophic discourse. Another tendency in

---

[1] For a bibliography of studies of *muthos* and words formed on *muth-* in archaic verse: Fowler 2011, 52 n. 31. For a short survey of the history of the word from antiquity to modern times: Meyer 1999, 63.
[2] Nagy 1989; answered by Griffith 1992, 170–71 (note the reference to Chantraine). Martin 2013, 47 echoes Nagy.
[3] Martin 1989, 44. Cf. the list in Nagy 2007, 54, which includes threats, invectives, and prophecies.
[4] Margolis/Laurence 2019, §2 ("The structure of concepts").
[5] Butchvarov 1999, 170.
[6] Morgan 2000, 34–35.
[7] I.e., *Vom Mythos zum Logos* (Nestle 1940). See the critique of Nestle by Most in an article entitled "From Logos to Mythos" (1999).

the history of *muthos* is its capacity for extension, as witnessed in Aristotle's use of *muthos* to designate the plot of a tragedy.

11.1 *Muthos* and *logos* from Homer and Hesiod to Herodotus

The approximately 160 examples of Homeric *muthos* in the sense of "speech" include a subgroup in which this word could be translated "story" just as easily as "speech."[8] Forms of μυθέομαι are also frequent (*Il*. 20x; *Od*. 37x). *Logos* is another matter, occurring only once in the *Iliad*: Patroclus cheered Eurypylus with *logoi* (ἔτερπε λόγοις, 15.393).[9] In this use it appears to be a synonym of *muthos* (cf. μύθοισιν τέρποντο, 11.643). Again in the *Odyssey*, a single occurrence: Calypso attempts to distract the mind of Odysseus from Ithaca (λόγοισι / θέλγει, 1.56–57), although here the connotation might be negative, as usually with this verb when someone plies someone else with words.[10] Words formed on *muth-* and on *leg-*/*log-* appear in the same context only once in Homer, in Alcinous' response to Odysseus' masterful recounting of his adventures: μῦθον δ' ὡς ὅτ' ἀοιδὸς ἐπισταμένως κατέλεξας (*Od*. 11.368).

In Hesiod, too, *logos* occurs infrequently—three times in the formula αἱμυλίοισι λόγοισιν / αἱμυλίους τε λόγους (*Theog*. 890; *Op*. 78, 789) and also personified, in the list of the baleful children of Eris (Λόγους τ' Ἀμφιλλογίας τε, *Theog*. 229). Once *logos* has a positive sense, when it introduces the authoritative account of the five races of men.[11] This is the first occurrence of this word in the singular.[12] In archaic lyric (Sim. 579 = fr. 257 Poltera), trimeter (Archil. 23.16 W²) and elegy (Theog. 418 W²) the singular *logos* sometimes claims truth but is still often negative. In sum, the interrelated semantic future of *muthos* and *logos* and their eventual differentiation in sense could not be predicted from Homer and Hesiod. The only intimations in hexameter are Demodocus' response to Odysseus, quoted above, and the verb μυθολογεύω (*Od*. 12.450, 453).

---

8 Martin 2013, 47: "Out of the larger group of speeches identified by the poet or his characters as *muthos*...we can specify a smaller subgroup that one could just as easily translate with 'story' rather than 'speech'. Or more accurately, they can be viewed as speeches with supporting evidence."
9 Nothing can be concluded from the fact that *logos* is a hapax in the *Il*. See Janko 1992, 15.393n.
10 Cf. *Od*. 1.56–57; 3.264; 12.40, 44 (Sirens' song); 14.387; 16.195; 18.282–83.
11 εἰ δ' ἐθέλεις, ἕτερόν τοι ἐγὼ λόγον ἐκκορυφώσω / εὖ καὶ ἐπισταμένως, *Op*. 106. See West 1978, 106–107n, who observes that "It is common to define the status of a story in advance."
12 For which the earliest comparandum is in Sim. 579.

In archaic lyric, however, φασι / φαῖσι / φάντι and λέγουσι / ὡς λόγος alternate as ways of introducing or referring to a mythical example.[13] This use of ὡς λόγος persists into classical Greek prose and verse (e.g., Aesch. *Eum.* 4; Hdt. 6.127; Pl. *Crat.* 396b7 and other places in Pl.). The discussion of Herodotus later in this section shows that *muthos* and *logos* are still for him synonyms in certain contexts, even if a distinction between the two begins in his work. The word μῦθος does not occur in Thucydides, although he once refers to the prevailing *logos* concerning the size of the Greek expedition against Troy, which continues what the poets said (οἵ τε ποιηταὶ εἰρήκασι καὶ ὁ λόγος κατέχει, 1.10.2). Here he is defending the received opinion, whereas elsewhere he opposes his own view of the Trojan War to Homer's (see below). Further, he says that he knows nothing of the Cyclopes and Laestrygonians, consigning the subject to the poets and whatever anyone happens to know about them (ἀρκείτω δὲ ὡς ποιηταῖς τε εἴρηται καὶ ὡς ἕκαστός πῃ γιγνώσκει περὶ αὐτῶν, 6.2.1; discussed in the Introduction).

With Xenophanes (6th–5th c.), for the first time in our sources after Demodocus, these two words are juxtaposed. In his stipulations for the proper conduct of a symposium he includes:

χρὴ δὲ πρῶτα μὲν θεὸν ὑμνεῖν εὔφρονας ἄνδρας
    εὐφήμοις μύθοις καὶ καθαροῖσι λόγοις   fr. 1.13–14 W²

Men in a festive state of mind should hymn the god
with stories of good omen and pure words.

Whether or not Xenophanes is contrasting *muthos* and *logos* has always seemed uncertain.[14] Some reasons for understanding a contrast can be seen. The sense of *muthoi* here is implied by its adjective (εὐφήμοις), the base of which, φα-, in the verbal form φασι(ν), already in the *Iliad* can mean "to tell a story about a divinity or hero" (2.783, of Typhoeus).[15] Xenophanes proceeds to expatiate on his advice: praise the man who reveals noble thoughts (ἐσθλά, 19), which would correspond to the apparently non-narrative λόγοι. Do not recount (διέπειν, 21) the battles of Titans or Giants or Centaurs, which would correspond, negatively, to the stories of good omen.

---

13 Edmunds 2006a.
14 Lesher 1992, 48 n. 3. Lesher's own view: "some contrast seems intended."
15 Cf. 5.638: Heracles; 24.615: the couches of the Nymphs on the mountain Sipylus. For other examples of this use of φασι(ν) in Homer and other poets: Edmunds 2006a.

The distinction appears certainly around 500 B.C.E. in Hecataeus, who begins his *Genealogies* with the declaration:

Ἑκαταῖος Μιλήσιος ὧδε μυθεῖται· τάδε γράφω, ὥς μοι δοκεῖ ἀληθέα εἶναι· οἱ γὰρ λόγοι πολλοί τε καὶ γελοῖοι, ὡς ἐμοὶ φαίνονται, εἰσίν. *FGrH* F 1a = *EGM* fr. 1

Thus speaks Hecataeus of Miletus: I write following things as they seem true to me; for the stories of the Greeks, as they seem to me, are many and foolish.[16]

His μυθεῖται, a denominative verb from *muthos*, keeps the fundamental Homeric sense of the noun: "authoritative utterance."[17] With his own utterance, intended as truthful, Hecataeus contrasts the stories of the Greeks, which are multiple and risible, that is, self-contradictory.[18] Like Xenophanes he makes a distinction but now one term is clearly positive and the other is negative.[19]

What will become the standard opposition between the two words appears first in Pindar. In *Nemean 7* (461 B.C.E.), he describes Homer's exaggeration of the sufferings of Odysseus:

ἐγὼ δὲ πλέον ἔλπομαι
λόγον Ὀδυσσέος ἢ πάθαν
   διὰ τὸν ἁδυεπῆ γενέσθ᾽ Ὅμηρον·

ἐπεὶ ψεύδεσί οἱ ποτανᾷ <τε> μαχανᾷ
σεμνὸν ἔπεστί τι· σοφία
   δὲ κλέπτει παράγοισα μύθοις. 20–23

I believe that Odysseus' story (λόγον)
has become greater than his actual suffering
because of Homer's sweet verse,

for upon his fictions and soaring craft
rests great majesty, and his skill
deceives with misleading tales (μύθοις).[20]

---

16 For a commentary on this fr.: *EGM* 2, 677–80.
17 Martin 2013, 45, referring to Martin 1989.
18 *EGM* 2, 667–68, 679–80.
19 Cf. Democritus ἀληθόμυθον χρὴ εἶναι, οὐ πολύλογον, 68 B 44 D-K ≈ ἀληθομυθέειν χρεών, οὐ πολυλογέειν, 68 B 225 D-K. The contrast appears only here in the pre-Socratics. For a survey, emphasizing the revaluation of *logos* in the pre-Socratics: Nesselrath 1999, 7–10.
20 Transl. Race 1997, 73.

Logos and *muthos* both refer to a story but are here contrasting terms (cf. *O.* 1.28/ 28b–29), one implicitly positive, the other negative.[21] Pindar seems not to be inventing the contrast for his immediate purposes but to assume familiarity. In the generation before him both Heraclitus and Parmenides had given primacy to *logos* in their philosophies. In the former it is a cosmic principle and, although he does not use *muthos*, criticism of myth by Heraclitus is implicit in the fragments on Hesiod and Homer (D-K 22 B 42, 57 = L-M 9 D21, D25a).[22] Parmenides establishes *logos* as the principle for the understanding of his doctrine (D-K 28 B 7.1–8.2 = L-M 19 D8.1–7) and he distinguishes within his own exposition between the truth of *logos* and the deceptiveness of his *epea* (D-K 28 B 8.50–52 = L-M 19 D8.55–57). What he says of his *epea* presumably applies also to the poets' and thus to the myths of which the poets' are the sources.[23]

To return to Pindar, *muthos* has a particular source, Homer, who appears again in the same contrast in Herodotus' discussion of the flooding of the Nile. Herodotus rejects the position (verb λέγω) according to which Ocean is the cause of the flooding (2.21) and adds that the one who speaks thus about Ocean refers his account to an "obscure *muthos*." (In other words, such a *muthos* cannot be used to corroborate a *logos*.) Herodotus knows of no such river. The name, he thinks, was invented by Homer or one of the earlier poets (2.23).[24] Herodotus uses *muthos* once more in his account of Egypt, this time apropos of a "foolish story," told by the Hellenes (verb λέγω) concerning the Egyptians' attempt to sacrifice Heracles to Zeus. He introduces this story with a generalization and then proceeds to the example. The Hellenes "thoughtlessly" tell many other such stories and this *muthos* is foolish, too (λέγουσι δὲ πολλὰ καὶ ἄλλα ἀνεπισκέπτως οἱ Ἕλληνες· εὐήθης δὲ αὐτῶν καὶ ὅδε ὁ μῦθος, 2.45.1). Here the adjective "foolish" and

---

[21] For a detailed comparison of *O.* 1.28–35 with Thuc. 1.21.1–22.4, highlighting similarities, while acknowledging the different bases of the opposition to myth as between poet and historian: Grethlein 2019, 314–20 (with 315 n. 3 for earlier comparisons of the two passages).
[22] Thus Meyer 1999, 49.
[23] I would thus somewhat amplify Meyer 1999, 50. Parmenides uses *muthos* twice, once in a Homeric sense, of the message that he is bringing to humans (D-K 28 B 2.1 = L-M 19 D6.1) and once, in similar fashion, of the truth of his own argument: μόνος δ' ἔτι μῦθος ὁδοῖο / λείπεται ὡς ἔστιν (D-K 28 B 8.1 = L-M 19 D8.6–7), "There only remains the word of the path [scil. that says] 'Is'" (trans. by L-M).
[24] Ὁ δὲ περὶ τοῦ Ὠκεανοῦ λέξας ἐς ἀφανὲς τὸν μῦθον ἀνενείκας οὐκ ἔχει ἔλεγχον· οὐ γάρ τινα ἔγωγε οἶδα ποταμὸν Ὠκεανὸν ἐόντα, Ὅμηρον δὲ ἤ τινα τῶν πρότερον γενομένων ποιητέων δοκέω τοὔνομα εὑρόντα ἐς ποίησιν ἐσενείκασθαι (2.23). "The one who speaks about Ocean, referring his story to that which is unknown, does allow disproof. For I do not know a river that is Ocean but I think that Homer or some one of the earlier poets found the name and introduced it into poetry." On this passage: Fowler 2011, 47.

the adverb "thoughtlessly" imply a criterion for Herodotus' judgment. The Hellenes do not make reasonable discriminations among the many stories that they tell. The comparison with Hecataeus' Ἑλλήνων λόγοι πολλοί is obvious (cf. ch. 4.3).

Herodotus consistently uses both λέγω, as in the passage just cited, and also λόγος of what others say. At the same time his own work is a *logos*.[25] "I am obliged to say what is said (*ta legomena*) but I am not at all obliged to believe it and let this pledge hold for my entire *logos*."[26] Herodotus sometimes uses *logos* or *logoi* of a large unit of his work.[27] Within such a unit the smaller *logoi* of others are included and one of these may stand in a subordinate relation to another, with the result that

> we have a definite distinction between inner and outer structure, the former easy to define, the latter of great diversity. The result is a system of superimposed structures based in different kinds of interconnections.[28]

An example is Herodotus' recounting the Athenian invocation of Boreas, apropos of the storm that destroyed part of the Persian fleet at Magnesia.[29]

> The story is told (*legetai de logos*) that the Athenians, in response to an oracle, invoked Boreas, another response having come to them that they should invoke their son-in-law as a helper. Boreas, according to the account (*logos*) of the Greeks, had an Attic wife, Oreithyia the daughter of Erechtheus. Because of this marriage, the Athenians, as the report (*phatis*) goes, reckoning that Boreas was their son-in-law and having stationed their fleet at Euboean Chalchis, when they saw that the storm was increasing, or even sooner, sacrificed

---

25 Immerwahr 1966, 6 and n. 14; 14–15.
26 Ἐγὼ δὲ ὀφείλω λέγειν τὰ λεγόμενα, πείθεσθαί γε μὲν οὐ παντάπασιν ὀφείλω (καί μοι τοῦτο τὸ ἔπος ἐχέτω ἐς πάντα τὸν λόγον), 7.152.3. Cf. τοῖσι μέν νυν ὑπ' Αἰγυπτίων λεγομένοισι χράσθω ὅτεῳ τὰ τοιαῦτα πιθανά ἐστι· ἐμοὶ δὲ παρὰ πάντα τὸν λόγον ὑπόκειται ὅτι τὰ λεγόμενα ὑπ' ἑκάστων ἀκοῇ γράφω, 2.123.1. For Herodotus' use of *logos* of his work: Powell 1938, s.v. λόγος 4e (31x).
27 Immerwahr 1966, 14 n. 34 cites the Assyrian (1.184) and the Libyan (2.16.3) *logoi*, etc. Herodotus uses *logoi* in this way also to point ahead to a later part of his work (ἐν τοῖσι ὄπισθε λόγοισι σημανέω, 7.213.3).
28 Immerwahr 1966, 15.
29 My discussion is limited to this example. Powell 1938, s.v. λόγος 4d lists eight places where *logos* means "tale", not including 7.189. A full investigation would have to consider other ways of introducing a traditional story. I have not discussed λόγιος, which Luraghi 2009 argues, does not refer to a story-teller.

and called upon Boreas and Oreithyia to assist them and destroy the ships of the barbarians, as earlier at Athos.³⁰

Herodotus will not vouch for the efficacy of the invocation of Boreas. "At any rate the Athenians say (*legousi*) that Boreas having helped them formerly then too brought about those results and having returned (to Athens) they established a shrine of Boreas by the river Ilissus" (7.189.3; for the reference to the myth in Pl. *Phdr*. cf. ch. 2.3).

This passage illustrates, in the first place, an interconnection of *logoi*. There is the one that the Athenians tell about the Athenian invocation of Boreas and Oreithyia and also the one about Boreas as the husband of Oreithyia. (His abduction of her is not mentioned.) The first of these is also referred to as a *phatis*. Herodotus refrains from giving an opinion on the causal connection made by the Athenians between oracle, response and the storm but he shows no skepticism concerning the *logoi*. In this respect, they differ from the two *muthoi* discussed in the preceding paragraph. Further, the interconnection between logoi in effect bridges the gap between a *spatium mythicum* and a *spatium historicum* (cf. ch. 4.1). The myth (Boreas and Oreithyia) lies on one side and history (Athenian application of myth) lies on the other.

11.1.1 *Historia* in Herodotus

Another Herodotean word, ἱστορία, comes to refer to myth, amongst other things, in the mythographical tradition. Herodotus is the first to use this word, formed on Attic-Ionic ἵστωρ with aspiration from the internal sigma (cf. ἴστωρ, *Il*. 18.501), although he does not use it to refer to myth.³¹ The word *historia* expresses both the activity of the *histōr*, in the sense of "the one who witnesses", and also the results of that activity. As for the latter, Herodotus asserts, for example, that he will not name the native leaders of certain contingents of the Persian force because "he is not constrained by necessity to give an account of his

---

30 Λέγεται δὲ λόγος ὡς Ἀθηναῖοι τὸν Βορέην ἐκ θεοπροπίου ἐπεκαλέσαντο, ἐλθόντος σφι ἄλλου χρηστηρίου τὸν γαμβρὸν ἐπίκουρον καλέσασθαι. Βορέης δὲ κατὰ τὸν Ἑλλήνων λόγον ἔχει γυναῖκα Ἀττικήν, Ὠρείθυιαν τὴν Ἐρεχθέος· κατὰ δὴ τὸ κῆδος τοῦτο οἱ Ἀθηναῖοι, ὡς φάτις ὅρμηται, συμβαλλόμενοί σφι τὸν Βορέην γαμβρὸν εἶναι, ναυλοχέοντες τῆς Εὐβοίης ἐν Χαλκίδι ὡς ἔμαθον αὐξόμενον τὸν χειμῶνα ἢ καὶ πρὸ τούτου, ἐθύοντό τε καὶ ἐπεκαλέοντο τόν τε Βορέην. καὶ τὴν Ὠρείθυιαν τιμωρῆσαί σφι καὶ διαφθεῖραι τῶν βαρβάρων τὰς νέας, ὡς καὶ πρότερον περὶ Ἄθων (7.189.1–2).
31 Chantraine 1973, 187.

investigation" (τῶν ἐγώ, οὐ γὰρ ἀναγκαίη ἐξέργομαι ἐς ἱστορίης λόγον, οὐ παραμέμνημαι, 7.96.1).³² Here the *historia* would have consisted of the names of the native leaders. The result of someone's research might also be a myth or myths and herein lies the possibility of the semantic extension of *historia* in mythography.

This use of *historia* appears in an apophasis in Callimachus' "Acontius and Cydippes" He says that he will not tell the story of the marriage of Zeus and Hera:

Ἥρην γὰρ κοτέ φασι – κύον, κύον, ἴσχεο, λαιδρέ
  θυμέ, σύ γ' ἀείσῃ καὶ τά περ οὐχ ὁσίη·
ὤναο κάρτ' ἕνεκ' οὔ τι θεῆς ἴδες ἱερὰ φρικτῆς,
  ἐξ ἂν ἐπεὶ καὶ τῶν ἤρυγες ἱστορίην.
ἦ πολυιδρείη χαλεπὸν κακόν, ὅστις ἀκαρτεῖ
  γλώσσης· ὡς ἐτεὸν παῖς ὅδε μαῦλιν ἔχει. *Aet.* 75.4–9 Pf.

> For they say that once upon a time Hera—dog. dog, refrain, my shameless soul! you would sing even of that which is not lawful to tell. It is a great blessing for you that you have not seen the rites of the dread goddess (Demeter) or you would have spewed up their story. Surely much knowledge is a grievous thing for him who does not control his tongue; this man is really a child with a knife.³³

Callimachus introduces the myth with the conventional φασι (cf. above). Having stopped himself, he says that if he had participated in the Eleusinian Mysteries—fortunately he has not—he would have divulged the *historia* of them (either the ritual or the foundational myth or both). He concludes by saying in effect that it would be better not to have πολυιδρεία "much knowledge." The second element of this word (-ιδρ-) has the zero-grade of the stem of οἶδα "I know" seen also in *historia*, which, to repeat, is formed on ἵστωρ (< ϝιδ-τωρ).³⁴ No matter what the exact reference of *historia* as used of the Eleusinian Mysteries, Callimachus is clearly putting the telling of such matters in a category in which it is a form of knowledge with a quasi-technical name.³⁵

---

32 Cf. the use of ἱστορέω in the perfect passive: "The results of my researches show clearly that Heracles is an ancient god" (τὰ μέν νυν ἱστορημένα δηλοῖ σαφέως παλαιὸν θεὸν Ἡρακλέα ἐόντα, 2.44.5). For the two senses of ἵστωρ: *DELG* s.v. οἶδα A. For "witness" Benveniste 1969, 173–74 stresses the visual but Herodotus' *historia* included listening (τὸ δ' ἀπὸ τούτου ἀκοῇ ἤδη ἱστορέων, etc.).
33 Transl. Trypanis 1958.1, 55.
34 For ἵστωρ *DELG* s.v. οἶδα A (with references for discussion of the initial aspiration).
35 The *historia* of the Eleusinian Mysteries might have included an account of the initiate's progress through the underworld. In Ar. *Ran.* Dionysus, determined to go to Hades in order to bring back Euripides, goes first to Heracles for advice. Heracles describes what Dionysus will see: first

The fortune of the word *historia* in mythography was great and varied. Sometimes it refers to a myth, sometimes to something else, polis history, geography, or genealogy. Ekaterini Vassilaki shows a variety of such uses in the scholia to Pindar. Apropos of a mythical scholium on *Olympian* 4, introduced by ἡ δὲ ἱστορία τοιαύτη, Charles Delattre raised the question of the source of the *historia*. Whereas Vassilaki saw "une narration relevant du champ de la mythologie" or "version courante, canonique d'un mythe précis, de la tradition mythologique, de l'arrière-plan légendaire", Delattre proposed various sources—the passage in Pindar, which the scholiast has only paraphrased, or some other source, written or oral, here transposed and adapted by the scholiast, or some combination. He doubted that a mythical *historia* ever comes from tradition and was led to the counter-thesis.[36] He proposed to redefine *historia* as "énoncé", with particular reference to the use of *historia* in MH and in the *Progymnasmata* (rhetorical exercises) of Theon. He emphasized the use of this word as a generic marker in the text, appearing usually at the beginning or the end of the passage, and as also designating or signaling, with the name of an author, another collection, an anterior corpus.[37] But, as I have argued in this book, a myth is always an *énoncé*, always a retold story, in whatever medium and at whatever length. The story that is retold was already there, as often in the memory of the teller as in a written text. Whether or not one uses the word "tradition", the distinction between Delattre's sense of *historia* and Vassilaki's seems to break down. He has emphasized features of *historiai* that are internal to their separate presentations and to the collections in which they appear, whereas she has emphasized the external, antecedent forms that each instance must presuppose.

11.2 Thucydides

Concluding his survey of earlier Greek history, the so-called "Archaeology", Thucydides, too, contrasts his own findings with the accounts found in poets, who exaggerate, and in logographers, who are more enticing than truthful

---

an enormous lake which must be crossed; after that, snakes and thousands of other beasts (136–44); then vast muck and ever-flowing diarrhea, where the sinners lie (145–46; cf. 273–75). West 1983, 23–24 showed, with reference to Plato *Rep.* 363c3–d2 and *Phd.* 69c3–7, that the sinners lying in muck were Eleusinian doctrine.[35] And not Orphic, *pace* Graf 1974, 103–7; Bremmer 2002, 16. For the passage in *Phd.* as Eleusinian see especially Clinton 2003, 55–56.

36 Vassilaki 2015, 100; Delattre 2016: 89–90. For observations on the variety of senses of *historia* see also Fowler 2019, 36 n. 22.
37 Delattre 2016, 105.

(ἀληθέστερον). Their accounts belong to τὸ μυθῶδες "the domain of *muthos*" (1.21.1).[38] To this extent, the contrast is the same as the one in Pindar and Herodotus. But Thucydides opposes to the poets and to the logographers his own kind of reasoning, to which he refers with the word τεκμήρια "inferences drawn from evidence."[39] He also uses the argument from τὸ εἰκός, as in the mythographical digression on Procne and Philomela (ch. 4 Introduction sub fin.), which Simon Hornblower calls "quasi-legal."[40] In particular, he opposes his own interpretation of the Trojan War to that of Homer, who, as a poet, was likely to exaggerate.[41] Thucydides has taken a step beyond Herodotus in establishing the criterion of evidence as the basis of the contrast.[42]

But both historians seek to oppose a new kind of discourse, even if it is different in each case, to another kind, represented by Homer and the poets and the *logographoi*. In the passage on Ocean discussed above, Herodotus begins by asserting that this river is unknown and thus does not allow disproof. We would say that the proposition is unfalsifiable. Both the historians are engaged, much less explicitly but no less confidently, in the Socratic application of a method. In the philosopher's case the goal is to reach, by means of the elenchus, the concepts of piety (*Euthyphro*), friendship (discussed in the *Lysis*), courage (the *Laches*), knowledge (the *Theaetetus*), or justice (the *Republic*).[43] The historians' goal for their new kinds of discourse is truth or a truthful discourse.[44] They are engaged in a non-philosophic but ambitious concept-formation. The result is formation of the counter-concept of myth, which now becomes, to borrow a phrase from Claude Calame, a self-conscious "indigenous category."

The qualification "non-philosophic" should be emphasized. In the history of myth among the Greeks one can distinguished between first- and second-order thinking. These terms require a brief introduction. The term "first-order thinking" occurs again and again in philosophical discussion of mathematics and logic. In such texts "first" refers to the mathematical or logical languages that are used to

---

[38] For the generic article: Smyth 1122.
[39] For this interpretation of this word: Hornblower 1991, 135 on 1.20.1. The common opinion that Thuc. is implicitly criticizing Herodotus is surveyed by Rood 2019, 333–36, who concludes: "There is no reason to think that Thucydides' condemnation of the mythodic was specifically aimed at Herodotus."
[40] Hornblower 1991, 22.
[41] τῇ Ὁμήρου αὖ ποιήσει..., ἣν εἰκὸς ἐπὶ τὸ μεῖζον μὲν ποιητὴν ὄντα κοσμῆσαι, 1.10.3.
[42] See Hornblower 1987, ch. 4 ("Uses of Evidence") and 106–107 for ὡς εἰκός.
[43] Earl 2020, §1.
[44] Hdt.: Εἰ ἀληθέως (2.56); πολλὸν τῆς ἀληθείης ἀπολελειμμένοι (2.106); etc.; Thuc.: ἐπὶ τὸ προσαγωγότερον τῇ ἀκροάσει ἢ ἀληθέστερον (1.21.1).

build theories. In other fields, such as history, first-order thinking concerns substantive concepts that are primary while second-order thinking has to do with argumentation concerning verification of these concepts. In archaic and classical Greece, first-order thinking began to oppose myth explicitly with Xenophanes (ch. 5.1) and implicitly in pre-Socratic thought.[45] But both Herodotus and Thucydides use second-order thinking when they object to explanations given in myth and advance their own criteria instead.

How the formation of the concept of myth as described here fits into the story of myth's replacement by logos (cf. introduction to this chapter) is another question. This binarism bit the dust along with many others in the past deconstructive generation.[46] Early on, Geoffrey Lloyd had already, on other grounds, changed the question about the relation of the two terms. He saw a change in awareness concerning reasoning but not a shift in logic or rationality itself. He posed the question how that change came about. "…[T]he problem is one of trying to understand how *that* occurred—that is, the conditions under which such second-order questions come to be asked—not one of trying to explain the substitution of one logic, or rationality, for another."[47]

Muthos, unqualified by the contrast with or the opposition to *logos* that has been discussed up to this point, begins to have a meaning corresponding to our "myth" also in Euripides. Characters in various tragedies use *muthos* to refer to certain stories that they have heard—a cosmogony (*Melanippe the Wise* fr. 484 Radt; quoted in ch. 2.2) and the Judgment of Paris (Eur. *IA* 72). Or to refer to stories that they tell (verb μυθέομαι)—about Iolaus (Eur. *Ion* 196).[48] These are stories that we would call "myths."[49] In the cosmogony that Melanippe heard from her mother two divinities alone initiate all the forms of life including humans. In Hesiod's vastly more elaborate theogony, Earth, one of three original divinities, bears Sky. The constrictive union of Sky with Earth is ended by his castration (154–210).[50] Melanippe's story, which ends with an anthropogony, is mainly a cosmogony. Earth and Sky (or Heaven, as οὐρανός is sometimes translated) are also a feature of Orphic theogonies.[51] The women in *Ion* who say that they tell stories about Iolaus as they work at their looms also refer to six other myths that they have discerned in sculptures at

---

45 After Laks 2018 [2006] one uses the term "pre-Socratic" with apology, as a convenience.
46 See Buxton 1999, 11.
47 Lloyd 1979, 123–24. For a survey and critique of Lloyd on myth and reason see Honorato 2020.
48 For other Euripidean examples: Nesselrath 1999, 13 n. 39.
49 As Nesselrath 1999, 13 points out.
50 See West 1966, 211–12 on the widespread myth of the separation of heaven and earth.
51 Orphic theogonies: West 1983, 235 and see Index s.v. Ge. But Melanippe's cosmogony could not be defined as Orphic: see Collard et al. 1995, 269–70 for its various affinities.

Delphi.⁵² Presumably they might have told these stories, too, at their looms or on some other occasion. The Pythia describes, in the prologue to Aeschylus' *Eumenides*, female creatures whom she has found in the temple of Apollo surrounding Orestes (46–51). They are, she says, like women whom she has seen in a painting (γεγραμμένας), who are carrying off the food of Phineus (50–51). Although she does not name the women as the Harpies, she has said enough to show that she could tell the whole story if it served her purpose. But she has made her point, which is their gruesome aspect.

A bifurcation in the sense of *muthos* between pejorative, as also in the examples from Pindar and the two historians, and non-pejorative, as in the uses of this word by characters in Euripides, has emerged. In particular, *muthos* in the pejorative sense is false either as exaggeration or as complete fabrication (as also in Democritus 68 B 297 D-K, concerning stories about the afterlife).⁵³ This division of two senses of *muthos* continues in the fourth century. At the beginning of the *Panathenaicus*, Isocrates says that in his youth he chose to avoid mythical discourse.⁵⁴ Nevertheless, "Myth…is useful in Isocratean discourse because it sets out examples that he thinks should be followed and sets out patterns that are consistent with Isocratean themes found elsewhere."⁵⁵ In a protreptic treatise addressed to a certain Demonicus, for example, Isocrates refers to Zeus's begetting Heracles and Tantalus, "as the *muthoi* say and everyone believes" (ὡς οἱ μῦθοι λέγουσι καὶ πάντες πιστεύουσι, 50), with no suggestion that this myth is unreliable. Isocrates takes a Thucydidean stance toward the Trojan War. In his encomium for the Cyprian king Evagoras, he takes this war as the standard of comparison for the king's achievements. If, says Isocrates, the *muthoi* were stripped away

---

52 (a) The son of Zeus (Heracles) slays the Hydra (191–92); (b) a man (Bellerophon) on a horse (Pegasus) kills a three-bodied creature (Chimaera) (201–204); (c) the rout of the Giants (206–207); (d) a woman brandishing a gorgon-emblazoned shield against Enceladus—Athena (209–11); (e) Zeus incinerates Mimas (212–15); (f) Bromios (Dionysus) kills another of the Giants (unnamed) (216–18). Only in the case of (b) could there be a suspicion that the women are unable to tell the story. On this passage in *Ion* see Woodford 2011, 157–60.
53 With Democritus cf. Xenophanes' πλάσματα τῶν προτέρων (ch. 2.2); Palaephatus' ἔπλασαν (ch. 4 init); Pl. *Rep.* 377b6: μύθους πλασθέντας; *Tim.* 26e4: πλασθέντα μῦθον. The words πλάσμα/πλάττειν are negative in these places. Papadopoulou 1999 traces the history of these words in Greek authors and in tragic scholia and shows a "range of…connotations…from 'falsehood' to 'creative invention,'" the latter intimated already at Hes. *Theog.* 27–28.
54 νεώτερος μὲν ὢν προῃρούμην γράφειν τῶν λόγων οὐ τοὺς μυθώδεις οὐδὲ τοὺς τερατείας καὶ ψευδολογίας μεστούς, *Panath.* 1.
55 Papillon 1996, 12; cf. 15. Isoc. is consistent, however, in using μυθώδης / -ες (5x) in a negative sense (Papillon 1996, 14). For the positive sense he uses μῦθος (4x), or μυθολογέω (3x). Cf. παραμυθέω (1x).

from the Trojan War and we should behold the truth (εἰ τοὺς μύθους ἀφέντες τὴν ἀλήθειαν σκοποῖμεν, 9.66), we would find that Evagoras has accomplished greater feats than the heroes.[56] Like Thucydides Isocrates sees mythical elaboration but does not doubt that the Trojan War took place.

11.3 Plato

The negative sense of *muthos*, which appeared in the fifth century, is articulated by Isocrates and takes a definitive form in Plato.[57] Luc Brisson collected a large number of Platonic passages in which *muthos* is an unverifiable and non-argumentative form of discourse by contrast with *logos*.[58] Markus Janka, however, in his semantic study of the occurrences of *muthos* and *logos* in the same context in Plato observed that the number of places in which they are opposed is relatively small (nine places in all). These places he subdivided into three categories. The discourse of *muthos* is deficient with respect to truth, or seriousness, or ethical-religious standards.[59] Janka emphasizes what he calls the convergence of the two kinds of discourse, which he finds in a preponderance of the places in which both are referred to.

The question of *logos* as a philosophic concept or method in Plato cannot, however, be decided by statistics. What is demonstrated again and again by a certain use of *logos* can be taken as a principle for Socratic-Platonic philosophy, whether or not *logos* and *muthos* appear as opposed terms in the context. As for the myths that are told by Socrates or another speaker in a dialogue, they can be explained not as an affirmation of philosophic status equal to that of *logos* but as stop-gaps at points at which philosophic logos falls silent. Such points are reached in discourse on life after death, or a place like Atlantis lying outside the known world, or cosmology, or autochthony.[60] "Plato" (i.e., Socrates or another speaker) uses traditional myths or combines them into new myths or invents his

---

[56] The extensive discussion of *muthos* and *logos* in Isoc. in Calame 1999 is at the service of his oft-stated thesis: "The speculative and symbolic aspect as well as the argumentative applications of the discursive and narrative manifestations which we call 'myths' render futile any effort expended in the attempt to define the domain of 'mythology' *vis-à-vis* that of literature" (142). See Fowler 2011, 50 n. 24.
[57] For Isocrates: *Panath.* 1 (232) quoted in n. 54 above.
[58] Brisson 1998, 89–112.
[59] Janka 2014, 35–38.
[60] See the list of myths in Brisson 1998, 143.

own myths.⁶¹ (For combination compare Euripides' construction of the plot of *IT*: ch. 6.4.) The terms with which Plato refers to these myths recall the variation of earlier times: besides μῦθος also μυθολόγημα and λόγος.

For the opposition of *muthos* and *logos* in Plato, διαμυθολογέω and διαλέγεσθαι should also be considered. Protagoras, in the eponymous dialogue, replying to Socrates' request for a demonstration that excellence (ἀρετή) is teachable, asks if his demonstration should be a *muthos* ("as an older man speaking to younger men") or a *logos*. He begins with the former (*Prot.* 320c2–4) and at a certain point he explicitly shifts to the latter (324d6–7).⁶² Socrates later asserts, against the entirety of Protagoras' speech, his own kind of *logos*, to which he refers as διαλέγεσθαι (335a9–b6).⁶³ (Compare Socrates' extensive exposition and defense of this method in *Euthydemus*.)

At the beginning of the third of the three speeches which the *Apology* comprises (38c1–42a5), Socrates invites his friends among the jurors to stay on: "nothing prevents us from conversing for as long as it is possible" (οὐδὲν γὰρ κωλύει διαμυθολογῆσαι πρὸς ἀλλήλους ἕως ἔξεστιν, 39e5).⁶⁴ Socrates is the only one to speak. He describes beliefs concerning the afterlife which he characterizes as popular (τὰ λεγόμενα, 40c7, κτλ.).⁶⁵ He hopes to meet and converse with, amongst others, Palamedes and Telamonian Ajax "and any other of men from the past who died because of an unjust judgment, comparing my own experiences with theirs…and, most important, to spend my time questioning and examining them as I do those here, to see which of them is wise and which thinks he is but is not" (41a8–b7). Socrates sums up the elenchus to which he is referring as διαλέγεσθαι καὶ συνεῖναι καὶ ἐξετάζειν. Within, then, a discourse announced as διαμυθολογῆσαι, the happy prospect of διαλέγεσθαι returns.⁶⁶

---

61 Partenie 2018§2. For a typology of Platonic myths: Most 2012.
62 μυθολόγημα is a rare word but it is the deverbative of the more common μυθολογέω.
63 Brisson 1994, 137 = 1998, 171: "In Plato, *muthos*, which until then was essentially a 'speech' noun, did not come to designate a nonfalsifiable and a nonargumentative discourse until the emergence of a *logos* which claimed to be a verifiable and/or argumentative discourse" (I have corrected an error in the translation). See Schwyzer 2.449–50 on δια- as the preverb in διαλέγεσθαι: "die Sonderung des Verschiedenen erzielt Klarheit, Genauigkeit"; thus the translation of this verb "bei sich genau überlegen."
64 One of three occurrences of διαμυθολογέω in Pl. The other two places are *Phaed.* 70b6; *Leg.* 632e4 (where note, in the immediate context, παραμύθια, implicitly the result of διαμυθολογεῖν.
65 These are the beliefs of those who have been initiated into the Eleusinian Mysteries, as I argue in Edmunds 2013.
66 Janka's discussion of this passage does not refer to διαλέγεσθαι (2014, 35).

11.4 Beast fable (αἶνος)

Besides the kinds of myth that have been discussed under the heading *muthos* there was another kind of named story recognized in ancient Greek sources, the beast fable (αἶνος), of which Hesiod's "Hawk and Nightingale" (*Op.* 202–212) and Archilochus' "Eagle and Fox" (fr.174 W²) and "Monkey and Fox" (fr. 185 W²) are examples.[67] These fables come to be attributed to Aesop, but without a fixed terminology. Herodotus referred to him as the *logopoios* (2.134.3) and his fables are often called *logoi* (as by Trygaeus at Ar. *Pax* 129) or *muthoi* (as by Socrates at Pl. *Phaedo* 60c1, 61b6).[68] *Ainos* never differentiated itself from these two words as *muthos* differentiated itself from *logos*. But the stories called *ainoi* were used to make a point just as *muthoi* were.[69]

11.5 Aristotle

Aristotle uses μυθολογεῖν (29x), μῦθος (21x), μυθικῶς (5x) and μυθώδης (5x). To say that the conceptual opposition between myth and logos is finally fixed in Aristotle is an exaggeration.[70] On the one hand, Aristotle does indeed repudiate myth. He concludes an argument concerning first principles, in which he rejects Hesiod and his ilk, by saying "but it is not worth seriously considering matters cleverly presented in myths" (ἀλλὰ περὶ μὲν τῶν μυθικῶς σοφιζομένων οὐκ ἄξιον μετὰ σπουδῆς σκοπεῖν, *Met.* 1000ᵃ18–19). On the other hand, in a remarkable passage, which comes as a comment on an argument concerning the prime mover, Aristotle says that the substances that he has been discussing have been handed down from remote antiquity in the form of myths (1074ᵇ1–14). These myths were elaborated in the course of time, but their original thought, that these substances were gods, is an inspired utterance (θείως...εἰρῆσθαι, 1074ᵇ9).[71] (Aristotle does not

---

[67] For a survey of the fable: Holzberg 2002.
[68] For a survey of the terminology: van Dijk 1997, 88–90. Socrates also calls Aesop's fables *logoi* in the same context (*Phaedo* 60d1).
[69] For *ainos* as a form of argumentation: Edmunds 2016a, 42–43.
[70] Meyer 1999, 36.
[71] Ross 1924.2, 395 on 1074a38–1074b14 for other places in which Aristotle finds "elements of truth in popular religion" or myth. "Towards the *details* of popular belief Aristotle adopts a somewhat contemptuous attitude" (his emphasis). For a translation and discussion of this passage: Johansen 1999, 287–88, in a valuable survey of the places in which Aristotle accommodates myth to his argument. For another translation and discussion: Segev 2017, 126–27. Segev's chapter on myth in Aristotle, apart from his conflation of myth and religion ("the myths of traditional Greek

refer to poets but his implicit distinction between the truth of a myth and its poetic elaboration reminds of Thucydides.)

In the *Poetics muthos* is a technical term for the plot of a tragedy, received from the old myths, which "it is not possible to undo."[72] Orestes killed Clytemnestra, Aristotle says, meaning that this mythical fact cannot be changed. The *muthos* is the "principle and the soul of tragedy."[73] The term thus retains the nonpejorative sense that this word has in the examples from the fifth century and from Isocrates given above.[74] At the same time, despite his stricture on the received myths, Aristotle countenanced some degree of invention on the part of the poet within adherence to the received myths.[75] What he was allowing was, however, nothing more than the variation usual in myths. Aristotle also casually uses *muthos* in a positive or at least open sense. He uses Sardanapalus as one of his examples of a monarch who was killed because of someone's contempt of him—"as someone seeing him carding wool with the women (if the ones who tell mythical stories [οἱ μυθολογοῦντες] are telling the truth; but if not in his case it still might happen in someone else's case)" (*Pol.* 1312ᵃ1–4).[76]

11.6 Conclusion

In the fifth century *muthos* for the first time becomes independent of the rhetorical senses that it has in Homer and becomes an apparently colloquial way of referring to stories about the past that anyone can tell. At the same time, first in Pindar and then in Herodotus and Thucydides (in particular his use of τὸ μυθῶδες) myth acquires a new more general sense. In the historians, when it is opposed to their own kinds of discourse, myth becomes, precisely because of this opposition, a rudimentary concept and, as such, negative. Isocrates has grasped this new concept, as the prooemium to the *Panathenaicus* shows, but he does not hesitate to use myths for his own purposes. In Aristotle and Plato, beside stricter formulations of the opposition, myths persist. Plato, under certain circumstances, composed myths of his own.

---

religion"), which is sometimes inapplicable to his examples, is also a valuable survey (125–39). I have not seen Neschke 1999.
72 τοὺς μὲν οὖν παρειλημμένους μύθους λύειν οὐκ ἔστιν, *Poet.* 1453ᵇ22–23.
73 ἀρχὴ μὲν οὖν καὶ οἷον ψυχὴ ὁ μῦθος τῆς τραγῳδίας, *Poet.* 1450α38–39.
74 Cf. Halliwell 1986, 23.
75 Edmunds 2014a, 12–14.
76 ἰδών τις ξαίνοντα μετὰ τῶν γυναικῶν (εἰ ἀληθῆ ταῦτα οἱ μυθολογοῦντες λέγουσιν· εἰ δὲ μὴ ἐπ' ἐκείνου, ἀλλ' ἐπ' ἄλλου γε ἂν γένοιτο τοῦτο ἀληθές).

Works Cited

Aarne, A. 1910. *Verzeichnis der Märchentypen*. FF Communications 3, Helsinki.
Abraham, K. 1909. *Traum und Mythus*, Leipzig.
Ackerman, R. 1987. *J.G. Frazer: His Life and Work*, Cambridge.
Ackerman, R. 1991. *The Myth and Ritual School: J.G. Frazer and the Cambridge Ritualists*, New York.
Aguirre Castro, M. 2005. "Expressions of Love and Sexual Union in Hesiod's *Catalogue of Women*," in: *Cuadernos de filología clásica: Estudios griegos e indoeuropeos* 15, 19–25.
Allan, W. 2006. "Divine Justice and Cosmic Order in Early Greek Epic," in: *JHS* 126, 1–35.
Allen, Nicholas J. 2011. "The Indo-European Background to Greek Mythology," in: Dowden/Livingstone (eds.), 2011, 341–56.
Allonge, M. 2005. "The Palaikastro Hymn and the Modern Myth of the Cretan Zeus," in: Princeton/Stanford Working Papers in Classics. http://www.princeton.edu/~pswpc/
Aloni, A. 1997. *Saffo: Frammenti*, Florence.
Andolfi, I. 2019. *Acusilaus of Argos' Rhapsody in Prose: Introduction, Text, and Commentary*, Trends in Classics Suppl. Vol. 70. Berlin (Non vidi.).
Arlen, S. 1990. *The Cambridge Ritualists: An Annotated Bibliography of the Works by and about Jane Ellen Harrison, Gilbert Murray, Francis M. Cornford, and Arthur Bernard Cook*, Metuchen, NJ.
Armstrong, R.H. 2011. "Psychoanalysis: The Wellspring of Myth?," in: Dowden/Livingstone (eds.) 2011, 471–86.
Arndt, W.F./F.W. Gingrich. 1979. *A Greek-English Lexicon of the New Testament and Other Early Christian Literature*. 2nd ed., Chicago.
Asheri, D./A. Lloyd/A. Corcella. 2007. *A Commentary on Herodotus: Books I–IV*. Ed. by O. Murray and A. Moreno. Trans. B. Graziosi, et al. Oxford.
Asper, M. 2007. "Medienwechsel und kultureller Kontext: Die Entstehung der griechischen Sachprosa," in: J. Althoff (ed.), *Philosophie und Dichtung im antiken Griechenland: Akten der 7. Tagung der Karl und Gertrud Abel-Stiftung am 10. und 11. Oktober 2002 in Bernkastel-Kues*, Philosophie der Antike 23, Stuttgart, 67–102.
Athanassaki, L. 2016. "Political and Dramatic Perspectives on Archaic Sculptures: Bacchylides' Fourth Dithyramb (Ode 18) and the Treasury of the Athenians in Delphi," in: V. Cazzato/A. Lardinois (eds.), *The Look of Lyric: Greek Song and the Visual*, Leiden, 16–49.
Azzolina, D.S. 1987. *Tale Type- and Motif-Indexes*. An Annotated Bibliography, New York.
Bachvarova, M.R. 2016. *From Hittite to Homer: The Anatolian Background of Ancient Greek Epic*, Cambridge.
Bachvarova, M.R. 2017. "The Hurro-Hittite Song of Release (Destruction of the City of Ebla)," in: C. López-Ruiz (ed.), *Gods, Heroes, and Monsters: A Sourcebook of Greek, Roman, and Near Eastern Myths in Translation*. 2nd ed., Oxford, 301–10.
Bachvarova, M.R./D. Dutsch/A. Suter (eds.) 2016, *The Fall of Cities: Commemoration in Literature, Folk Song, and Liturgy*, Cambridge. (Non vidi.)
Bakhtin, M. 1984. *Problems of Dostoevsky's Poetics*. Trans. and ed. Caryl Emerson, Minneapolis.
Bal, M. 1997. *Narratology: Introduction to the Theory of Narrative*. 2nd ed., Trans. Christine Van Boheemen, Toronto.

Baragwanath, E. 2012. "The Mythic Plupast in Herodotus," in: Grethlein/Krebs (eds.), 2012, 35–56.
Baragwanath, E. 2019. "Myth and History Entwined: Female Influence and Male Usurpation in Herodotus' Histories," in: J. Baines/H. van der Blom/Yi Samuel Chen/T. Rood (eds.), *Historical Consciousness and the Use of the Past in the Ancient World*, Sheffield, UK, 293–311.
Barlow, S.A. 1997. *Euripides: Trojan Women*, Oxford.
Barthes, R. 1970. *S/Z*, Paris.
Beck, W.R. 2019. *The Narrative of the Iliad: Time, Space, and Story*, PhD. diss. University of Pennsylvania.
Beck-Schachter, A. 2018. *The Goddess on Parade: Mobile Cult Statues in Archaic and Classical Greece*. Ph.D. diss. Rutgers, The State University of New Jersey, New Brunswick NJ.
Bellah, R.N. 2005. "Durkheim and Ritual," in: J.C. Alexander/P. Smith (eds.), *The Cambridge Companion to Durkheim*, Cambridge, 183–210.
Ben-Amos, D. 1971. "Toward a Definition of Folklore in Context," in: *Journal of American Folklore* 84, 3–15.
Benveniste, É. 1969. "Le serment en Grèce," in : *Le vocabulaire des institutions indo-européennes*. Vol. 2, Paris, 163–75.
Benveniste, É. 1970. "L'appareil formel de l'énonciation," in: *Langages* 17, 12–18.
Bérard, C. 1983. "Imagiers et artistes," in: *Études de lettres* 4, 2–4.
Bertelli, L. 1996. "'C'era una volta un mito...': Alla origine della storiografia greca," in: *De tuo tibi: Omaggio degli allievi a Italo Lana*, Bologna, 49–85.
Bertelli, L. 2001. "Hecataeus: From Genealogy to Historiography," in: N. Luraghi (ed.), *The Historian's Craft in the Age of Herodotus*, Oxford, 67–94.
Bettinetti, S. 2001. *La statua di culto nella pratica rituale greca*, Bari.
Bettini, M. 2012. "Introduzione," in: *I Quaderni del Ramo d'Oro On-Line* (extra seriem) 2012, ii-vii. http://www.qro.unisi.it/frontend/node/133
Bevilacqua, F. 2010. *Memorabili di Senofonte*, Turin.
Bies, W. 1999. "Mythologie," in: *EM*, cols. 1073–86.
Biles, Z.P./S.D. Olson. 2015. *Aristophanes: Wasps*, Oxford.
Binder, G. 1964. *Die Aussetzung des Königskindes: Kyros und Romulus*. Beiträge zur klassischen Philologie 10, Meisenheim am Glan.
Birus, H. 1987. "Vorschlag zu einer Typologie literarischer Namen," in: *LiLi: Zeitschrift für Literaturwissenschaft und Linguistik* 17 (67), 38–51.
Boedeker, D. 2012. "The Speaker's Past: Herodotus in the Light of Elegy and Lyric," in: Grethlein/Krebs (eds.), 2012, 17–34.
Bogatyrev, P./R. Jakobson. 1966 [1929]. "Die Folklore als eine besondere Form des Schaffens," in: R. Jakobson, *Selected Writings*, vol. 4. The Hague, 1–15 [Orig. pub. in *Donum natalicium Schrijnen*, Nijmegen/Utrecht, 900–913].
Bogatyrev, P./R. Jakobson. 1976 [1931]. "On the Boundary between Studies of Folklore and Literature," in: *Readings in Russian Poetics: Formalist and Structuralist Views*, ed. L. Matejka and K. Pomorska, trans. H. Eagle. Cambridge, MA, 91–93. [Orig. pub. as "K problematike razmezhivaniia folkloristiki i literaturovedeniia," in: Lud Slowianski 2, 229–33].
Bogatyrev, P./R. Jakobson. 1982 [1929]. "Folklore as a Special Form of Creativity," in: *The Prague School: Selected Writings, 1929–1946*, ed. P. Steiner, trans. M. Jacobson, Austin, 32–46. (Trans. of Bogatyrev/Jakobson 1966 [1929]).

Bosanquet, R.C. 1908–1909. "The Palaikastro Hymn of the Kouretes," in: *The Annual of the British School at Athens* 15, 339–356.
Bowie, A.M. 2019. *Homer: Iliad Book III*, Cambridge.
Braid, Donald. 2002. "Performanz," in: *EM* 10, cols. 730–43.
Braund, S.M./G.W. Most (eds.). 2003. *Ancient Anger: Perspectives from Homer to Galen*, Cambridge.
Brelich, A. 1958. *Gli eroi greci: un problema storico-religioso*, Rome.
Brelich, A. 1969. *Paides e partenoi*, Rome.
Bremer, J.M. 1987. "The So-Called 'Götterapparat' in *Iliad* XX–XXII," in: id./I.J.F. de Jong/J. Kalff (eds.), *Homer: Beyond Oral Poetry: Recent Trends in Homeric Interpretation*, Amsterdam, 31–46.
Bremmer, J.N. (ed.). 1987. *Interpretations of Greek Mythology*, London.
Bremmer, J.N. 1987. "What is a Greek Myth?," in: id. 1987, 1–9.
Bremmer, J.N. 2002. *The Rise and Fall of the Afterlife: The 1995 Read-Tuckwell Lectures at the University of Bristol*, London.
Bremmer, J.N. 2013. "Local Mythography: The Pride of Halicarnassus," in: Trzaskoma/Smith, 54–73.
Bremond, C. 1964. "Le message narratif," in: *Communications* 4, 4–32.
Bremond, C. 1966. "La logique des possibles narratifs," in: *Communications* 8, 60–76.
Bremond, C. 1973. *Logique du récit*, Paris.
Brillante, C. 1990. "History and the Historical Interpretation of Myth," in Edmunds (ed.), 93–138.
Brisson, L. 1994. *Platon: Les mots et les mythes*, Paris.
Brisson, L. 1998. *Plato the Myth Maker*. Trans. G. Naddaf, Chicago.
Brown, M.K. 2002. *The Narratives of Conon*, Munich.
Bulloch, A.W. 1985. *Callimachus: The Fifth Hymn*. Cambridge Classical Texts and Commentaries 26, Cambridge.
Burgess, J.S. 2001. *The Tradition of the Trojan War in Homer and the Epic Cycle*, Baltimore.
Burkert, W. 1966. "Kekropidensage und Arrephoria," in: *Hermes* 94, 1–25.
Burkert, W. 1972. *Homo Necans: Interpretationen altgriechischer Opferriten und Mythen*, Berlin.
Burkert, W. 1977. *Griechische Religion der archaischen und klassischen Epoche*, Stuttgart.
Burkert, W. 1979. *Structure and History in Greek Mythology and Ritual*, Berkeley/Los Angeles.
Burkert, W. 1983. *Homo Necans: The Anthropology of Ancient Greek Sacrificial Ritual and Myth*. Trans. P. Bing, Berkeley.
Burkert, W. 1984. *Die orientalisierende Epoche in der griechischen Religion und Literatur*, Heidelberg.
Burkert, W. 1985. *Greek Religion*. Trans. J. Raffan, Cambridge, MA.
Burkert, W. 1987. "Oriental and Greek Mythology," in: Bremmer (ed.), 10–40.
Burkert, W. 1992 [1984]. *The Orientalizing Revolution: Near Eastern Influence on Greek Culture in the Early Archaic Age*, Cambridge MA.
Burkert, W. 1993. "Mythos—Begriff, Struktur, Funktionen," in: F. Graf (ed.), *Mythos in mythenloser Gesellschaft*, Stuttgart, 9–24.
Burkert, W. 1997. *Homo Necans: Interpretationen altgriechischer Opferriten und Mythen*. 2nd ed., Berlin.
Burkert, W. 2011. *Griechische Religion der archaischen und klassischen Epoche*. 2nd ed., Stuttgart.

Burnet, J. 1924. *Plato's Euthyphro, Apology of Socrates and Crito*, Oxford.
Burris, S./J. Fish/D. Obbink. 2014. "New Fragments of Book 1 of Sappho," in: *ZPE* 189, 1–28.
Butchvarov, P. 1999. "conceptualism." In R. Audi (ed.), *The Cambridge Dictionary of Philosophy*. 2nd ed., Cambridge, 169–70.
Buxton R.G.A. 1994. *Imaginary Greece: The Contexts of Mythology*, Cambridge.
Buxton, R.G.A. (ed.). 1999. *From Myth to Reason? Studies in the Development of Greek Thought*, Oxford.
Buxton R.G.A. 1999. "Introduction," in: Buxton (ed.), 1–21.
Buxton R.G.A. 2009. *Forms of Astonishment: Greek Myths of Metamorphosis*, Oxford.
Buxton R.G.A. 2013. *Myths and Tragedies in Their Ancient Greek Contexts*, Oxford.
Cairns, D.L. 1993. *Aidōs: The Psychology and Ethics of Honour and Shame in Ancient Greek Literature*, Oxford.
Cairns, D.L. 2003. "Ethics, Ethology, Terminology: Iliadic Anger and the Cross-Cultural Study of Emotion," in: Braund/Most (ed.), 11–49.
Cairns, D.L./L. Fulkerson. 2015."Introduction," in: Cairns/Fulkerson (eds.), *Emotions between Greece and Rome*. BICS Suppl. 125, London, 1–22.
Calame, C. 1985. "La formulation de quelques structures sémio-narratives ou comment segmenter un texte," in: H. Parret/H.-G. Ruprecht, eds., *Exigences et perspectives de la sémiotique: recueil d'hommages pour Algirdas Julien Greimas*. Amsterdam, 135–47.
Calame, C. 1986. "Mythe et conte: La légende du Cyclope et ses transformations narratives," in: id., *Le récit en Grèce ancienne: Énonciations et representations de poètes*, Paris, 123–51.
Calame, C. 1987. "Spartan Genealogies: The Mythological Representation of a Spatial Organization," in: Bremmer (ed.), 153–86.
Calame, C. 1990. *Thésée et l'imaginaire athénien: légende et culte en Grèce antique*, Lausanne.
Calame, C. 1990. "Narrating the Foundation of a City: The Symbolic Birth of Cyrene," in: Edmunds, ed. 1990, 277–341.
Calame, C. 1991."'Mythe' et 'rite' en Grèce: Des catégories indigènes?" *Kernos* 4, 179–204.
Calame, C. 1996. *Mythe et histoire dans l'antiquité grecque: la création symbolique d'une colonie*, Lausanne.
Calame, C. 1999. "The Rhetoric of Mythos and Logos," in: Buxton (ed.), 119–43.
Calame, C. 2007. "Greek Myth and Greek Religion," in: Woodard (ed.), 259–85.
Calame, C. 2009. "The Abduction of Helen and the Greek Poetic Tradition: Politics, Reinterpretations and Controversies," in: U. Dill/Chr. Walde (eds.), *Antike Mythen: Medien, Transformationen und Konstruktionen*, Berlin, 645–61.
Calame, C. 2011a. "Myth and Performance on the Athenian Stage: Praxithea, Erechtheus, Their Daughters, and the Etiology of Autochthony," in: *CP* 106.1, 1–19.
Calame, C. 2011b. "Semiotics and Pragmatics of Myth," in: Dowden/Livingstone (eds.), 507–24.
Calame, C. 2014. "Narrative Semantics and Pragmatics: The Poetic Creation of Cyrene," in: Edmunds (ed.), 281–352.
Calame, C. 2015. *Qu'est-ce que la mythologie grecque?*, Paris.
Calder, W.M., III, ed. 1989. *The Cambridge Ritualists Reconsidered: Proceedings of the First Oldfather Conference, Held on the Campus of the University of Illinois at Urbana-Champaign April 27–30, 1989*.
Caldwell, R. 1990. "The Psychoanalytic Interpretation of Greek Myth," in: Edmunds (ed.), 344–89.

Cameron, A. 2004. *Greek Mythography in the Roman World*, New York.
Carbon, J.-M./V. Pirenne-Delforge. 2012. "Beyond Greek 'Sacred Laws'," in: *Kernos* 25, 163–82.
Chantraine, P. 1963–1973. *Grammaire Homérique*. 2 vols. (vol. 1 rev. 1973), Paris.
Chong-Gossard/J.H. K.O. 2016. "The Irony of Consolation in Euripides' Plays and Fragments," in: *Ramus* 45, 18–44.
Christopoulos, M. 2011. "*Casus belli*: Causes of the Trojan War in the Epic Cycle." In: E.D. Karakantza (ed.), *Classics@*6. The Center for Hellenic Studies. http://nrs.harvard.edu/urn-3:hlnc.jissue:ClassicsAt.Issue06.Reflecting_on_the_Greek_Epic_Cycle.2010.
Clarke, K. 2017. "Walking through History: Unlocking the Mythical Past," in: Hawes (ed.), 14–31.
Clauss, J.J./S.I. Johnston (eds.). 1997. *Medea: Essays on Medea in Myth, Literature, Philosophy, and Art*, Princeton, NJ.
Clinton, K. 2003. "Stages of Initiation in the Eleusinian and Samothracian Mysteries," in: M.B. Cosmopoulos (ed.), *Greek Mysteries: The Archaeology and Ritual of Ancient Greek Secret Cults*, London, 50–78.
Cohen, A. 2007. "Mythic Landscapes of Greece," in: Woodard (ed.), 305–30.
Collard, C./M. Cropp. 2008. *Euripides: Fragments*. 2 vols., Cambridge MA.
Collard, C./M. Cropp/K.H. Lee. 1995. *Selected Fragmentary Plays*. Vol. 1. Warminster, England.
Colpe, C. 1981. "Dumézil, Georges Edmond Raoul," in: *EM* 3, cols. 924–27.
Condello, F. 2009. *Sofocle: Edipo Re*, Siena.
Conrad, J.A. 1999. "Motivem," in: *EM* 9, cols. 1012–30.
Conrad, J.A. 2002. "Polyphem," in: *EM* 10, cols. 1174–84.
Cook, R.M. 1983. "Art and Epic in Archaic Greece," *Bulletin Antieke Beschaving* 58, 1–10.
Coray, M. 2009. In Latacz/Bierl (eds.) 2000ff. Vol. 6 (Book 19). Fasc. 2 (Commentary), Berlin.
Csapo, E. 2005. *Theories of Mythology*, Oxford.
Culler, J. 1975. *Structuralist Poetics: Structuralism, Linguistics, and the Study of Literature*, Ithaca NY.
Cumming, S. 2016. "Names," in: E.N. Zalta, ed., *The Stanford Encyclopedia of Philosophy* (Fall 2016 Edition). https://plato.stanford.edu/archives/fall2016/entries/names/.
Currie, B. 2012. "The *Iliad*, *Gilgamesh*, and Neoanalysis," in F. Montanari/A. Rengakos/C. Tsagalis (eds.), *Homeric Contexts: Neoanalysis and the Interpretation of Oral Poetry*, Berlin, 543–80.
Currie, B. 2015. "Cypria," in: Fantuzzi/Tsagalis (eds.), 281–305.
Dalgat, U.B. 1984. "Feuerraub," in: *EM* 4, cols. 1087–91.
Dammann, G. 2007. "Strukturalismus," in: *EM* 12, cols. 1406–16.
Danek, G. 2008. "Heroic and Athletic Contest in Bacchylides 17," in: *Wiener Studien* 121, 71–83.
Darwin, C.R. 1998 [1872]. *The Expression of the Emotions in Man and Animals*. 3rd ed., Oxford.
Davidson, O.M. 1980. "Indo-European Dimensions of Herakles in 'Iliad' 19.95–133," in: *Arethusa* 13, 197–202.
Davies, M. 2002. "The Folk-Tale Origins of the *Iliad* and *Odyssey*," in: *Wiener Studien* 115, 5–43.
Davies, M. 2003a. "Proppian Light on the Aristaeus Episode in Vergil's 'Fourth Georgic'," in: *Prometheus* 29.1, 57–64.
Davies, M. 2003b. "Philoctetes: Wild Man and Helper Figure," in: *Parola del Passato* 58, 347–55.

Davies, M. 2004. "Two Medieval Saints' Lives and the Judgement of Paris," in: *Prometheus* 30, 177–86.
Davies, M. 2005. "Dolon and Rhesus," in: *Prometheus* 31.1, 29–34.
Davies, M. 2009. "Folk-tale Vestiges in the Second Half of the 'Odyssey'," in: *Prometheus* 35.1, 1–10.
Davies, M. 2011a. "Folk-tale Elements in the *Cypria*," in: E.D. Karakantza (ed.), *Classics@6*. The Center for Hellenic Studies. http://nrs.harvard.edu/urn-3:hlnc.jissue:ClassicsAt.Issue06.Reflecting_on_the_Greek_Epic_Cycle.2010.
Davies, M. 2011b. "'Unpromising' Heroes and Heroes as Helpers in Greek Myth," in: *Prometheus* 37, 108–27.
de Man, P. 1983 [1969]. "Literary History and Literary Modernity," in: *Blindness and Insight: Essays in the Rhetoric of Contemporary Criticism*. 2d ed. Minneapolis, 142–65.
De Strycker, É./S.R. Slings. 1994. *Plato's Apology of Socrates: A Literary and Philosophical Study with a Running Commentary*, Leiden.
Dégh, L. 1984. "Erzählen, Erzählung," in: *EM* 4, 315–42.
Delattre, C. 2005. *Manuel de mythologie grecque*, Rosny-sous-Bois.
Delattre, C. 2016. "Référence et corpus dans les pratiques de commentaire: les emplois de *historia*," in: *Revue de Philologie* 90.2, 89–110.
Denecke, L. 1990. "Grimm, Wilhelm Carl," in: *EM* 6, cols. 186–95.
Detienne, M./J.-P. Vernant (eds.) 1979. *La cuisine du sacrifice en pays grec*, Paris.
Detienne, M./J.-P. Vernant (eds.) 1989. *The Cuisine of Sacrifice Among the Greeks*. Trans. Paula Wissing, Chicago.
Detienne, M. 1974. *Les jardins d'Adonis: la mythologie des aromates en Grèce*, Paris.
Detienne, M. 1977. *The Gardens of Adonis: Spices in Greek Mythology*. Trans. J. Lloyd, Atlantic Highlands NJ.
Detienne, M. 1981. *L'invention de la mythologie*, Paris.
Detienne, M. 1986. *The Creation of Mythology*, Chicago.
Devereux, G. 1973. "The Self-blinding of Oidipous in Sophokles," in: *Journal of Hellenic Studies* 93, 36–49.
Dewald, C. 2012. "Myth and Legend in Herodotus' First Book," in: E. Baragwanath/M. de Bakker (eds.), *Myth, Truth, and Narrative in Herodotus*, Oxford, 59–86.
Diggle, J. 1984. *Euripidis Fabulae*. Vol. 1, Oxford.
Dijk, G.-J. van. 1997. *Ainoi, Logoi, Mythoi: Fables in Archaic, Classical, and Hellenistic Greek Literature, with a Study of the Theory and Terminology of the Genre*, Leiden.
Dodd, D.B. 2003. "Preface," in: id./Faraone (eds.), xiii–xvi.
Dodd, D.B./C.A. Faraone (eds.) 2003. *Initiation in Ancient Greek Rituals and Narratives: New Critical Perspectives*, London.
Doherty, L. 2017. "Revisionism," in: Zajko/Hoyle (eds.), 153–64.
Domaradzki, M. 2011. "Theagenes of Rhegium and the Rise of Allegorical Interpretation," in: *Elenchos* 32.2, 205–28.
Dosse, F. 1997. *History of Structuralism*. Vol. 1 ("The rising sign, 1945–1966"). Trans. D. Glassman, Minneapolis MN.
Dover, K.J. 1978. *Greek Homosexuality*, London.
Dowden, K./N. Livingstone (eds.) 2011. *A Companion to Greek Mythology*, Chichester, West Sussex.
Dowden, K.H. 1992. *The Uses of Greek Mythology*, London.

Dowden, K.H. 2011a. "Telling the Mythology: From Hesiod to the Fifth Century," in: Dowden/Livingstone (eds.), 47–72.
Dowden, K.H. 2011b. "Initiation: The Key to Myth?," in: Dowden/Livingstone (eds.), 487–505.
Dowden, K.H./N. Livingstone. 2011. "Thinking through Myth, Thinking Myth Through," Dowden/Livingstone (eds.), 3–23.
Duchemin, J. 1952. "Les sources grecques et orientales de la Théogonie hésiodique," in: *L'information littéraire* 4, 146–51.
Duchemin, J. 1995. *Mythes grecs et sources orientales*. Ed. by B. Deforge, Paris.
Dumézil, G. 1995. *Mythe et épopée*s, Paris.
Dundes, A. 1962. "From Etic to Emic Units in the Structural Study of Folktales," in: *The Journal of American Folklore* 75, no. 296, 95–105 [Repr. as Dundes 2007b].
Dundes, A. 1964. *The Morphology of North American Indian Folktales*, Helsinki.
Dundes, A. 1976. "Structuralism and Folklore," in: *Studia Fennica* 20, 75–93. [Repr. as Dundes 2007d].
Dundes, A. 2007a. *Meaning of Folklore: The Analytical Essays of Alan Dundes*. Ed. by S.J. Bronner, Logan.
Dundes, A. 2007b. "From Etic to Emic Units in the Structural Study of Folktales," in: id. 2007a, 90–106, with a postscript "The Motif-Index and the Tale Type Index: A Critique", 107–53.
Dundes, A. 2007c. "The Symbolic Equivalence of Allomotifs: Towards a Method of Analyzing Folktales," in: id. 2007a, 317–324.
Dundes, A. 2007d. "Structuralism and Folklore," in: id. 2007a, 126–44, with a postscript "Binary Opposition in Myth: The Propp/Lévi-Strauss Debate in Retrospect", 145–53.
Durkheim, É. 1912. *Les formes élémentaires de la vie religieuse, le système totémique en Australie*, Paris.
Earl, D. 2020. "The Classical Theory of Concepts," in: *Internet Encyclopedia of Philosophy*. https://www.iep.utm.edu/conc-cl/.
Easterling, P.E. 2012. "tragedy, Greek," in: OCD^4, 1493–97.
Ecker, H.-P. 1996. "Legende," in: *EM* 1996, cols. 855–67.
Edmunds, L. (ed.) 1990. *Approaches to Greek Myth*, Baltimore MD.
Edmunds, L. (ed.) 2014. *Approaches to Greek Myth*. 2nd ed., Baltimore.
Edmunds, L. 1985. *Oedipus: The Ancient Legend and its Later Analogues*, Baltimore.
Edmunds, L. 1986. "Il corpo di Edipo: struttura psico-mitologica," in: B. Gentili/R. Pretagostini, (eds.), *Edipo: Il teatro greco e la cultura europea: Atti del convegno internazionale (Urbino 15–19 Nov. 1982)*, Rome, 237–53.
Edmunds, L. 1988. "The Body of Oedipus," in: *Psychoanalytic Review* 75.1, 51–65.
Edmunds, L. 1990a. "Introduction: The Practice of Greek Mythology," in: Edmunds (ed.), 1–20.
Edmunds, L. 1990b. Introduction to ch. 1 (Versnel), in: Edmunds (ed.), 23–25.
Edmunds, L. 1990c. Introduction to ch. 7 (Caldwell), in: Edmunds (ed.), 342–44.
Edmunds, L. 1990d. Introduction to ch. 8 (Sourvinou-Inwood), in: Edmunds (ed.), 393–94.
Edmunds, L. 1997. "Myth in Homer," in B. Powell/I. Morris (eds.), *New Companion to Homer*, Leiden, 415–41.
Edmunds, L. 2005. "Myth and Epic," in: Foley (ed.), 31–44.
Edmunds, L. 2006a. "The New Sappho: ἔφαντο (9)," in: *ZPE* 156, 23–26.
Edmunds, L. 2006b. *Oedipus*, London.
Edmunds, L. 2008. "Deixis in Ancient Greek and Latin Literature: Historical Introduction and State of the Question," in: *Philologia Antiqua* 1, 67–98.

Edmunds, L. 2013. "The Afterlife of Socrates: Plato, *Apology* 38c1–42a5," in: Luis Miguel Pino Campos/Germán Santana Henríquez (eds.), Καλὸς καὶ ἀγαθὸς ἀνήρ διδασκάλου παράδειγμα: *Homenaje al Profesor Juan Antonio López Férez*, Madrid, 243–50.
Edmunds, L. 2014a. "General Introduction," in: Edmunds, ed. 2014, 1–41.
Edmunds, L. 2014b. Introduction to ch. 4 (Nagy), in: Edmunds (ed.), 200–202.
Edmunds, L. 2014c. Introduction to ch. 6 (Calame), in: Edmunds (ed.), 280–81.
Edmunds, L. 2014d. Introduction to ch. 7 (Sourvinou-Inwood), in: Edmunds (ed.), 353–55.
Edmunds, L. 2014e. Introduction to ch. 8 (Segal), in: Edmunds (ed.), 407–408.
Edmunds, L. 2016a. *Stealing Helen: The Myth of the Abducted Wife in Comparative Perspective*, Princeton.
Edmunds, L. 2016b. "The Gods of Homer between Myth and Religon," in: Federico Gallo (ed.), *Omero: Quaestiones Disputatae*. Ambrosiana Graecolatina 5, Rome, 107–22.
Edmunds, L. 2016c. "Intertextuality without Texts in Archaic Greek Verse and the Plan of Zeus," in: *Syllecta Classica* 27, 1–27.
Edmunds, L. 2017. "Helen in Pseudo-Apollodorus Book 3," in: J. Pàmias (ed.), *Apollodoriana: Ancient Myths, New Crossroads*, Berlin, 82–99.
Edmunds, L. 2019. *Toward the Characterization of Helen in Homer: Appellatives, Periphrastic Denominations, and Noun-Epithet Formulas*. Trends in Classics Suppl. Vol. 87, Berlin.
Edmunds, L. Forthcoming(1). "Heracles' Sack of Troy in Mythographus Homericus (schol. D *Il.* 20.145)," in: J. Pàges/N. Villagra (eds.).
Edmunds, L. Forthcoming(2). "Sappho's Helen and Sappho's Homer (Frs. 16, 23, 166 V)," in: X. Riu (ed.), *Festschrift for Jaume Pòrtulas*.
Erbse, H. 1986. *Untersuchungen zur Funktion der Götter im homerischen Epos*, Berlin.
Fahr, W. 1969. *Theous Nomizein: Zum Problem der Anfänge des Atheismus bei den Griechen*, Hildesheim.
Fantham, E. 1992. "Strengths and Weaknesses of Current Ovidian Criticism," in: K. Galinsky (ed.), *The Interpretation of Roman Poetry: Empiricism or Hermeneutics?* Studien zur klassischen Philologie 67, Frankfurt am Main, 191–99.
Fantuzzi, M./C. Tsagalis (eds.) 2015. *The Greek Epic Cycle and Its Ancient Reception: A Companion*, Cambridge.
Faraone, C.A. 2011. "An Athenian Tradition of Dactylic Paeans to Apollo and Asclepius: Choral Degeneration or a Flexible System of Non-Strophic Dactyls?," in: *Mnemosyne* 64.2, 206–231.
Faraone, C.A./F.S. Naiden (eds.) 2012. *Greek and Roman Animal Sacrifice: Ancient Victims, Modern Observers*, Cambridge.
Feeney, D.C. 1998. *Literature and Religion at Rome: Cultures, Contexts, and Beliefs*, New York.
Fehling, D. 1977. *Amor und Psyche: Die Schöpfung des Apuleius und ihre Einwirkung auf das Märchen, eine Kritik der romantischen Märchentheorie*, Wiesbaden.
Fehling, D. 1984. "Die alten Literaturen als Quelle der neuzeitlichen Märchen," in: Siegmund (ed.), 79–92.
Finglass, P.J. 2011. *Sophocles: Ajax*. Cambridge Classical Texts and Commentaries 48, Cambridge.
Finglass, P.J. 2012a. "Sophocles' Theseus." In A. Markantonatos/B. Zimmermann (eds.), *Crisis on Stage: Tragedy and Comedy in Late Fifth-Century Athens*. Trends in Classics Suppl. Vol. 13, Berlin, 41–53.
Finglass, P.J. 2012b. "Ethnic identity in Stesichorus", in: *ZPE* 182, 39–44.
Finglass, P.J. 2013. "Demophon in Egypt," in: *ZPE* 184, 37–50.

Finglass, P.J. 2014. "A new fragment of Euripides' *Ino*," in: *ZPE* 189, 65–82.
Finglass, P.J. 2016. "Mistaken Identity in Euripides' *Ino*," in: P. Kyriakou/A. Rengakos (eds.), *Wisdom and Folly in Euripides*. Trends in Classics Suppl. Vol. 31, Berlin, 299–315.
Finglass, P.J. 2017a. "Further Notes on the Euripides Ino Papyrus (P. Oxy. 5131)," in: *Eikasmos* 28, 61–65.
Finglass, P.J. 2017b. "Ibycus or Stesichorus? Fr. S166 Page," in: *ZPE* 202, 19–28.
Finglass, P.J. 2020. "Phaedra between Homer and Sophocles: The Stesichorean Connexion," in: P. Cecconi/C. Tornau (eds.), *Städte und Stadtstaaten zwischen Mythos, Literatur und Propaganda*. Beiträge zur Altertumskunde 383, Berlin, 181–90.
Finkelberg, M. 2014. "Boreas and Oreithyia: A Case-Study in Multichannel Transmission of Myth," in: Scodel, 87–100.
Fludernik, M. 1996. *Towards a 'Natural' Narratology*, London.
Foley, J.M. (ed.) 2005. *A Companion to Ancient Epic*, Oxford.
Foley, J.M. 1991. *Immanent Art: From Structure to Meaning in Traditional Oral Epic*, Bloomington.
Forbes Irving, P.M.C. 1990. *Metamorphosis in Greek Myths*, Oxford.
Ford, A. 1999. "Reading Homer from the Rostrum: Poems and Laws in Aeschines' Against Timarchus," in: S. Goldhill/R. Osborne (eds.), *Performance Culture and Athenian Democracy*, Cambridge, 231–56.
Ford, A. 2002. *The Origins of Criticism Literary Culture and Poetic Theory in Classical Greece*, Princeton NJ.
Ford, A. 2019. "Mythographic Discourse among non-Mythographers: Pindar's *Ol*. 1, Plato's *Phaedrus* and Callimachus' *Hymn to Zeus*," in: Romano/Marincola (eds.), 5–28.
Forster, E.M. 1927. *Aspects of the Novel*, London.
Foucault, M. 1969. *L'Archéologie du savoir*, Paris.
Foucault, M. 1972. *The Archaeology of Knowledge and the Discourse on Language*. Trans. A.M. Sheridan Smith, New York.
Fowler, R.L. 1998. "Genealogical Thinking, Hesiod's *Catalogue*, and the Creation of the Hellenes," in: *Proceedings of the Cambridge Philological Society* 44, 1–19.
Fowler, R.L. 2009. "Thoughts on Myth and Religion in Early Greek Mythography," in: *Minerva* 22, 21–39.
Fowler, R.L. 2011. "Mythos and Logos," in: *JHS* 131, 45–66.
Fowler, R.L. 2015. "History," in: E. Eidinow/J. Kindt (eds.), *The Oxford Handbook of Ancient Greek Religion*, Oxford, 195–209.
Fowler, R.L. 2017a. "Apollodorus and the Art of the Variant," in: Pàmias (ed.), 158–75.
Fowler, R.L. 2017b. "Greek Mythography," in: Hoyle/Zajko (ed.), 15–27.
Fowler, R.L. 2019. "Myth(ography), History, and the Peripatos," in: Romano/Marincola (eds.), 29–53.
Foxhall, L./H.-J. Gehrke/N. Luraghi (eds.) 2010. *Intentional History: Spinning Time in Ancient Greece*, Stuttgart.
Frangeskou, V. 1999. "Tradition and Originality in Some Attic Funeral Orations," in: *CW* 92.4, 315–336.
Frazer, J.G. 1911–15. *The Golden Bough*. 12 vols., London.
Frazer, J.G. 1921. *Apollodorus: The Library*. Loeb Library, Cambridge MA.
Furley, W.D./J.M. Bremer. 2001. *Greek Hymns: Selected Cult Songs from the Archaic to the Hellenistic Period*. 2 vols, Tübingen.

Gadamer, H.-G. 1993 [1981]a. "Mythologie und Offenbarungsreligion," in: id., *Gesammelte Werke*. Tübingen, 174–78. [Orig. pub. in: F. Böckle et al. (eds.), *Christlicher Glaube in moderner Gesellschaft*. Vol. 2. Freiburg im Breisgau, 13–19].

Gadamer, H.-G. 1993 [1981]b. "Der Mythos im Zeitalter der Wissenschaft," in: id., *Gesammelte Werke*. Tübingen, 180–88. [Orig. pub. in: F. Böckle et al. (eds.), *Christlicher Glaube in moderner Gesellschaft*, Freiburg, 20–29].

Gantz, Timothy. 1993. *Early Greek Myth: A Guide to Literary and Artistic Sources*. Baltimore, MD.

Garvie, A.F. 1994. *Homer: Odyssey Books VI–VIII*, Cambridge.

Gayton, A.H. 1935. "The Orpheus Myth in North America," in: *Journal of American Folklore* 48, 263–93.

Genette, G. 1972. *Figures*. 3 vols., Paris.

Genette, G. 1980. *Narrative Discourse: An Essay in Method*. Trans. by J.E. Lewin, Ithaca. [Orig. pub. "Discours du récit", part of *Figures III*, Paris 1972].

Gennep, A. van. 1909. *Les rites de passage: Étude systématique des rites de la porte et du seuil, de l'hospitalité, de l'adoption, de la grossesse et de l'accouchement, de la naissance, de l'enfance, de la puberté, de l'initiation, de l'ordination, du couronnement des fiançailles et du mariage, des funérailles, des saisons, etc.*, Paris.

Giannini, A.. 1965. *Paradoxographorum Graecorum Reliquiae*, Milan.

Girard, R. 1972. *La violence et le sacré*, Paris.

Girard, R. 1977. *Violence and the Sacred*. Trans. P. Gregory, Baltimore.

Goethe, J.W. von. 1842. *Maximes et réflexions*, Paris.

Goldberg, C. 1998. *Some Suggestions for Future Folktale Indexes*, in: W. Heissig/R. Schott (eds.), *Die heutige Bedeutung oraler Traditionen / The Present-Day Importance of Oral Traditions*. Nordrhein-Westfälische Akademie der Wissenschaften, Abh. 102. Opladen, 249–62.

González, J.M. 2013. *The Epic Rhapsode and His Craft: Homeric Performance in a Diachronic Perspective*. Hellenic Studies Series 47, Washington, DC.

Gordon, R. 2012. "mysteries," in: *OCD*[4], 990–91.

Gotteland, S. 2001. *Mythe et rhétorique: les exemples mythiques dans le discours politique de l'Athènes classique*, Paris.

Graf, F. 1974. *Eleusis und die orphische Dichtung Athens in vorhellenistischer Zeit*, Berlin.

Graf, F. 1987. *Griechische Mythologie: Eine Einführung*, Munich.

Graf, F. 1993 [1987]. *Greek Mythology. An Introduction*. Trans. by T. Marier, Baltimore.

Graf, F. 1997. "Medea the Enchantress from Afar: Remarks on a Well-Known Myth," in: Clauss/Johnston (eds.), 21–43.

Graf, F. 2003a."Cult," in: H. Cancik/H. Schneider (eds.), *Brill's New Pauly: Encyclopaedia of the Ancient World*, Leiden, 980–87.

Graf, F. 2003b. "Initiation: A Concept with a Troubled History," in: Dodd/Faraone (eds.), 3–24.

Graf, F. 2012a. "ritual," in: *OCD*[4], 1263–64.

Graf, F. 2012b. "One Generation after Burkert and Girard: Where Are the Great Theories?," in: C.A. Faraone/F. Naiden (eds.), *Greek and Roman Animal Sacrifice: Ancient Victims, Modern Observers*, Cambridge, 32–51.

Graf, F. 2020. "Greece and Rome" (III) and "Christianity" (IV). In Johannes Renger/Karl Jansen-Winkeln/Beate Ego/Fritz Graf. 2020. "Prayer." In Hubert Cancik/Helmuth Schneider (eds.), *Brill's New Pauly*. (Date of access May 6, 2020.)

Graf, F. et al. 2000. "Prolegomena", in: Latacz/Bierl (eds.), Munich.

Greenwood E. (2006). *Thucydides and the Shaping of History*, London.
Greimas, A.J./J. Cortès. 1979. *Sémiotique: Dictionnaire raisonné de la théorie du langage*, Paris.
Greimas, A.J./J. Cortès. 1982. *Semiotics and Language: An Analytical Dictionary. Semiotics and Language: An Analytical Dictionary*. Trans. L. Crist/D. Patte, et al., Bloomington IN.
Grethlein, J./C.B. Krebs (eds.) 2012. *Time and Narrative in Ancient Historiography: The 'Plupast' from Herodotus to Appian*, Cambridge.
Grethlein, J. 2006. *Das Geschichtsbild der Ilias: Eine Untersuchung aus phänomenologischer und narratologischer Perspektive*, Göttingen.
Grethlein, J. 2019. "'Stories Embroidered Beyond Truth': Reading Herodotus and Thucydides in Light of Pindar's *Olympian* 1," in: J. Baines/H. van der Blom/Yi Samuel Chen/T. Rood (eds.), *Historical Consciousness and the Use of the Past in the Ancient World*, Sheffield, UK, 313–28.
Griffin, J. 1980. *Homer on Life and Death*, Oxford.
Griffith, R.D. 1992. Rev. of *Cambridge History of Literary Criticism*, Vol. 1., in: *Phoenix* 46.2, 170–73.
Griffiths, M. 1983. *Prometheus Bound*, Cambridge.
Grimm, W. 1857. "Die Sage von Polyphem." *Abhandlungen der Kgl. Akademie der Wissenschaften zu Berlin*, phil.-hist. Klasse, 1–30. [Repr. in *Kleinere Schriften*. Ed. by G. Hinrichs. Vol. 4. Gütersloh, 428–62]. https://archive.org/details/diesagevonpolyp00unkngoog/page/n35/mode/1up
Grube, G.M.A. 1981. *The Trial and Death of Socrates: Euthyphro, Apology, Crito, and Death Scene from Phaedo*. 2nd ed., Indianapolis.
Hainsworth, B. 1969. *Homer*. G&R New Surveys 3, Oxford.
Hall, J.M. 2007. "Politics and Greek Myth," in: Woodard (ed.), 331–54.
Halliwell, S. 1986. *Aristotle's Poetics*, London.
Halliwell, S. 1987. *The Poetics of Aristotle: Translation and Commentary*, London.
Hansen, W. 1997a. "Homer and the Folktale," in: Powell/Morris (eds.), 442–62.
Hansen, W. 1997b. "Mythology and Folktale Typology: Chronicle of a Failed Scholarly Revolution," in: *Journal of Folklore Research* 34.3, 275–280.
Hansen, W. 2002a. *Ariadne's Thread: A Guide to International Tales Found in Classical Literature*, Ithaca, NY.
Hansen, W. 2002b. "Perseus," in: *EM* 10, cols. 755–58.
Hansen, W. 2007. "Prometheus and Loki: The Myth of the Fettered God and His Kin," in: *Classica et Mediaevalia* 58, 65–117.
Hansen, W. 2017. *The Book of Greek and Roman Folktales, Legends, and Myths*, Princeton.
Hansen, W. 2020. "Mythic Aetiologies of Loss," in: N.P. Roubekas/T. Ryba (eds.), *Explaining, Interpreting, and Theorizing Religion and Myth: Contributions in Honor of Robert A. Segal*, Leiden, 265–81.
Hare, J.E. 1981. *Plato's Euthyphro*, Bryn Mawr.
Harris, O. 2017. *Lacan's Return to Antiquity: Between Nature and the Gods*, London.
Harris, W.V. 1989. *Ancient literacy*, Cambridge MA.
Harrison, J.E. 1912. *Themis: A Study of the Social Origins of Greek Religion*, Cambridge. https://babel.hathitrust.org/cgi/pt?id=inu.30000130228368&view=1up&seq=40.
Harrison, T. 2000. *Divinity and History: The Religion of Herodotus*, Oxford.
Harrison, T. 2007. "The Use of Literary Texts in the Study of Greek Religion," in: D. Ogden (ed.), *A Companion to Greek Religion*, Malden, MA, 373–84.

Harrison, T. 2015. "Belief vs. Practice," in: E. Eidinow/J. Kindt (eds.), *The Oxford Handbook of Greek Religion*, Oxford.
Hawes, G. (ed.) 2017. *Myths on the Map: The Storied Landscapes of Ancient Greece*, Oxford.
Hawes, G. 2014a. *Rationalizing Myth in Antiquity*, Oxford.
Hawes, G. 2014b. "Story Time at the Library: Palaephatus and the Emergence of Highly Literate Mythology," in: Scodel (ed.), 125–47.
Hawes, G. 2017. "Walking through History: Unlocking the Mythical Past," in: ead. (ed.), 14–31.
Headland, T.N./K.L. Pike/M. Harris (eds.) 1990. *Emics and Etics: The Insider/Outsider Debate*, Newbury Park, CA.
Heath, J. 2019. *The Bible, Homer, and the Search for Meaning in Ancient Myths: Why We Would Be Better Off with Homer's Gods*, London. (Non vidi.)
Heiden, B. 2007. "The Muses' Uncanny Lies: Hesiod, 'Theogony' 27 and Its Translators," in: *AJP* 128.2, 153–75.
Henderson, J. 1991. *The Maculate Muse: Obscene Language in Attic Comedy*. 2nd ed., Oxford.
Henrichs, A. 1987. "Three Approaches to Greek Mythography," in: Bremer (ed.), 242–77.
Henrichs, A. 2008. "What Is a Greek Priest?" In B. Dignas/K. Trampedach (eds.), *Practitioners of the Divine: Greek Priests and Religious Figures from Homer to Heliodorus*. Hellenic Studies Series 30. Washington, DC, 1–16.
Heubeck, A./A. Hoekstra. 1989. *A Commentary on Homer's* Odyssey, Vol. II (Books IX–XVI), Oxford.
Heubeck, A. 2003. *Omero: Odissea*. Vol. 3 (Books 9–12). 2nd ed., Milan.
Higbie, C. 2007. "Hellenistic Mythographers," in: Woodard (ed.), 237–254.
Holzberg, N. 2002. *The Ancient Fable: An Introduction*. Trans. C. Jackson-Holzberg, Bloomington.
Honorato, D. 2020. "The Dichotomy Myth and Reason Revisited from the Perspective of Geoffrey E.R. Lloyd: A Critical Assessment," in: *Humanitas* 75, 25–47.
Hornblower, S. 1987. *Thucydides*, Baltimore.
Hornblower, S. 1991. *A Commentary on Thucydides*. Vol. 1 (Books 1–3), Oxford.
Hornblower, S. 2008. *A Commentary on Thucydides*. Vol. 3 (Books 5.25–8.109), Oxford.
Hoyle, H./V. Zajko (eds.) 2017. *A Handbook to the Reception of Classical Mythology*, Hoboken, NJ.
Hunter, R. (ed.) 2005. *The Hesiodic Catalogue of Women: Constructions and Reconstructions*, Cambridge.
Hunter, R. 2016. "'Palaephatus', Strabo, and the Boundaries of Myth," in: *CP* 111, 245–61.
Huß, B. 1999. *Xenophons Symposion: Ein Kommentar*, Stuttgart.
Icard-Gianolio, N. 2004. "Vols d'images cultuelles," in: *ThesCRA* 2, 488–94.
Isler, G. 1993. "Jung, Carl Gustav," in: *EM* 7, cols. 743–50.
Immerwahr, H.R. 1966. *Form and Thought in Herodotus*. American Philological Association Monographs 23, Cleveland OH.
James, H. 1884. "The Art of Fiction," in: *Longman's Magazine* 4, 502–21. [Repr. in *Literary Criticism*. Ed. by L. Edel. 1, 44–65].
James, W. 1884. "What Is an Emotion?," in: *Mind* 9, 188–205.
Janka, M./C. Schäfer (eds.) 2014. *Platon als Mythologe: Neue Interpretationen zu den Mythen in Platons Dialogen*. 2nd ed., Darmstadt.
Janka, M. 2014. "Semantik und Kontext: *Mythos* und Verwandtes im *Corpus Platonicum*," in: Janka/Schäfer (eds.), 23–46.
Janko, R. 1992. *The Iliad: A Commentary*. Vol. 4 (Books 13–16), Cambridge.

Jannidis, F. 2004. *Figur und Person: Beitrag zu einer historischen Narratologie*, Berlin.
Jeanmaire, H. 1939. *Couroi et Courètes: Essai sur l'éducation spartiate et sur les rites d'adolescence dans l'antiquité hellénique*, Lille.
Johansen, H.F./E.W. Whittle. 1980. *Aeschylus: The Suppliants*. 3 vols., Copenhagen.
Johansen, T,K. 1999. "Myth and *logos* in Aristotle," in: Buxton (ed.), 279–91.
Johnston, S.I. 2017. "The Comparative Approach," in: Hoyle/Zajko (eds.), 139–51.
Jones, E. 1910. "The Oedipus-Complex as an Explanation of Hamlet's Mystery: A Study in Motive," in: *American Journal of Psychology* 21.1, 72–113.
Jones, E. 1949. *Hamlet and Œdipus*, Garden City, NY.
Jones, W.H.S. 1933. *Pausanias: Description of Greece*. Vol. 3. Loeb Classical Library, Cambridge, MA.
Jong, I.J.F. de. 1997. "Narrator Language versus Character Language: Some Further Explorations," in: F. Létoublon (ed.), *Hommage à Milman Parry. Le style formulaire de l'épopée homérique et la théorie de l'oralité poétique*, Amsterdam, 293–302.
Jong, I.J.F. de. 2001a. *A Narratological Commentary on the Odyssey*, Cambridge.
Jong, I.J.F. de. 2001b. "The Origins of Figural Narrative in Antiquity," in: W. Van Peer/S. Chapman (eds.), *New Perspectives on Narrative Perspective*, Albany, 67–81.
Jong, I.J.F. de. 2012. *Homer: Iliad Book XXII*, Cambridge.
Jong, I.J.F. de. 2014. *Narratology and Classics: A Practical Guide*, Oxford.
Jung, C.G. 1976. *Gesammelte Werke*. Vol. 9.1, Zurich.
Kant, I. 1923 [1793]. *Kant's Werke*. Vol. 8, Berlin/Leipzig.
Kant, I. 1983 [1793]. *Perpetual Peace, and Other Essays on Politics, History, and Morals*. Trans. T. Humphrey, Indianapolis.
Katrinaki, M. 2010. "Theseus," in: *EM* 13, 498–500.
Katz, J.T. 2009. "The Prehistory and Analogues of Hesiod's Poetry," in: A.C. Loney/S. Scully (eds.), *The Oxford Handbook of Hesiod*, New York. https://www.oxfordhandbooks.com/view/10.1093/oxfordhb/9780190209032.001.0001/oxfordhb-9780190209032-e-35
Kearns, E. 2012a. "religion, Greek," in: OCD^4, 1262–63.
Kearns, E. 2012b. "religion, Greek, terms relating to," in: OCD^4, 1263–64.
Kearns, E. 2014c. "theoxenia," in: OCD^4, 1463.
Kirk, G.S. 1970. *Myth: Its Meaning and Functions in Ancient and Other Cultures*, Cambridge.
Kirk, G.S. 1974. *The Nature of Greek Myths*, Harmondsworth.
Kirk, G.S. 1985. *The Iliad: A Commentary*. Vol. 1 (Books 1–4), Cambridge.
Koerner, E.F.K. 1998. "Noch einmal on the History of the Concept of Language as a 'système où tout se tient,'" in: *Cahiers Ferdinand de Saussure* 51, 21–40.
Kolesnikoff, N. 1993a. "Shklovskii, Viktor Borisovich," in: Makaryk (ed.), 471–72.
Kolesnikoff, N. 1993b. "Story/plot," in: Makaryk (ed.), 631–32.
Kovacs, D. 2016. "On a New Fragment of Euripides' Ino (P. Oxy. 5131)," in: *ZPE* 199, 3–6.
Krieter-Spiro, M. 2009. In: Bierl/Latacz (eds.) (2000ff.). Vol. 3 (Book 3). Fasc. 2 (Commentary), Berlin.
Kripke, S.A. 1980. *Naming and Necessity*, Oxford.
Kripke, S.A. 2013. *Reference and Existence: The John Locke Lectures*. Oxford.
Kullmann, W. 1960. *Die Quellen der Ilias (Troischer Sagenkreis)*, Wiesbaden.
Kurke, L. 2005. "Choral Lyric as 'Ritualization': Poetic Sacrifice and Poetic Ego in Pindar's Sixth Paean," in: *CA* 24.1, 81–130.
Kvideland, R. 1996. "Konglomerat, Konglomeratmärchen," in: *EM* 8, cols. 133–34.

La Caze, M./H.M. Lloyd. 2011. "Editors' Introduction: Philosophy and the 'Affective Turn'," in: *Parrhesia* 13, 1–13.
Laks, A. 2006. *Introduction à la philosophie présocratique*, Paris.
Laks, A. 2018 [2006]. *The Concept of Presocratic Philosophy: Its Origin, Development, and Significance*. Trans. G.W. Most, Princeton.
Lambert, W.G. 1960. *Babylonian Wisdom Literature*, Oxford.
Lambert, W.G./P. Walcot. 1965. "A New Babylonian Theogony and Hesiod," in: *Kadmos* 4, 64–72.
Laplanche, J./J.-B. Pontalis. 1973. *The Language of Psycho-Analysis*. Trans. D. Nicholson-Smith, London.
LaPorte, J. 2018. "Rigid Designators," in: Edward N. Zalta, ed., *The Stanford Encyclopedia of Philosophy* https://plato.stanford.edu/archives/spr2018/entries/rigid-designators/
Latacz, J. 2000. "Zur Struktur der Ilias," in: Graf et al. (eds.), 145–57.
Lateiner, D. 2016. Rev. of Cairns/Fulkerson 2015. *Bryn Mawr Classical Review* 2016.01.12.
Lauwers, J./J. Opsomer/H. Schwall (eds.) 2018. *Psychology and the Classics: A Dialogue of Disciplines*, Berlin.
Lehmann, A. 2011. "Vergessen und Erinnern," in: *EM* 14, cols. 5–14.
Lesher, J.H. 1992. *Xenophanes of Colophon: Fragments*, Toronto.
Létoublon, F. 2011. "Homer's Use of Myth," in: Dowden/Livingstone (eds.), 27–45.
LeVen, P. 2014. *The Many-Headed Muse: Tradition and Innovation in Late Classical Greek Lyric Poetry*, Cambridge.
Lévi-Strauss, C. 1955. "The Structural Study of Myth," in: *Journal of American Folklore* 68, 428–44.
Lévi-Strauss, C. 1957. "La geste d'Asdiwal," in: *Annuaires de l'École Pratique des Hautes Études* 66, 3–43.
Lévi-Strauss, C. 1958. "La structure des mythes," in: id., *Anthropologie structurale*. Paris.
Lévi-Strauss, C. 1963. "The Structural Study of Myth," in: id., *Structural Anthropology*. Trans. C. Jacobson/Br.G. Schoepf, New York, 206–31.
Lévi-Strauss, C. 1964–1971. *Mythologiques*, Paris.
Lévi-Strauss, C. 1973. *Anthropologie structurale deux*, Paris.
Lévi-Strauss, C. 1983. *Le regard éloigné*, Paris.
Lévi-Strauss, C. 1985. "Myth and Forgetfulness," in: id., *The View from Afar*. Trans. J. Neugroschel/P. Hoss, New York, 186–91.
Lewis, S. 2011. "Women and Myth," in: Dowden/Livingston (eds.), 443–58.
Leys, R. 2011. "The Turn to Affect: A Critique," in: *Critical Inquiry* 37, 434–72.
Linderski, J. 2012. "Palladium," in: *OCD*[4], 1070.
Lindquist, K.A./E.H. Siegel/K.S. Quigley/L. Feldman Barrett. 2013. "The Hundred-Year Emotion War: Are Emotions Natural Kinds or Psychological Constructions? Comment on Lench, Flores, and Bench (2011)," in: *Psychological Bulletin* 139.1, 255–63.
http://www.affective-science.org/pubs/2013/Lindquistetal_PB2013.pdf
Liveley, G. 2017. "Orpheus and Eurydice," in: Zajko/Hoyle (eds.), 287–98.
Livingstone, A./B. Haskamp. 2011. "Near Eastern Mythologies," in: Dowden/Livingstone (eds.), 357–82.
Livingstone, N. 2011. "Instructing Myth: From Homer to the Sophists," in: Dowden/Livingstone (eds.), 125–39.
Lloyd, G.E.R. 1979. *Magic, Reason and Experience: Studies in the Origin and Development of Greek Science*, Cambridge.

Lloyd-Jones, H. 1983. *The Justice of Zeus*, 2nd ed., Berkeley.
López-Ruiz, C. 2010. *When the Gods Were Born: Greek Cosmogonies and the Near East*, Cambridge MA.
López-Ruiz, C. 2014. "Greek and Near Eastern Mythologies," in: Edmunds (ed.), 154–99.
Lord, A.B. 1971[1948]. "Homer, Parry, and Huso," in: Parry (ed.), 465–78.
Louden, B. 2006. *Iliad: Structure, Myth, and Meaning*, Baltimore, MD.
Louden, B. 2019. *Greek Myth and the Bible*, Abingdon, UK. (Non vidi.)
Lowe, N. J. 2000. *The Classical Plot and the Invention of Western Narrative*, Cambridge.
Lozynsky, Y. 2014. *Ancient Greek Cult Hymns: Poets, Performers and Rituals*. Ph.D. diss. University of Toronto.
Luraghi, N. 2009. "The Importance of Being λόγιος," in: *CW* 102.4, 439–56.
Mackie, H.S. 2011. "Storytelling," in: *HE* 3, 826–28.
Maehler, H. 2004. *Bacchylides: A Selection*, Cambridge.
Makaryk, I.R. (ed.) 1993. *Encyclopedia of Contemporary Literary Theory: Approaches, Scholars, Terms*, Toronto.
Malkin, I. 1994. *Myth and Territory in the Spartan Mediterranean*, Cambridge.
Malkin, I. 2012a. "nymphs," in: *OCD*[4], 1027.
Malkin, I. 2012b. "votive offerings," in: *OCD*[4], 1564–65.
Mannhardt, W./W. Heuschkel. 1875–1877. *Wald- und Feldkulte*, 2 vols., Berlin.
Margolin, U. 2007. "Character," in: D. Herman (ed.), *The Cambridge Companion to Narrative*, Cambridge, 66–79.
Margolis, E./S. Laurence. 2019. "Concepts," in: E.N. Zalta (ed.), *The Stanford Encyclopedia of Philosophy*. https://plato.stanford.edu/archives/sum2019/entries/concepts/
Marincola, J. 1997. *Authority and Tradition in Ancient Historiography*, Cambridge.
Martin, R.P. 1989. *The Language of Heroes: Speech and Performance in the Iliad*, Ithaca, NY.
Martin, R.P. 1993. "Telemachus and the Last Hero Song." *Colby Quarterly* 29.3, 222–40.
Martin, R.P. 2013. "The 'Myth Before the Myth Began'," in: J. Falaky Nagy (ed.), *Writing Down the Myths*, Turnhout, 45–66.
Martin, R.P. 2015. "Epic," in: E. Eidinow/J. Kindt (eds.), *The Oxford Handbook to Greek Religion*, Oxford, 151–64.
Mastronarde, D.J. 2002. *Euripides: Medea*, Cambridge.
Mastronarde, D.J. 2017. *Preliminary Studies on the Scholia to Euripides*, Berkeley CA.
Meillet, A. 1915. *Introduction à l'étude comparative des langues indo-européennes*. 4th ed., Paris.
Meisner, D.A. 2018. *Orphic Tradition and the Birth of Gods*, Oxford.
Meister, K. 2006a. "Atthis," in: H. Cancik/H. Schneider (eds.), *BNP*. English ed. by C.F. Salazar.
Meister, K. 2006b. "Genealogy" II (Greece), in: H. Cancik et al. (eds.), *BNP*.
Meuli, K. 1975. "Griechische Opferbräuche," in: id., *Gesammelte Schriften*, Basel, 2.907–1021.
Meyer, M.F. 1999. "Die Bedeutungsgenese der Begriffe *mythos* und *logos* in der griechischen Antike," in: *Archiv für Begriffsgeschichte* 41, 35–63.
Mikalson, J.D. 1983. *Athenian Popular Religion*, Chapel Hill.
Mikalson, J.D. 1991. *Honor Thy Gods: Popular Religion in Greek Tragedy*, Chapel Hill.
Mills, S. 1997. *Theseus, Tragedy and the Athenian Empire*, Oxford.
Mitchell, A.G. 2004. "Humor in Greek Vase Painting," in: *Revue archéologique* 37.1, 3–32.
Mitchell, A.G. 2009. *Greek Vase Painting and the Origins of Visual Humor*, Cambridge. (Non vidi.)

Montanari, F./A. Rengakos/C. Tsagalis (eds.) 2012. *Homeric Contexts: Neoanalysis and the Interpretation of Oral Poetry*, Berlin.
Morgan, K. 2000. *Myth and Philosophy from the Presocratics to Plato*, Cambridge.
Most, G.W. 1999. "From Logos to Mythos," in: Buxton (ed.), 26–47.
Most, G.W. 2002. "Freuds Narziß: Reflexionen über einen Selbstbezug," in: A.-B. Renger (ed.), *Narcissus: Ein Mythos von der Antike bis zum Cyberspace*, Stuttgart, 117–31.
Most, G.W. 2012. "Plato's Exoteric Myths," in: C. Collobert/P. Destrée/F.J. Gonzales (eds.), *Plato and Myth. Studies on the Use and Status of Platonic Myths.* Mnemosyne Supplements, 337, Leiden, 13–24.
Most, G.W. 2017. "Postface: The Mazes of Mythography," in: Pàmias (ed.), 227–34.
Munson, R.V. 2017. "Thucydides and Myth: A Complex Relation to Past and Present," in: S. Forsdyke/E. Foster/ R.K. Balot (eds.), *Oxford Handbook of Thucydides*, Oxford, 257–66.
Nägelsbach, K.F. von. 1861. *Homerische Theologie*, 2nd ed., Nürnberg.
Nagy, G. 1989. "Early Greek Views of Poets and Poetry," in: G.A. Kennedy (ed.), *The Cambridge History of Literary Criticism*, Vol. 1, Cambridge, 1–77.
Nagy, G. 1990. *Greek Mythology and Poetics*, Ithaca. http://chs.harvard.edu/CHS/article/display/1283
Nagy, G. 1999 [1979]. *The Best of the Achaeans: Concepts of the Hero in Archaic Greek Poetry*, Rev. ed. Baltimore.
Nagy, G. 2002. "The Language of Heroes as Mantic Poetry," in: M. Reichel/A. Rengakos (eds.), *Epea Pteroenta: Beiträge zur Homerforschung*. Festschrift für Wolfgang Kullmann zum 75. Geburtstag, Stuttgart, 141–50.
Nagy, G. 2005. "The Epic Hero," in: Foley (ed.), 71–89.
Nagy, G. 2007. "Homer and Greek Myth," in: Woodard (ed.), 52–82.
Nagy, G. 2011. "Lord, A.B.," in: *HE* 2, 487–89.
Nagy, J.F. 2014. "Hierarchy, Heroes, and Heads: Indo-European Structures in Greek Myth," in: Edmunds (ed.), 202–44.
Naiden, F.S. 2013. *Smoke Signals for the Gods: Ancient Greek Sacrifice from the Archaic through Roman Periods*, New York.
Neer, R. 2004. "The Athenian Treasury at Delphi and the Material of Politics," in: *CA* 63, 63–93.
Neri, C./F. Cinti. 2017. *Saffo: Poesie, frammenti e testimonianze*, Santarcangelo di Romagna (RN).
Neschke, A. 1999. "Mythe et histoire d'après Aristote," in : D. Bouvier/C. Calame (eds.), *Philosophes et historiens anciens face aux mythes*, Paris, 105–17.
Nesselrath, H.-G. 1995. "Myth, Parody, and Comic Plots: The Birth of Gods and Middle Comedy," in: G.W. Dobrov (ed.), *Beyond Aristophanes: Transition and Diversity in Greek Comedy*, Atlanta, GA, 1–28.
Nesselrath, H.-G. 1999. "Mythos—Logos—Mytho-Logos," in: P. Rusterholz/R. Moser (eds.), *Form und Funktion des Mythos in archaischen and modernen Gesellschaften*, Bern, 1–26.
Nestle, W. 1940. *Vom Mythos zum Logos: Die Selbstentfaltung des griechischen Denkens von Homer bis auf die Sophistik und Sokrates*, Stuttgart.
Neu, E. 1996. *Das hurritische Epos der Freilassung*, Wiesbaden.
Niederhoff, B. 2011. "Focalization," in: *the living handbook of narratology*. http://wikis.sub.uni-hamburg.de/lhn/index.php/Focalization
Nünlist, R./I.J.F. de Jong. 2000. "Homerische Poetik in Stichwörtern," in: Graf et al. (eds.), 159–71.

Ogden, D. 2013. *Drakōn: Dragon Myth and Serpent Cult In the Greek and Roman Worlds*, Oxford.
Oldfather, C.H. 1935. *Diodorus of Sicily*, Vol. 2, Loeb Classical Library, Cambridge MA.
Oliver, J.H. 1972. "The Conversion of the Periegete Pausanias," in: *Homenaje a Antonio Tovar ofrecido por sus discípulos, colegas y amigos*, Madrid, 319–21.
Osborne, R. 2005. "Ordering Women in Hesiod's Catalogue," in: Hunter (ed.), 5–24.
Otto, WF. 1933. *Dionysos: Mythos und Kultus*, Frankfurt am Main.
Page, D. 1955. *Sappho and Alcaeus: An Introduction to the Study of Lesbian Poetry*, Oxford.
Pàges, J. 2007. *Mythographus homericus: estudi i edició comentada*, Barcelona.
Pàges, J. 2017. "Apollodorus' *Bibliotheca* and the Mythographus Homericus: An Intertextual Approach," in: Pàmias (ed.), 66–81.
Pàmias, J. (ed.) 2017. *Apollodoriana: Ancient Myths, New Crossroads*, Berlin.
Pàmias, J. 2008. *Ferecides d'Atenes: Històries*, 2 vols., Barcelona.
Pàmias, J. 2015. "Acusilaus of Argos and the Bronze Tablets," in: *HSCP* 108, 53–75.
Pàmias, J. Forthcoming(1). "The Origins of Mythography as a Genre," in: S. Smith/S. Trzaskoma (eds.), *Oxford Handbook of Greek and Roman Mythography*, Oxford.
Pàmias, J. Forthcoming(2). "Greek Mythographic Tradition," in: R.D. Woodard (ed.), *Cambridge History of Mythology and Mythography*, Cambridge.
Papadopoulou, T. 1999. "Literary Theory and Terminology in the Greek Tragic Scholia: The Case of πλάσμα," in: *BICS* 43, 203–210.
Papillon, T.L. 1996. "Isocrates and the Use of Myth," in: *Hermathena* 161, 9–22.
Parker, R.C.T. 2005. *Polytheism and Society at Athens*, Oxford.
Parker, R.C.T. 2012a. "sacrifice, Greek," in: OCD^4, 1306–1307.
Parker, R.C.T. 2012b. "sacred laws," in: OCD^4, 1305.
Parry, M. 1971. *The Making of Homeric Verse*. Ed. A. Parry, Oxford.
Partenie, C. 2018. "Plato's Myths," in: E.N. Zalta (ed.), *The Stanford Encyclopedia of Philosophy*. https://plato.stanford.edu/archives/fall2018/entries/plato-myths/>.
Pascal, R. 1977. *The Dual Voice: Free Indirect Speech and its Functioning in the Nineteenth-century European Novel*, Manchester.
Pasquier, D. 1993. "Hélène et les garçons: une éducation sentimentale," in : *Esprit* 6, 124–144.
Patterson, LE. 2010. *Kinship Myth in Ancient Greece*, Austin.
Patterson, LE. 2013. "Geographers as Mythographers: The Case of Strabo," in: Trzaskoma/Smith (eds.), 201–21.
Pavlou, M. 2012. "Bacchylides 17: Singing and Usurping the Paean," in: *Greek, Roman, and Byzantine Studies* 52, 510–539.
Pedrick, V. 2007. *Euripides, Freud, and the Romance of Belonging*, Baltimore.
Peels, S. 2015. *Hosios: A Semantic Study of Greek Piety*, Leiden.
Pelling, C. 2009. "Bringing Autochthony Up-to-Date: Herodotus and Thucydides," in: *CW* 102.4, 471–483.
Pellizer, E. 1982. *Favole d'identità, Favole di paura: Storie di caccia e altri racconti della Grecia antica*, Roma.
Pellizer, E. 1984. "L'eco, lo specchio e la reciprocità amorosa: Una lettura del tema di Narciso," in: *QUCC* n.s. 17, 21–35.
Pellizer, E. 1986. "Riflessioni sulla dinastia dei Labdaci," in: B. Gentili/R. Pretagostini (eds.), *Edipo: Il teatro greco e la cultura europea: Atti del convegno internazionale (Urbino 15–19 Nov. 1982)*, Rome, 549–54.

Pellizer, E. 1987. "Reflections, Echoes and Amorous Reciprocity: On Reading the Narcissus Story," in: Bremmer 1987, 107–120.
Pellizer, E. 1988. "L'enfant et "oracle: Ésquisse d'une analyse sémio-narrative," in : C. Calame (ed.), *Métamorphoses du mythe en Grèce antique*, Geneva, 71–83.
Pellizer, E. 1991. *La peripezia dell'eletto: Racconti eroici della Grecia antica*, Palermo.
Pellizer, E. 2011. "L'initiation ratée: Retour au *Chasseur noir*," in: *Gaia* 14, 157–69. https://www.persee.fr/doc/gaia_1287-3349_2011_num_14_1_1559
Petropoulou, M.-Z. 2008. *Animal Sacrifice in Ancient Greek Religion, Judaism, and Christianity, 100 BC–AD 200*, Oxford.
Pickard-Cambridge, W.A. 1984. "Topics," in: J. Barnes (ed.), *The Complete Works of Aristotle*, 2 vols., Princeton, 1.165–277.
Pike, K.L. 1967. *Language in Relation to a Unified Theory of the Structure of Human Behavior*, 2nd ed., The Hague.
Pirenne-Delforge, V. 2008. *Retour à la source: Pausanias et la religion grecque*. Kernos Suppl. 20, Liège.
Pirenne-Delforge, V. 2009. "Under Which Conditions Did the Greeks 'Believe' in Their Myths? The Religious Criteria of Adherence," in: U. Dill/C. Walde (eds.), *Antike Mythen: Medien, Transformationen und Konstruktionen*, Berlin, 38–54.
Pirenne-Delforge, V. 2010. "Reading Pausanias: Cults of the Gods and Representation of the Divine," in: J.N. Bremmer/A. Erskine (eds.), *The Gods of Ancient Greece: Identities and Transformations*, Edinburgh, 375–87.
Pohlenz, M. 1937. *Herodot: der erste Geschichtschreiber des Abendlandes*, Leipzig.
Polinskaya, I. 2013. *A Local History of Greek Polytheism: Gods, People, and the Land of Aigina, 800–400 B.C.E.*, Leiden.
Porter, J.I./M. Buchan. 2004. "Introduction," in: *Helios* 31, 1–19.
Powell, B./I. Morris (eds.) 1997. *New Companion to Homer*, Leiden.
Powell, J.E. 1938. *A Lexicon to Herodotus*, Cambridge.
Pretzler, M. 2005. "Pausanias and Oral Tradition," in: *CQ* 55.1, 235–49.
Price, H.H. 1969. *Belief: The Gifford Lectures Delivered at the University of Aberdeen in 1960*, London.
Propp, V. 1968 [1928]. *Morphology of the Folktale*. Trans. L. Scott. 2nd ed. of the translation rev. by L.A. Wagner, Austin.
Pulleyn, S. 1997. *Prayer in Greek Religion*, Oxford.
Race, W. 1997. *Pindar*, Vol. 2, Loeb Classical Library, Cambridge MA.
Rank, O. 1909. *Der Mythus von der Geburt des Helden*, Leipzig.
Rausmaa, P.-L. 1977. "Aarne, Antti Amatus," in: *EM* 1, cols. 1–4.
Ready, J.L./C.C. Tsagalis (eds.) 2018. *Homer in Performance: Rhapsodes, Narrators, and Characters*, Austin TX.
Ready, J.L. 2018. *The Homeric Simile in Comparative Perspectives: Oral Traditions from Saudi Arabia to Indonesia*, Oxford.
Rees, A.D./B.R. Rees. 1961. *Celtic Heritage: Ancient Tradition in Ireland and Wales*, New York.
Renehan, R. 1987. "Review Article: *Curae Callimacheae*," in: *CP* 82.3, 240–254.
Riu, X. 2017. *Aristòtl: Poètica*, Barcelona.
Roazen, P. 1971. *Freud and his Followers*, New York.
Robert, L. 1960. "Recherches épigraphiques: V. Inscriptions de Lesbos," in: *REA* 62, 285–315. [Repr. in *Opera minora selecta*. Vol. 2, Amsterdam, 801–31].
Robinson, P. 1993. *Freud and his Critics*, Berkeley.

Rodighiero, A. 2018. "Raccontare cantando nella tragedia greca: due casi da *Agamennone* e *Troiane*," in: G. Ieranò/P. Taravacci (eds.), *Il racconto a teatro: dal dramma antico al Siglo de Oro alla scena contemporanea*, Trent, 37–73.

Röhrich, L. 1987. "Geographisch-historische Methode," in: *EM* 9, cols. 954–57.

Romani, S. 2015. "Il mito di Arianna," in: M. Bettini/S. Romani. *Il mito di Arianna: Immagini e racconti dalla Grecia a oggi*, Turin, 33–234.

Romano, A.J./J. Marincola (eds.) 2019. *Host or Parasite? Mythographers and their Contemporaries in the Classical and Hellenistic Periods*, Berlin.

Romano, A.J./J. Marincola. 2019. "Introduction," in: Romano/Marincola (eds.), 1–3.

Rood, T. 2019. "Thucydides and Myth," in: J. Baines/H. van der Blom/Yi Samuel Chen/T. Rood (eds.), *Historical Consciousness and the Use of the Past in the Ancient World*. Sheffield, UK, 331–44.

Ross, W.D. 1924. *Aristotle's Metaphysics*, 2 vols., Oxford.

Rossum-Steenbeek, M. van. 1997. *Greek Readers' Digests? Studies on a Selection of Subliterary Papyri*, Leiden.

Rowe, C. 2012. "logographers," in: *OCD*[4], 856.

Ruiz-Montero, C./M. Dolores Sánchez Alacid. 2005. "La estructura de la 'Vida de Esopo': Análisis functional," in: *Habis* 36, 243–52.

Russo, J./M. Fernández-Galiano/A. Heubeck. 1989. *A Commentary on Homer's* Odyssey, Vol. 3 (Books 17–24), Oxford.

Russo, J. 2011. "Parry, Milman," in: *HE* 2, 629–31.

Rusten, J. 1982. "Dicaearchus and the Tales from Euripides," in: *GRBS* 23, 357–67.

Rusten, J. 2011. "Scenes from Old or Middle Comedy on Fourth-Century South Italian Vases" (ch. 11), in: Id. (ed.), *The Birth of Comedy: Texts, Documents, and Art from Athenian Comic Competitions, 486–280*, Baltimore, 434–54.

Rusten, J. 2012. "paradoxographers," in: *OCD*[4], 1080.

Rutherford, I. 2009. "Hesiod and the Literary Traditions of the Near East," in: F. Montanari/A. Rengakos/C.C. Tsagalis (eds.), *Homeric Contexts: Neoanalysis and the Interpretation of Oral Poetry*, 9–35.

Rutherford, R.B. 1993. *The Iliad: A Commentary*. Vol. 6 (Books 21–24), Cambridge.

Ryan, M.-L./E. van Alphen. 1993. "Narratology," in: Makaryk (ed.), 110–16.

Ryan, M.-L. 2013. "Possible Worlds," in: *the living handbook of narratology*. http://www.lhn.uni-hamburg.de/article/possible-worlds

Ryan, P. 1997. "Menexenus," in: J. Cooper (ed.), *Plato: Complete Works*, Indianapolis IN, 950–64.

Saïd, S. 2008. *Approches de la mythologie grecque: Lectures anciennes et modernes*, Paris.

Saïd, S. 2014. "Between Mythography and Historiography: Diodorus' Universal Library," in: E.K. Emilsson/A. Maravela/M. Skoie (eds.), *Paradeigmata: Studies in Honour of Øivind Andersen*, Athens, 67–86.

Sanders, Ed. 2014. *Envy and Jealousy in Classical Athens: A Socio-Psychological Approach. Emotions of the Past*, Oxford.

Saussure, F. de. 1972. *Cours de linguistique général*. Edited by C. Bally/A. Sechehaye with the collaboration of A. Riedlinger, Paris.

Saussure, F. de. 1986. *Course in General Linguistics*. Trans. of Saussure 1972 by R. Harris, La Salle, Ill.

Sauzeau, P./A. Sauzeau. 2012. *La quatrième fonction: altérité et marginalité dans l'idéologie des Indo-Européens*, Paris.

Schmitt, A. 2014. "Mythos bei Platon," in: M. Janka/C. Schäfer (eds.), *Platon als Mythologe: Neue Interpretationen zu den Mythen in Platons Dialogen*, 2nd ed., Darmstadt, 81–111.
Schwitzgebel, E. 2019. "Belief," in: E.N. Zalta (ed.), *The Stanford Encyclopedia of Philosophy* (Fall 2019 Edition). https://plato.stanford.edu/archives/fall2019/entries/belief/
Scodel, R. (ed.) 2014. *Between Orality and Literacy: Communication and Adaptation in Antiquity*, Leiden.
Scodel, R. 2005. "Tragedy and Epic," in: R. Bushnell (ed.), *A Companion to Tragedy*, Malden MA, 181–92.
Seckler, M. 1962. "Glaube," in: H. Fries (ed.), *Handbuch theologischer Grundbegriffe*, Vol. 1, Munich, 528–48.
Segal, R.A. 1999. *Theorizing about Myth*, Amherst MA.
Segal, R.A. 2014. "Greek Myth and Psychoanalysis," in: Edmunds (eds.), 409–55.
Segev, M. 2017. *Aristotle on Religion*, Cambridge.
Shapiro, H.A. 1998. *Art and Cult under the Tyrants in Athens*, 2nd ed., Mainz am Rhein.
Shapiro, H.A. 2014. "Staging the Birth of Helen in Athens and South Italy," in: P. Valavanis/E. Manakidou (eds.), *Egraphsen kai Epoiesen: Essays on Greek Pottery and Iconography in Honour of Professor Michalis Tiverios*, Thessaloniki, 355–63.
Shaw, C.A. 2014. *Satyric Play: The Evolution of Greek Comedy and Satyr Drama*, Oxford.
Shklovsky, V. 1925. *O teorii prozy*, Moscow/Leningrad.
Shklovsky, V. 1990. *Theory of Prose*. Trans. by Benjamin Sher. Elmwood Park IL.
Siegmund, W. (ed.) 1984. *Antiker Mythos in unseren Märchen*, Kassel.
Sinn, U. 2004. "Einleitung," in: *ThesCRA* 4, 1–5.
Small, J.P. 1997. *Wax Tablets of the Mind: Cognitive Studies of Memory and Literacy in Classical Antiquity*, London.
Snell, B. 1953. *The Discovery of the Mind: The Greek Origins of European Thought*. Trans. T.G. Rosenmeyer, Oxford.
Snell, B. 1975. *Die Entdeckung des Geistes: Studien zur Entstehung des europäischen Denkens beiden Griechen*, 4th ed., Göttingen.
Sommerstein, A.H. 2005. "Tragedy and Myth," in: R. Bushnell (ed.), *A Companion to Tragedy*. Malden MA, 163–180.
Sommerstein, A.H. 2019. *Aeschylus: Suppliants*, Cambridge.
Sourvinou-Inwood, C. 2011. *Athenian Myths and Festivals: Aglauros, Erechtheus, Plynteria, Panathenaia, Dionysia*, Oxford.
Sourvinou-Inwood, C. 2014. "Myths in Images: Theseus and Medea as a Case Study," in: Edmunds (ed.), 355–406. [Repr. from Edmunds 1990, 395–445].
Steinbock, B. 2013. *Social Memory in Athenian Public Discourse: Uses and Meanings of the Past*, Ann Arbor, MI.
Steinbock, B. 2013. *Social Memory in Athenian Public Discourse: Uses and Meanings of the Past*, Ann Arbor.
Steiner, A. 2007. *Reading Greek Vases*, Cambridge.
Steiner, De. T. 2002. *Images in Mind: Statues in Archaic and Classical Greek Literature and Thought*, Princeton.
Stern, J. 1996. *Palaephatus: On Unbelievable Tales (Peri apiston)*, Wauconda IL.
Stern, J. 1999. "Rationalizing Myth in Palaephatus," in: Buxton (ed.), 215–22.
Stewart, C./J. North. 2012. "belief," in: *OCD*[4], 227–28.

Strijdom, J. 2007. "The Uses of Ancient Greek Myths: From Social-historical Description to Ideological Criticism," in: *Myth & Symbol* 4.2, 39–48. https://doi.org/10.1080/10223820802503194
Sulimani, I. 2011. *Diodorus' Mythistory and the Pagan Mission: Historiography and Culture-heroes in the First Pentad of the Bibliotheke*, Leiden.
Taplin, O. 1992. *Homeric Soundings: The Shaping of the Iliad*, Oxford.
Taplin, O. 1993. *Comic Angels and Other Approaches to Greek Drama through Vase-Paintings*, Oxford.
Thiel, H. van. 2014. *Scholia D in Iliadem*. 2nd ed. Universitäts- und Stadtbibliothek Köln, Elektronische Schriftenreihe der Universitäts- und Stadtbibliothek vol. 7.
Thomas, R. 1989. *Oral Tradition and Written Record in Classical Athens*, Cambridge.
Thomas, R. 1992. *Literacy and Orality in Ancient Greece*, Cambridge.
Thomas, R. 2012. "genealogy," in: *OCD*[4], 608.
Thomas, R. 2019. *Polis Histories, Collective Memories and the Greek World*, Cambridge.
Thompson, S. 1946. *The Folktale*, New York.
Thompson, S. 1977 [1946]. *The Folktale*, 3rd ed., Berkeley.
Thomsen, A. 1909. "Der Trug des Prometheus," in: *ARW* 12, 460–90.
Todorov, T. 1966a. *Théorie de la littérature: Textes des formalistes russes réunis, présentés et traduits par Tzvetan Todorov*, Paris.
Todorov, T. 1966b. "Les catégories du récit littéraire," in: *Communications* 8, 125–51.
Todorov, T. 1969. *Grammaire de Décaméron*, The Hague.
Toye, D.L. 2009. "Akousilaos of Argos (2)," in: *BNJ* 2 F 39.
Trypanis, C.A. 1958. *Callimachus*, 2 vols., Loeb Classical Library, Cambridge MA.
Trzaskoma, S.M. 2013. "Introduction," in: id./R. Scott Smith (eds.), xv–xxiv.
Trzaskoma, S.M. 2017. "Mythography," in: D.S. Richter/W.A. Johnson (eds.), *The Oxford Handbook of the Second Sophistic*, Oxford, 463–76.
Trzaskoma, S.M./R. Scott Smith (eds.) 2013. *Writing Myth: Mythography in the Ancient World*, Leuven.
Trzaskoma, St.M./R. Scott Smith. 2011. "Mythography," in: Oxford Bibliographies https://www.oxfordbibliographies.com/view/document/obo-9780195389661/obo-9780195389661-0142.xml#firstMatch
Tsagalis, C.C. 2009. "Poetry and Poetics in the Hesiodic Corpus," in: F. Montanari/A. Rengakos/id., *Brill's Companion to Hesiod*, Leiden, 131–177.
Tsagalis, C.C. 2015. "Telegony," in: Fantuzzi/Tsagalis (eds.), 380–41.
Tsagalis, C.C. 2018. "Performance Contexts for Rhapsodic Recitals in the Archaic and Classical Periods," in: Ready/Tsagalis (eds.), 29–75.
Tybjerg, T. 1993. "Wilhelm Mannhardt: A Pioneer in the Study of Rituals," in: T. Alhbäck, (ed.), *The Problem of Ritual*, Stockholm, 27–37.
Uther, H.-J. 1996. "Type- and Motif-Indices 1980–1995: An Inventory," in: *Asian Folklore Studies* 55.2, 299–317.
Uther, H.-J. 2010a. "Typenkataloge," in: *EM* 13, cols. 1073–3284.
Uther, H.-J. 2010b. "Typus," in: *EM* 13, cols. 1084–90.
Vansina, J. 1985. *Oral Tradition as History*, Madison WI.
Vassilaki, E. 2015. "Entre histoire et légende. Recherche sur les emplois des mots ἱστορία, ἱστορεῖν, ἱστοριογράφος et ἱστορικός dans les scholies aux Olympiques de Pindare," in: *Dialogues d'histoire ancienne* Suppl. 13, 93–117.

Veldhuis, N. 2001. "The Solution of the Dream: A New Interpretation of Bilgames' Death," in: *Journal of Cuneiform Studies* 53, 133–148.
Verhasselt, G. 2015. "The Hypotheses of Euripides and Sophocles by 'Dicaearchus'." *GRBS* 55.3, 608–636.
Vernant, J.-P. 1969. *Mythe et pensée chez les Grecs: Études de psychologie historique*. 2nd ed., Paris.
Vernant, J.-P. 1972. "'Œdipe' sans complexe," in : id./P. Vidal-Naquet, *Mythe et tragédie en Grèce ancienne*, Paris, 75–98.
Vernant, J.-P. 1974. *Mythe et société en Grèce ancienne*, Paris.
Vernant, J.-P. 1980a. *Myth and Society in Ancient Greece*. Transl. Janet Lloyd. Sussex
Vernant, J.-P. 1980b. "Between the Beasts and the Gods: From the Gardens of Adonis to the Mythology of Spices," in: Vernant 1980a, 143–82.
Vernant, J.-P. 1980c. "The Reason of Myth," in: Vernant 1980a, 203–46.
Vernant, J.-P. 1983 [1969]. "Hesiod's Myth of the Races: An Essay in Structural Analysis," in: id., *Myth and Thought among the Greeks*, London, 3–32.
Vernant, J.-P. 1989. "At Man's Table: Hesiod's Foundation Myth of Sacrifice," in: M. Detienne/id. (eds.), *The Cuisine of Sacrifice Among the Greeks*, Chicago, 21–86.
Versnel, H.S. 1990a. "What's Sauce for the Goose is Sauce for the Gander: Myth and Ritual, Old and New," in: Edmunds (ed.), 25–90.
Versnel, H.S. 1990b. *Inconsistencies in Greek and Roman Religion: Transition and Reversal in Myth*, Leiden.
Versnel, H.S. 2014. "What's Sauce for the Goose is Sauce for the Gander: Myth and Ritual, Old and New," in: Edmunds (ed.), 86–151.
Versnel, H.S. 2011. *Coping with the Gods: Wayward Readings in Greek Theology*, Leiden.
Vetta, Massimo. 1980. *Theognis. Elegiarum liber secundus*, Rome.
Veyne, P. 1983. *Les Grecs ont-ils cru à leurs mythes?: Essai sur l'imagination constituante*, Paris.
Veyne, P. 1988. *Did the Greeks Believe in Their Myths? An Essay on the Constitutive Imagination*. Trans. Paula Wissing, Chicago.
Vian, F. 1963. *Les origines de Thèbes: Cadmos et les Spartes*, Paris.
Vidal-Naquet, P. 1981. *Le chasseur noir: Formes de penseé et formes de société dans le monde grec*, Paris.
Villagra, N. 2008 (2009). "Los Τραγωδούμενα de Asclepíades de Tragilo: una obra mitográfica," in: *Faventia* 30.1–2, 285–95.
Villagra, N. 2012. "Commenting on Asclepiades of Tragilos: Methodological Considerations on a Fragmentary Mythographer," in: A. Castro et al. (eds.), *Learning from the Past: Methodological Considerations in Studies of Antiquity and Middle Ages*. British Archaeological Reports International Series, Oxford, 289–96.
Visser, M. 1982. "Worship Your Enemy: Aspects of the Cult of Heroes in Ancient Greece," in: *HTR* 75, 403–28.
Voigt, V. 1977. "Anordnungsprinzipien," in: *EM* 1, cols. 565–76.
Voigt, V. 1999. "Morphologie des Erzählguts," in: *EM* 9, cols. 921–32.
Voigt, V. 2002. "Propp, Vladimir Jakovlevič," in: *EM* 10, cols. 1435–42.
von den Hoff, R. 2002. "Die Pracht der Schalen und die Tatkraft des Heros. Theseuszyklen auf Symposiongeschirr in Athen," in: W.D. Heilmeyer (ed.), *Die griechische Klassik: Idee oder Wirklichkeit*, Mainz, 331–337.

von den Hoff, R. 2009. "Heracles, Theseus and the Athenian Treasury at Delphi," in: P. Schultz/ R. von den Hoff (eds.), *Structure, Image, Ornament: Architectural Sculpture in the Greek World*, Oxford, 96–104.
von den Hoff, R. 2010. "Media for Theseus, or: The Different Images of the Athenian Polis-Hero," in: Foxhall/Gehrke/Luraghi (eds.), 161–88.
von Hahn, J.G. 1864. *Griechische und albanesische Märchen*, 2 vols., Leipzig.
von Hendy, A. 2002. *The Modern Construction of Myth*, Bloomington.
Wachter, R. 1991. "The Inscriptions on the François Vase," in: *Museum Helveticum* 48.2, 86–113.
Walcot, P. 1966. *Hesiod and the Near East*, Cardiff.
Walker, H.J. 1995a. *Theseus and Athens*, Oxford.
Walker, H.J. 1995b. "The Early Development of the Theseus Myth," in: *Rheinisches Museum für Philologie* NF 138.1, 1–33.
Walsh, D. 2008. *Distorted Ideals in Greek Vase-Painting: The World of Mythological Burlesque*, Cambridge. (Non vidi.)
Watkins, C. 1995. *How to Kill a Dragon: Aspects of Indo-European Poetics*, New York.
Watkins, C. 2011. *The American Heritage Dictionary of Indo-European Roots*, 3rd ed., Boston.
Watt, I. 1957. *The Rise of the Novel: Studies in Defoe, Richardson, and Fielding*, Berkeley.
Wees, H. van. 1992. *Status Warriors: War, Violence, and Society in Homer and History*, Amsterdam.
Werber, G. 1987. "Frazer, James George," in: *EM* 5, cols. 220–27.
West, M.L. 1966. *Hesiod: Theogony*, Oxford.
West, M.L. 1978. *Hesiod: Works and Days*, Oxford.
West, M.L. 1983. *The Orphic Poems*, Oxford.
West, M.L. 1985. *The Hesiodic Catalogue of Women*, Oxford.
West, M.L. 1993. *Greek Lyric Poetry*, Oxford.
West, M.L. 1997. *The East Face of Helicon: West Asiatic Elements in Greek Poetry and Myth*, Oxford.
West, M.L. 2007. *Indo-European Poetry and Myth*, Oxford.
West, M.L. 2011. "History and Prehistory: The Troy Saga," in: *Hellenica*, Vol. 1 (Epic), Oxford, 97–112.
West, M.L. 2013. *The Epic Cycle: A Commentary on the Lost Troy Epics*, Oxford.
West, M.L. 2014. "Nine Poems of Sappho," in: *ZPE* 191, 1–12.
West, Stephanie. 1991a. "Christa Wolf's *Kassandra*: A Classical Perspective," in: *Oxford German Studies* 20–21, 164–85.
West, Stephanie. 1991b. "Herodotus' Portrait of Hecataeus," in: *JHS* 111, 144–160.
West, Stephanie. 2012. "Some Reflections on Alpamysh," in: Montanari/Rengakos/Tsagalis (eds.), 531–41.
Wilamowitz-Moellendorff, U. von. 1931–1932. *Der Glaube der Hellenen*, 2 vols., Berlin.
Wild, Min. 2020. "Romance versus realism." *TLS* July 10, 4–5.
Willcock, M.M. 1964. "Paradeigmata in the *Iliad*," in: *CQ* 14, 140–52.
Wohl, V.J. 2008. "The Romance of Tragedy and Psychoanalysis: A Review Article," in: *Helios* 35, 89–110. Review of Pedrick 2007.
Wolf, Chr. 1983. *Kassandra: Erzählung*, Darmstadt.
Woodard, R.D. 2007. "Hesiod and Greek Myth," in: Woodard (ed.), 83–165.

Woodard, R.D. 2020. "The Disappearance of Telipinu in the Context of Indo-European Myth," in: R.I. Kim/J. Mynárová/P. Pavuk (eds.), *Hrozný and Hittite: The First Hundred Years: Proceedings of the International Conference Held at Charles University, Prague*, 11–14 November 2015, Amsterdam, 583–602.

Woodard, R.D. (ed.) 2007. *The Cambridge Companion to Greek Mythology*, Cambridge.

Woodford, S. 1994. "Theseus and the Minotaur," in: *LIMC* "Th." Section VIII, 940–43.

Woodford, S. 2011. "Displaying Myth: The Visual Arts," in: Dowden/Livingstone (eds.), 157–78.

Würzbach, N. 1999. "Motiv," in: *EM 9*, cols. 947–54.

Zaccarini, M. 2015, "The Return of Theseus to Athens: A Case Study in Layered Tradition and Reception," in: *Histos* 9, 174–198.

Zajko, V./E. O'Gorman (eds.) 2013. *Classical Myth and Psychoanalysis: Ancient and Modern Stories of the Self*, Oxford.

Zajko, V./H. Hoyle (eds.) 2017. *A Handbook to the Reception of Classical Mythology*, Hoboken NJ.

Zajko, V. 1998. "Myth as Archive," in: *History of the Human Sciences* 11.4, 103–19.

Zajko, V. 2007. "Women and Greek Myth," in: Woodard (ed.), 387–406.

Zuntz, G. 1955. *The Political Plays of Euripides*, Manchester.

Index Nominum et Rerum

Aarne, Antti 122, 127
Abraham, Karl 99
Achaean army 23
Achaeans 24, 30, 81
Achilles 23, 24, 26, 30, 32, 37, 38, 112, 113, 116, 120
Acragas 65
Actaeon 46
Adler, Alfred 100
Adonis 95
Adrastus 22
Aeëtes 33
Aegean 7
Aegeus 7–8, 10–13, 33, 57
Aeginetans 92
Aegle 8
Aeneas 91, 152
Aether 68
Aethra 2
Afanás'ev, A.N. 128, 135
Agamemnon 23, 24, 26, 29, 37, 132, 140, 151
Aiaia 38
Aigla 77
Aiolos 44
Aitolia 44
Ajax, Oïlean 8, 90
Ajax, Telamonian 65, 169
Akeso 77
Alcestis and Eurydice 20
Alcibiades 52
Alcinous 157
Aleppo 112
Alexander 59
Alkmeonids 11
allegoresis 62
Allen, Nicholas 111–112, 114, 124
Amazons 9, 25
Amphitrite 6
Amyclae 44
Amyclae throne 6
Anatolia 124
Anatolian languages, Hittite 112
Andromeda 36

Antiope 8–10
Anzu, cf. Zu 117
Aphiaraus 69
Aphidna 2
Aphrodite 114, 115–16
Apollo 6, 30, 77, 78, 84, 85, 91, 136
–temple at Delphi 82, 167
Apollodorus xvii, xxvii
Arcadia 69, 136
Arcadian goatherd xvii
Arcadians 22, 23
Argo 57
Argonauts 21, 31
Argos 21, 22, 44
argumentum ex love 29
Ariadne 2–5, 7–9, 30, 33
Arion 22
–and the dolphin 60
Aristagoras 52
Arkteia 137
Arktos 136
Arrephoria festival 97
Artemis 22, 92, 132
–Tauropolos 91
Asclepius 77, 78
Ashurbanipal, library of 117
Astyanax 47
Atalanta 136
Athena 11, 81, 90, 91, 93, 114
–Polias, Promachos, Ergane 82, 83
Athenians 25, 84, 92
Athens Ch. 1 *passim*, 22, 33, 34, 75
Atlantis 168
Atrahasis 119
Atreids 53, 145, 146
Atthidographers 50
Atthidography 51
Attica 25, 91
Aulis 53, 132
Australian National University 49, 144
autochthony, Athenian 26, 27
autogenesis 110, 119
Auxesia 93
Bal, Mieke 139–40

"Barcelona school, the" 49, 58
Barthes, Roland 38–39
belief-in ch. 5 *passim*
belief-that ch. 5 *passim*
Benveniste, Émile 139
Bérard, Claude 13
Berlin 121
Bogatyrev, Petr xxiii, 147, 148
Boiotia 44
Boreas 21, 161–62
Brauron 91
Brazil 109
Bremer, Jan Maarten 78
Bremond, Claude 128–29
Breton, André xxii
Brisson, Luc 168
Buphonia 89
Burgess, Jonathan 123
Burkert, Walter xviii, xix, xxiv, xxv, 36, 47, 48, 82, 88–89, 94, 97, 98, 100, 106, 107, 108, 109, 119, 125, 126, 127, 128, 130, 132, 133, 134–35, 136, 137, 138, 143, 144, 146–47, 148, 149
Buxton, Richard v, 72, 132
Cadmus 105
Cadmus and Harmonia, marriage of 87
Calame, Claude vi, xxiii, 2, 10, 11, 44, 129–30, 131, 138, 141, 152–53, 165
Caldwell, Richard 101–102
Callimachus xv
Callisto 130, 131, 134, 135–37, 146
Calydonian boar hunt 45
Calypso 157
"Cambridge school" 94, 110
Campbell, Joseph 99
Carians 92
Cassandra 90, 151, 152
Castor and Polydeuces 24
catasterism 58, 136
Ceans 6
Cecrops 26, 69, 97
Centaur Μάρφσος 46
Centaurs 4, 34, 158
Cercyon 10
Chaos 68
Charybdis 22
Cheiron 136

Chest of Cypselus 4
Chios xvii, 75
Cimon 2
Circe 20, 38, 143
Cleisthenes 2–3, 10–11
Clytemnestra 171
Cnossos 4, 5, 8, 31
Colchis 31, 50, 57
Colonus Hippius 22
Cook, Robert 123
Corinth 34, 44
Corone 85
Coronis 77
Cranaos 26
"Crane Dance" 1
–"Crane, The" 5
Crete 6–7, 31, 96
Creusa 85
Cronus 69
cult ch. 6 *passim*
Cyclic Epic 37, poets xvii
Cyclopes xvi
Cyclops 123, 158
Cyme 60
Daedalus 4
daimones 71
daimonian 71
Damia and Auxesia 92
Danaids 22
Daphne 136
Darwin, Charles 40, 95
Daulia 53, 54
Deianira 34
Delattre, Charles v, xxii, 107–108, 164
Delian League 6
Delium 28
–battle of 84
Delos 1, 5–6
Delphi 11, 22, 84, 85, 167
Delphic oracle 52
Demodocus 157
Derveni papyrus 118
Detienne, Marcel xviii, xx
Deucalion 120
Diomedes 81, 90, 91, 93
Dion (Macedonia) 75, 77
Dionysus 95, 125, 145

Dionysus and Ariadne, marriage of 20
Dioscouroi 2, 7, 31, 69
Doležel, Lubomír 42
Dowden, Ken v, xxvi, 98, 132, 137
Duchemin, Jacqueline 118
Dumézil, Georges 107, 108, 114–15, 111–112, 120
Dundes, Alan 134–35, 144
Durkheim, Émile 98
Earth 113, 166
Ebla 112, 113
Eblaites 112, 113
Echemus 25
Eco, Umberto 42
Egypt 22, 160
Eleatic Stranger 18
Eleusinian Mysteries 81, 163
Eleusinians 28
Eleusis 21, 22
Eleutherae 21
Embaros 137
"Eniautos-Daimon" 97
Enkidu 116
Enlil 117, 119
Epidaurians 92
Epione 77
Epopeus 30
Er, myth of 152
Erbse, Helmut 66
Erechtheidae 28
Erechtheis 27
Erechtheum 84
Erechtheus 26, 28, 83, 84, 85
Erichthonius 26
Eros 8, 68
Erythrae 75
Euhemerism 62
Euhemerist 95
Eumolpus 28, 84
Eurotas 44
Eurydice 153
Eurypylus 157
Eurystheus 24, 34
Euthyphro 29, 66–67, 70, 83
Evagoras 167–68
Fabre-Serris, Jacqueline 49
Feeney, Denis 73

Festa, Nicolaus 61
fleece, golden 34
"floating gap" 51
Flood, Biblical 119
Foley, John Miles 42
folklore v
folktale motifs 122
–magic ring 121
–No Man or Nobody ruse 121
–ogre 121
folktales xxiv
Forbes Irving 136, 137
Ford, Andrew 52
Formalists, Russian 128
Foucault, Michel 72
Fowler, Robert xvii, xviii, xxiii, xxiv, xxv, xxvi, xxvii, xxviii, 1, 44, 49, 50, 51, 52, 59, 143, 144, 149, 154
François Vase 1, 4, 45, 47
Frazer, James George 95, 96, 98, 108
Freud, Sigmund v, 91–100, 101–102, 109, 124, 153
–Freudian 149
functions, Dumézilian 114
functions, Proppian 106, 127, 128–29, 133, 134, 141
funeral oration 27
Furley, William D. 78
Gaia 68
Ganymedes 31
Genette, Gérard 37, 139–40
Geryons 34
Giants 158
Goethe, Johann Wolfgang von 68
Golden Fleece, quest for 153
Graf, Fritz xix–xxi, 71, 72, 94
Graziani, Françoise 49
Greece 145, 146
Greimas, Algirdas Julien 108, 128–29, 141
Grimm brothers 122
Grimm, Wilhelm 121
Halai 91
Halliwell, Stephen 39
Hamlet 99
Hansen, William 36, 122, 123, 144
Harma (Chariot), town of 22

Harpagos 60
Harpies 167
Harris, William 17
Harrison, Jane Ellen 95, 96–97, 98, 109, 155
Harrison, Thomas 72
Haskamp, Birgit 124
Hawes, Greta 49, 52
Hecabe 81
Hecataeus of Miletus xvii, 45
Hector 37, 81, 112, 114, 115
Helen 2, 8–9, 30, 33, 37, 38, 53, 113, 114, 115–16, 120
–birth from an egg 151, 153
Helenus 90, 114
Henrichs, Albert 46, 58, 130–32, 135, 137
Hephaestus xviii, 4
Hephaisteion 11
Hera xviii, 24, 34, 92, 114, 145, 163, of Samos 93
Heracle 8
Heracles 1–2, 11, 20, 21, 24, 30, 31, 34, 36, 69, 82, 143, 153, 160, 167
Heraclids 25
Hermione 113
Hesione 30, 31, 36
Hippias 18
Hippo 136
Hippolyte 10
Hippolytus 33
Horkos 45
Hornblower, Simon 7, 165
Hurrian 112
Hurrian-Hittite tablets 112
Hygieia 77
Hylus 25
Iaso 77
Ilios 8
incredibilia 60
Indian Ocean 62
Indo-European languages 114
–proto-Indo-European 111
Indo-European myth v, 116–17
Indo-European people 110
Inkalis 112, 113
Ino 85
Io 2, 134, 135, 136

Iolaus 166
Iolcus 50, 57
Ionian revolt 52
Iphicles 24
Iphigeneia 91–92, 132, 137
Ishara 112
Isthmus of Corinth 25, 85
Ithaca 142–43, 157
Jacoby, Felix 51
Jakobson, Roman xxiii, 94, 139, 147, 148
James, Henry 39
James, William 40
Janka, Markus 168
Janko, Richard 151
Jason 33, 34, 57
Jeanmaire, Henri 98
Jesus 89, 95
Jocasta 43, 102
Jones, Ernest 99
Jong, Irene de 139–40
Jung, Carl v, 94, 98–99, 100, 102
–Jungian 149
Kant, Emmanuel 104–105, 133, 149
Kerényi, Carl 99
Kingship in Heaven 119
Kirk, Geoffrey 100, 118
Kore 33
Koronis 77
Kouretes 97
Kripke, Saul 42, 48
Kronos 83
Kullmann, Wolfgang 37
Labdacids 65, 130
Labdacus 105
Lacan, Jacques 102
Lacedaemon 44
Lacedaemonian army 26
Lacedaemonians 26
Laestrygonians xvi, 158
Laius 101, 43, 105
Lamb (Ἀρνη), a spring 22, 69
Lamia 18
Laomedon 30, 31
Lapiths 77
Laurium, silver mines xvii
Lelex 85
Leto 136

Leucippus 136, 137
Leucothea 85
Lévi-Strauss, Claude xx, xxvii, 10, 94, 103–107, 108, 109, 117–18, 128, 132, 146, 147–48, 149
Libya 59
literacy 17
Livingstone, Alasdair 124
Livingstone, Niall v, xxvi
Lloyd, Geoffrey 166
Lord, Albert 145
Lorenz, Konrad 89
Lycaon 69
Lyceum 56
Machaon 77
Macron 91
Magnesia 161
Mannhardt, Wilhelm 108
Mantinea 22, 23, 69, 142–43
"Mapping Ancient Narratives, Territories, Objects" (MANTO) 49, 144
Marathonian Bull 10–13
Martin, Richard 38, 157
Mastronarde, Donald 34
Mecone 85, 86
Medea 9, 11–13, 33, 34, 35, 48, 50, 57, 90
Medes 13
Media 13
Medus 13
Megarians 85
Megistos Kouros 97
Melanippe xxv, 68, 166
Meleager 3
Meletus 71
Melicertes 85
Menelaus 30, 113
Menexenus 27
Menodotos of Samos 92
Messa, temenos in 145, 146
Messene 22
Messenia 44, 85
metamorphosis 57, 58
Meuli, Karl 88
Miletus 52
Mill, John Stuart 42
Mills, Sophie 33, 34
Miltiades 65

Minos 6–7, 14, 31, 33
Minotaur 1, 3, 5–6, 31, 33
Momus 120
Morgan, Kathryn 20
morphology, Proppian 108, 125, 127–28, 135, 141
Most, Glenn 100
motifs 123, 126 cf. folktale motifs
Mounychia 137
Muses 142
Mycenae xvi
Mycenaeans 25
Nagy, Gregory 38, 110
Nagy, Joseph 115, 120
Naxos 5
Near Eastern myth, ancient v, 110, 116–21, 124
Neda xvii
Neleus 44
Neoptolemus 84
Nereids 45
Nereus 45
Nestor 2, 30, 31, 153
Neumann, Eric 99
Night 45, 68
Nile 160
Ninurta 117
Niobe 69
Nünlist, René 140
Ocean 160
Odysseus 2, 26, 37, 38, 90, 91, 93, 123, 142–43, 152, 153, 157, 159
Oedipus 30, 43, 47, 101, 105, 146, 149
Oedipus Complex 96, 101, 124
Oedipus myth xxvii–xxviii, 109, 124
Olympus xviii
Orchomenus 143
Oreithyia 21, 52, 162
Orestes 22, 91–92, 167, 171
Orontes 112
Orpheus 20
Orphic theogony 118, 166
Osiris 95
Pactyes the Lydian 60
Pàges, Joan 58
Paian 77
Palaemon 85

Palaikastro 96
Palamedes 169
Palladion 90, 91, 93
Pallas 12
–sons of 12
Panakeia 77
Panathenaic festival 83
Pandion 54
Pandora 86
Paris 9, 115–16
–Judgement of 114, 120, 166
"Paris, School of" 102, 108
Parry, Milman 144–45
Paterson, Lee 72
Patroclus 37, 112, 116, 157
Pausanias xv, xvii, 23, 69, 142–43
Pavel, Thomas 42
Peels, Saskia 71
Peirithous 8, 33
Peisistratids 10
Peisistratus 1, 2, 5, 11
Pelasgus 22
Peleus and Thetis, marriage of 87
Pelias 34
–daughters of 57
Pellizer, Ezio 108, 130–31, 136, 137
Peloponnesus 21, 25
Pelops 52
Penelope 38, 142–43, 153
Pericles 2
–son of 28, 84
Perieres 44
Periphetes 10
Persephone 8
Perseus 36
Philomela 53–54, 165
Philyra 136
Phineus 167
Phlegyas 77
Phocis 43, 53
Phoenix 30, 45
Pike, Kenneth xxv–xxvi, 75, 134
Plataea, battle of 25
Podaleirios 77
Polycrates, and the ring 60
Polydamas 115

Polymnia (Réseau de recherche sur les mythographes anciens et modernes) 49
Polyphemus 121, 123
Polyphonte 136
Polyxena 151
Poseidon 6, 30, 31, 69, 85
–Poseidon-Erechtheus 84
Potniae 43
Priam 8, 114
Price, H.H. 64
Price, Simon 73
Procne 53–54, 165
Procrustes 10
Prodicus 20
Proitides 136
Prometheus 29, 82, 85–86, 87–89, 93, 146
Propp, Vladimir 36, 106, 108, 125, 127, 128–29, 133, 134, 135, 141, 144
Ptolemais (Egypt) 75
Ptoliporthes 143
Pulleyn, Simon 78
Pylades 22, 91–92
Pythia 167
Rank, Otto 99
Ready, Jonathan xxiv
Rees, Alwyn 114
Rees, Brinley 114
Rhea 23
Rhegium 22
Robertson Smith, William 98, 108
Rodighiero, Andrea 53
Rutherford, R.B. 118–19
Ryan, Marie-Laure 42
"sacred laws" 70, 80
Saïd, Suzanne xxii
Salmoneus 44
Samos 92
Sardanapalus 171
Saronic Gulf 10
satyrs 150
Saussure, Ferdinand de xxiii, xxiv, 94, 103, 128, 148, 154
Sciron 10
Scyros 8
Seckler, Max 74

Index Nominum et Rerum — **203**

segmentation 121
Seven against Thebes 21, 22, 25
Shapiro, Alan 151
Shaw, Carl 150
Shield of Achilles 4, 5
Shklovsky, Viktor 128
Sicily xvi
Sicyon 86
Sicyonians 86
Sinis 10
Sky 66–67, 166
Skyros 2
Smith, R. Scott 49
Smith, William Robertson 96
Snell, Bruno 66
Socrates 20, 21, 27, 28, 33, 52, 66–67, 70, 71, 73, 79, 83, 84, 142, 152, 169
Solon 1, 60
Sommerstein, Alan 34, 43
Sourvinou-Inwood, Christiane 9, 12–13
South Slavic heroic epic 144
Sow of Crommyon 10
Sparta 21, 25, 44, 143
Spartoi 105
spatium historicum 51
spatium mythicum 51
Sphinx 102
Stern, Jacob 61
Stoa Poikile 11
Storm God, i.e., Hurrian Teshub, Hittite Tarhun 112
Sun Goddess of the Earth 112
symposium 19–20, 158
synoecism 3, 10
Syria 112
T., Christa 152
Tammuz 95
Tantalus 167
Tartarus 68
Taurians 91–92
Tauris 22, 92
Taygete 44, 136
Tegeans 25, 26
Teiresias 38, 131
Telegonus 38, 143
Telemachus 30, 38, 143
Telephus 144

Tell Mardikh 112
Teres 53–54
Tereus 53, 54
Thales 31
Theano 81, 90
Theban War 65, 120
Thebes 21, 22, 25, 65, 105
Themis 120
theognony 18, 67–68, 166
Theron 65
Theseus v, xv, Ch. 1 *passim*, 21, 30, 31, 33, 34, 35, 48, 90, 125, 153
Thesprotia 143
Thesssaly 44
Thetis 45, 120
Thoas 91
Thomas, Rosalind 59
Thompson, Stith xxviii, 122, 126, 135, 144
Thrace 54
Thracians 54
Thucydides xvii, 22, the "Archaeology" xvi, 7
Titans 66, 87, 158
Todorov, Tzvetan 138, 139
tragedy 16
trifunctionality 114
Troezen 10
Trojan War xvi, xvii, 15, 25, 29, 38, 59, 65, 112, 113, 114, 115, 120, 146, 152, 167–68
Trojans 47, 81
Tros 31, 114, 115–16, 120, 145, 146, 152, 153
Troy xvi, 30, 38, 53, 65, 84, 90, 93
Tylor, E.B. 108
types, folktale 122, 123, 126, cf. typology
Typhoeus 158
typology 121, 125, 126–27, cf. folktale types
Tyrrhenian pirates 92
Universitat Autònoma, Barcelona 49
Uther, Hans-Jörg 122
van Gennep, Arnold 98
Vassilaki, Ekaterini 164
Vernant, Jean-Pierre 86–88, 89, 93–94, 100, 102, 107, 130, 146, 149
Versnel, H.S. 73, 75, 95, 97
Veyne, Paul 64, 70, 72, 73, 79

Vidal-Naquet, Pierre 98
Villagra, Nereida 58
von Günderrode, Caroline 152
von Hahn, Johann Georg 122, 126
Wachter, Rudolf 46
Walcot, Peter 118
Watkins, Calvert 111
West, Martin 27, 44, 29, 87, 111, 118, 119
West, Stephanie 152
Wolf, Christa 152
women as myth-tellers 18–19
Woodard, Roger v

Xenophon 25
Yugoslavia 144, 145
Zeus xviii, 23, 24, 30, 31, 53, 66, 69, 83, 86, 88, 112, 113, 120, 137, 145
–comical 151
–deception of 151, 160, 163, 167
–Lycaean 69
–Dictaean 96
Zu, cf. Anzu 117
Zuni myths 104, 149
Zuntz, Günther 57

Index Locorum

Acusilaus of Argos
FGrH 2 F 39 = EMG 2, fr. 39   115
FGrH 2 F 6a-c = EGM fr. 6a-c   68
FGrH 2 F 5 = EGM fr. 6d   68
FGrH 2 T 2 = EGM Test. 1   55

Aeschylus
Ag.
104   53
105–106   53
511–13   53
551–55   53
Eum.
4   158
46–51   167
50–51   167
1011   27
PV
461   29
872   82
Suppl.
291–92   22
fr. 387A Radt   43

Alcaeus
fr. 129 V   145

Alcman
fr. 5 PMG/PMGF   68
fr. 21 PMG/PMGF   7, 9 n. 40

Antiphanes
Poiēsis
fr. 189 K-A   43

Apollonius Rhod.
1.101   27 n. 58

Apollodorus
2.5.12   8
3.14.8   53 n. 28
Epit.
1.8–9   4
3.21   92

5.13   90 n. 59
5.22   91 n. 60
1.5–6   12 n. 59

Apollonius Dysc.
2.2.494   27

Aristophanes
Nub.
902–907, 1079–82   28 n. 63
Eq.
1015, 1030   27 n. 58
Pax
129   170
129–30, 133–34, 135–36   28
Ran.
136–44   163 n. 35
145–46   164 n. 35
273–75   164 n. 35
Vesp.
566   28

Archilochus
fr. 23.16 W^2 157
fr. 174 W^2 170
fr. 185 W^2 170

Aristotle
EN
1181b7, b17
Met.
1000a 18–19   170
1074a38–1074b14   170 n. 71
1074b1–14   170
1074b9   170
Poet.
1449a36   35 n. 7
1449b4   35 n. 7
1449b12–13   16
1449b37–38   36 n. 10
1450a16   35
1451a19–21   3
1450a38–39   171 n. 73
1451b5–10   35

1453b22–23	16, 171 n. 72	fr. 1.6–7 B	113 n. 19
1454a17–19	35	fr. 13 B	7, 9 n. 40
1455b17–23	15 n. 3	*Il. parv.*	
1459a35	15	arg. 17–18 B	90 n. 59
1461a13	35 n. 7	25 B	93 n. 69
Pol.		*Ilioupersis*	
1312a 1–4	171	arg. 15–16 B	91 n. 60
Rhet.		*Minyas*	
1355b 26	23 n. 38	fr. 7.26	3
1393a 28–1394a 5	28 n. 62	*Oedipodea*	
Topics		arg. B	xxviii
105b 12–14	56 n. 39	*Teleg.*	
		arg. 1 Pàmia	143
Athenaeus		arg. 17–20 B	38 n. 25
13.557a–b	3	fr. 5 B	38 n. 25

Bacchyl.
Dith.
17   6, 31

Diod. Siculus
4.1.1–4	59 n. 56
4.1.5	59
4.8.5	35 n. 6
4.60.4–5–61.1–3	6
4.61.4	4
4.63	8
10.27	13

Callimachus
Aet.
75.4–9 Pf.	163
Hecale	
fr. 232 Pf.	13 n. 63
fr. 233 Pf.	13 n. 63
Hymns	
4.307–15	5
5.1	90 n. 58
fr. 612 Pf.	53
frs. 407–411 Pf.	58 n. 50

Diog. Laert.
2.40   70 n. 33

Dionysius of Halicarnassus
Ant. Rom. 1.69   91

Conon
FGrH 26 F 1 [XXXIV.4]

Epimenides
FGrH 457 F 4–6b, 8, 10–13, 21 =
EGM frs. 1, 6–18   68 n. 23

Democritus
68 B 44 D-K	159 n. 19
68 B 225 D-K	159 n. 19
68 B 297 D-K	167

Eratosth.
Cat. 1 Pàmias   136

Erythraean Paean
75–78   *passim*

Demosthenes
60.4	26 n. 55
60.27	28 n. 59

Etym. Magn.
s.v. Ἱππία   22

Epic Cycle
Cypria
arg. 22–29 B   30

Euripides
Andr.
1161–65   84 n. 21

Bacch.		852	27 n. 58
286–97	51 n. 19	*Supp.*	
El.		387	27 n. 58
1282–83	113 n. 19	681	27 n. 58
Erechth.		702	27 n. 58
fr. 370.59–60 Kannicht	84 n. 18	713	27
fr. 370.93–94 Kannicht	84 n. 19	754–59	21 n. 29
Hel.		schol. Eur. *Phoen* 1760	xxviii
39–41	113 n. 19		
HF		**Gilgamesh**	
1166	27	SV Tablet 11	119
Hipp.			
151	27 n. 58	**Hecataeus**	
IA		*FGrH* F 1a = *EGM* 1, fr. 1	54, 159
72	166		
Ion		**Hellanicus**	
24, 1060	27 n. 58	*FGrH* 323a F3= *EGM* 1, fr. 40	27
191–218	*passim* 167 n. 52	*FGrH* 323a F14 = *EGM* 1, fr. 164	6
196	166	*FGrH* 4 F 166 = *EGM* 1, fr. 166	8
196–200	14	*FGrH* 4 T 18 = *EGM* 1, test. 18	154
269–70	84 n. 20		
277–83	84	**Heraclitus**	
281–82	84	D-K 22 B 42, 57 = L-M 9 D21, D25a	160
296	27		
721–24	85 n. 26	**Herodorus**	
1056	27 n. 58	*FGrH* 31 F 26 = *EGM* 1, fr. 25**b	9 n. 38
IT			
87–88	22	**Herodotus**	
Med.		1.23–4	60
hypoth. 10–11	57	1.64.2	1
hypoth. 11–18	57	1.108–19	60
hypoth. 20–24	57	1.157–60	60
9–10	57	1.184	161 n. 27
285	34	158.5	26 n. 53
486–87	57	2.106	165 n. 44
505	57	2.123.1	161 n. 26
663–823	57	2.134.3	170
679	101	2.143.1–4	17
824	27 n. 58	2.148.1	62 n. 68
1282–89	19, 85 n. 29	2.16.3	161 n. 27
Melanippe the Wise		2.18.1	62 n. 68
fr. 484 Radt	19, 166	2.21	160
Or.		2.23	160, 160 n. 24
1639–42	113 n. 19	2.29.1	62 n. 68
Phoen.		2.44.2	62 n. 68
26–28	xxviii	2.44.3	62 n. 68
38	43	2.44.5	163 n. 32

2.45.1	54 n. 33, 160	154–210	166
2.53 6	7 n. 19	226–33	45
2.56	165 n. 44	229	157
2.75.1	62 n. 68	240–64	45
3.40–43	60	312	45 n. 63
3.122.2	51	468–91	23, 69
5.83–86	passim 92	523–33	82
5.85	93	535	87
5.124–25	52	535-61	86
6.117.3	62 n. 68	562–69	86
6.127	158	570–612	86
7.152.3	161 n. 26	585	86
7.157	26 n. 53	613–16	86
7.159.1	26 n. 53	630–720	66
7.161.3	26 n. 53	672	45 n. 63
7.189.1–2	161	890	157
7.189.3	162	fr. 280.26 M-W	3
7.213.3	161 n. 27	fr. 298 M-W	3, 8
7.224.1	62 n. 68		
7.96.1	163	**Homer**	
9.16	69 n. 27	*Il.*	
9.26.1–5	25	1.5	113
9.26–28.1	25	1.260–73	30
9.27.1–4	25	1.265	2, 4
9.27.4–6	26	1.351–52	38 n. 22
9.28.1	26	1.396–400	30
		1.397	30 n. 68
Hesiod		1.399	30 n. 68
Cat.		1.400	30 n. 68
fr. 1.6–7 M-W	87	1.416–18	38 n. 22
fr. 163 M-W	136	1.505–6	38 n. 22
fr. 204.95 M-W	113	1.590–94	xviii
Op.		2.509	45 n. 63
42–105	86	2.522	26 n. 53
78	157	2.546–552	84 n. 20
90–105	86	2.549–51	82
106	157 n. 11	2.550	84 n. 20
156–73	65	2.556	45 n. 63
202–212	170	2.685	45 n. 63
789	157	2.719	45 n. 63
Scut.		2.732	77
182	2	2.783	158
Theog.		3.46–48	9
27–28	142, 167 n. 53	3.46–51	115 n. 28
116	68	3.46–53	9
116–22	68	3.144	2, 7
151	45 n. 63	3.399–403	47

4.393	45 n. 63	11.275	xxviii
5.638	158 n. 15	11.321–25	2, 4
5.786	45 n. 63	11.325	4 n. 23
6.237–311	81	11.620–25	24
6.298	81	11.630–33	2
6.301–311	passim 81	11.631	2
6.303	90	11.368	157
7.125	26 n. 53	12.40	157 n. 10
8.362–69	24	12.44	157 n. 10
9.260–99	26	12.450	157
9.404–405	82	12.453	157
9.524–605	30	14.387	157 n. 10
9.529–99	46	15.170–78	38
14.323–24	24	16.195	157 n. 10
15.25–29	24	18.282–83	157 n. 10
15.393	157	23.296	143 n. 5
15.639–40	24	schol. *Od.*	
16.777–867	37	11.271	xviii n. 55
18.39–48	45		
18.59–60	38 n. 22	**Hyg.**	
18.95–96	38 n. 22	*Astr.*	
18.117–18	24	2.5	6 n. 28
18.394–99	xviii	*Fab.*	
18.458	38 n. 22	42	4
18.509–40	113		
18.590–92	4	**Hymn to Dictaean Zeus**	
19.78–144	24	96–98	passim
19.83	26		
19.147	26	**Hymn. Hom.**	
21.277–78	38 n. 22	15.4–6	24
21.443–45	30		
24.506–507	47	**Hyperides**	
24.615	158 n. 15	6.7 Jensen	26 n. 55
Od.			
1.56–57	157	**Ibycus**	
3.130–85	153	S151 PMGF	9 n. 40
3.130–200	30		
3.165–72	145 n. 15	**Inscriptions**	
3.264	157 n. 10	IG^3 474–79	84 n. 23
4.235–64	90 n. 59	IG^3 873	84 n. 24
5.333–35	85		
7.78–81	84 n. 20	**Isocrates**	
10.310–22	20 n. 22	1.50	167
10.371–87	20 n. 22	4.24–25	26 n. 55
11.121–34	38	9.66	168
11.266–68	24	*Panath.*	
11.274	xxviii n. 54	1	167 n. 54

Istros
FGrH 334 F 10   10

Lucian
De salt. 34   5

Lysias
2.17   26 n. 55

Melissus
D-K 30 B 1 = L-M 21 D2a   61, 61 n. 65

Menodotos of Samos
Athen. 672a–e = *FGrH* 541 F 1   92 n. 68

New Testament
Ev. Jo.
3.13   74

Old Testament
Genesis
6:11–9:19   119

Ovid
Met.
3.222   46
3.224   46

Papyri
P. Oxy. LXXVIII 5131   85 n. 29

Palaephatus
pref.   47, 60
26.18   49

Parmenides
D-K 28 B 2.1 = L-M 19 D6.1   160 n. 23
D-K 28 B 7.1–8.2 =
LM 19 D8.1–7   160
D-K 28 B 8.1 =
L-M 19 D8.6–7   160 n. 23
D-K 28 B 8.50–52 =
L-M 19 D8.55–57 1   60

Pausanias
1.15.3   11
1.17.2–6   6 n. 28
1.17.3   6 n. 29
1.30.4   22
1.38.3   28 n. 61
1.42.7   85
2.2.1   85
3.18.9, 11   6
3.26.1   85 n. 30
4.34.4   85
6.3.8   69
7.2.6   8
7.152   69
8.2.4   69
8.8.2   23 n. 36, 24
8.8.3   69
8.12.5–6   142
8.38.3   xvii
9.40.3   4 n. 22
10.24.4   84 n. 21

Pherecydes
FGrH 3 F 2 = *EGM* 1, fr. 2   65
FGrH 3 F 18a = *EGM* 1, fr. 18a   16
FGrH 3 F 148 = *EGM* 1, fr. 148   4, 4 n. 23
FGrH 3 F 149 = *EGM* 1, fr. 149   65
FGrH 3 F 151 = *EGM* 1, fr. 151   8
FGrH 3 T 1 = *EGM* test. 1**   55 n. 37

Pindar
Nem.
7.20–23   159
Ol.
1.5–9   53
1.28/28b–29   160
1.28–35   160 n. 21
2.35–45   65
Paean
6.105–22   84
fr. 175 Sn.   8
schol. Nem. 10.80–82   24 n. 42

Plato
Alc. 1
127d9–129a9   52
Apol.
24b8–c1   70 n. 33
24c1   71 n. 35
26c7   71

27a5–6	70 n. 33	376b11–377c5	xx
27c8–9	71	376e1–end	17 n. 14
27d1–28a1	71	377b1–2	15
38c1–42a5	169	377b6	167 n. 53
39e5	169	377c6–d5	xx
40c7	169	377e6–378a6	67
41a8–b7	169	379a–353c	142
Crat.		381e2	68
396b7	158	391c8–d1	33
Euthyphr.		414d–e	28 n. 60, 84 n. 25
5e5–6	67 n. 15	607b5	142
6b3	67	620c5–7	152
6b3	71	*Soph.*	
6b5–6	83	242c8–9	18
6b6–c4	83	*Symp.*	
6c3–4	67	179b4–180a4	20
6c5–7	83	*Tim.*	
Hipp. mai.		26e4	167 n. 53
285d6–e1	18 n. 16		
285e10–286a2	18 n. 16	**Plutarch**	
Leg.		*Comp. Thes. et Rom.*	
632e4	169 n. 64	6.1	8
886a	67 n. 16	*Thes.*	
Menex.		15.1	6
237b2–3	26 n. 55	17.3	6
237b2–c3	27 n. 56	19.1–2	8
Phaed.		20	3
70b6	169 n. 64	20.1	4 n. 23, 8
60c1	170	21	5
61b6	170	26.1	9
69c3–7	164 n. 35	29.4	21 n. 29
Phaedr.		35.4	8
229b4–e4	21		
229e3	52	**ps.-Aristotle**	
230a1–6	52	"On Marvellous Things Heard"	
230a2	69 n. 27	830a 5–847b10	58
243a2–b3	53		
Polit.		**Sappho**	
268e4–5	18	fr. 17 V 145	*passim*
Prot.		fr. 17 V	146
320c2–4	169	fr. 206 V	3
320c8–323a4	20	fr. 44 V	146
324d6–7	169		
335a9–b6	169	**Scholia, Homeric**	
347b8–348a2	20	b *Il.* 1.108–109	92
Rep.		D *Il.*18.590	5
363c3–d2	164 n. 35	B *Il.* 20.67	66

D *Il.* 20.145 — 31 n. 69
D *Il.* 20.307 — 115
MV *Od.* 11.322 — 4 n. 23
V *Od.* 11.271 — xxviii n. 55

Servius
Aen. 6.21 — 3

Simonides
fr. 11.7–9 W² — 84 n. 21
fr. 550 *PMG* =
fr. 248 Poltera — 7
fr. 579 *PMG* = f
r. 257 Poltera — 157, 157 n. 12

Sophocles
Aj.
202 — 27 n. 58
434–46 — 31 n. 69
91–93 — 90 n. 58
Ant.
982 — 27 n. 58
OC
83 — 7 n. 33
OT
711–14 — 101 n. 48
732–34 — 43
787–9 — 101 n. 48
825–26 — 101 n. 48
976 — 101 n. 48

Stesichorus
fr. 86 F — 9 n. 40
fr. 91a F — 53
fr. 97 F 43 — 43 n. 51
fr.183 F — 45 n. 64

Strabo
1.2.8 — 18 n. 15
1.2.35 — 49
8.3.9 — 49
9.2.11 — 22
11.5.3 — 59 n. 58
17.3.3 — 59 n. 59

Thales
D-K 11 A 22 = L-M D10, R34a — 31

Theagenes of Rhegium
D-K 8 A 2 — 66

Theocritus
Id. 13.2 — 68

Theognis
418 W² — 157
1231–34 — 8

Thucydides
1.4 — 7
1.10.2 — xvi n. 6, 158
1.10.2, 1.11.2 — xvi n. 7
1.10.3 — 165 n. 41
1.11.2 — xvi n. 8
1.1–21 — 52 n. 21
1.21.1 — xvii n. 13, 165, 165 n. 44
1.21.1–22.4 — 160 n. 21
1.24 — 28 n. 60
1.98.2 — 7
2.15 — 10
2.15.1 — 28 n. 61, 83 n. 17
2.15–16 — 52 n. 21
2.29 — 53, 53 n. 28
2.36.1 — 26 n. 55
3.204.1 — 1
4.24.5 — 22
4.109.3 — 7
6.1–5 — 52 n. 21
6.2.1 — xvi n. 9, 158

Vatican Mythographer 1
48 — 12 n. 59

Vergil
Aen.
6.617–18 — 8

Xenophon
Apol.
10 — 70 n. 33
11 — 70
Mem.
1.3.6–7 — 20
2.1.21 — 20

2.1.21–34	20
3.5.10	28, 84
Symp.	
3.2	20
8.40	28 n. 61, 83 n. 17
9.2	20

Xenophanes
D-K 21 B 1.13-14 =	
(I) B 1.13–14 W^2	158
D-K 21 B 1.19–22 =	
(I) B 1.19–22 W^2	19 n. 20
D-K 21 B 11 =	
L-M 8D8	65, 83
D-K 21 B 23–26 =	
L-M 8D16-20	65
D-K 21 B 34 =	
L-M 8D49	65

Xenophon
Cynegeticus
3.4–4.8	47
7.5	46

www.ingramcontent.com/pod-product-compliance
Lightning Source LLC
Chambersburg PA
CBHW030646230426
43665CB00011B/983